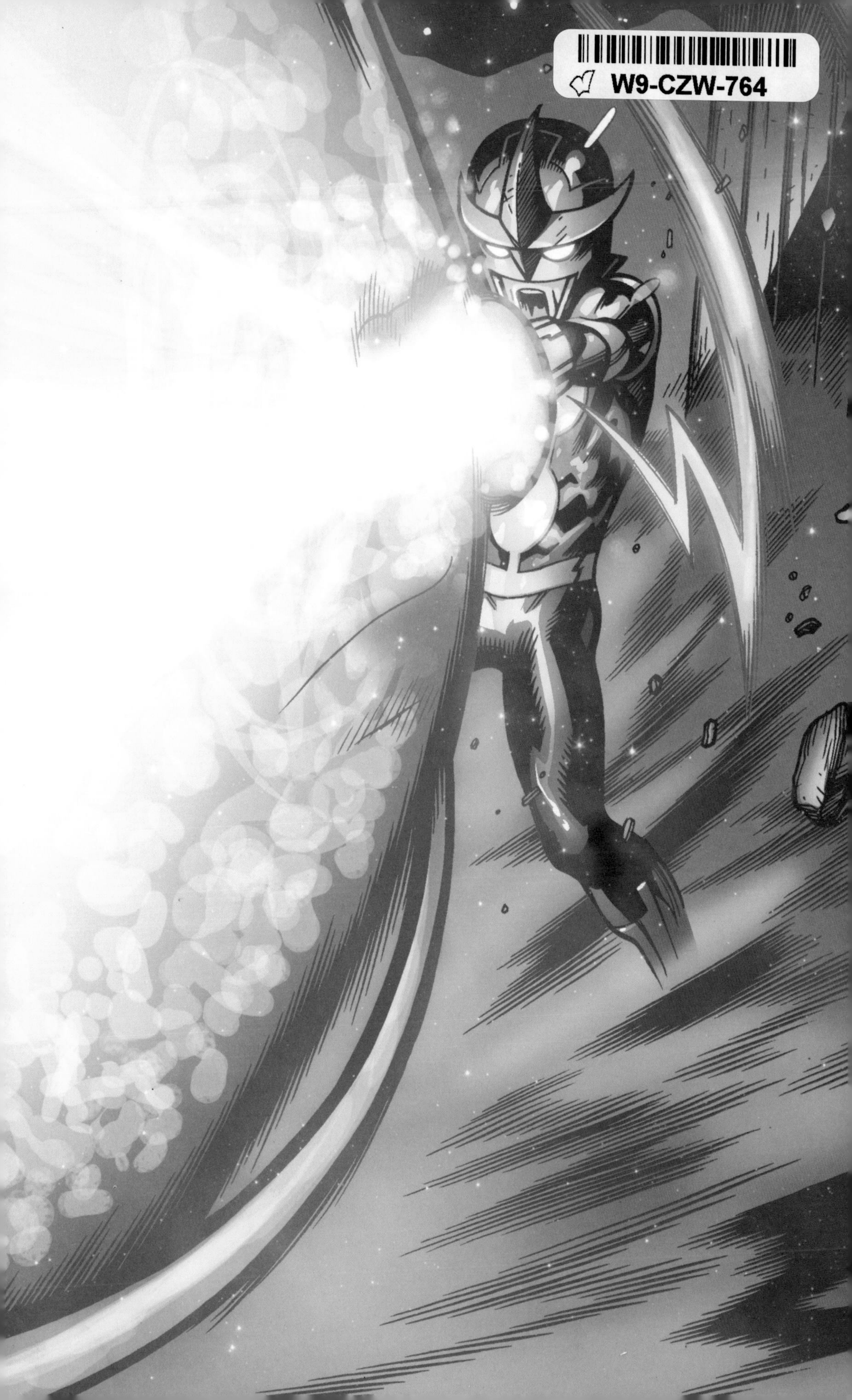

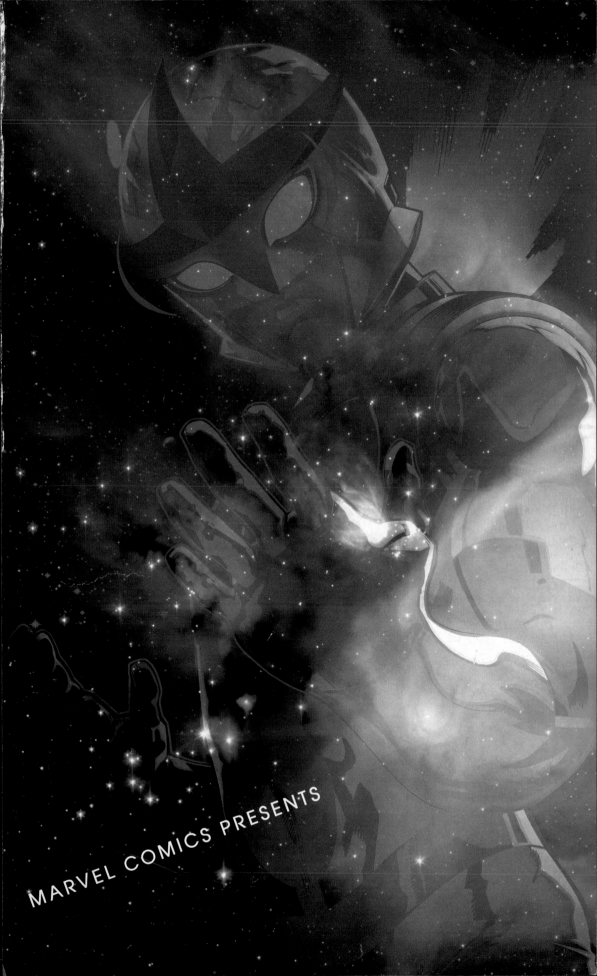

MARVEL COMICS PRESENTS

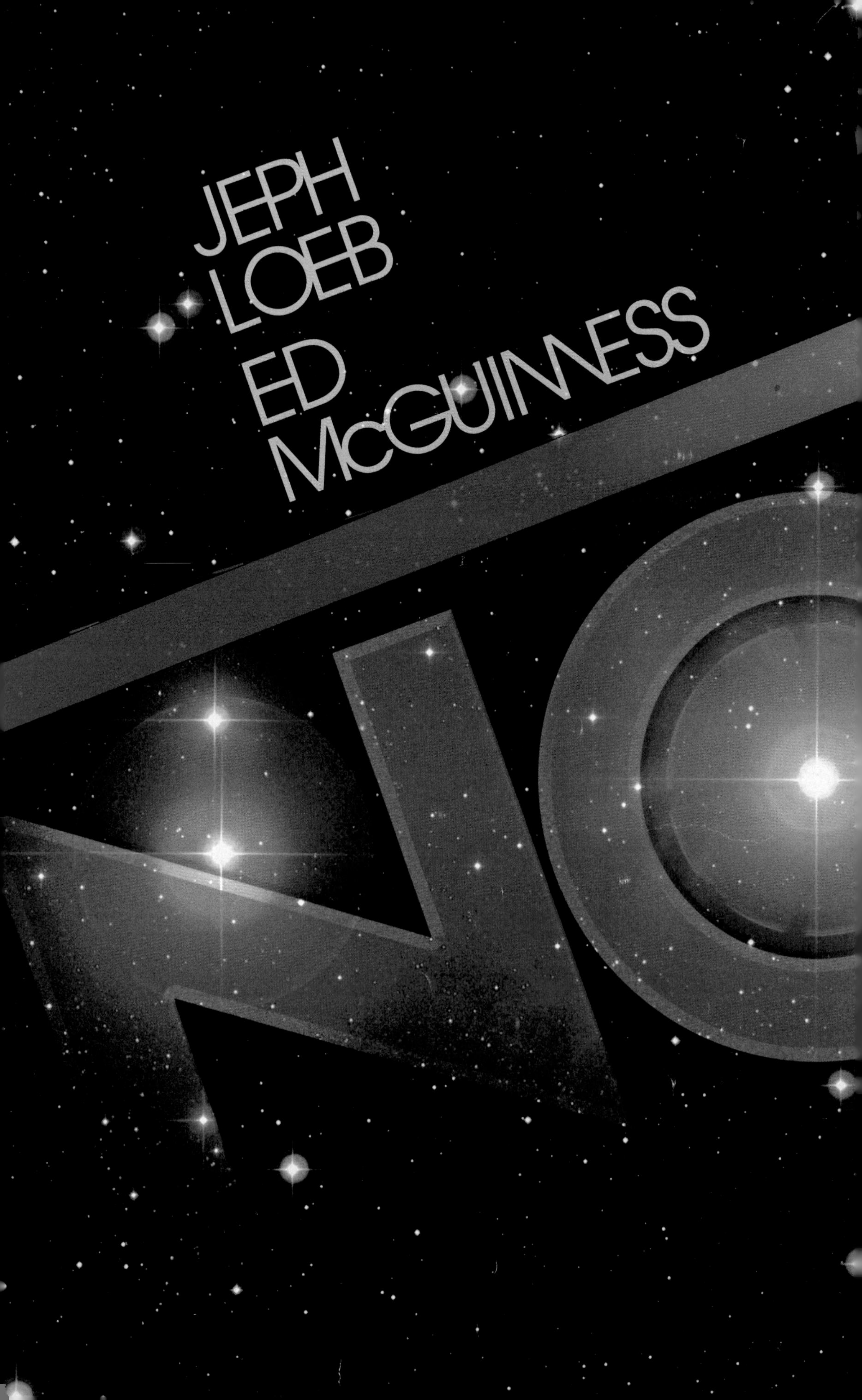
JEPH
LOEB
ED
McGUINNESS

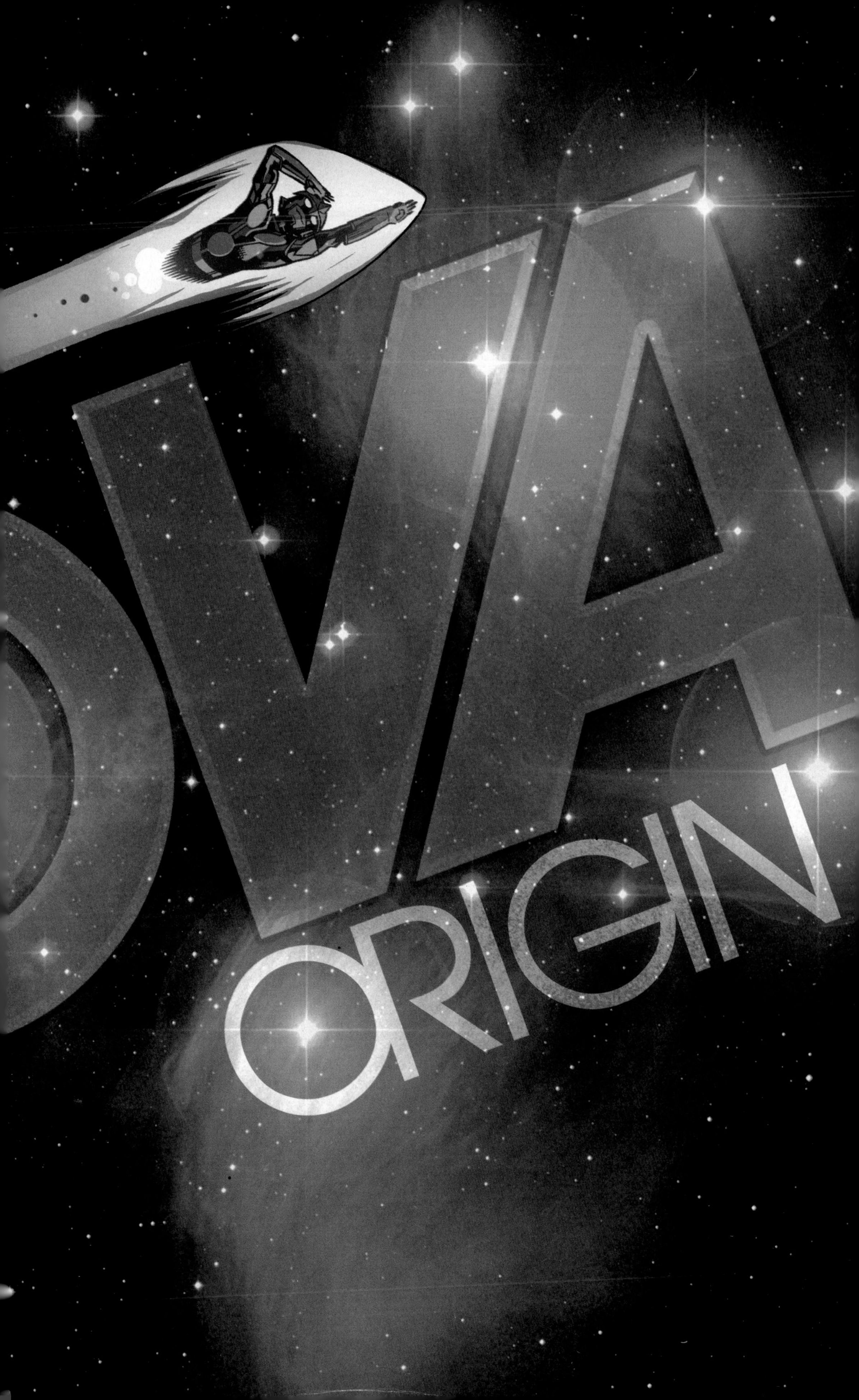
ORIGIN

WRITER JEPH LOEB
PENCILS ED McGUINNESS
INKS DEXTER VINES WITH ED McGUINNESS (#5)
COLORS MARTE GRACIA (#1-4 & "DIAMONDHEAD")
& EDGAR DELGADO (#5)

LETTERS COMICRAFT'S ALBERT DESCHESNE
COVER ART ED McGUINNESS, DEXTER VINES & MARTE GRACIA
ASSISTANT EDITOR ELLIE PYLE
ASSOCIATE EDITOR SANA AMANAT
EDITOR STEPHEN WACKER

COLLECTION EDITOR JENNIFER GRÜNWALD
ASSISTANT EDITORS ALEX STARBUCK & NELSON RIBEIRO
EDITOR, SPECIAL PROJECTS MARK D. BEAZLEY
SENIOR EDITOR, SPECIAL PROJECTS JEFF YOUNGQUIST
SVP OF PRINT & DIGITAL PUBLISHING SALES DAVID GABRIEL
BOOK DESIGN JOHN ROSHELL @ COMICRAFT
STARFIELD IMAGES COURTESY NASA/JPL-CALTECH

EDITOR IN CHIEF AXEL ALONSO
CHIEF CREATIVE OFFICER JOE QUESADA
PUBLISHER DAN BUCKLEY
EXECUTIVE PRODUCER ALAN FINE

NOVA: ORIGIN. Contains material originally published in magazine form as NOVA #1-5 and MARVEL NOW! POINT ONE #1. First printing 2013. ISBN# 978-0-7851-6838-6. Published by MARVEL WORLDWIDE, INC., a subsidiary of MARVEL ENTERTAINMENT, LLC. OFFICE OF PUBLICATION: 135 West 50th Street, New York, NY 10020. Copyright © 2012 and 2013 Marvel Characters, Inc. All rights reserved. All characters featured in this issue and the distinctive names and likenesses thereof, and all related indicia are trademarks of Marvel Characters, Inc. No similarity between any of the names, characters, persons, and/or institutions in this magazine with those of any living or dead person or institution is intended, and any such similarity which may exist is purely coincidental. Printed in the U.S.A. ALAN FINE, EVP - Office of the President, Marvel Worldwide, Inc. and EVP & CMO Marvel Characters B.V.; DAN BUCKLEY, Publisher & President - Print, Animation & Digital Divisions; JOE QUESADA, Chief Creative Officer; TOM BREVOORT, SVP of Publishing; DAVID BOGART, SVP of Operations & Procurement, Publishing; C.B. CEBULSKI, SVP of Creator & Content Development; DAVID GABRIEL, SVP of Print & Digital Publishing Sales; JIM O'KEEFE, VP of Operations & Logistics; DAN CARR, Executive Director of Publishing Technology; SUSAN CRESPI, Editorial Operations Manager; ALEX MORALES, Publishing Operations Manager; STAN LEE, Chairman Emeritus. For information regarding advertising in Marvel Comics or on Marvel.com, please contact Niza Disla, Director of Marvel Partnerships, at ndisla@marvel. com. For Marvel subscription inquiries, please call 800-217-9158. Manufactured between 7/5/2013 and 8/19/2013 by R.R. DONNELLEY, INC., SALEM, VA, USA.

10 9 8 7 6 5 4 3 2 1

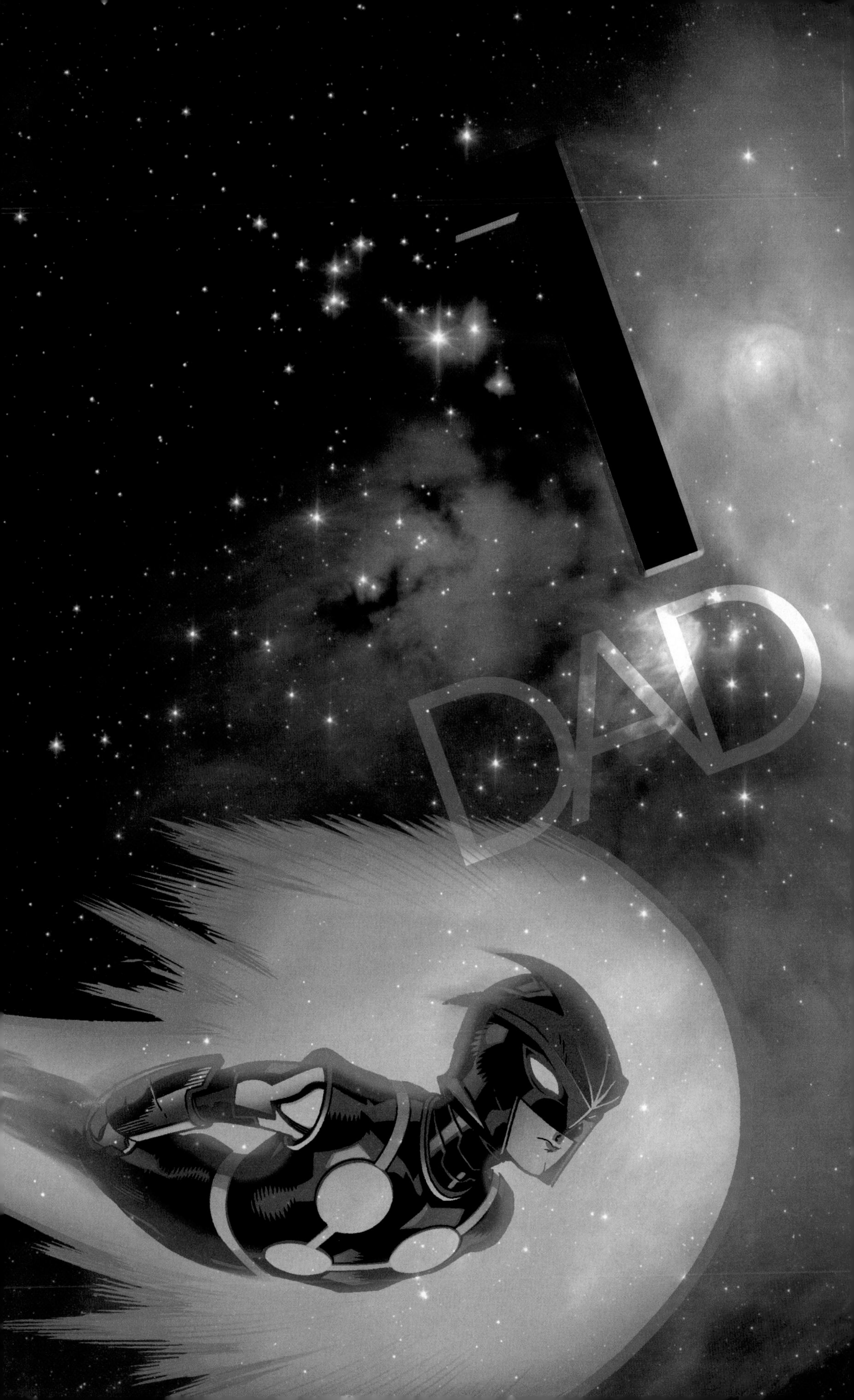
DAD

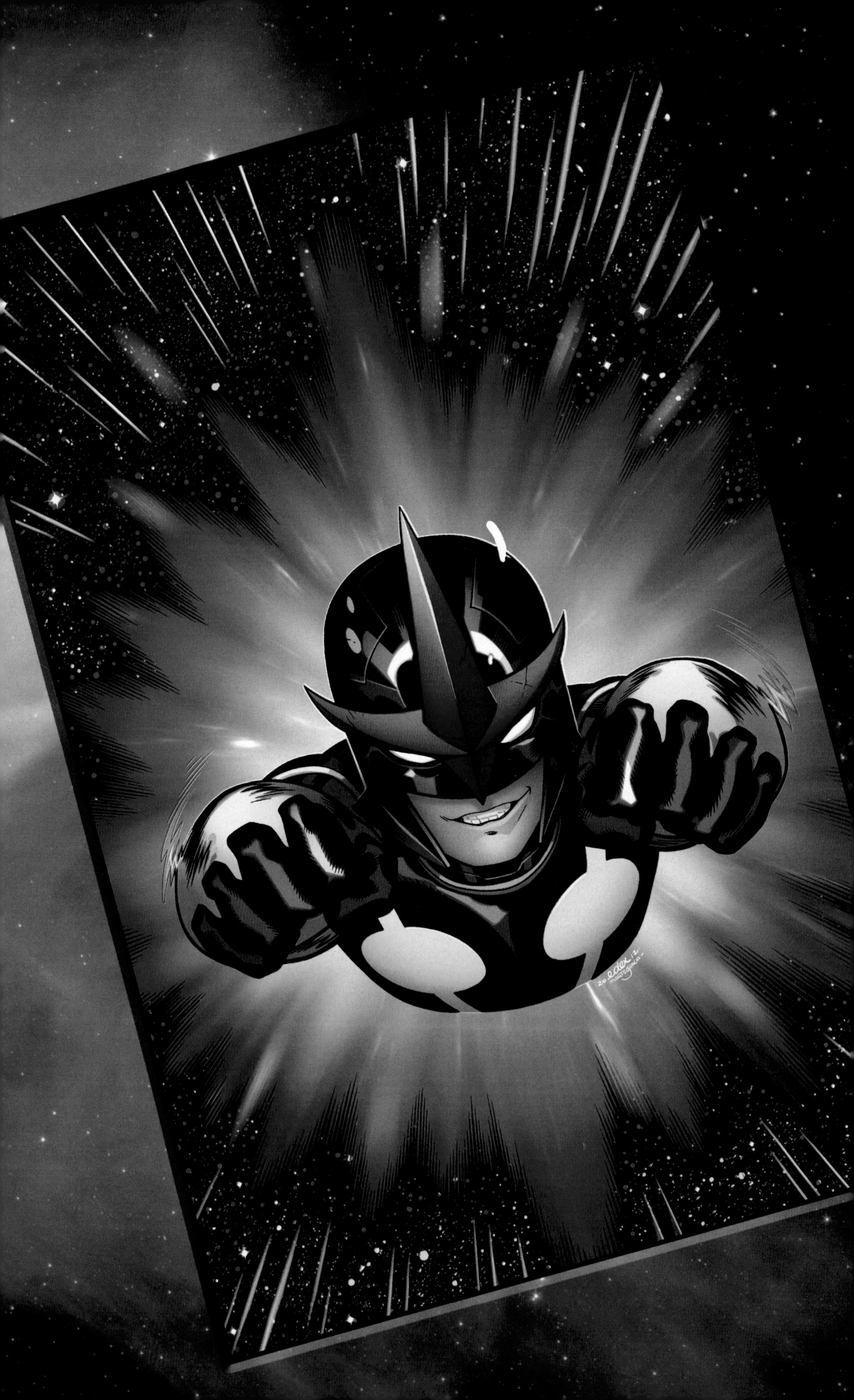

PREVIOUSLY...

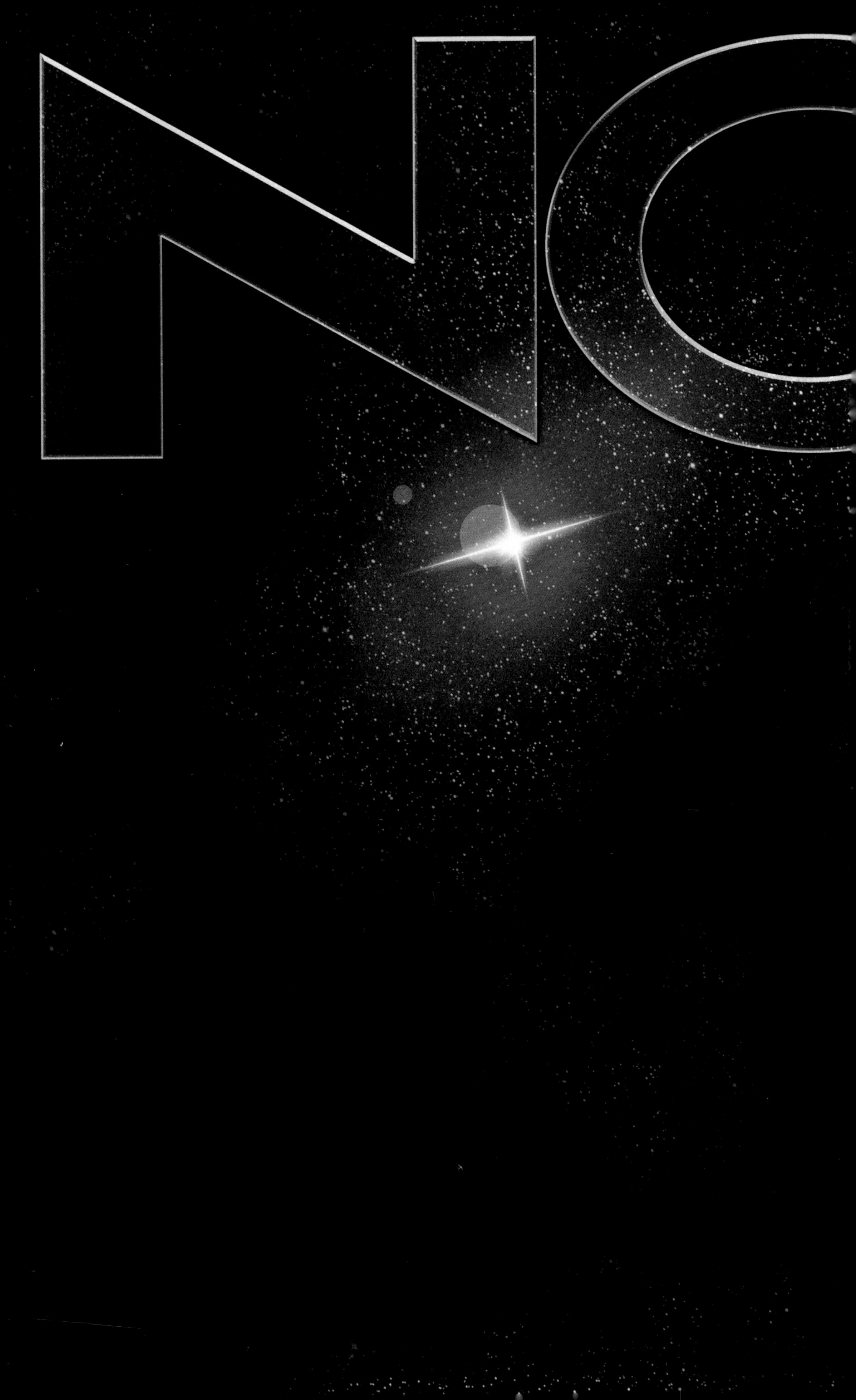
NO

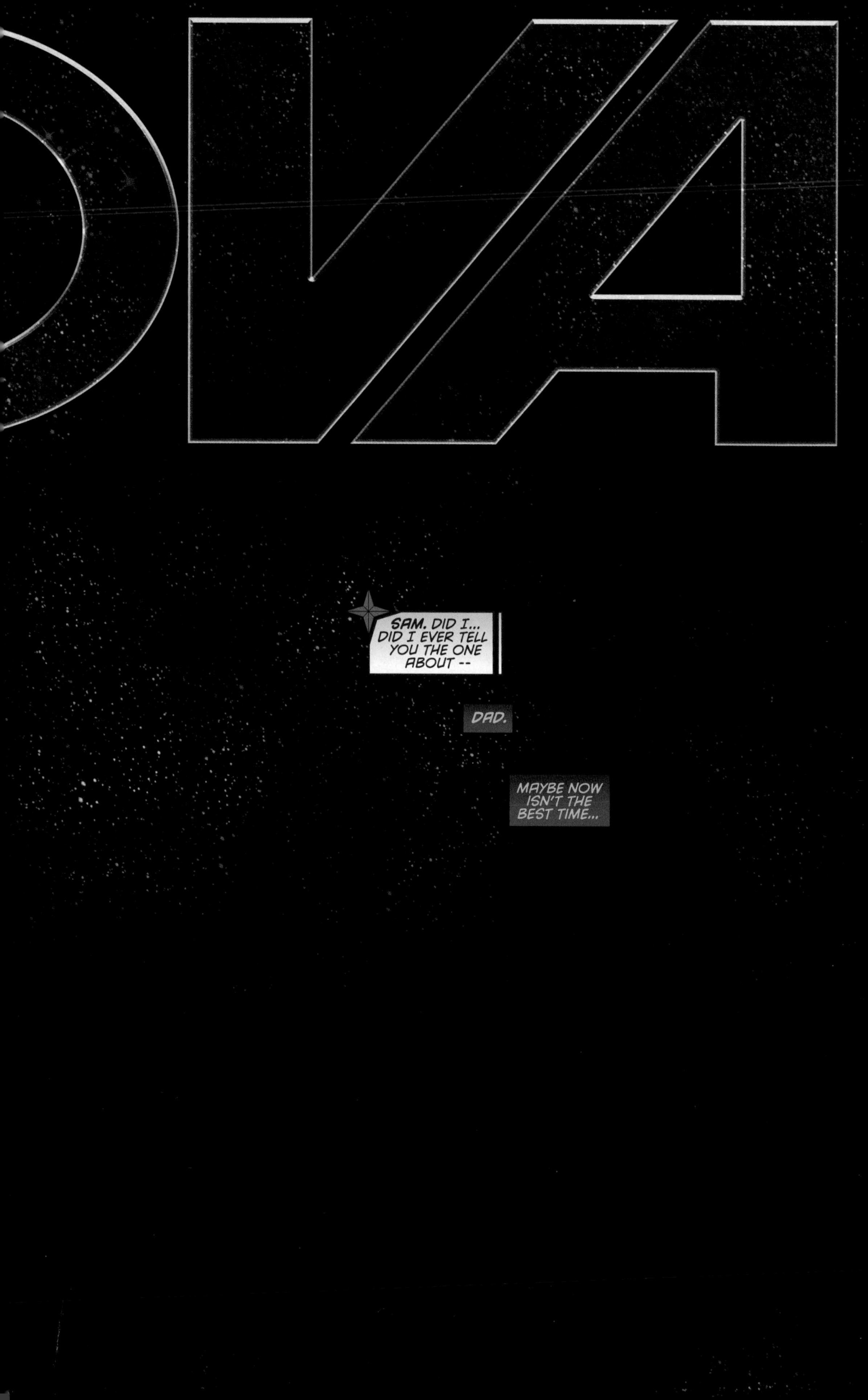
SAM. DID I... DID I EVER TELL YOU THE ONE ABOUT --
DAD.
MAYBE NOW ISN'T THE BEST TIME...

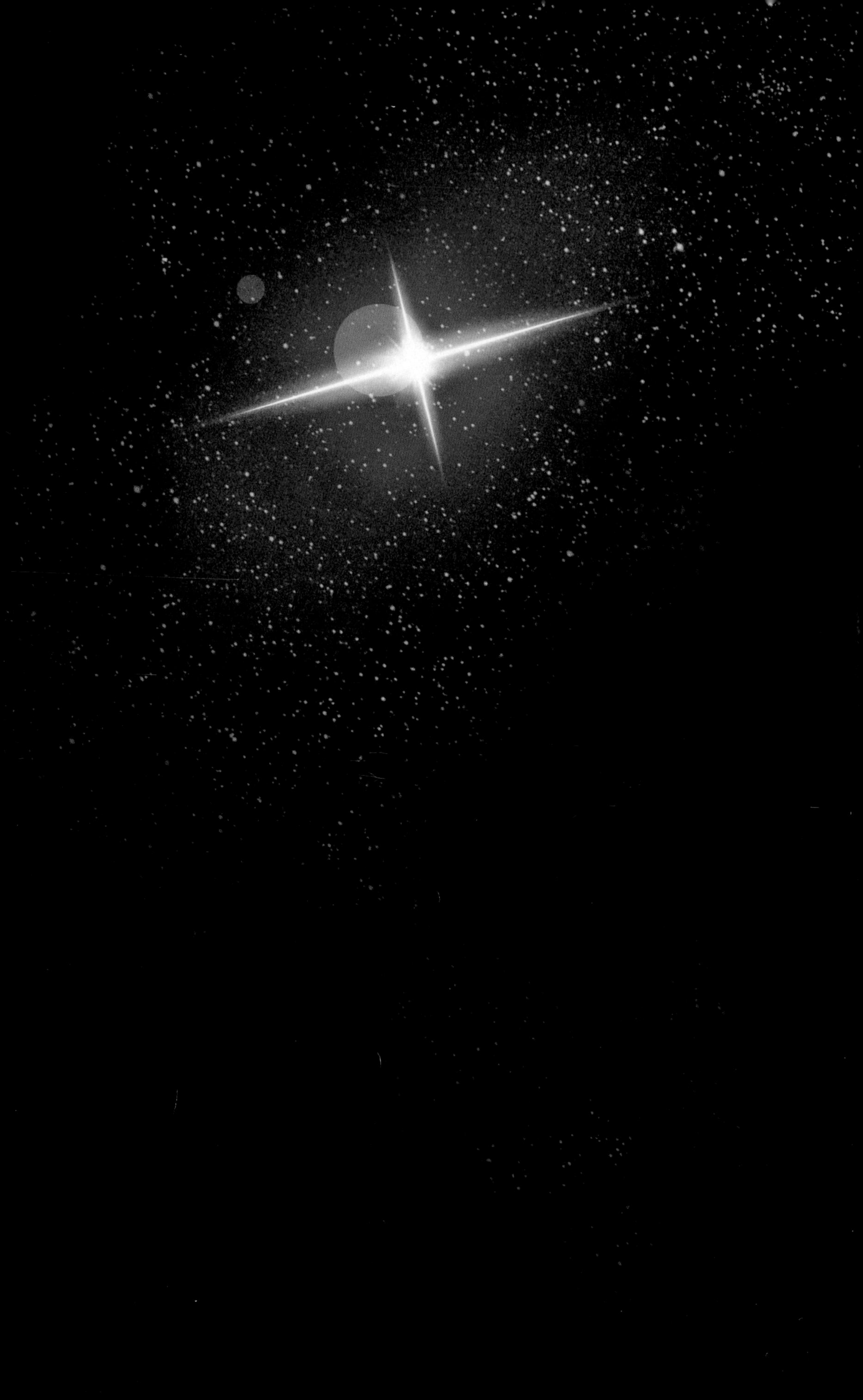

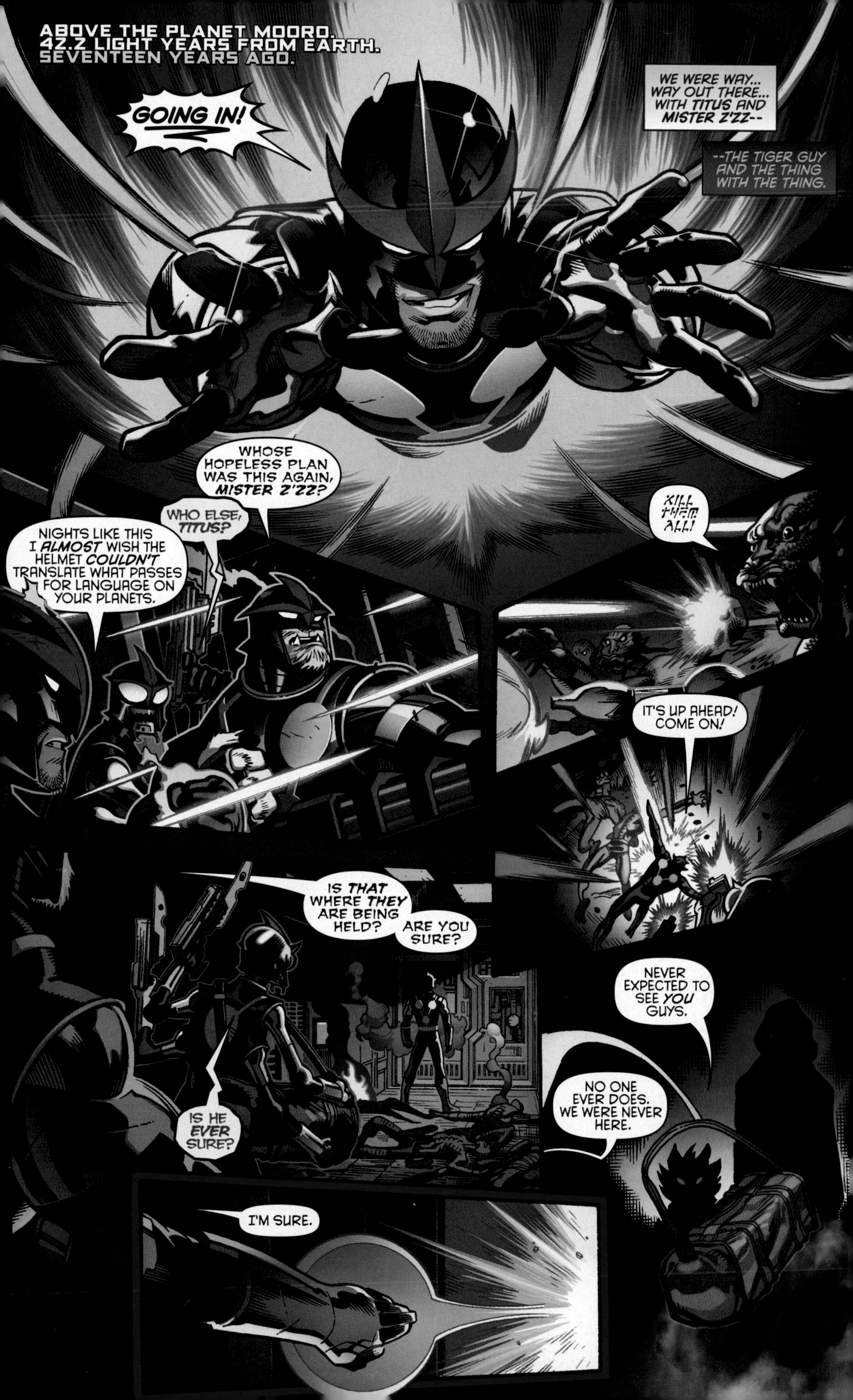

ABOVE THE PLANET MOORO.
42.2 LIGHT YEARS FROM EARTH.
SEVENTEEN YEARS AGO.
GOING IN!
WE WERE WAY... WAY OUT THERE... WITH TITUS AND MISTER Z'ZZ--
--THE TIGER GUY AND THE THING WITH THE THING.
WHOSE HOPELESS PLAN WAS THIS AGAIN, MISTER Z'ZZ?
WHO ELSE, TITUS?
NIGHTS LIKE THIS I ALMOST WISH THE HELMET COULDN'T TRANSLATE WHAT PASSES FOR LANGUAGE ON YOUR PLANETS.
KILL THEM ALL!
IT'S UP AHEAD! COME ON!
IS THAT WHERE THEY ARE BEING HELD?
ARE YOU SURE?
IS HE EVER SURE?
I'M SURE.
NEVER EXPECTED TO SEE YOU GUYS.
NO ONE EVER DOES. WE WERE NEVER HERE.

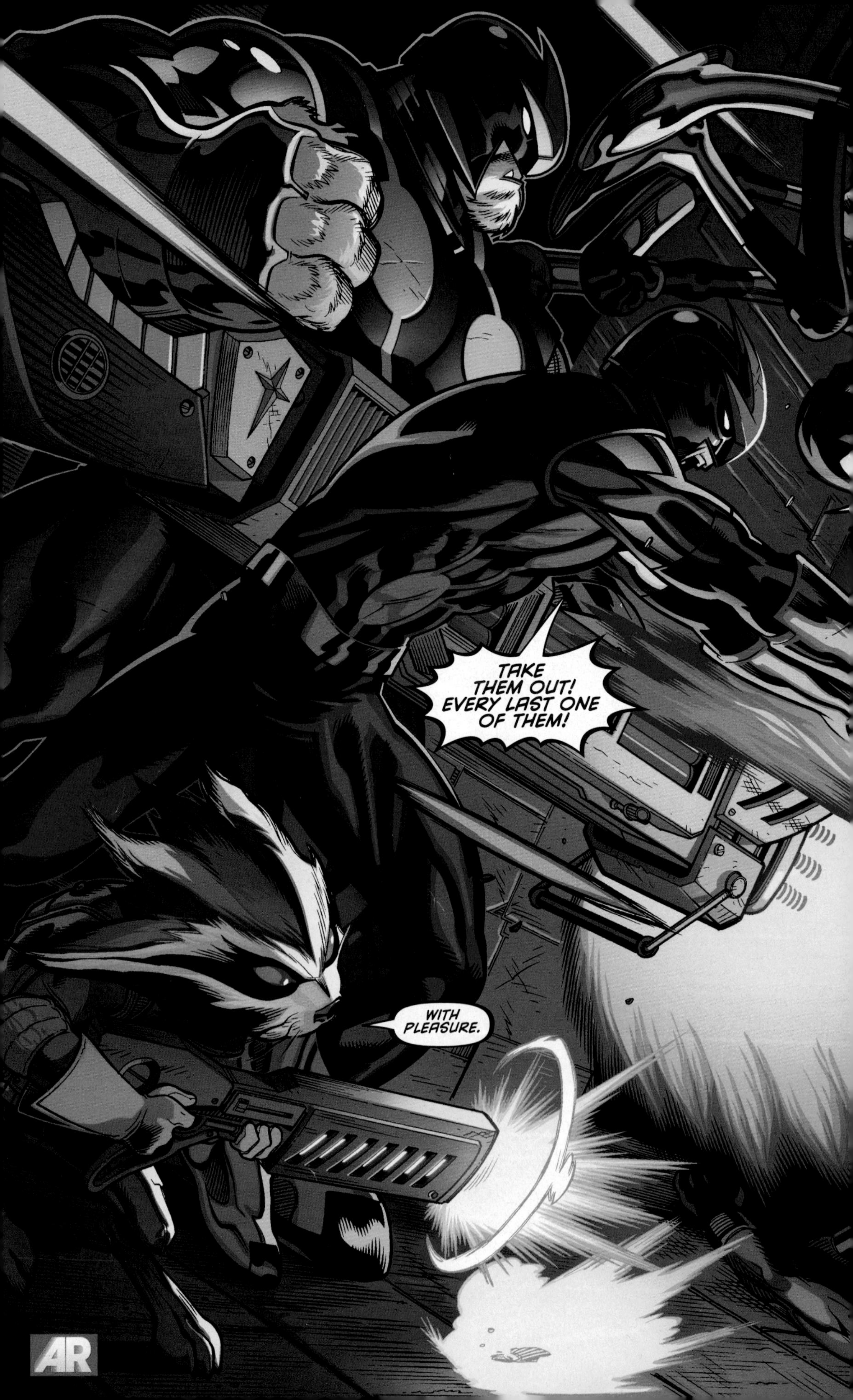
TAKE THEM OUT! EVERY LAST ONE OF THEM!
WITH PLEASURE.

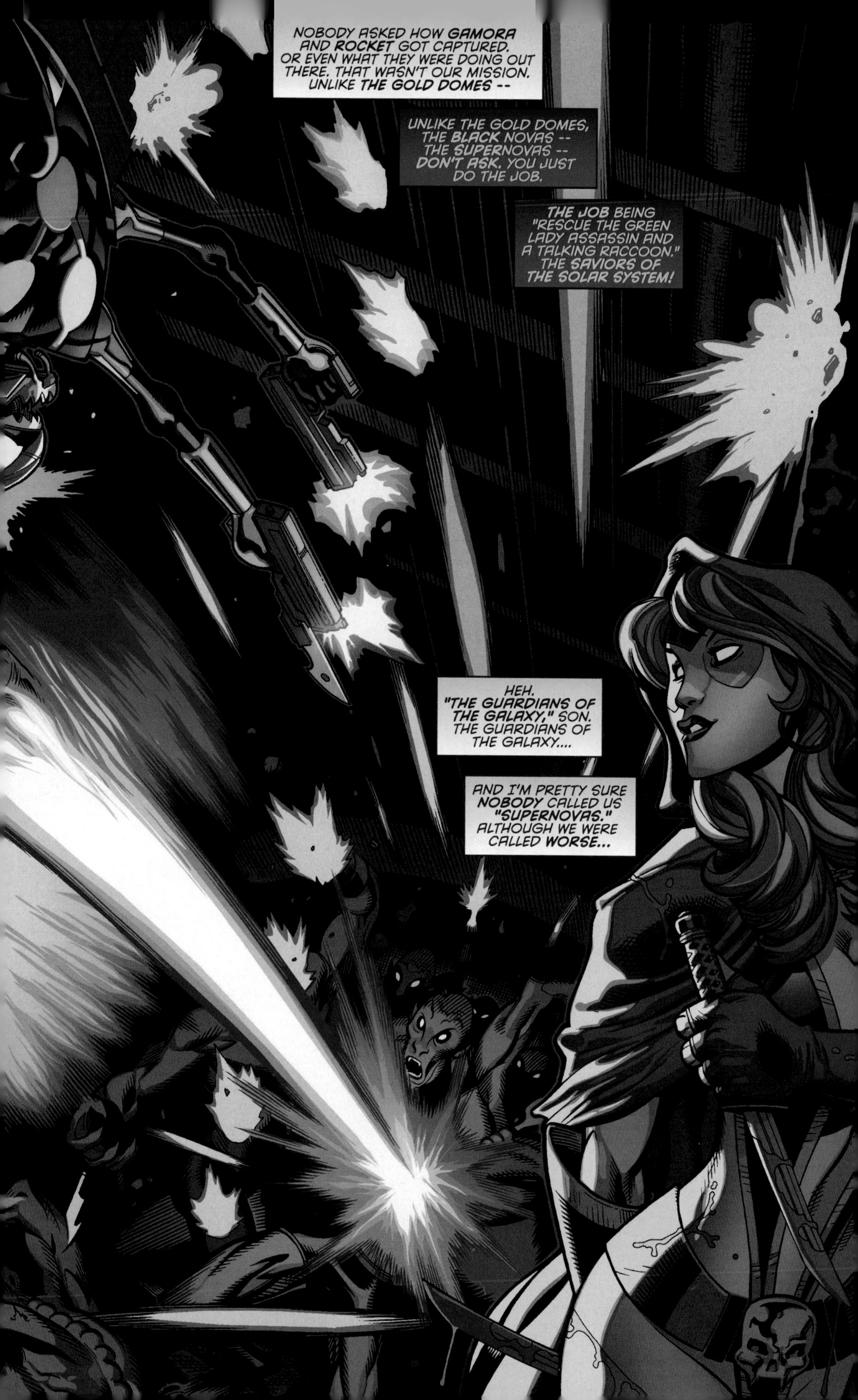
NOBODY ASKED HOW GAMORA AND ROCKET GOT CAPTURED. OR EVEN WHAT THEY WERE DOING OUT THERE. THAT WASN'T OUR MISSION. UNLIKE THE GOLD DOMES --
UNLIKE THE GOLD DOMES, THE BLACK NOVAS -- THE SUPERNOVAS -- DON'T ASK. YOU JUST DO THE JOB.
THE JOB BEING "RESCUE THE GREEN LADY ASSASSIN AND A TALKING RACCOON." THE SAVIORS OF THE SOLAR SYSTEM!
HEH. "THE GUARDIANS OF THE GALAXY," SON. THE GUARDIANS OF THE GALAXY....
AND I'M PRETTY SURE NOBODY CALLED US "SUPERNOVAS." ALTHOUGH WE WERE CALLED WORSE...

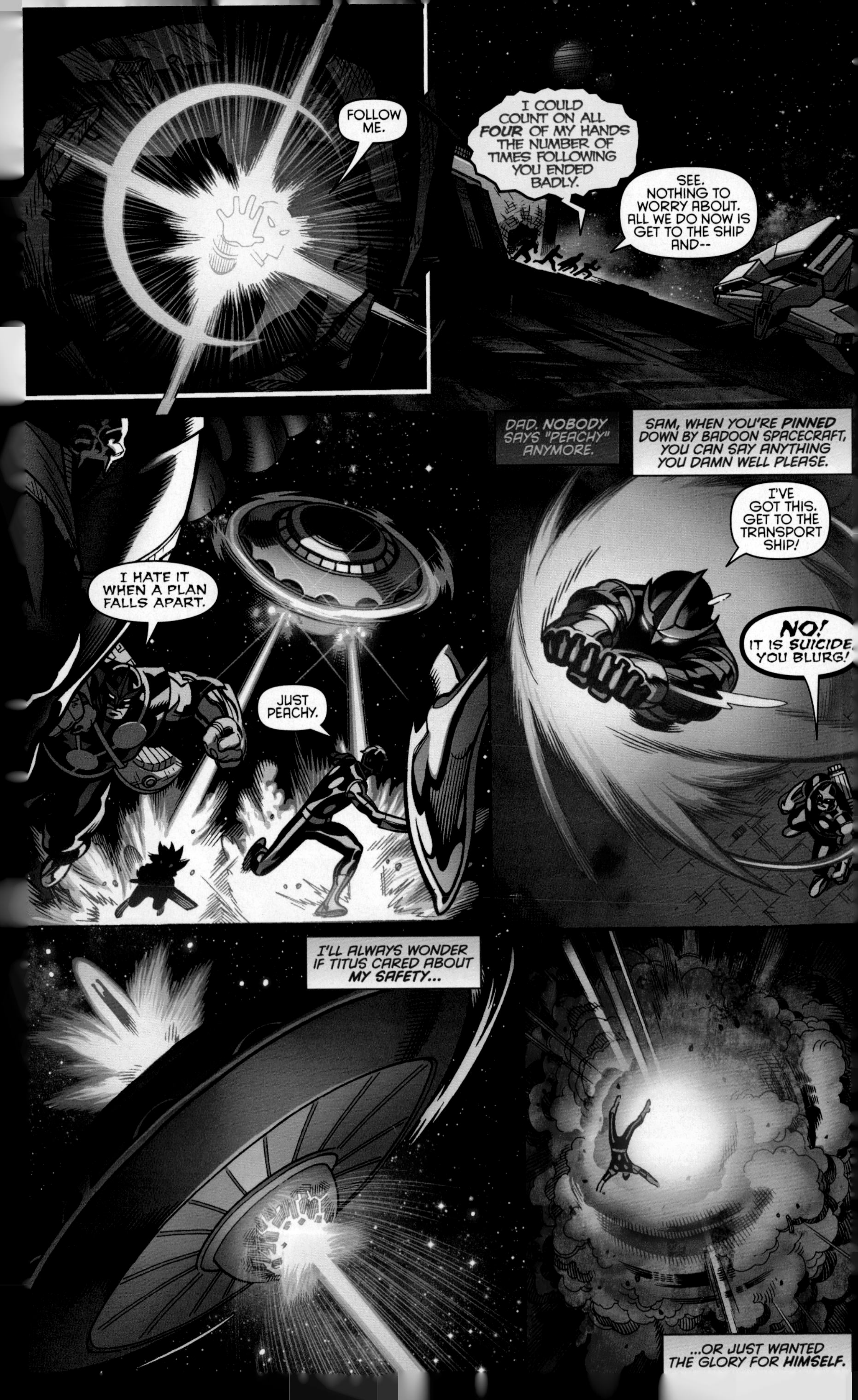
FOLLOW ME.
I COULD COUNT ON ALL FOUR OF MY HANDS THE NUMBER OF TIMES FOLLOWING YOU ENDED BADLY.
SEE. NOTHING TO WORRY ABOUT. ALL WE DO NOW IS GET TO THE SHIP AND--
I HATE IT WHEN A PLAN FALLS APART.
JUST PEACHY.
DAD. NOBODY SAYS "PEACHY" ANYMORE.
SAM, WHEN YOU'RE PINNED DOWN BY BADOON SPACECRAFT, YOU CAN SAY ANYTHING YOU DAMN WELL PLEASE.
I'VE GOT THIS. GET TO THE TRANSPORT SHIP!
NO! IT IS SUICIDE, YOU BLURG!
I'LL ALWAYS WONDER IF TITUS CARED ABOUT MY SAFETY...
...OR JUST WANTED THE GLORY FOR HIMSELF.

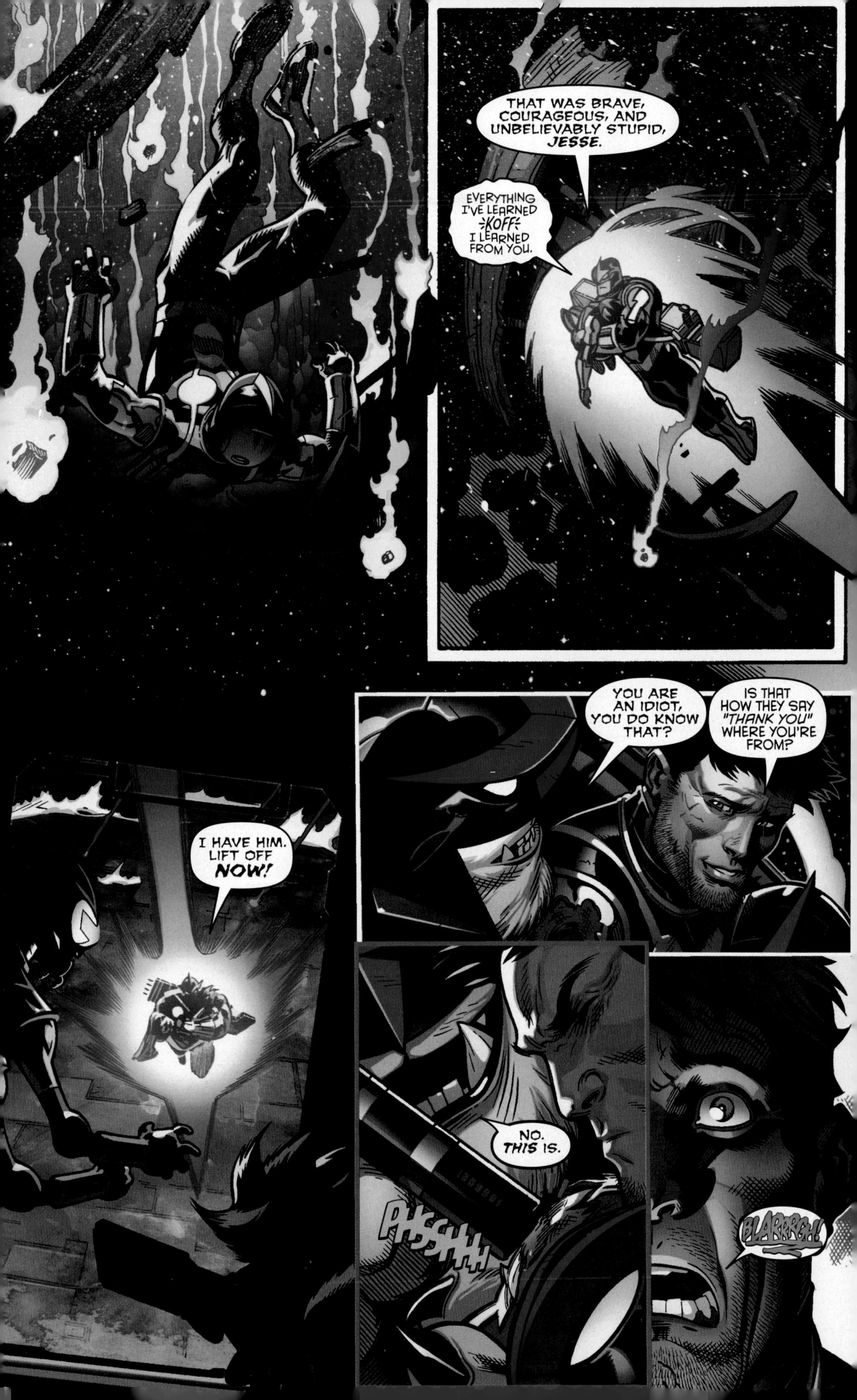
THAT WAS BRAVE, COURAGEOUS, AND UNBELIEVABLY STUPID, JESSE.
EVERYTHING I'VE LEARNED *KOFF* I LEARNED FROM YOU.
I HAVE HIM. LIFT OFF NOW!
YOU ARE AN IDIOT, YOU DO KNOW THAT?
IS THAT HOW THEY SAY "THANK YOU" WHERE YOU'RE FROM?
NO. THIS IS.
PHSSHHH
BLARRRGH!

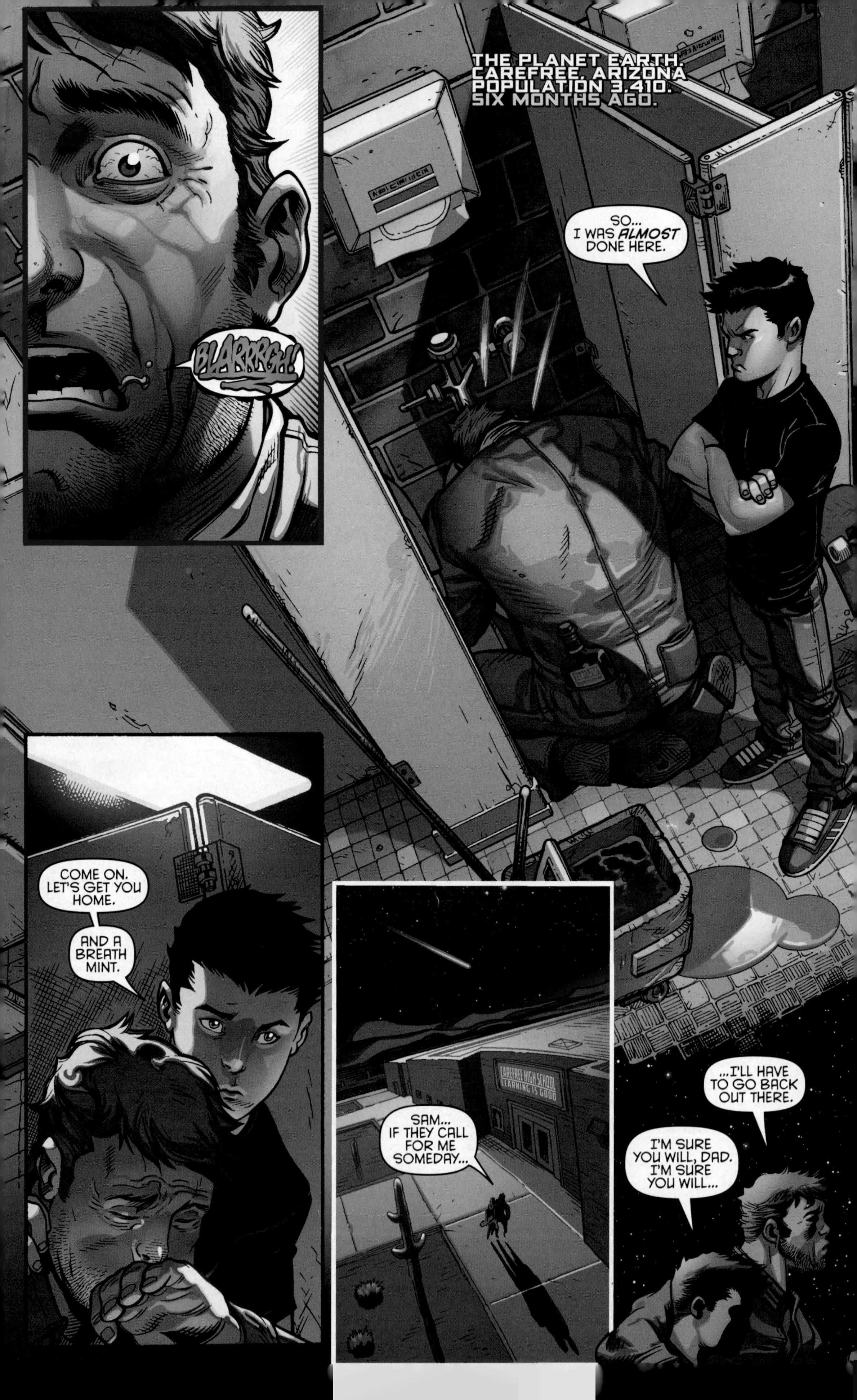
BLARRRGH!
THE PLANET EARTH.
CAREFREE, ARIZONA
POPULATION 3,410.
SIX MONTHS AGO.
SO... I WAS ALMOST DONE HERE.
COME ON. LET'S GET YOU HOME.
AND A BREATH MINT.
CAREFREE HIGH SCHOOL
LEARNING IS GOOD
SAM... IF THEY CALL FOR ME SOMEDAY...
...I'LL HAVE TO GO BACK OUT THERE.
I'M SURE YOU WILL, DAD. I'M SURE YOU WILL...

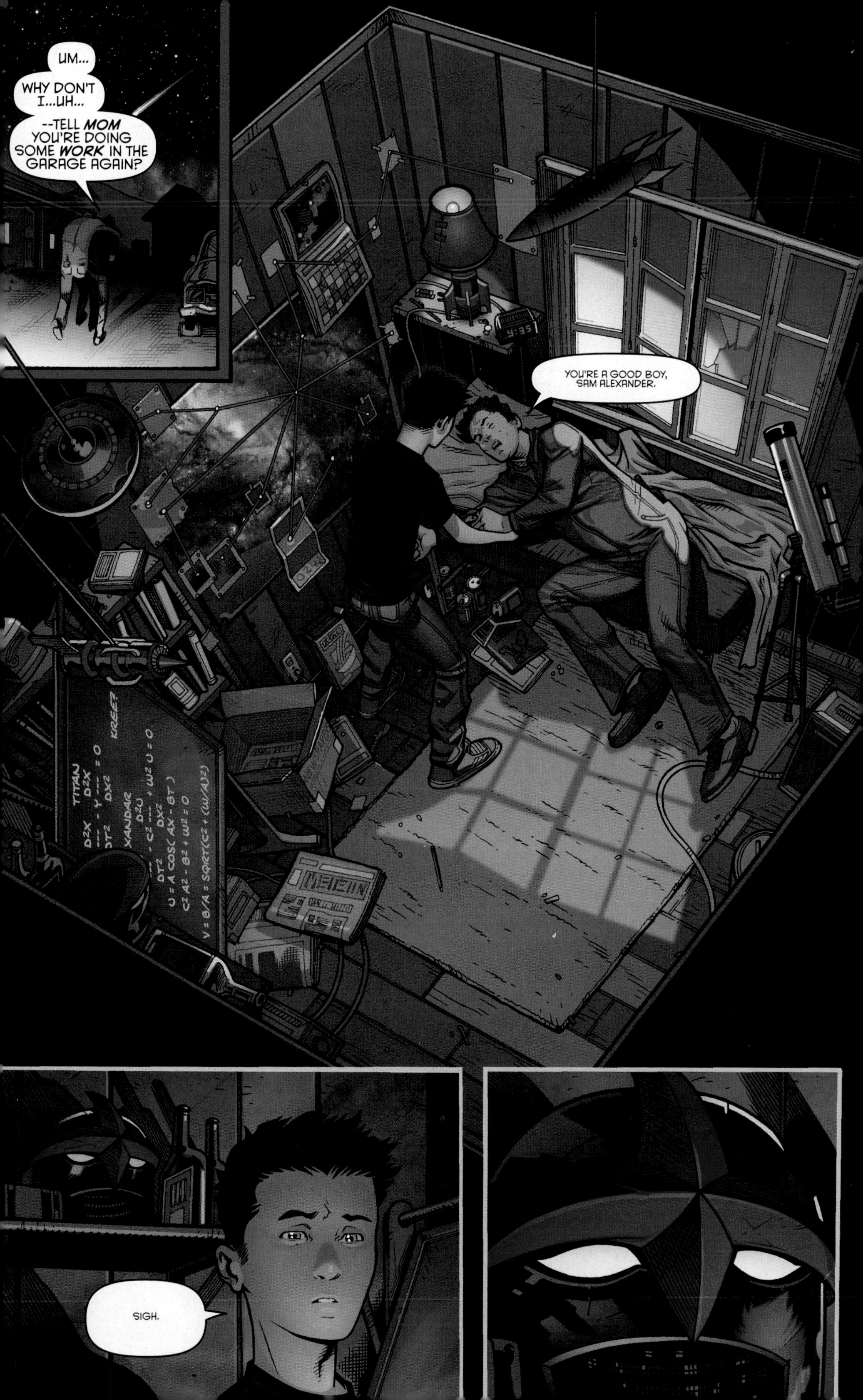
UM...
WHY DON'T I...UH...
--TELL MOM YOU'RE DOING SOME WORK IN THE GARAGE AGAIN?
YOU'RE A GOOD BOY, SAM ALEXANDER.
SIGH.

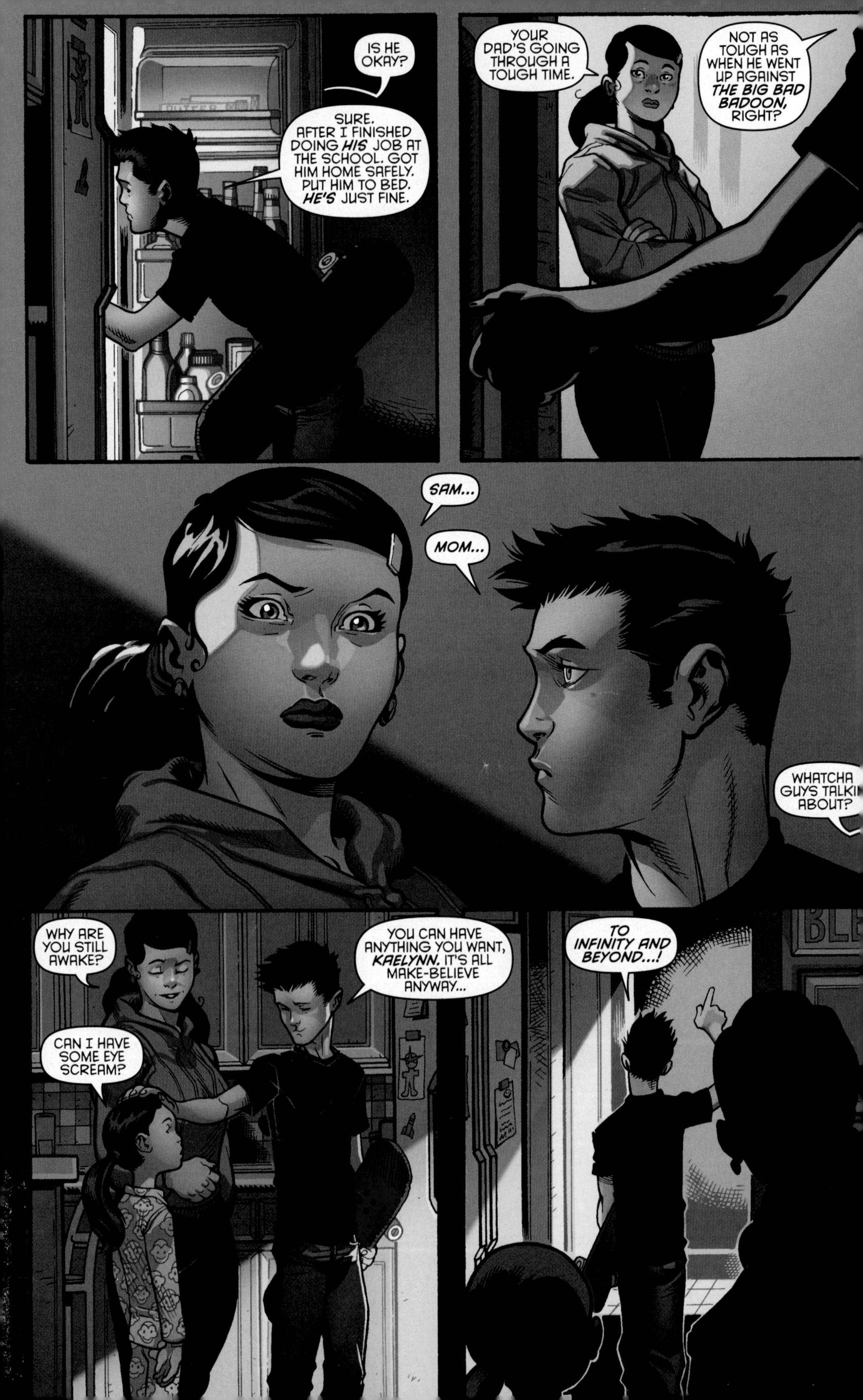
IS HE OKAY?
SURE. AFTER I FINISHED DOING HIS JOB AT THE SCHOOL. GOT HIM HOME SAFELY. PUT HIM TO BED. HE'S JUST FINE.
YOUR DAD'S GOING THROUGH A TOUGH TIME.
NOT AS TOUGH AS WHEN HE WENT UP AGAINST THE BIG BAD BADOON, RIGHT?
SAM...
MOM...
WHATCHA GUYS TALKI ABOUT?
WHY ARE YOU STILL AWAKE?
CAN I HAVE SOME EYE SCREAM?
YOU CAN HAVE ANYTHING YOU WANT, KAELYNN. IT'S ALL MAKE-BELIEVE ANYWAY...
TO INFINITY AND BEYOND...!

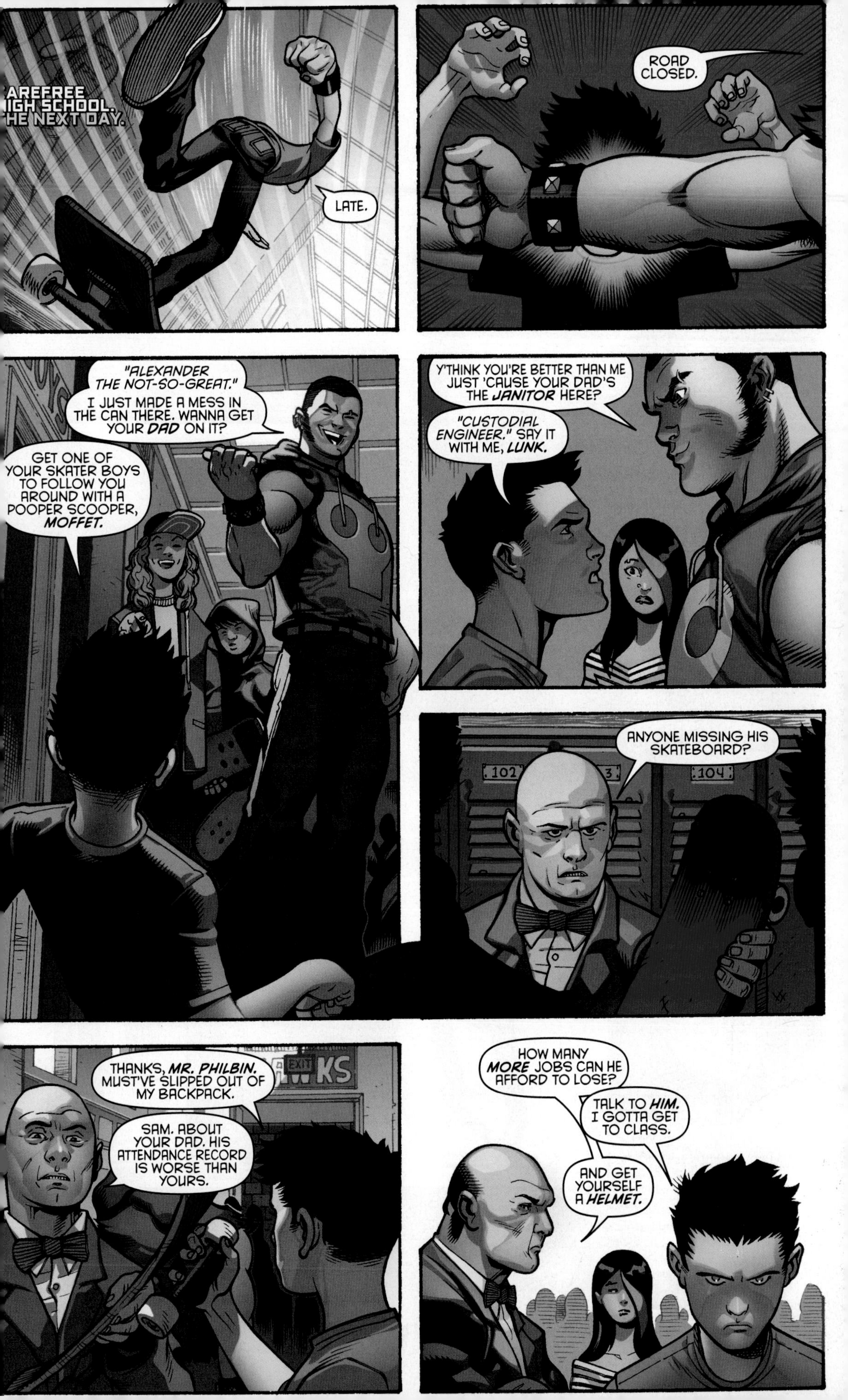

AREFREE
IGH SCHOOL.
HE NEXT DAY.
LATE.
ROAD CLOSED.
"ALEXANDER THE NOT-SO-GREAT." I JUST MADE A MESS IN THE CAN THERE. WANNA GET YOUR DAD ON IT?
GET ONE OF YOUR SKATER BOYS TO FOLLOW YOU AROUND WITH A POOPER SCOOPER, MOFFET.
Y'THINK YOU'RE BETTER THAN ME JUST 'CAUSE YOUR DAD'S THE JANITOR HERE?
"CUSTODIAL ENGINEER." SAY IT WITH ME, LUNK.
ANYONE MISSING HIS SKATEBOARD?
102
104
THANKS, MR. PHILBIN. MUST'VE SLIPPED OUT OF MY BACKPACK.
SAM. ABOUT YOUR DAD. HIS ATTENDANCE RECORD IS WORSE THAN YOURS.
EXIT
HOW MANY MORE JOBS CAN HE AFFORD TO LOSE?
TALK TO HIM. I GOTTA GET TO CLASS.
AND GET YOURSELF A HELMET.

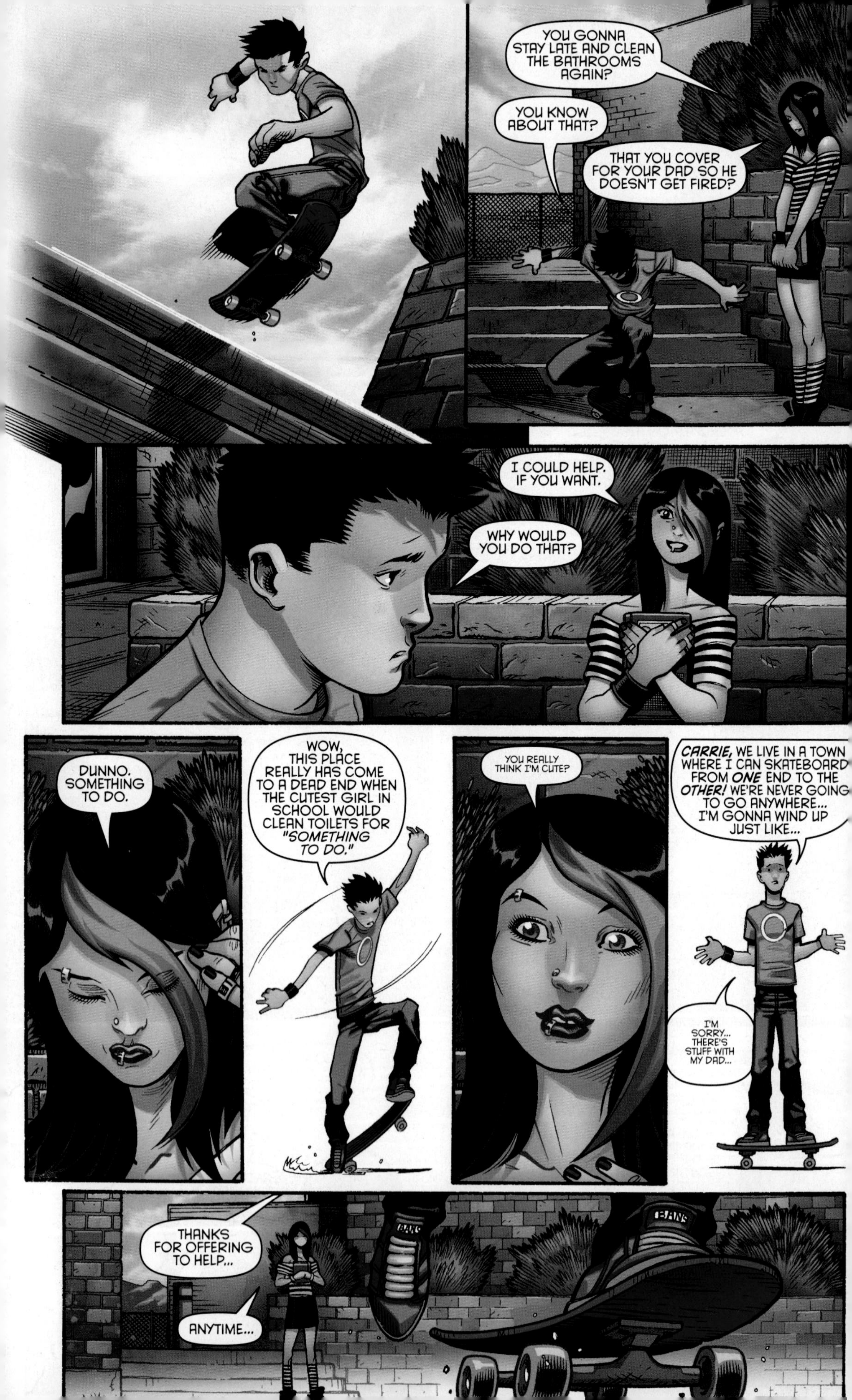
YOU GONNA STAY LATE AND CLEAN THE BATHROOMS AGAIN?
YOU KNOW ABOUT THAT?
THAT YOU COVER FOR YOUR DAD SO HE DOESN'T GET FIRED?
I COULD HELP. IF YOU WANT.
WHY WOULD YOU DO THAT?
DUNNO. SOMETHING TO DO.
WOW, THIS PLACE REALLY HAS COME TO A DEAD END WHEN THE CUTEST GIRL IN SCHOOL WOULD CLEAN TOILETS FOR "SOMETHING TO DO."
YOU REALLY THINK I'M CUTE?
CARRIE, WE LIVE IN A TOWN WHERE I CAN SKATEBOARD FROM ONE END TO THE OTHER! WE'RE NEVER GOING TO GO ANYWHERE... I'M GONNA WIND UP JUST LIKE...
I'M SORRY... THERE'S STUFF WITH MY DAD...
THANKS FOR OFFERING TO HELP...
ANYTIME...

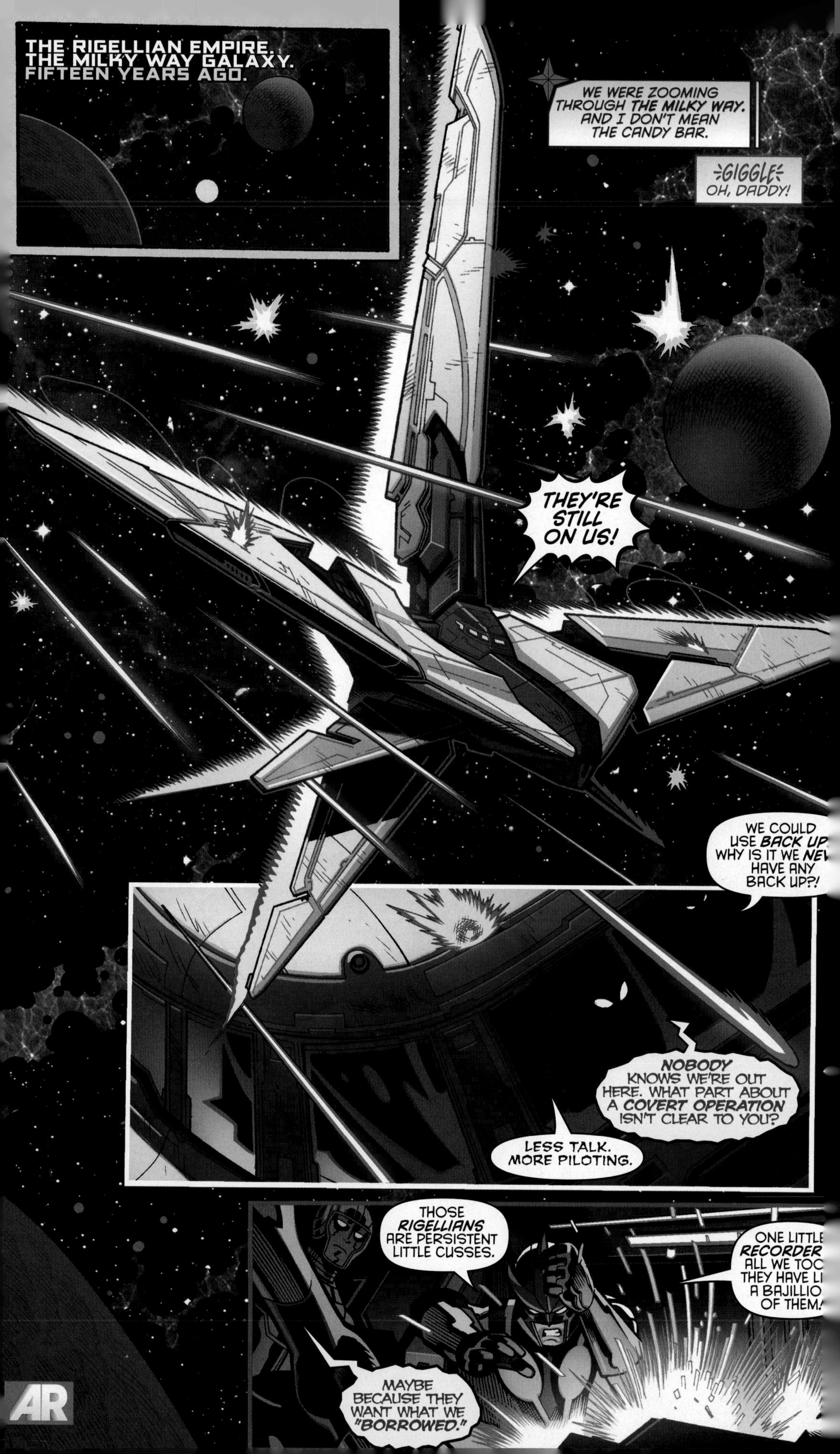
THE RIGELLIAN EMPIRE.
THE MILKY WAY GALAXY.
FIFTEEN YEARS AGO.
WE WERE ZOOMING THROUGH THE MILKY WAY. AND I DON'T MEAN THE CANDY BAR.
GIGGLE OH, DADDY!
THEY'RE STILL ON US!
WE COULD USE BACK UP WHY IS IT WE NEV HAVE ANY BACK UP?!
NOBODY KNOWS WE'RE OUT HERE. WHAT PART ABOUT A COVERT OPERATION ISN'T CLEAR TO YOU?
LESS TALK. MORE PILOTING.
THOSE RIGELLIANS ARE PERSISTENT LITTLE CUSSES.
ONE LITTLE RECORDER ALL WE TOO THEY HAVE L A BAJILLIO OF THEM.
MAYBE BECAUSE THEY WANT WHAT WE "BORROWED."

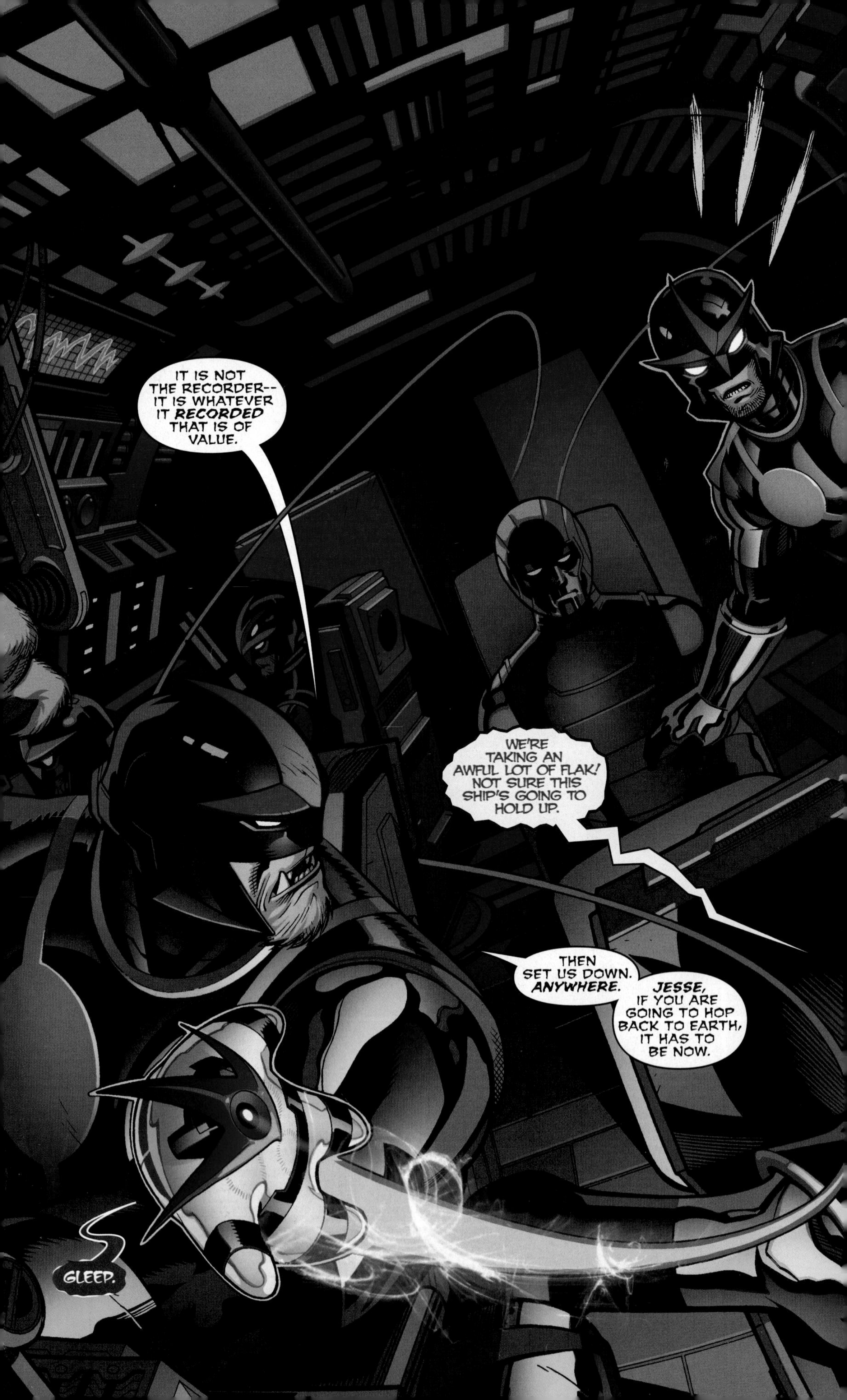
IT IS NOT THE RECORDER-- IT IS WHATEVER IT *RECORDED* THAT IS OF VALUE.
WE'RE TAKING AN AWFUL LOT OF FLAK! NOT SURE THIS SHIP'S GOING TO HOLD UP.
THEN SET US DOWN. *ANYWHERE.*
JESSE, IF YOU ARE GOING TO HOP BACK TO EARTH, IT HAS TO BE NOW.
GLEEP.

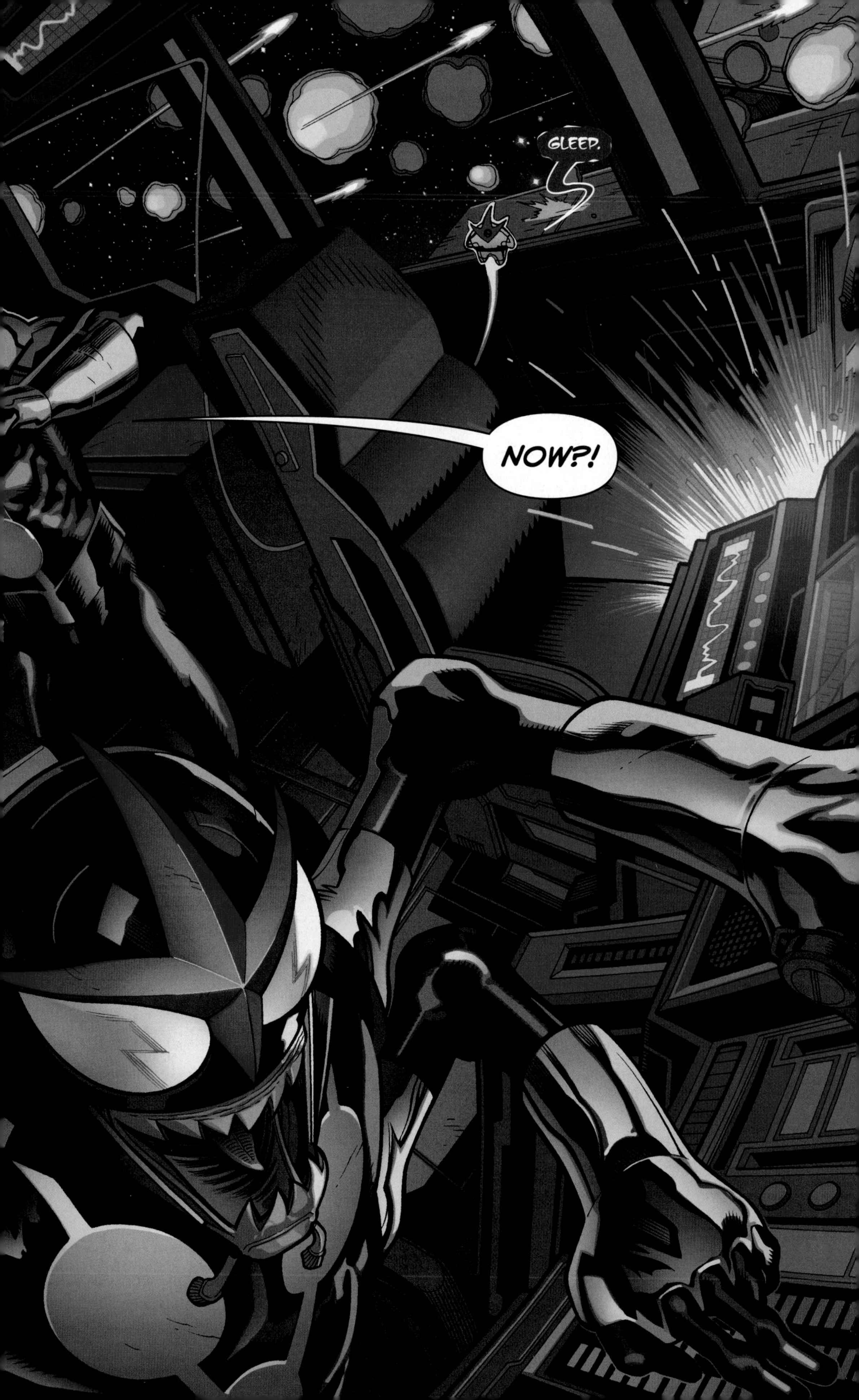
GLEEP.
NOW?!

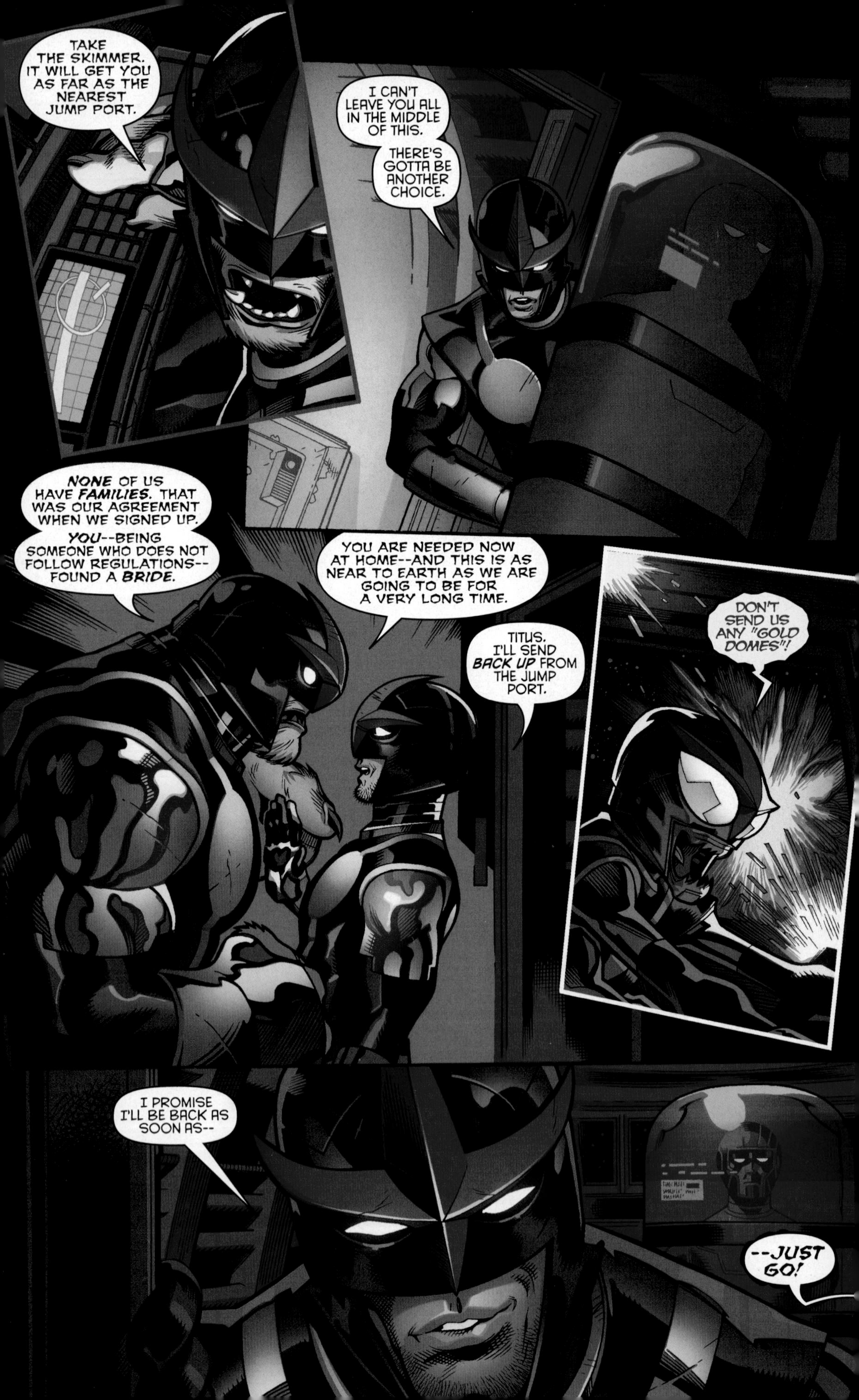
TAKE THE SKIMMER. IT WILL GET YOU AS FAR AS THE NEAREST JUMP PORT.
I CAN'T LEAVE YOU ALL IN THE MIDDLE OF THIS.
THERE'S GOTTA BE ANOTHER CHOICE.
NONE OF US HAVE *FAMILIES*. THAT WAS OUR AGREEMENT WHEN WE SIGNED UP.
YOU--BEING SOMEONE WHO DOES NOT FOLLOW REGULATIONS--FOUND A *BRIDE*.
YOU ARE NEEDED NOW AT HOME--AND THIS IS AS NEAR TO EARTH AS WE ARE GOING TO BE FOR A VERY LONG TIME.
TITUS. I'LL SEND *BACK UP* FROM THE JUMP PORT.
DON'T SEND US ANY *"GOLD DOMES"*!
I PROMISE I'LL BE BACK AS SOON AS--
--*JUST GO!*

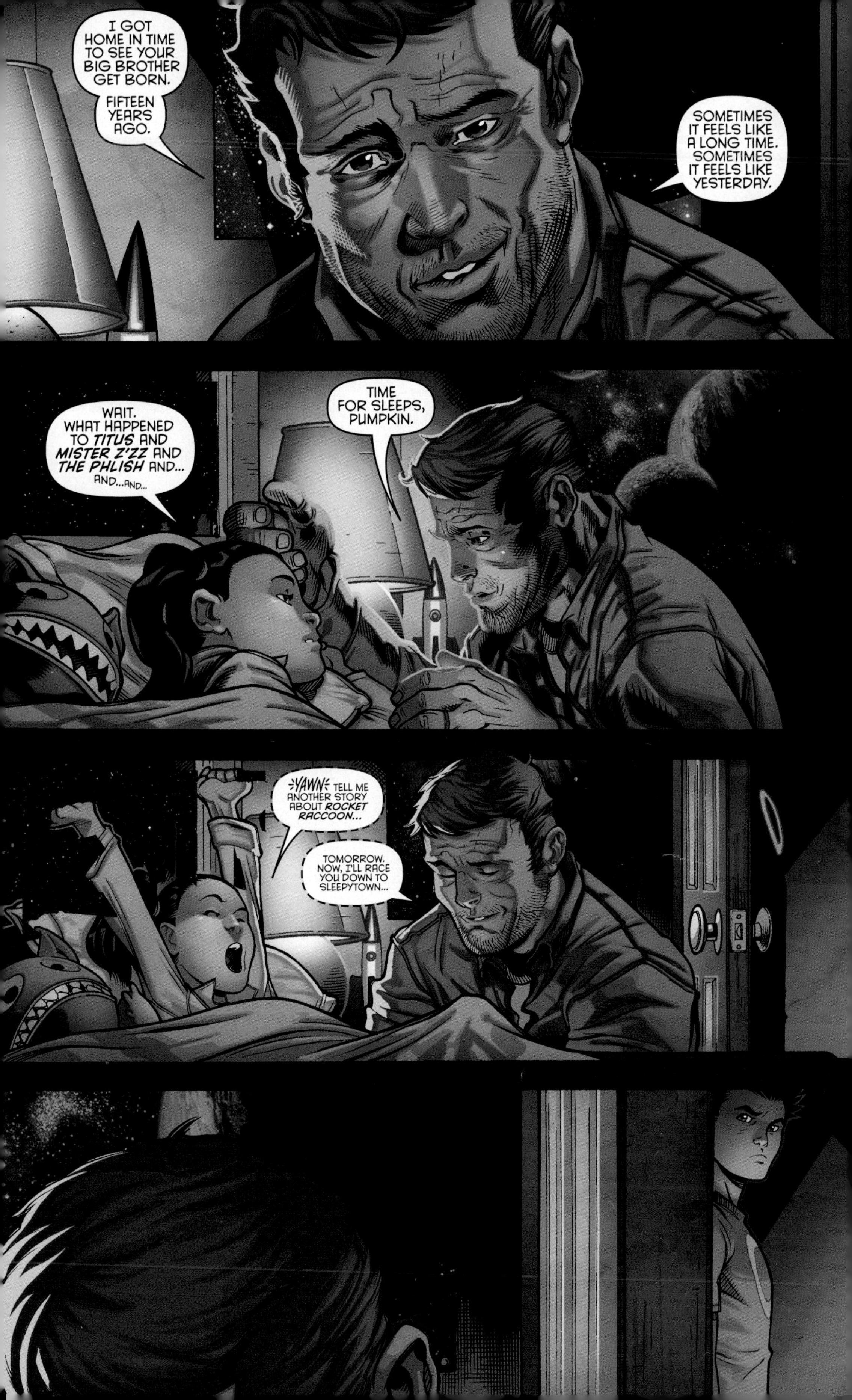
I GOT HOME IN TIME TO SEE YOUR BIG BROTHER GET BORN.
FIFTEEN YEARS AGO.
SOMETIMES IT FEELS LIKE A LONG TIME. SOMETIMES IT FEELS LIKE YESTERDAY.
WAIT. WHAT HAPPENED TO TITUS AND MISTER Z'ZZ AND THE PHLISH AND... AND...AND...
TIME FOR SLEEPS, PUMPKIN.
YAWN TELL ME ANOTHER STORY ABOUT ROCKET RACCOON...
TOMORROW. NOW, I'LL RACE YOU DOWN TO SLEEPYTOWN...

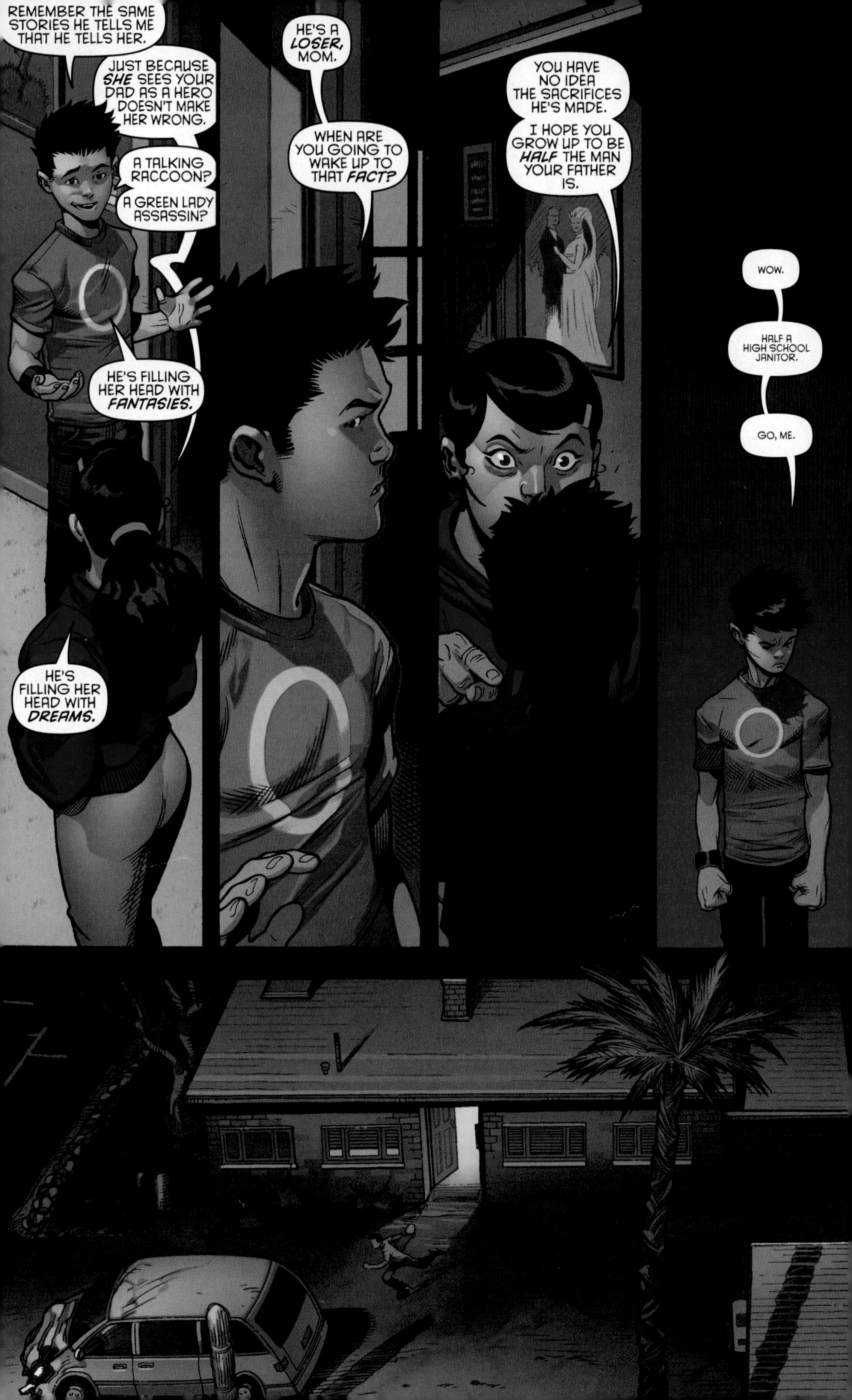
REMEMBER THE SAME STORIES HE TELLS ME THAT HE TELLS HER.
JUST BECAUSE *SHE* SEES YOUR DAD AS A HERO DOESN'T MAKE HER WRONG.
A TALKING RACCOON?
A GREEN LADY ASSASSIN?
HE'S FILLING HER HEAD WITH *FANTASIES.*
HE'S FILLING HER HEAD WITH *DREAMS.*
HE'S A *LOSER,* MOM.
WHEN ARE YOU GOING TO WAKE UP TO THAT *FACT?*
YOU HAVE NO IDEA THE SACRIFICES HE'S MADE.
I HOPE YOU GROW UP TO BE *HALF* THE MAN YOUR FATHER IS.
WOW.
HALF A HIGH SCHOOL JANITOR.
GO, ME.

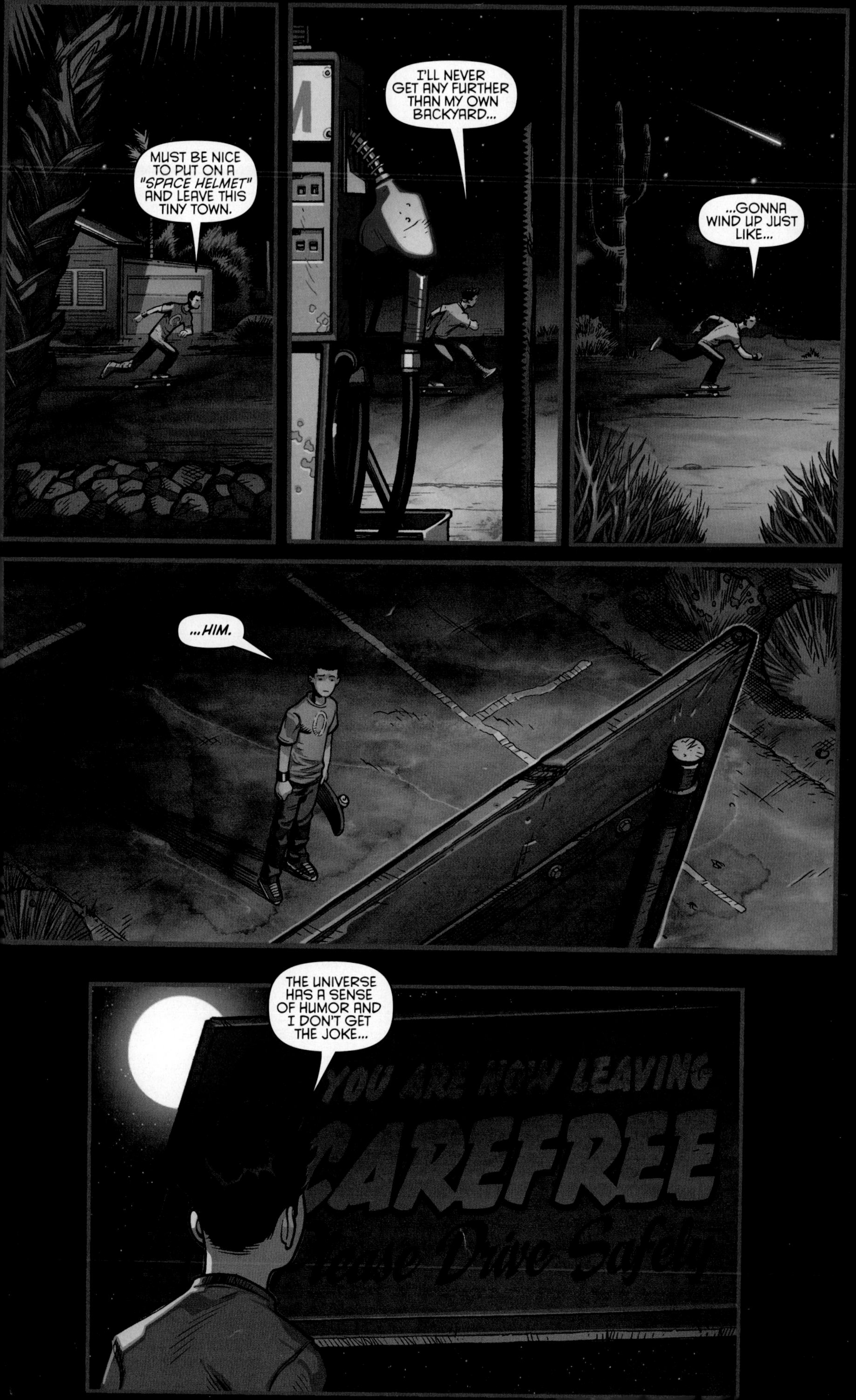
MUST BE NICE TO PUT ON A "SPACE HELMET" AND LEAVE THIS TINY TOWN.
I'LL NEVER GET ANY FURTHER THAN MY OWN BACKYARD...
...GONNA WIND UP JUST LIKE...
...HIM.
THE UNIVERSE HAS A SENSE OF HUMOR AND I DON'T GET THE JOKE...
YOU ARE NOW LEAVING
CAREFREE

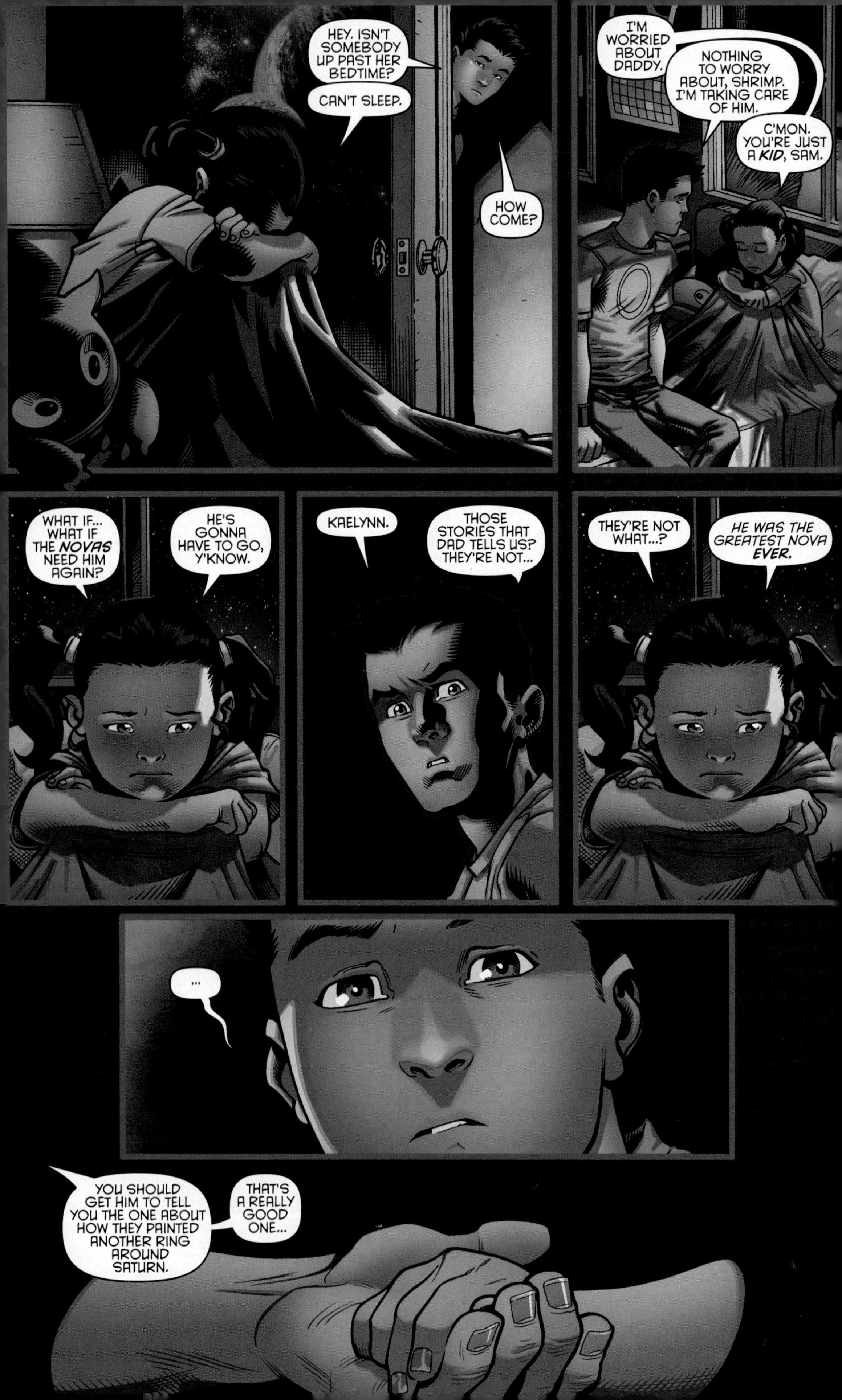
HEY. ISN'T SOMEBODY UP PAST HER BEDTIME?
CAN'T SLEEP.
HOW COME?
I'M WORRIED ABOUT DADDY.
NOTHING TO WORRY ABOUT, SHRIMP. I'M TAKING CARE OF HIM.
C'MON. YOU'RE JUST A *KID*, SAM.
WHAT IF... WHAT IF THE *NOVAS* NEED HIM AGAIN?
HE'S GONNA HAVE TO GO, Y'KNOW.
KAELYNN.
THOSE STORIES THAT DAD TELLS US? THEY'RE NOT...
THEY'RE NOT WHAT...?
HE WAS THE GREATEST NOVA ***EVER.***
...
YOU SHOULD GET HIM TO TELL YOU THE ONE ABOUT HOW THEY PAINTED ANOTHER RING AROUND SATURN.
THAT'S A REALLY GOOD ONE...

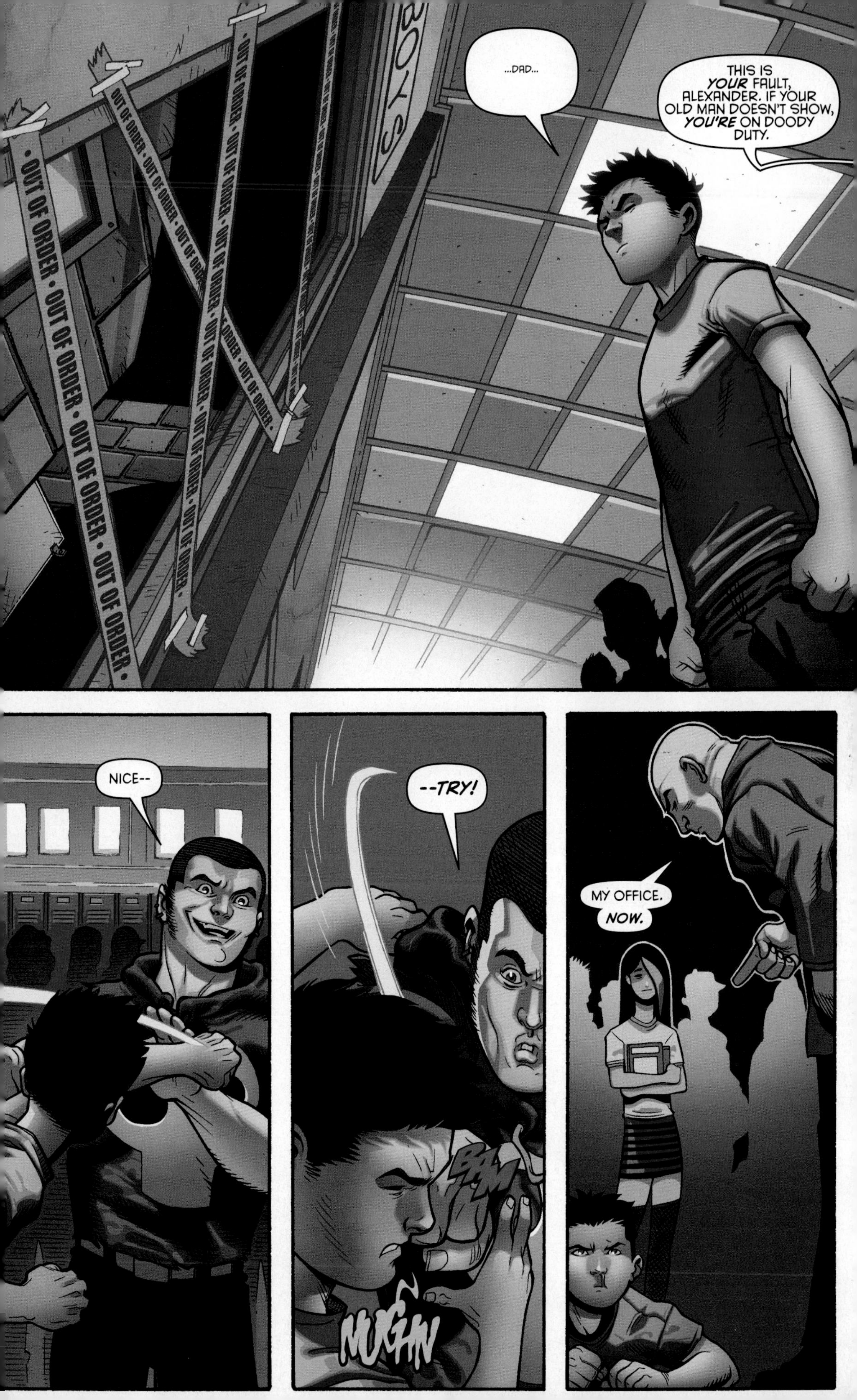
OUT OF ORDER
BOYS
...DAD...
THIS IS YOUR FAULT, ALEXANDER. IF YOUR OLD MAN DOESN'T SHOW, YOU'RE ON DOODY DUTY.
NICE--
--TRY!
BAM
MUGHN
MY OFFICE. NOW.

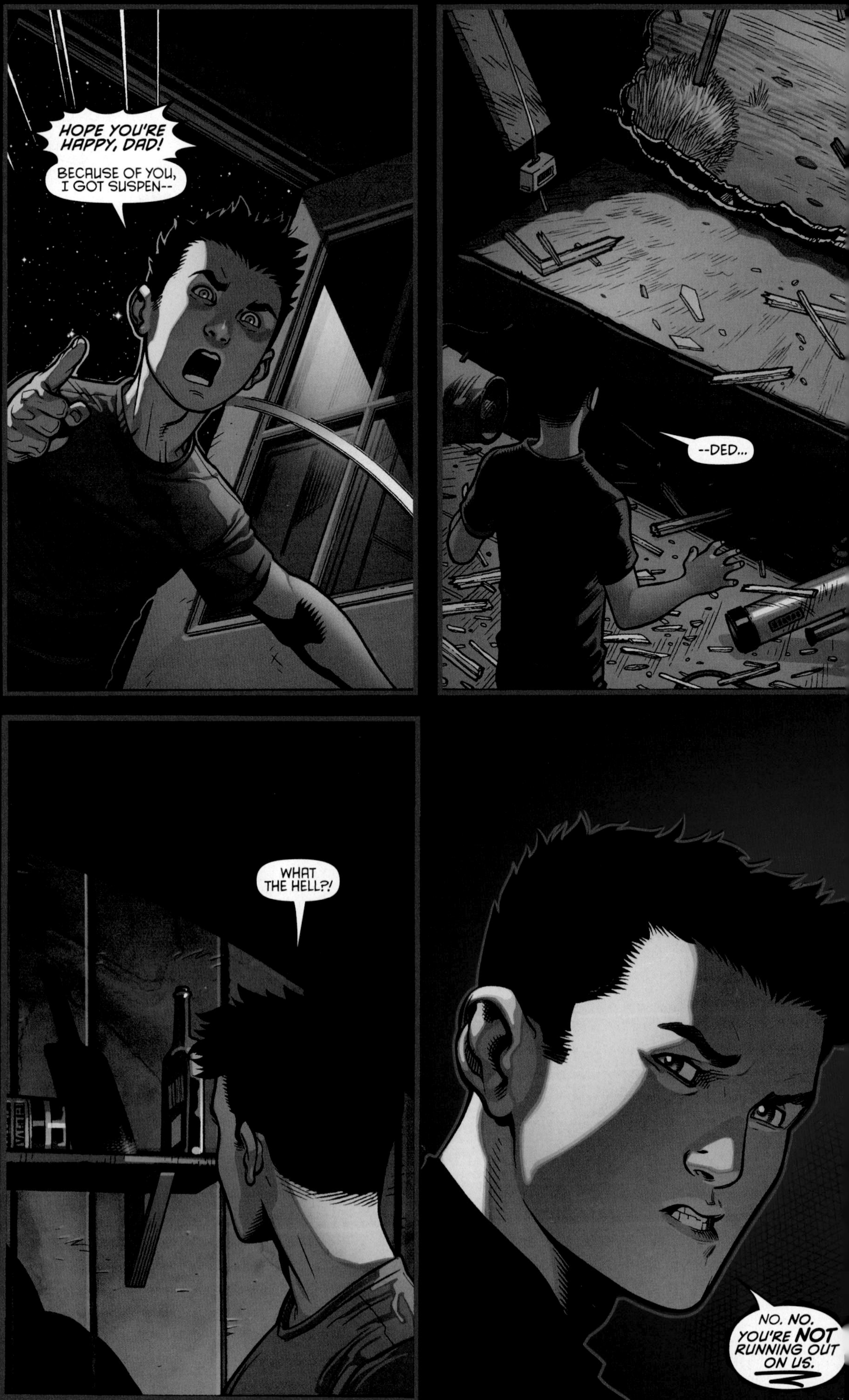
HOPE YOU'RE HAPPY, DAD!
BECAUSE OF YOU, I GOT SUSPEN--
--DED...
WHAT THE HELL?!
NO. NO. YOU'RE NOT RUNNING OUT ON US.

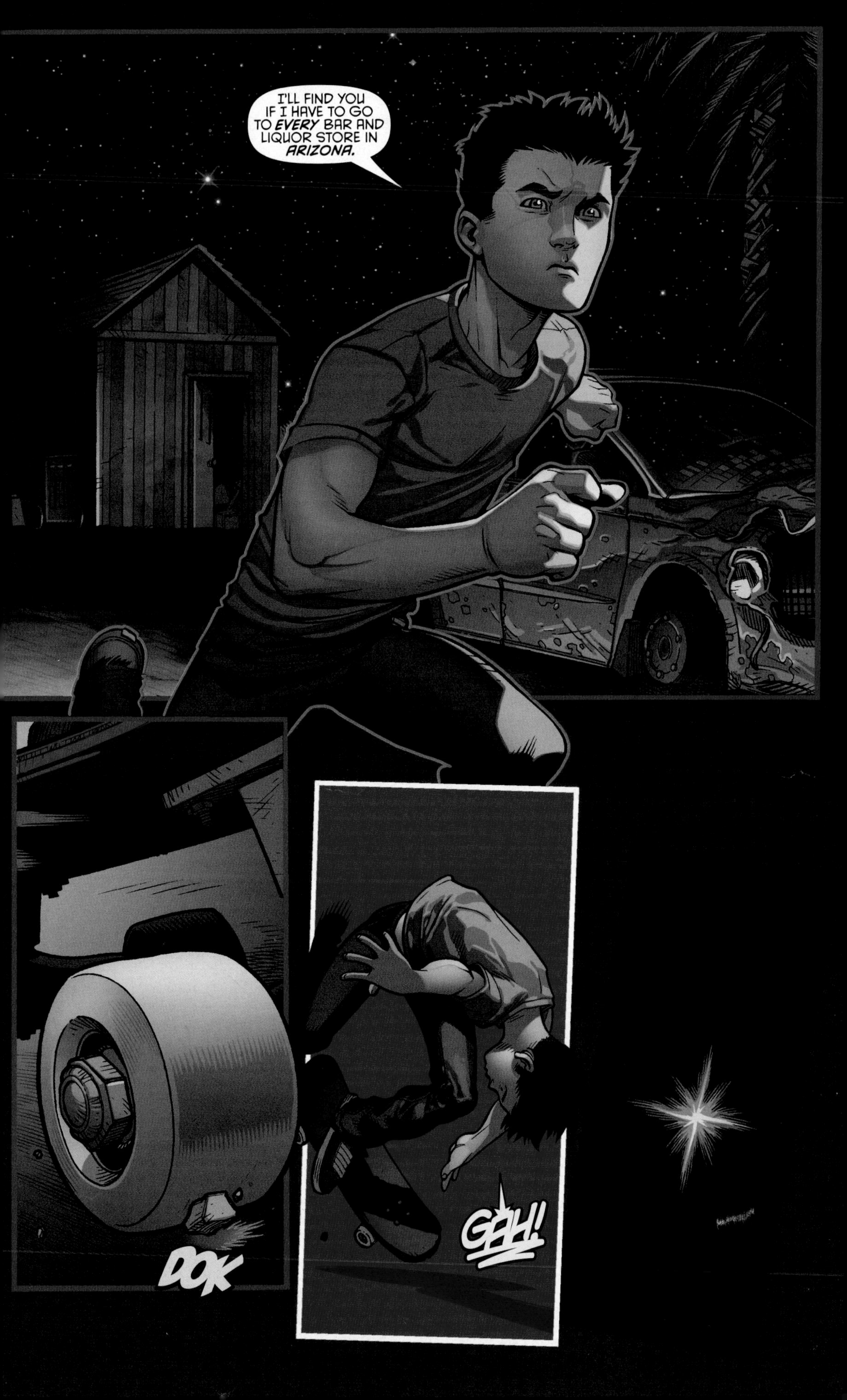
I'LL FIND YOU IF I HAVE TO GO TO *EVERY* BAR AND LIQUOR STORE IN *ARIZONA.*
DOK
GAH!

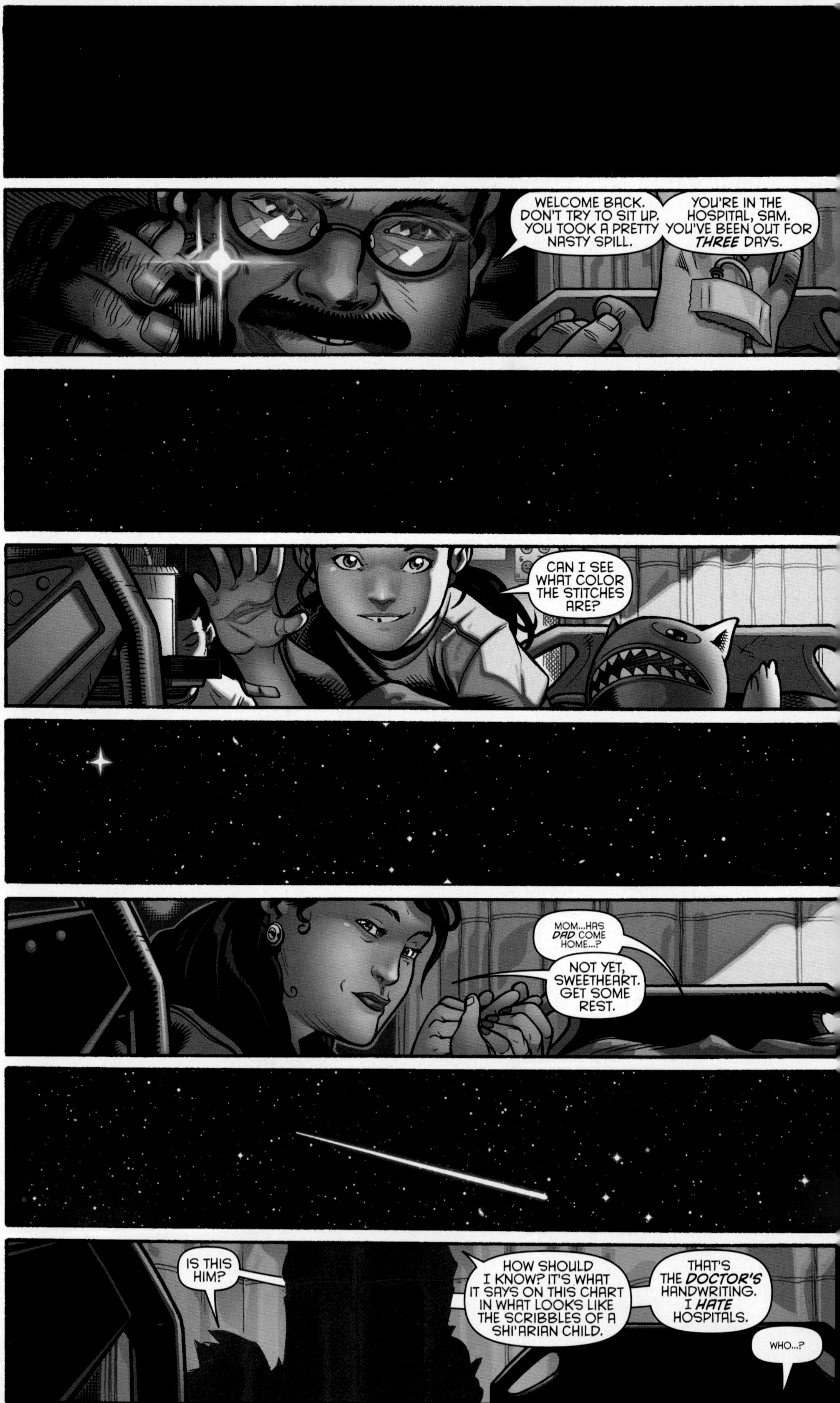
WELCOME BACK. DON'T TRY TO SIT UP. YOU TOOK A PRETTY NASTY SPILL.
YOU'RE IN THE HOSPITAL, SAM. YOU'VE BEEN OUT FOR *THREE* DAYS.
CAN I SEE WHAT COLOR THE STITCHES ARE?
MOM...HAS *DAD* COME HOME...?
NOT YET, SWEETHEART. GET SOME REST.
IS THIS HIM?
HOW SHOULD I KNOW? IT'S WHAT IT SAYS ON THIS CHART IN WHAT LOOKS LIKE THE SCRIBBLES OF A SHI'ARIAN CHILD.
THAT'S THE *DOCTOR'S* HANDWRITING. I *HATE* HOSPITALS.
WHO...?

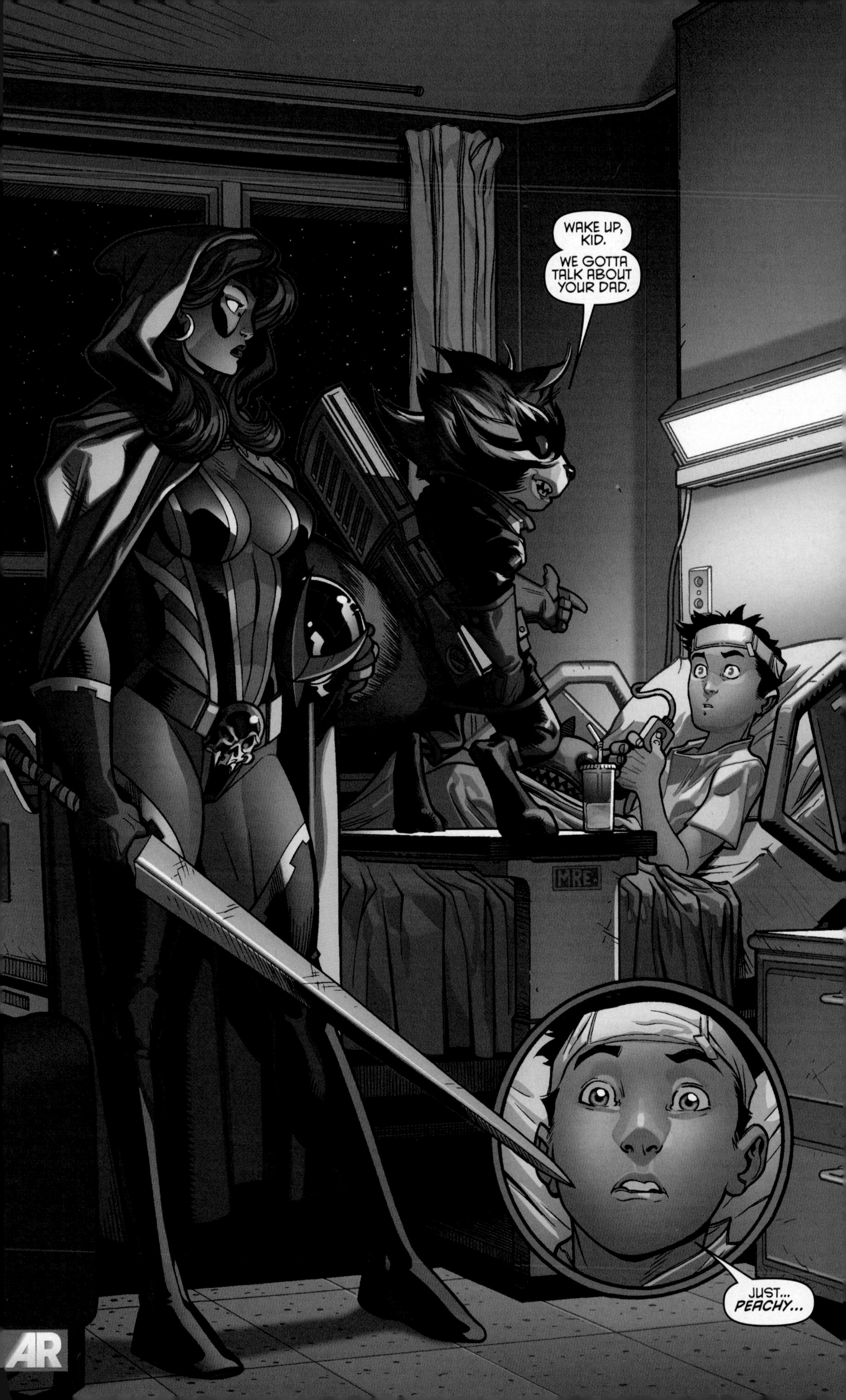
WAKE UP, KID.
WE GOTTA TALK ABOUT YOUR DAD.
JUST... *PEACHY*...
AR

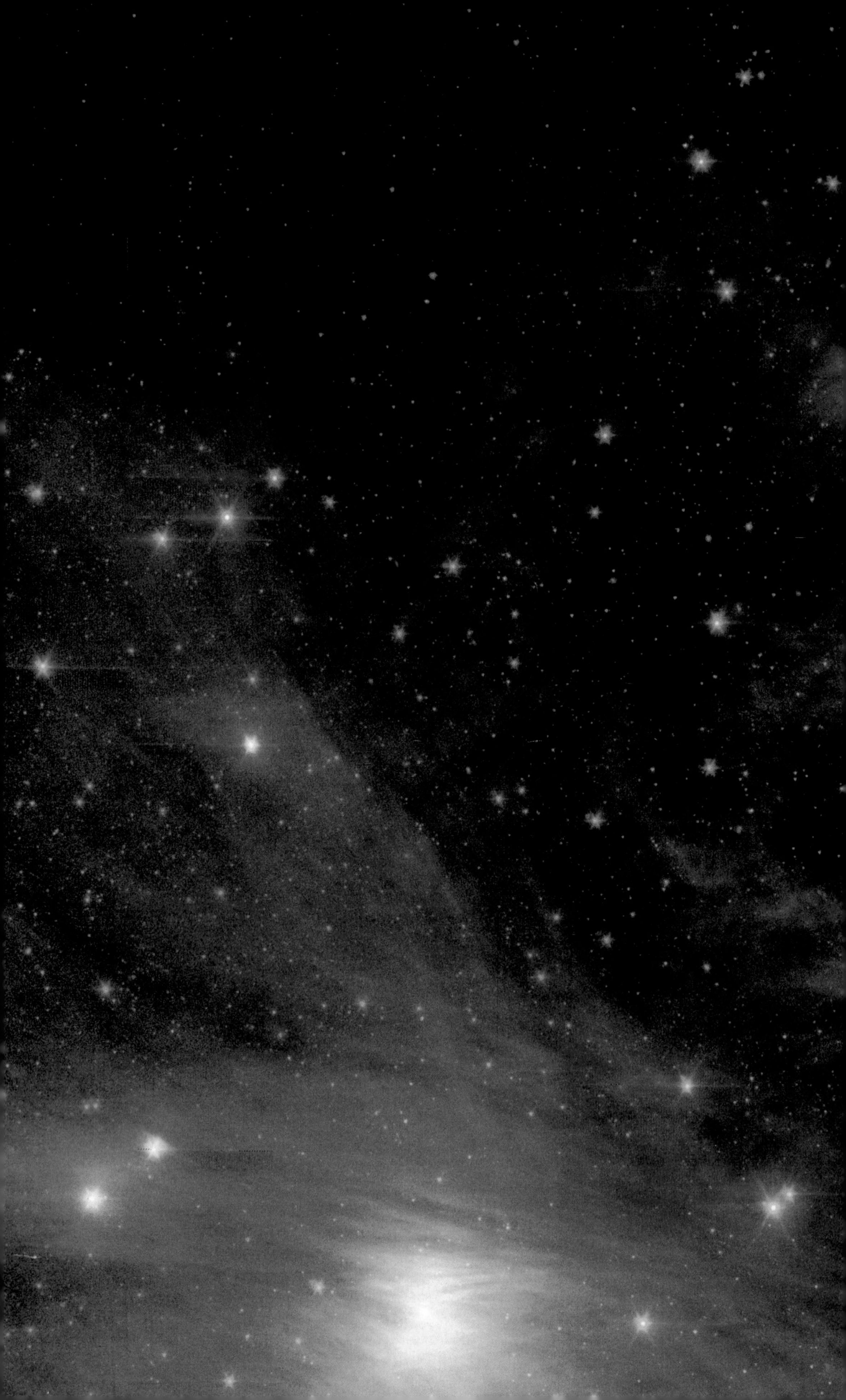

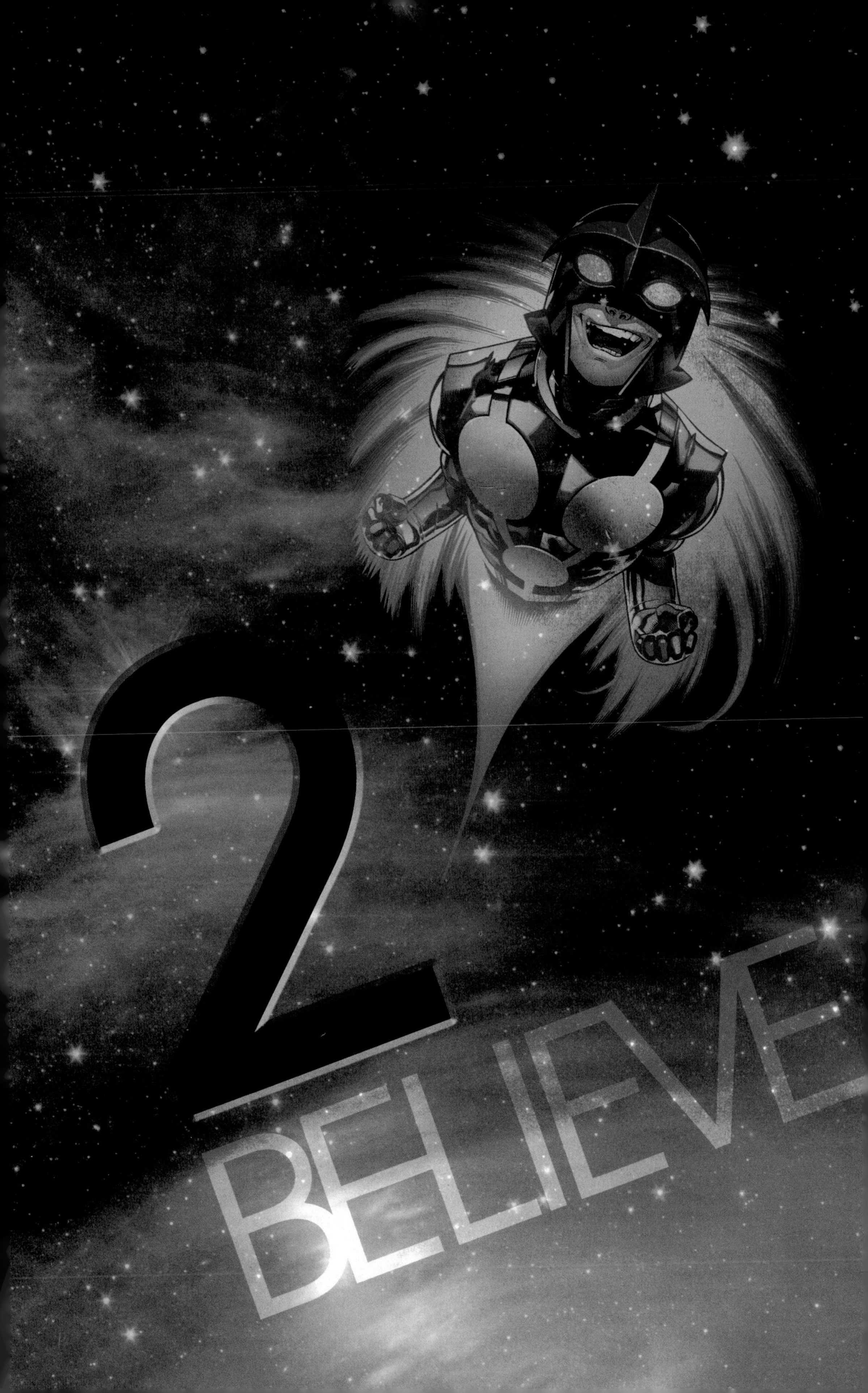
2
BELIEVE

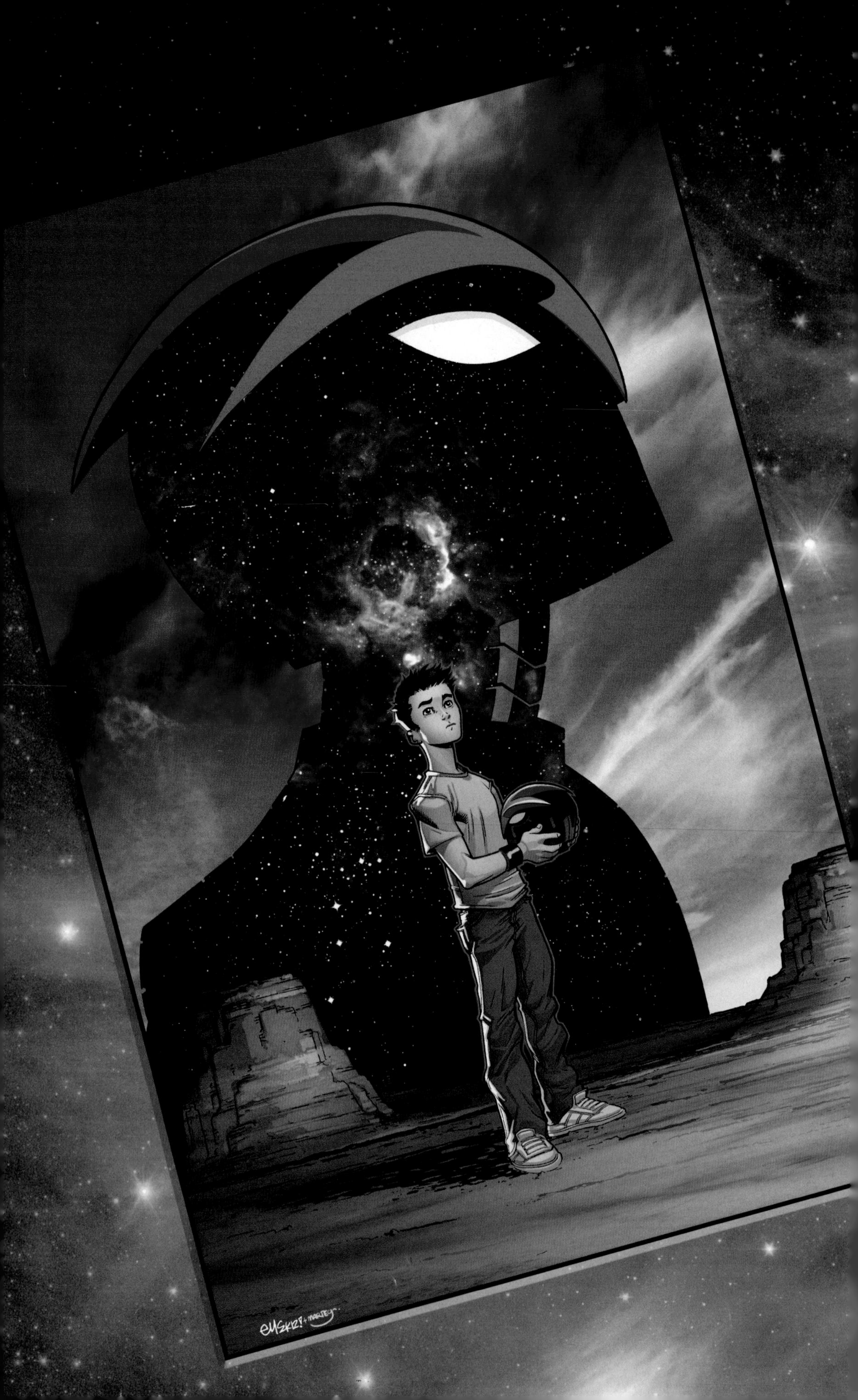

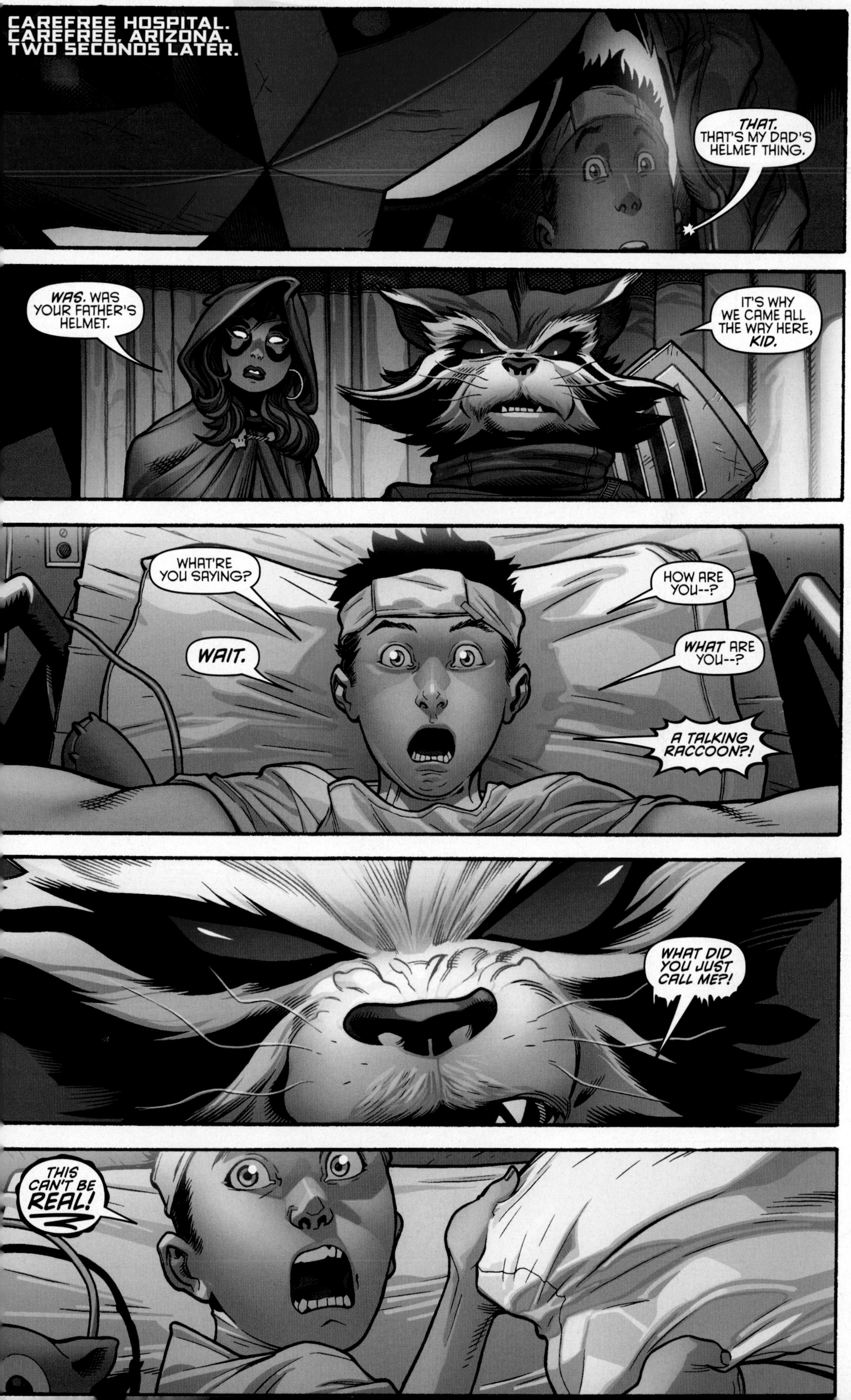
CAREFREE HOSPITAL. CAREFREE, ARIZONA. TWO SECONDS LATER.
THAT. THAT'S MY DAD'S HELMET THING.
WAS. WAS YOUR FATHER'S HELMET.
IT'S WHY WE CAME ALL THE WAY HERE, KID.
WHAT'RE YOU SAYING?
WAIT.
HOW ARE YOU--?
WHAT ARE YOU--?
A TALKING RACCOON?!
WHAT DID YOU JUST CALL ME?!
THIS CAN'T BE REAL!

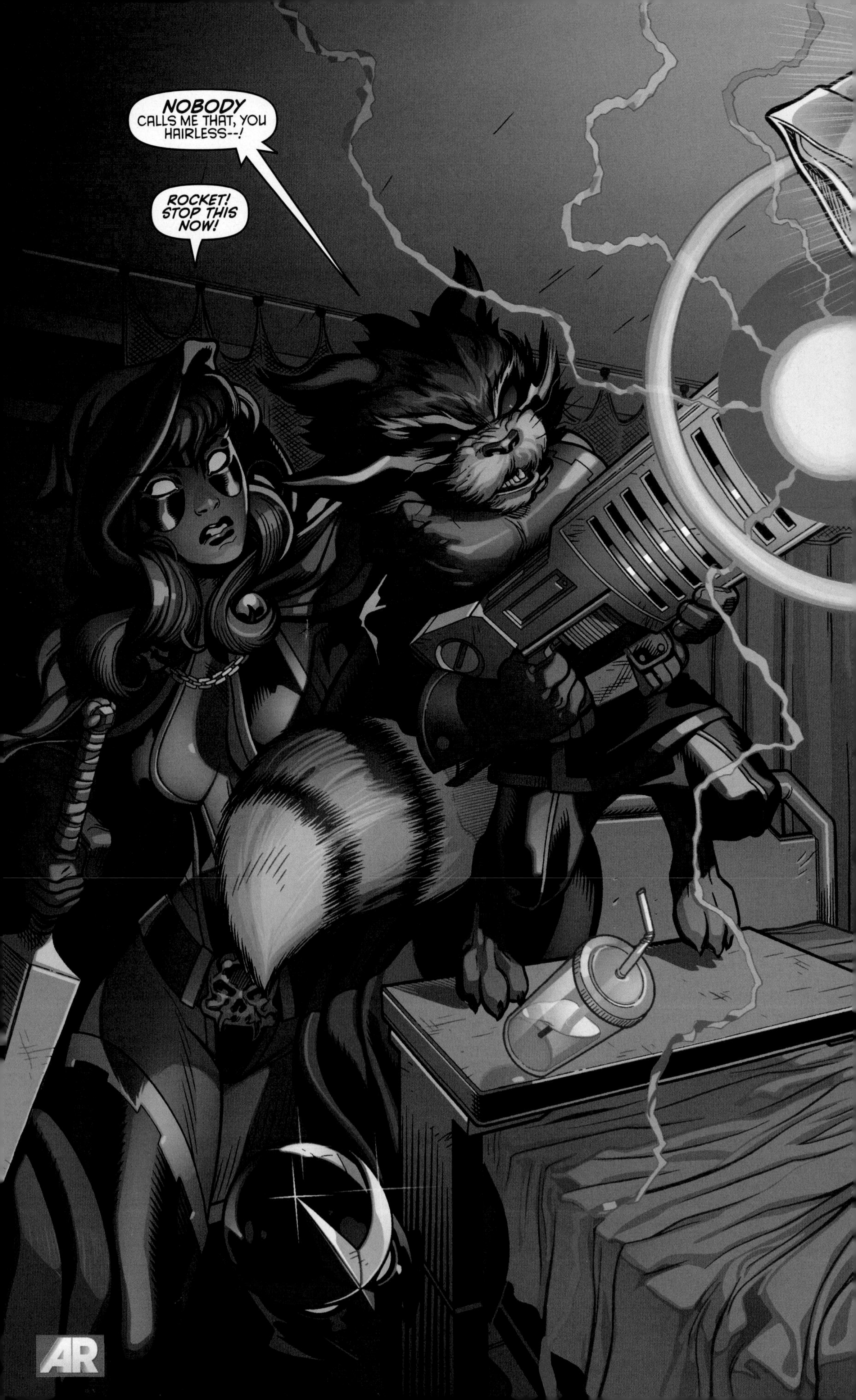
NOBODY CALLS ME THAT, YOU HAIRLESS--!
ROCKET! STOP THIS NOW!

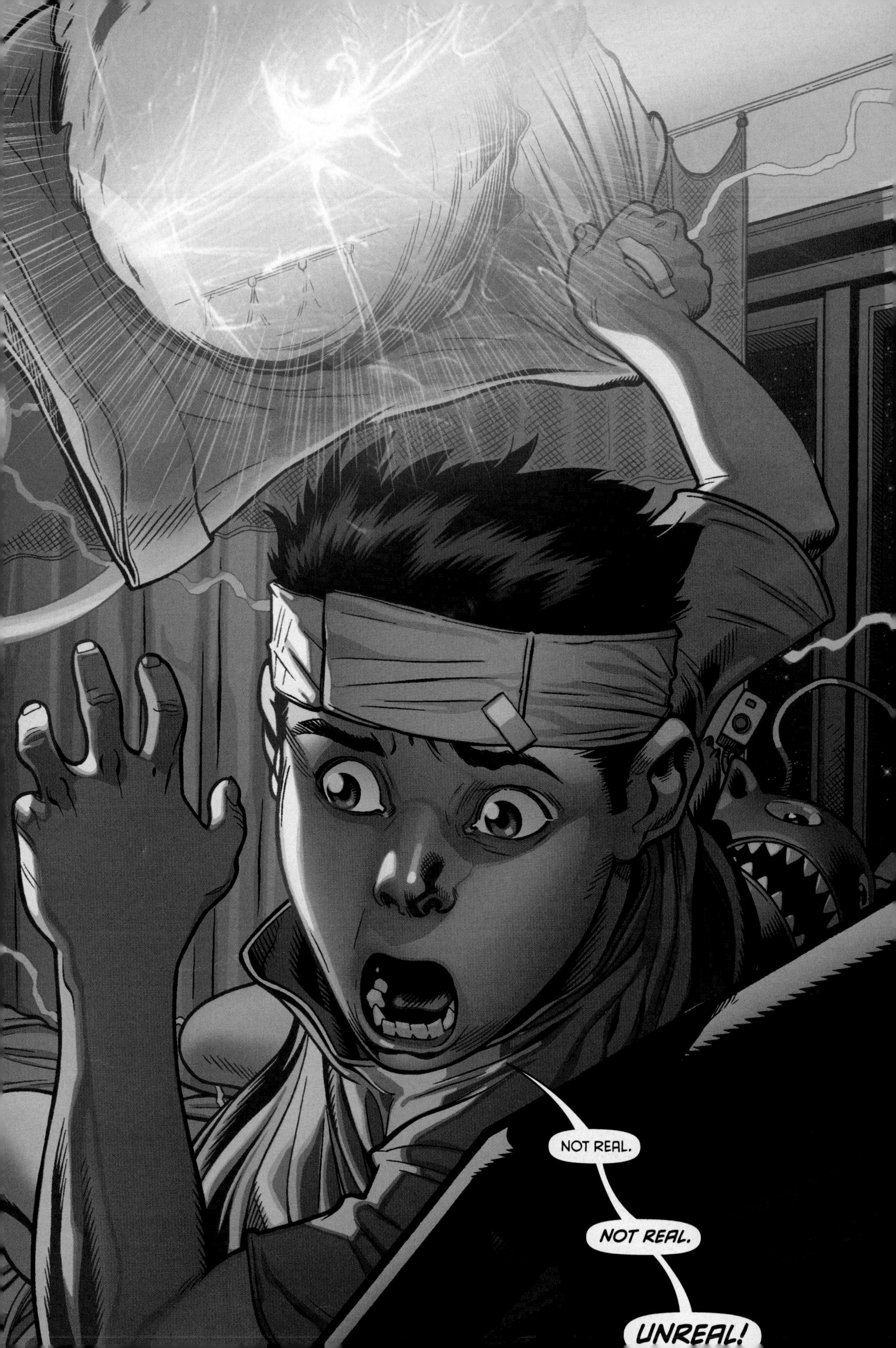
NOT REAL.
NOT REAL.
UNREAL!

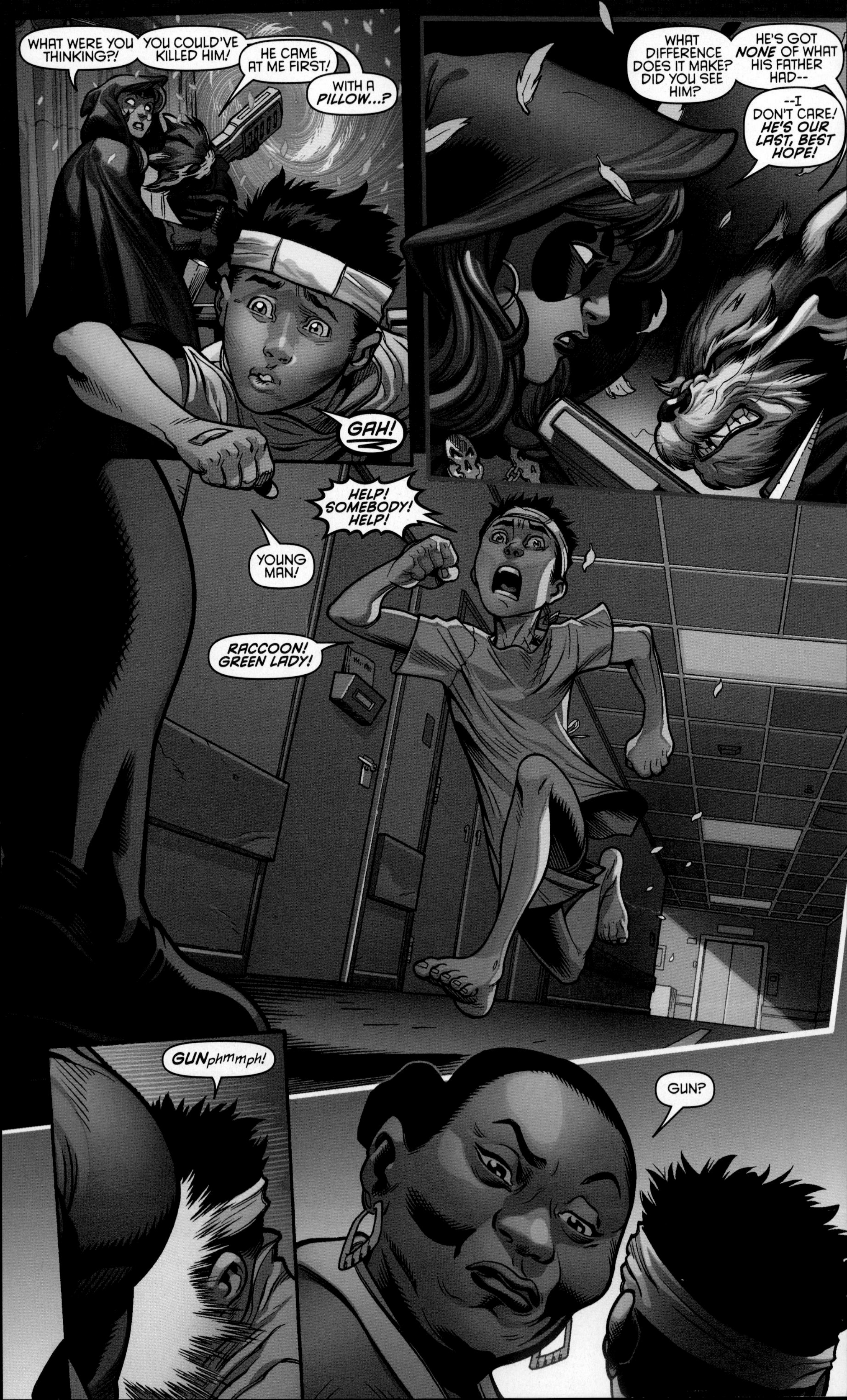
WHAT WERE YOU THINKING?!
YOU COULD'VE KILLED HIM!
HE CAME AT ME FIRST!
WITH A PILLOW...?
GAH!
WHAT DIFFERENCE DOES IT MAKE? DID YOU SEE HIM?
HE'S GOT NONE OF WHAT HIS FATHER HAD--
--I DON'T CARE! HE'S OUR LAST, BEST HOPE!
HELP! SOMEBODY! HELP!
YOUNG MAN!
RACCOON! GREEN LADY!
GUNphmmph!
GUN?

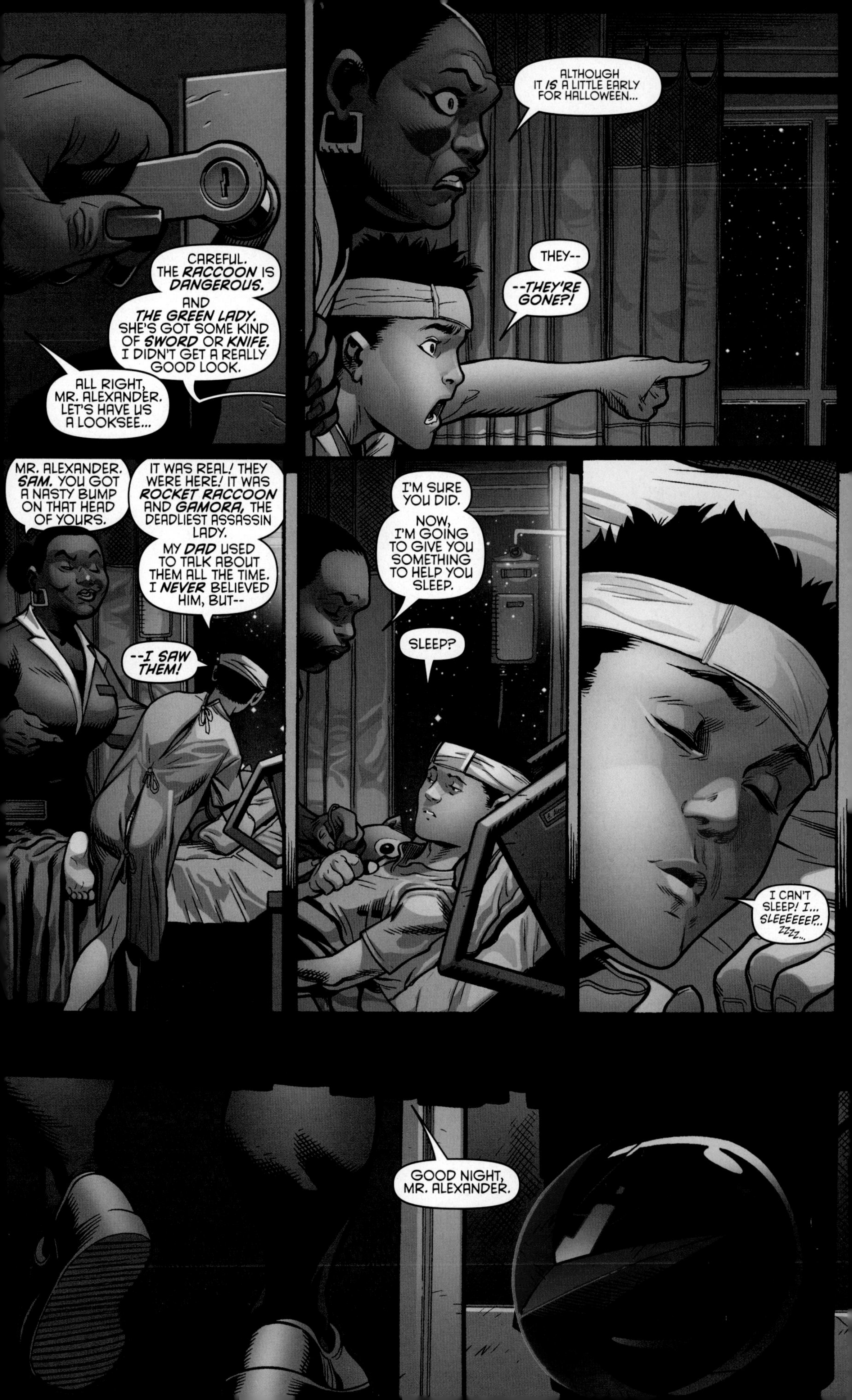
CAREFUL. THE RACCOON IS DANGEROUS.
AND THE GREEN LADY. SHE'S GOT SOME KIND OF SWORD OR KNIFE. I DIDN'T GET A REALLY GOOD LOOK.
ALL RIGHT, MR. ALEXANDER. LET'S HAVE US A LOOKSEE...
ALTHOUGH IT IS A LITTLE EARLY FOR HALLOWEEN...
THEY--
--THEY'RE GONE?!
MR. ALEXANDER. SAM. YOU GOT A NASTY BUMP ON THAT HEAD OF YOURS.
IT WAS REAL! THEY WERE HERE! IT WAS ROCKET RACCOON AND GAMORA, THE DEADLIEST ASSASSIN LADY.
MY DAD USED TO TALK ABOUT THEM ALL THE TIME. I NEVER BELIEVED HIM, BUT--
--I SAW THEM!
I'M SURE YOU DID.
NOW, I'M GOING TO GIVE YOU SOMETHING TO HELP YOU SLEEP.
SLEEP?
I CAN'T SLEEP! I... SLEEEEEEP... ZZZZ...
GOOD NIGHT, MR. ALEXANDER.

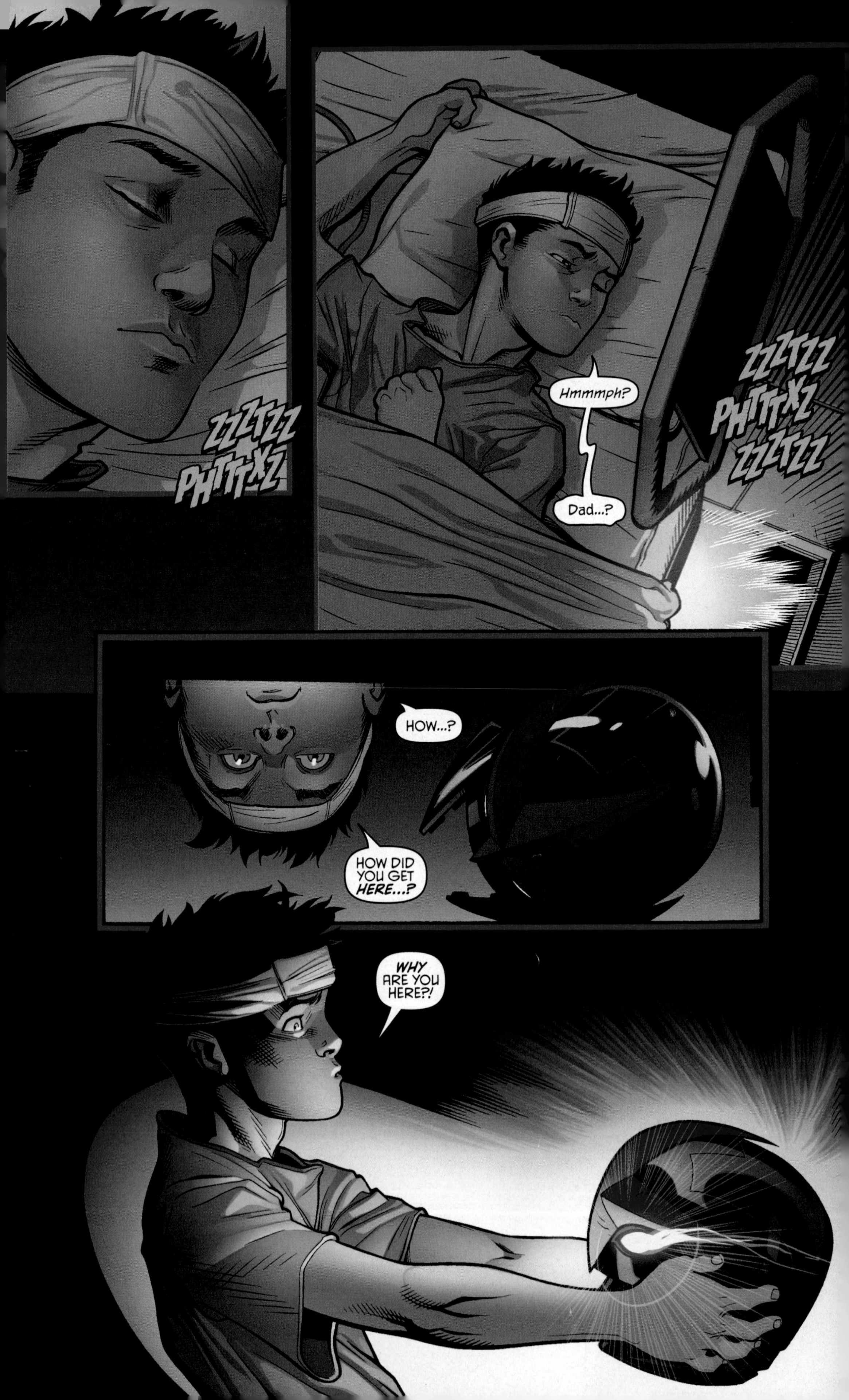
ZZZTZZ
PHTTTXZ
Hmmmph?
Dad...?
ZZZTZZ
PHTTTXZ
ZZZTZZ
HOW...?
HOW DID YOU GET HERE...?
WHY ARE YOU HERE?!

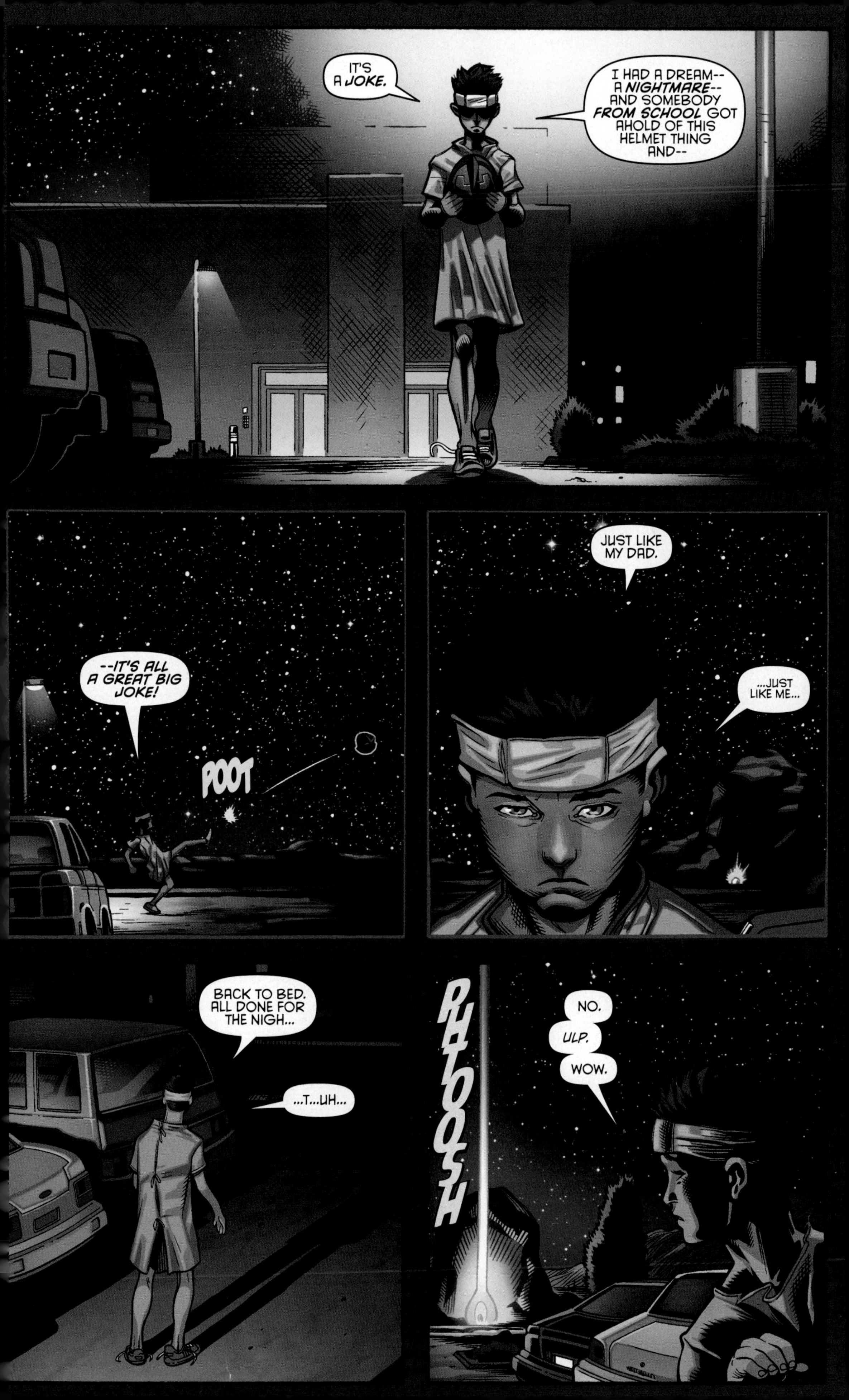
IT'S A JOKE.
I HAD A DREAM-- A NIGHTMARE-- AND SOMEBODY FROM SCHOOL GOT AHOLD OF THIS HELMET THING AND--
--IT'S ALL A GREAT BIG JOKE!
POOT
JUST LIKE MY DAD.
...JUST LIKE ME...
BACK TO BED. ALL DONE FOR THE NIGH...
...T...UH...
PHOOOSH
NO.
ULP.
WOW.

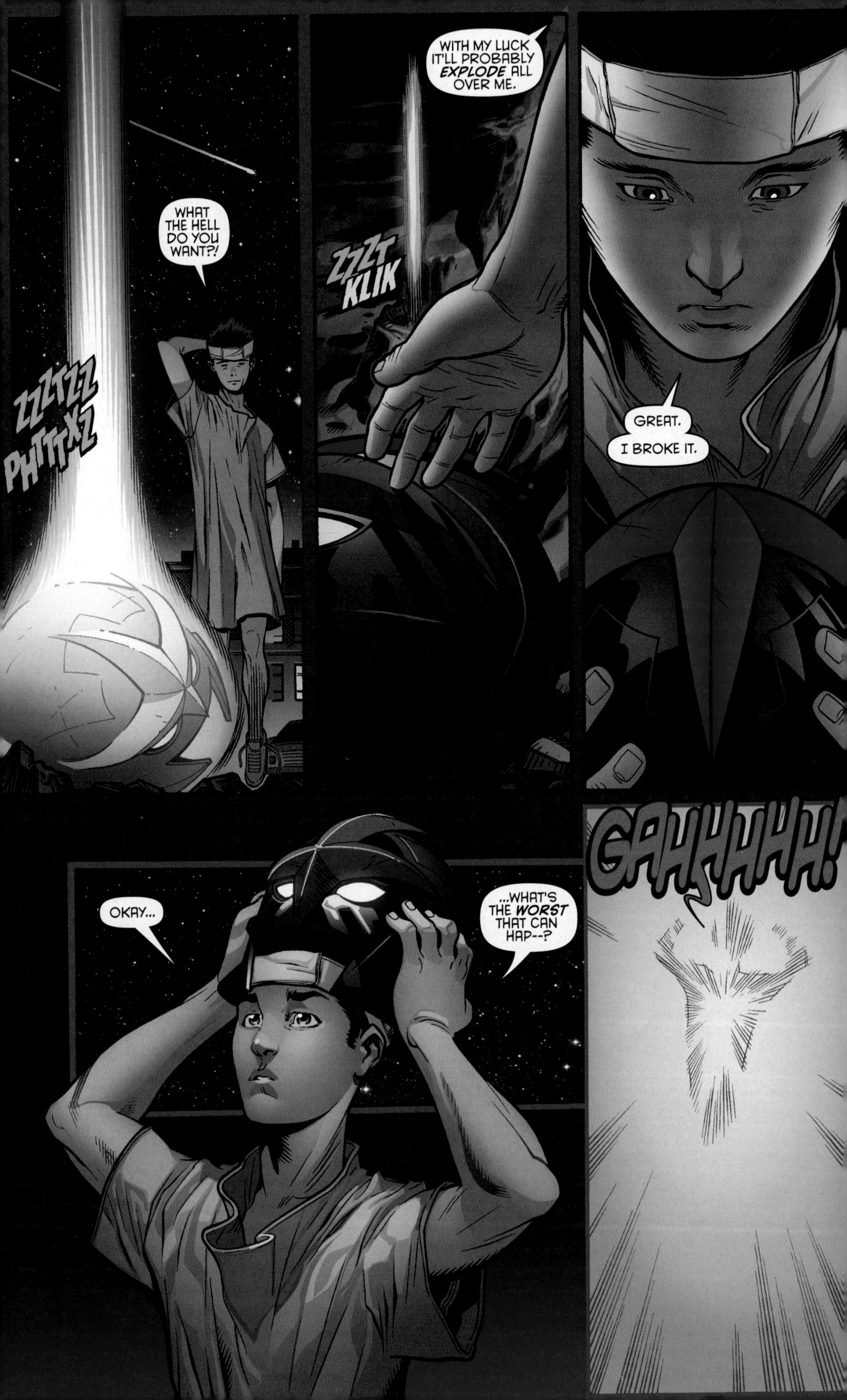
WHAT THE HELL DO YOU WANT?!
ZZZTZZ PHTTTXZ
WITH MY LUCK IT'LL PROBABLY EXPLODE ALL OVER ME.
ZZZT KLIK
GREAT. I BROKE IT.
OKAY...
...WHAT'S THE WORST THAT CAN HAP--?
GAHHHHH!

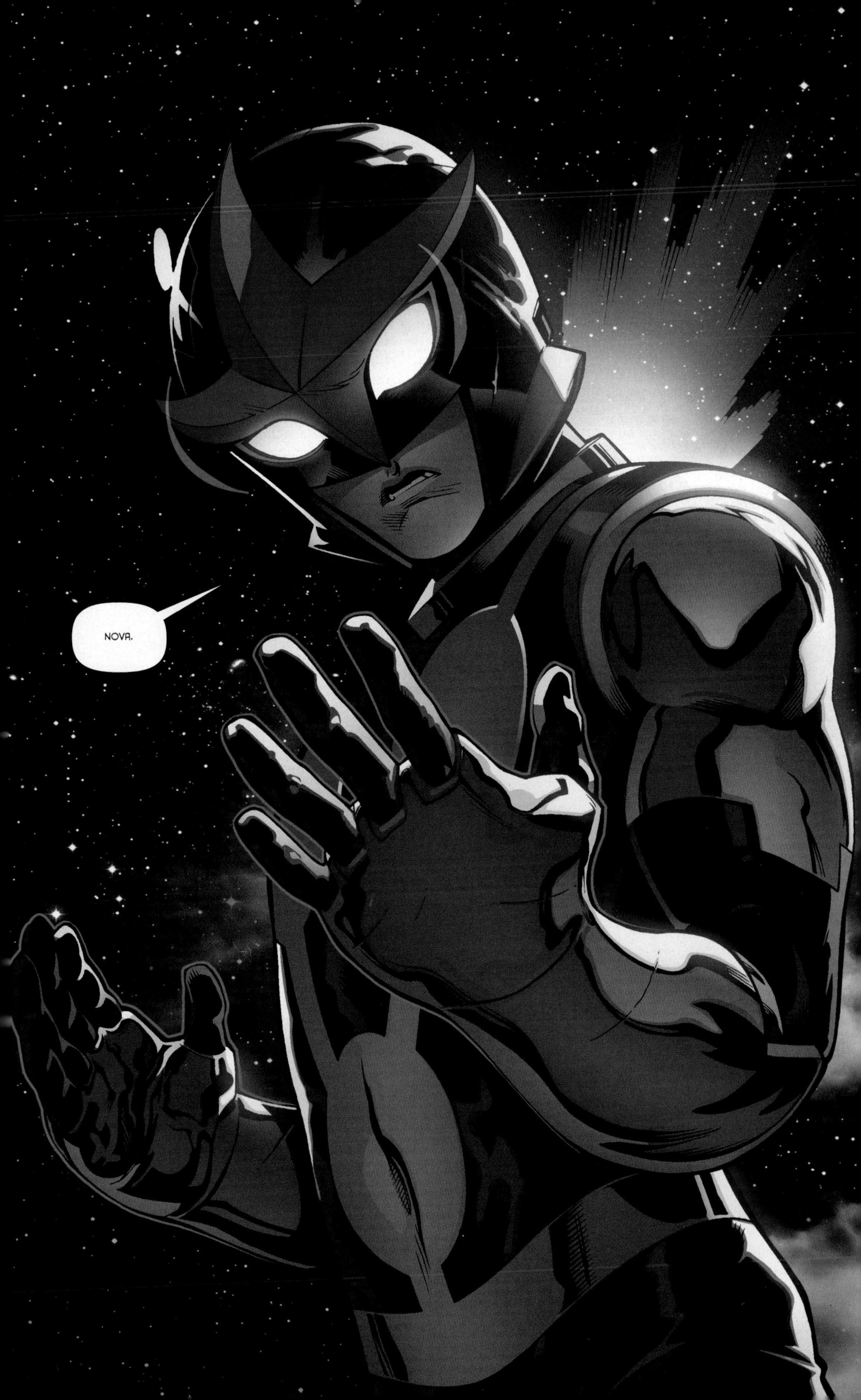
NOVA.

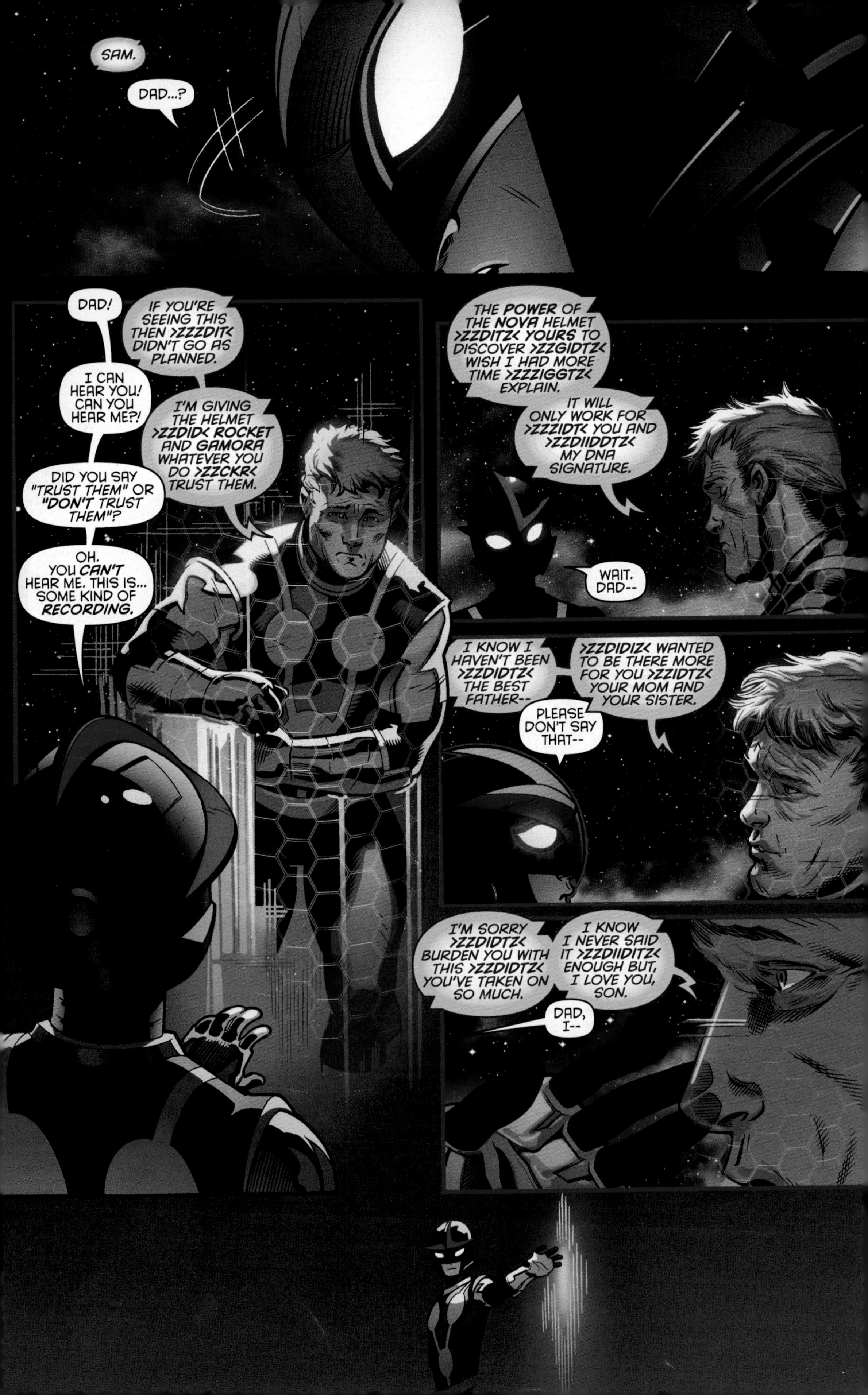

SAM.
DAD...?
DAD!
IF YOU'RE SEEING THIS THEN >ZZZDIT< DIDN'T GO AS PLANNED.
I CAN HEAR YOU! CAN YOU HEAR ME?!
I'M GIVING THE HELMET >ZZDID< ROCKET AND GAMORA WHATEVER YOU DO >ZZCKR< TRUST THEM.
DID YOU SAY "TRUST THEM" OR "DON'T TRUST THEM"?
OH. YOU CAN'T HEAR ME. THIS IS... SOME KIND OF RECORDING.
THE POWER OF THE NOVA HELMET >ZZDITZ< YOURS TO DISCOVER >ZZGIDTZ< WISH I HAD MORE TIME >ZZZIGGTZ< EXPLAIN.
IT WILL ONLY WORK FOR >ZZZIDT< YOU AND >ZZDIIDDTZ< MY DNA SIGNATURE.
WAIT. DAD--
I KNOW I HAVEN'T BEEN >ZZDIDTZ< THE BEST FATHER--
>ZZDIDIZ< WANTED TO BE THERE MORE FOR YOU >ZZIDTZ< YOUR MOM AND YOUR SISTER.
PLEASE DON'T SAY THAT--
I'M SORRY >ZZDIDTZ< BURDEN YOU WITH THIS >ZZDIDTZ< YOU'VE TAKEN ON SO MUCH.
I KNOW I NEVER SAID IT >ZZDIIDITZ< ENOUGH BUT, I LOVE YOU, SON.
DAD, I--

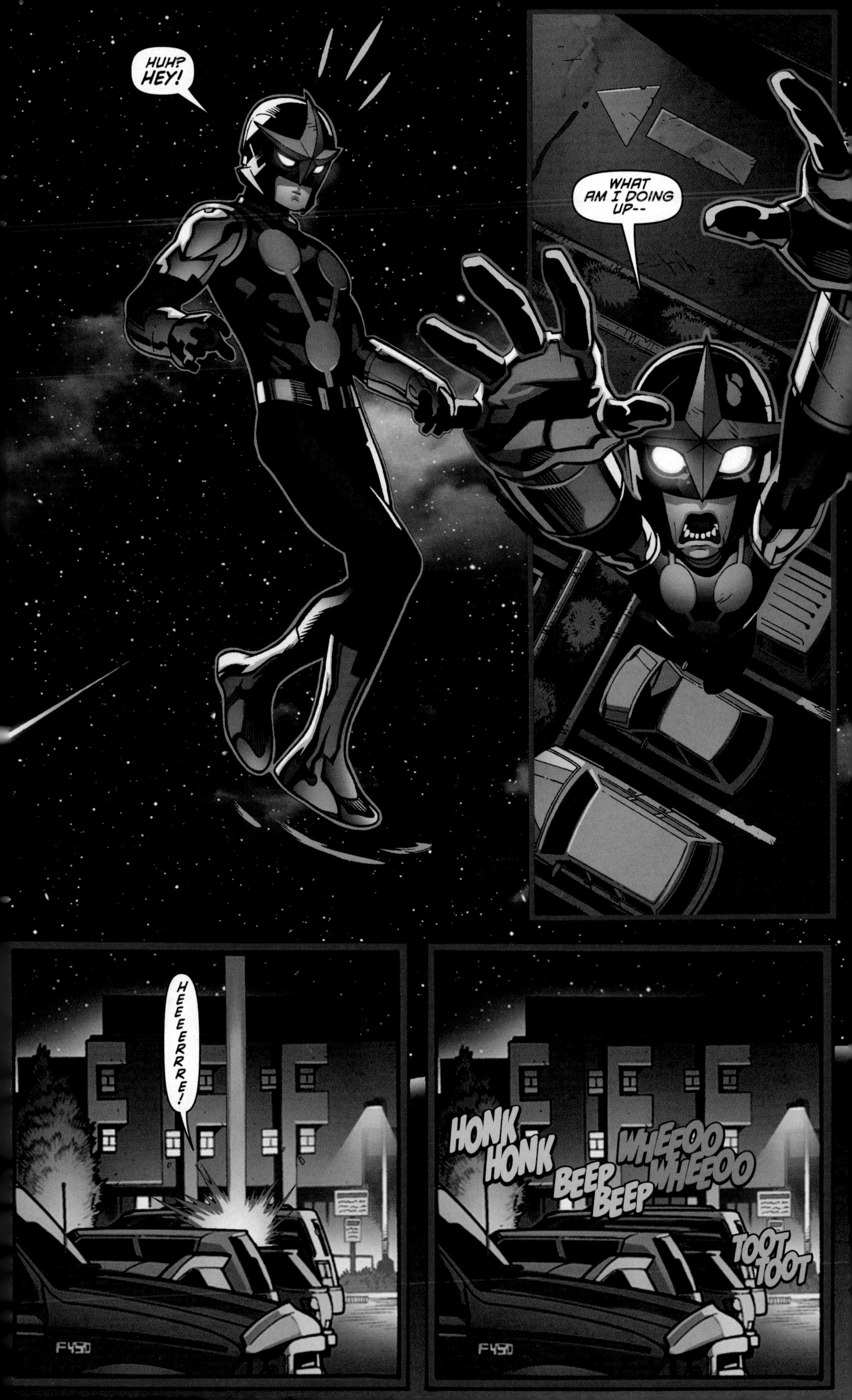
HUH? HEY!
WHAT AM I DOING UP--
HEEEERRRE!
F450
HONK HONK
BEEP BEEP
WHEEOO WHEEOO
TOOT TOOT
F450

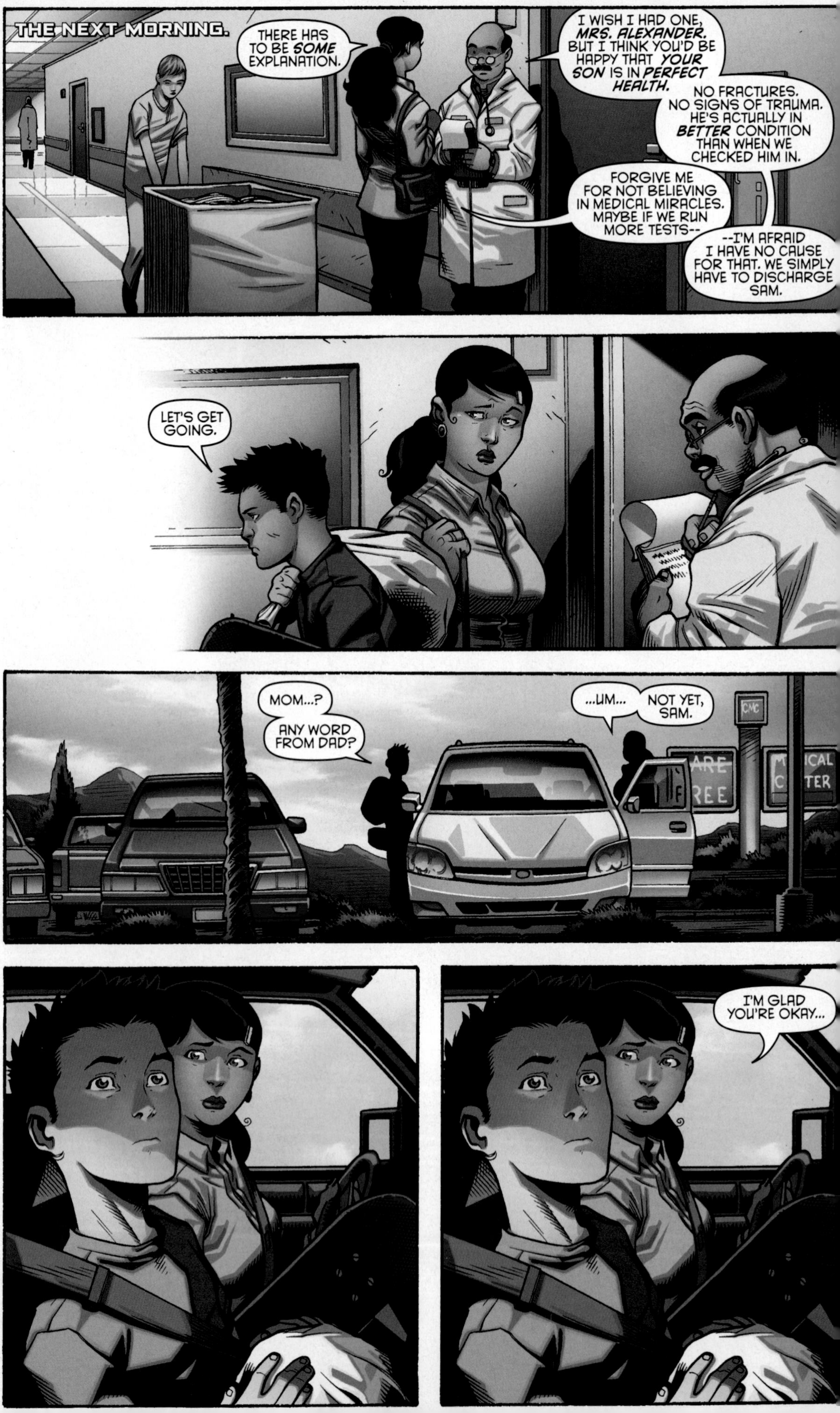
THE NEXT MORNING.
THERE HAS TO BE SOME EXPLANATION.
I WISH I HAD ONE, MRS. ALEXANDER. BUT I THINK YOU'D BE HAPPY THAT YOUR SON IS IN PERFECT HEALTH.
NO FRACTURES. NO SIGNS OF TRAUMA. HE'S ACTUALLY IN BETTER CONDITION THAN WHEN WE CHECKED HIM IN.
FORGIVE ME FOR NOT BELIEVING IN MEDICAL MIRACLES. MAYBE IF WE RUN MORE TESTS--
--I'M AFRAID I HAVE NO CAUSE FOR THAT. WE SIMPLY HAVE TO DISCHARGE SAM.
LET'S GET GOING.
MOM...?
ANY WORD FROM DAD?
...UM...
NOT YET, SAM.
CMC
MEDICAL CENTER
I'M GLAD YOU'RE OKAY...

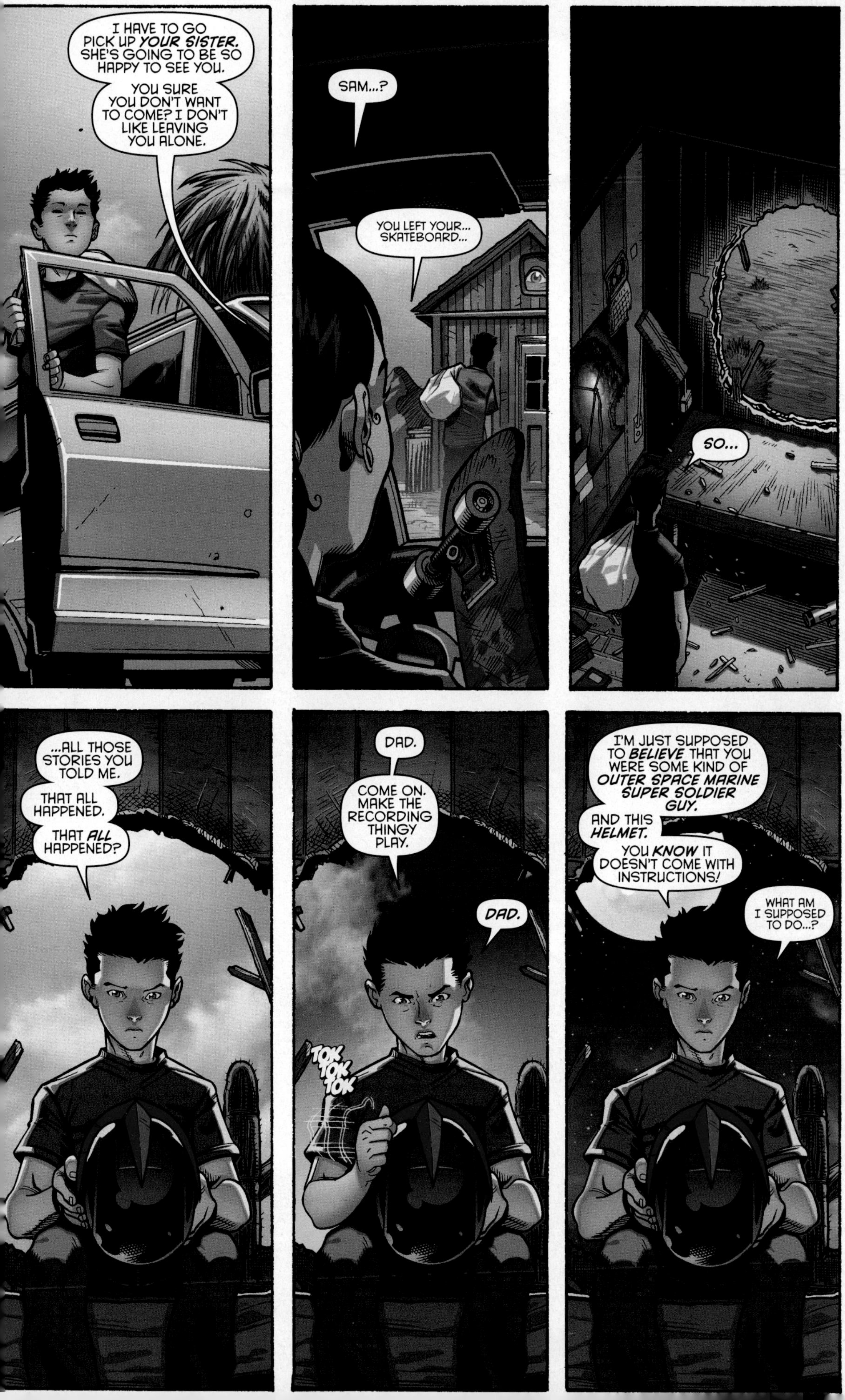
I HAVE TO GO PICK UP YOUR SISTER. SHE'S GOING TO BE SO HAPPY TO SEE YOU.
YOU SURE YOU DON'T WANT TO COME? I DON'T LIKE LEAVING YOU ALONE.
SAM...?
YOU LEFT YOUR... SKATEBOARD...
SO...
...ALL THOSE STORIES YOU TOLD ME.
THAT ALL HAPPENED.
THAT ALL HAPPENED?
DAD.
COME ON. MAKE THE RECORDING THINGY PLAY.
DAD.
TOK TOK TOK
I'M JUST SUPPOSED TO BELIEVE THAT YOU WERE SOME KIND OF OUTER SPACE MARINE SUPER SOLDIER GUY.
AND THIS HELMET.
YOU KNOW IT DOESN'T COME WITH INSTRUCTIONS!
WHAT AM I SUPPOSED TO DO...?

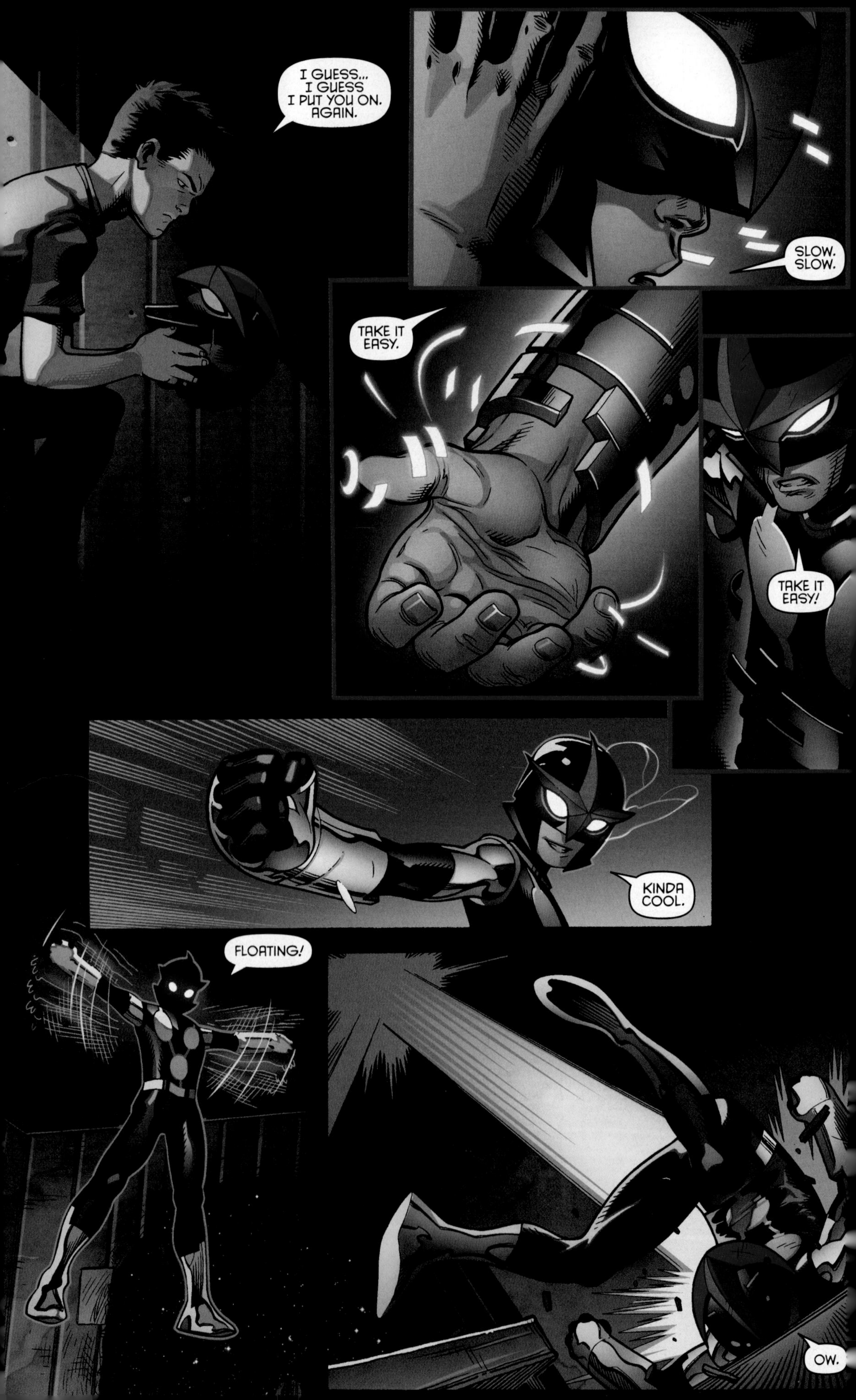
I GUESS...
I GUESS
I PUT YOU ON.
AGAIN.
SLOW.
SLOW.
TAKE IT
EASY.
TAKE IT
EASY!
KINDA
COOL.
FLOATING!
OW.

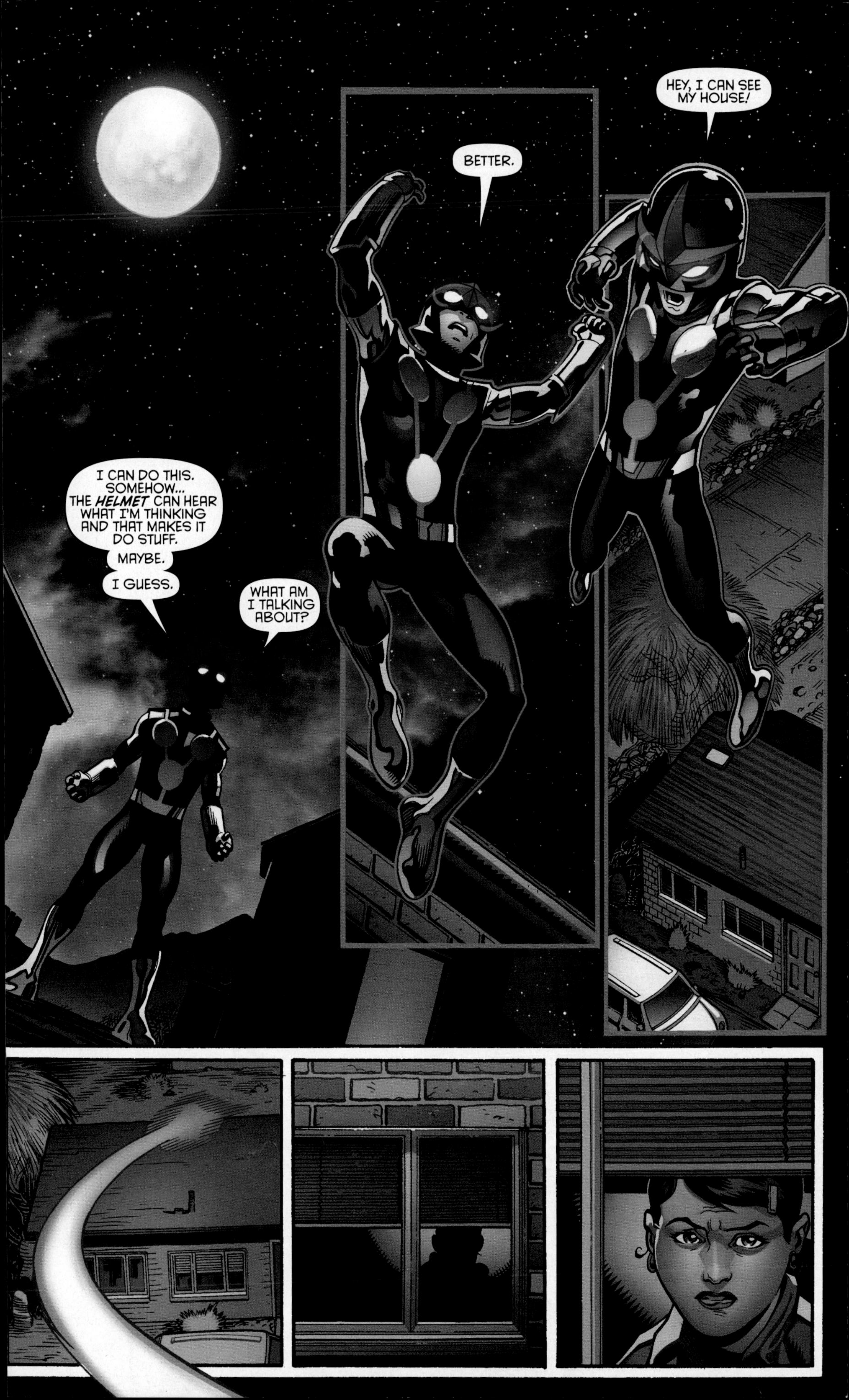
I CAN DO THIS. SOMEHOW... THE HELMET CAN HEAR WHAT I'M THINKING AND THAT MAKES IT DO STUFF.
MAYBE.
I GUESS.
WHAT AM I TALKING ABOUT?
BETTER.
HEY, I CAN SEE MY HOUSE!

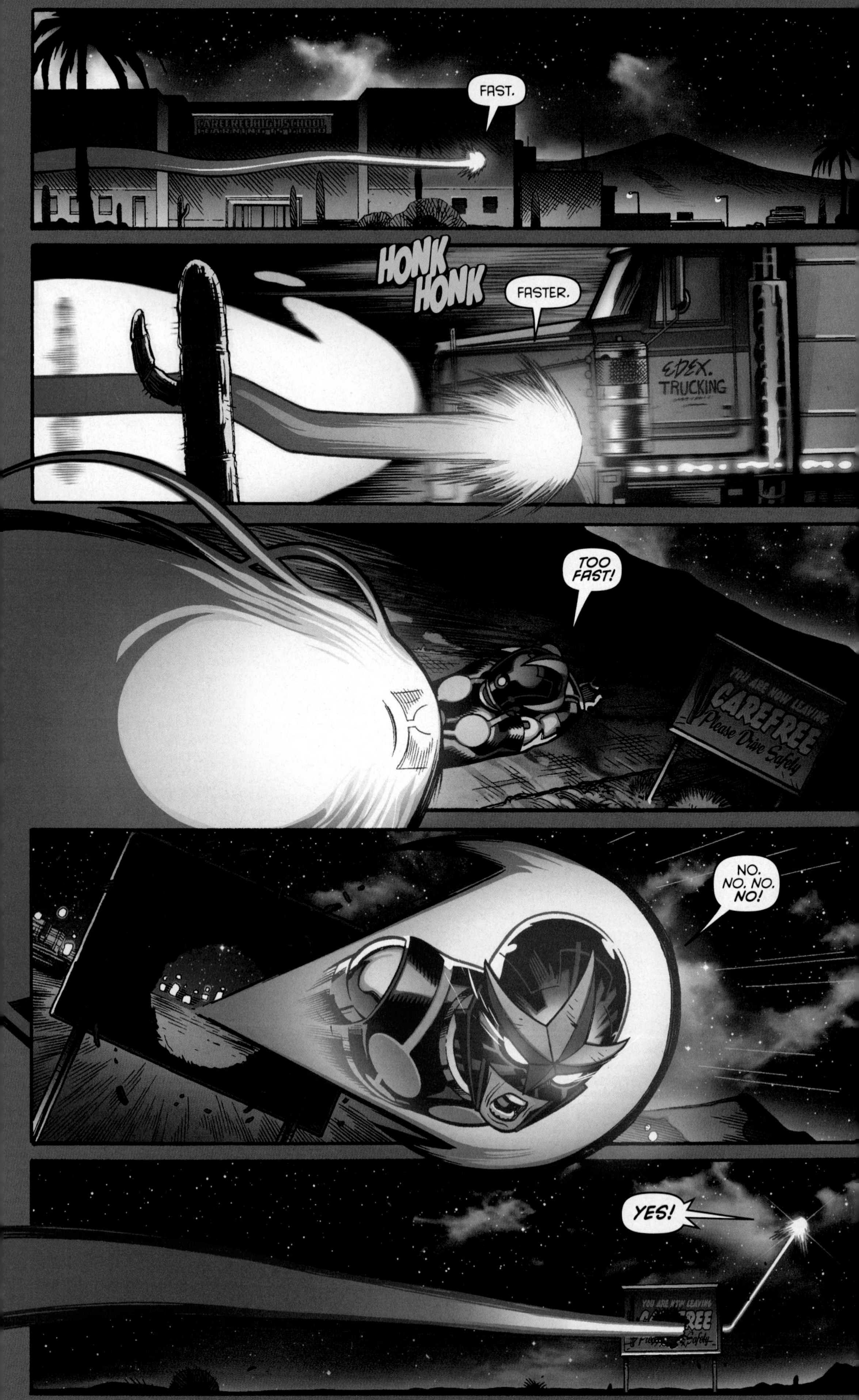
CAREFREE HIGH SCHOOL
FAST.
HONK
HONK
FASTER.
EDEX.
TRUCKING
TOO FAST!
YOU ARE NOW LEAVING
CAREFREE
Please Drive Safely
NO. NO, NO. NO!
YES!

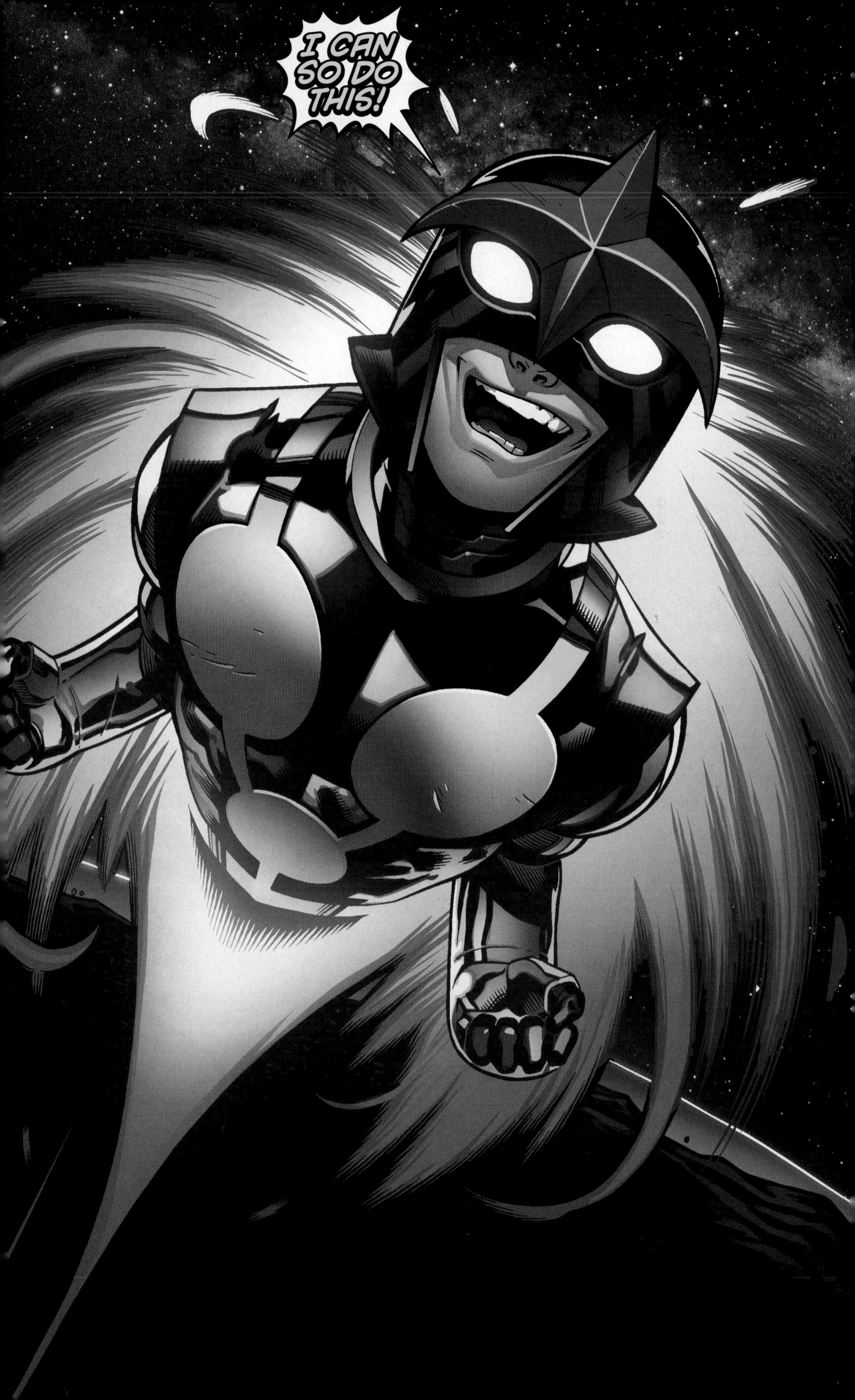
I CAN SO DO THIS!

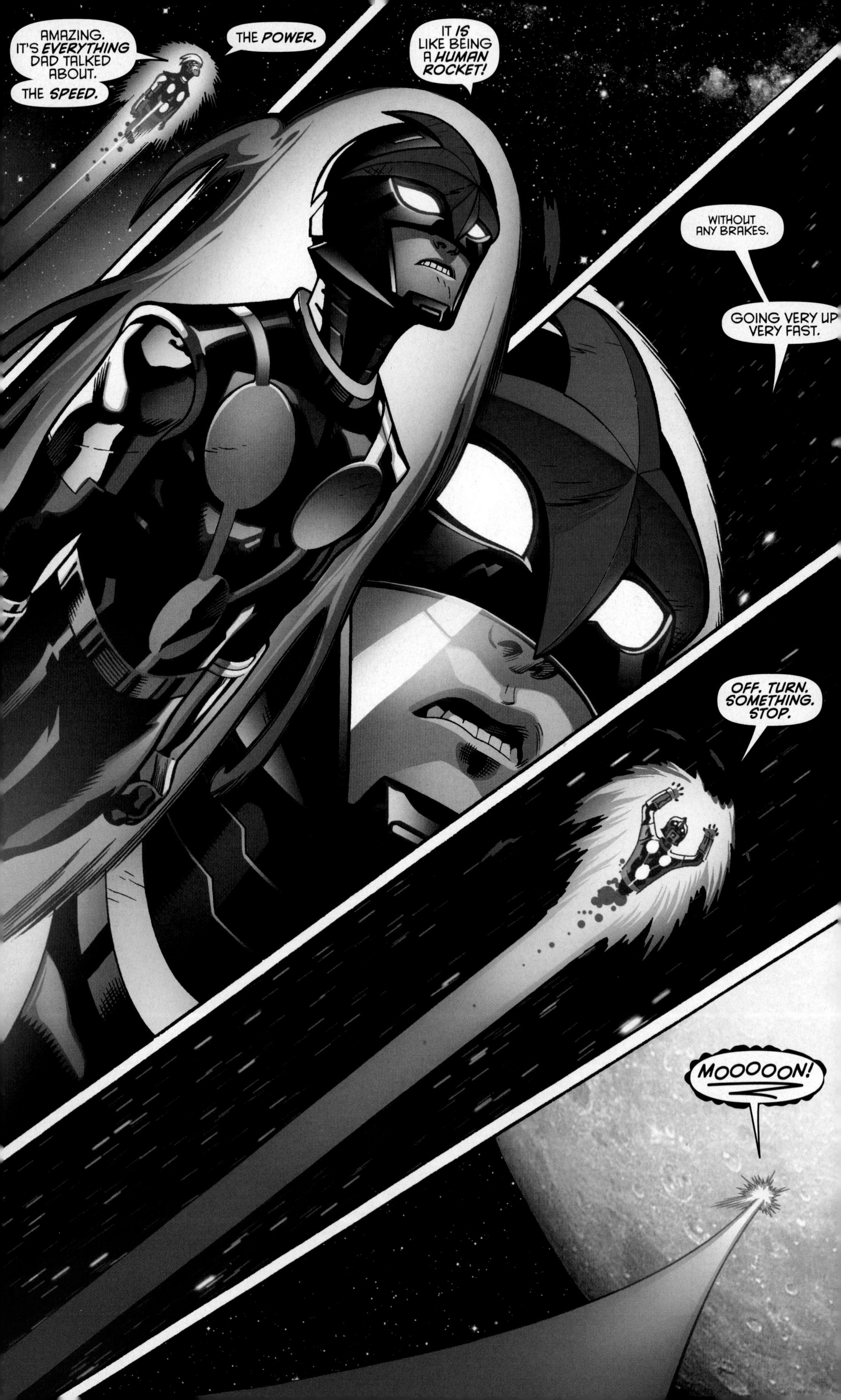
AMAZING. IT'S *EVERYTHING* DAD TALKED ABOUT.
THE *SPEED.*
THE *POWER.*
IT *IS* LIKE BEING A *HUMAN ROCKET!*
WITHOUT ANY BRAKES.
GOING VERY UP VERY FAST.
OFF. TURN. SOMETHING. STOP.
MOOOOON!

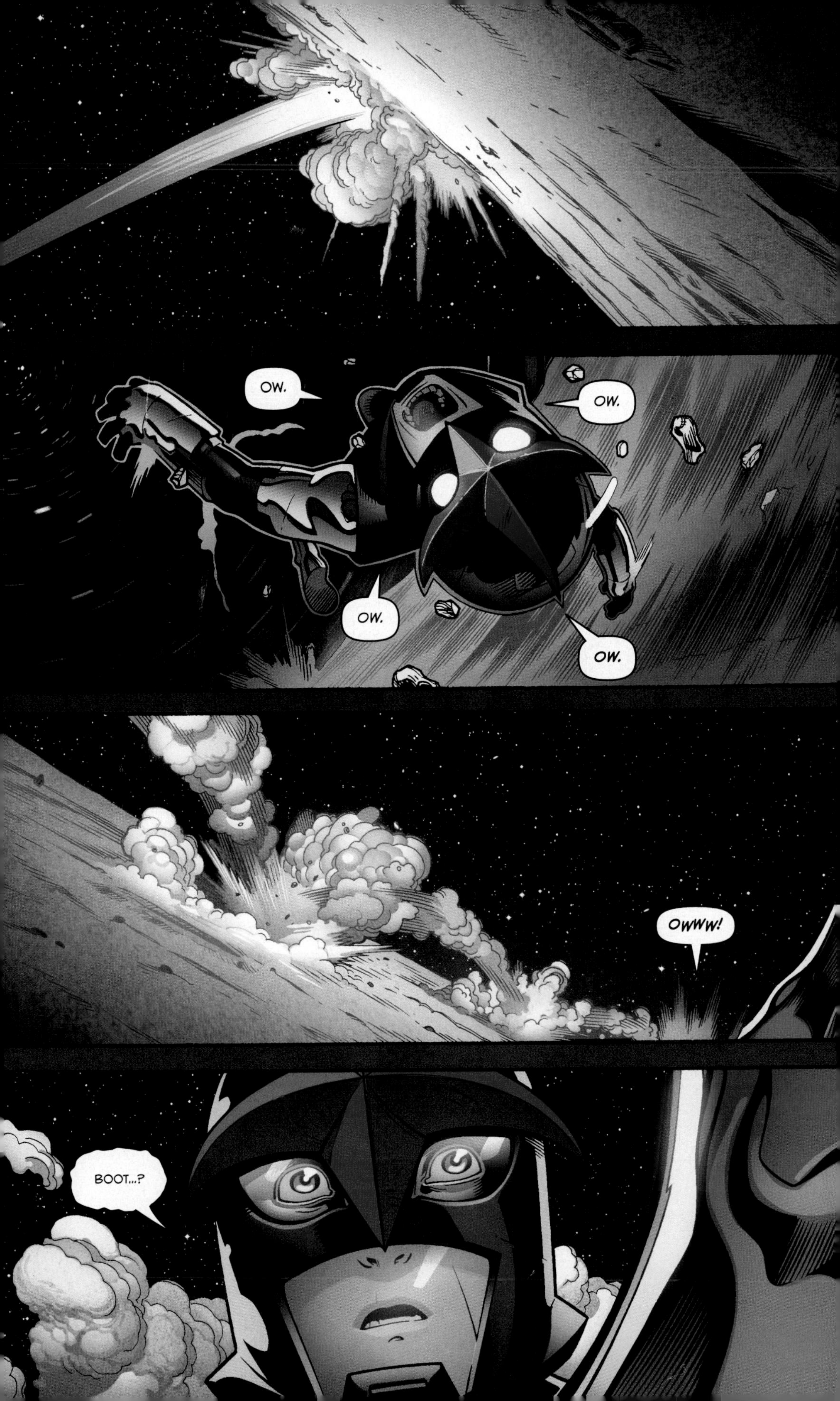
OW.
OW.
OW.
OW.
OWWW!
BOOT...?

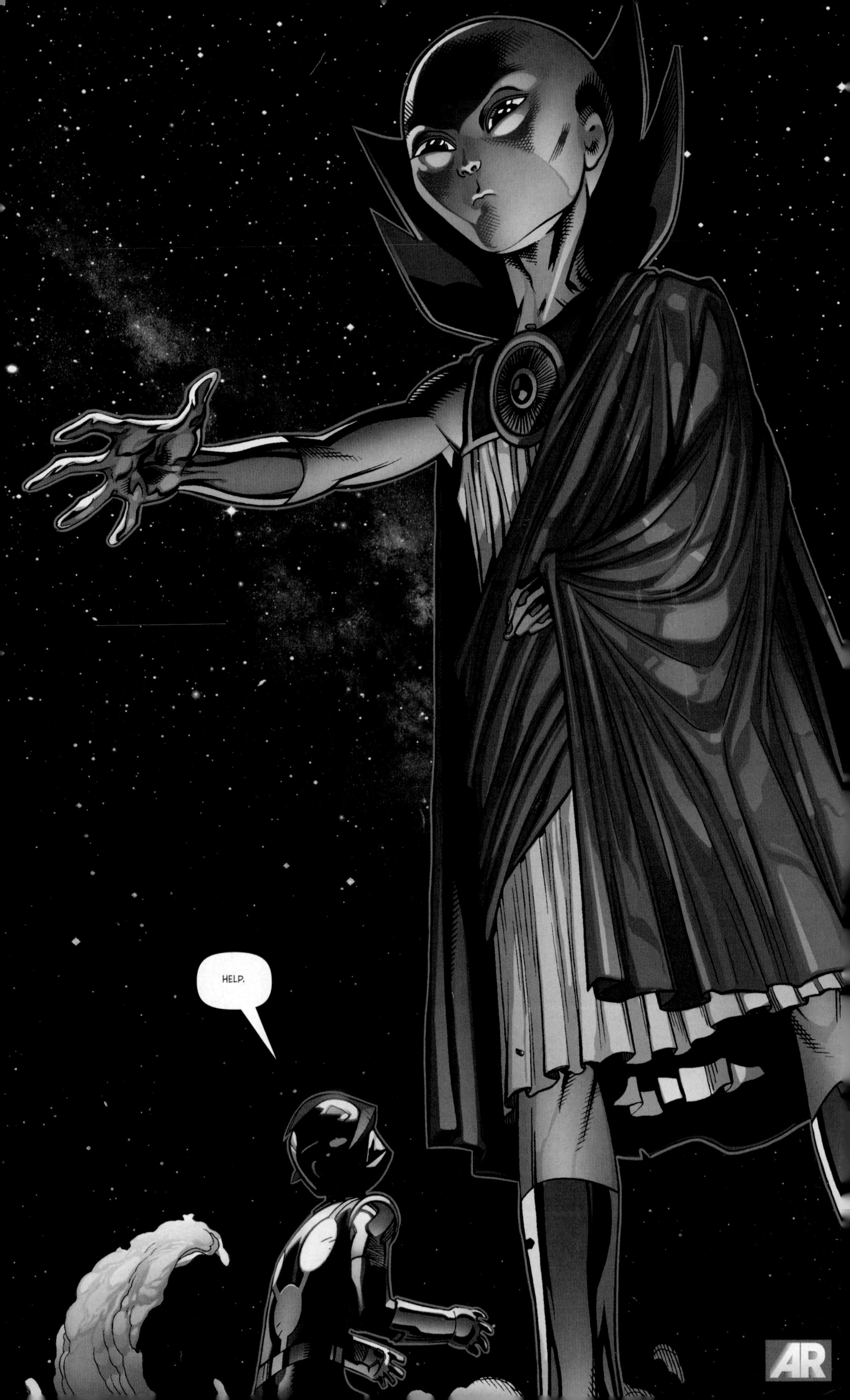
HELP.

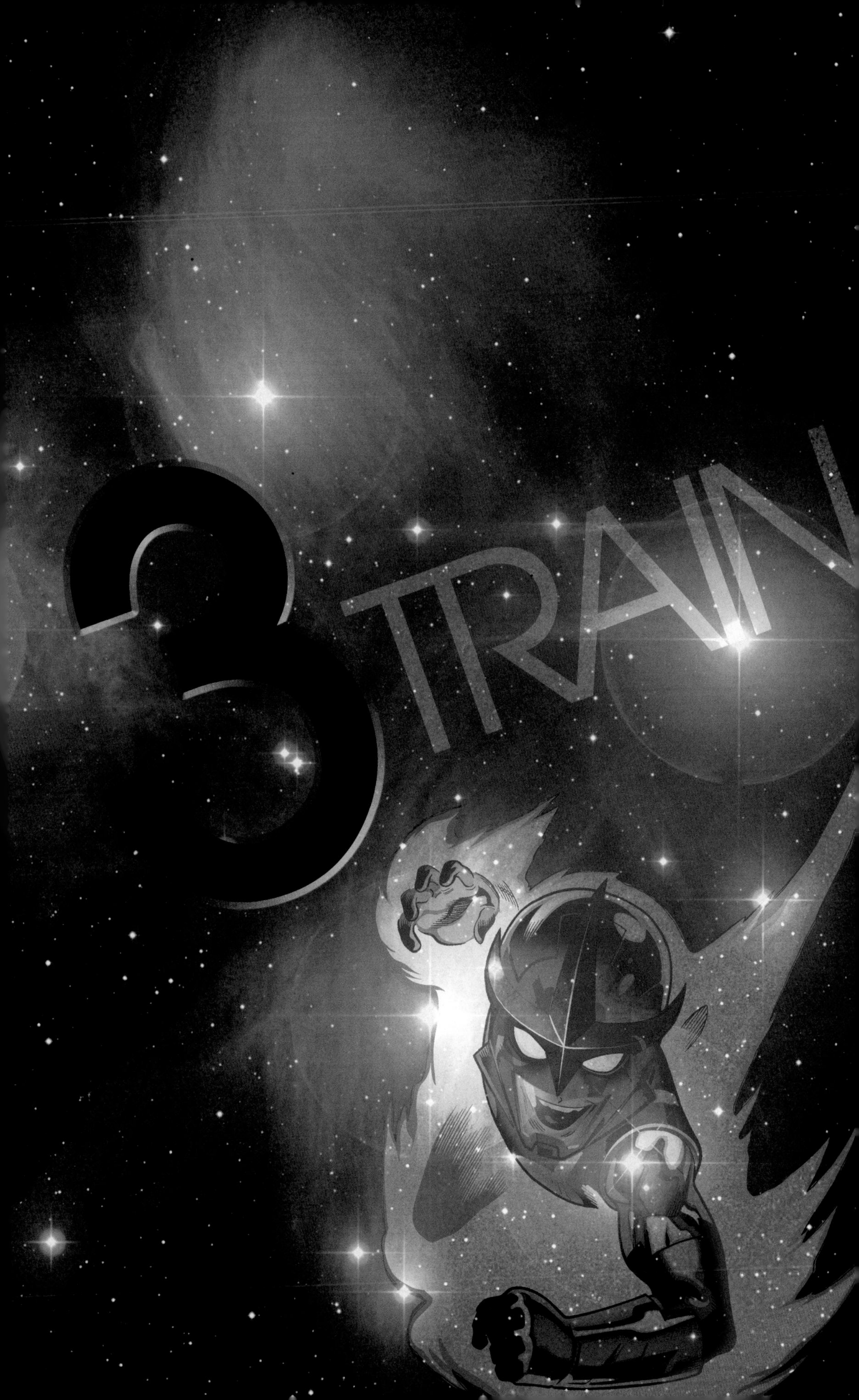
3
TRAV

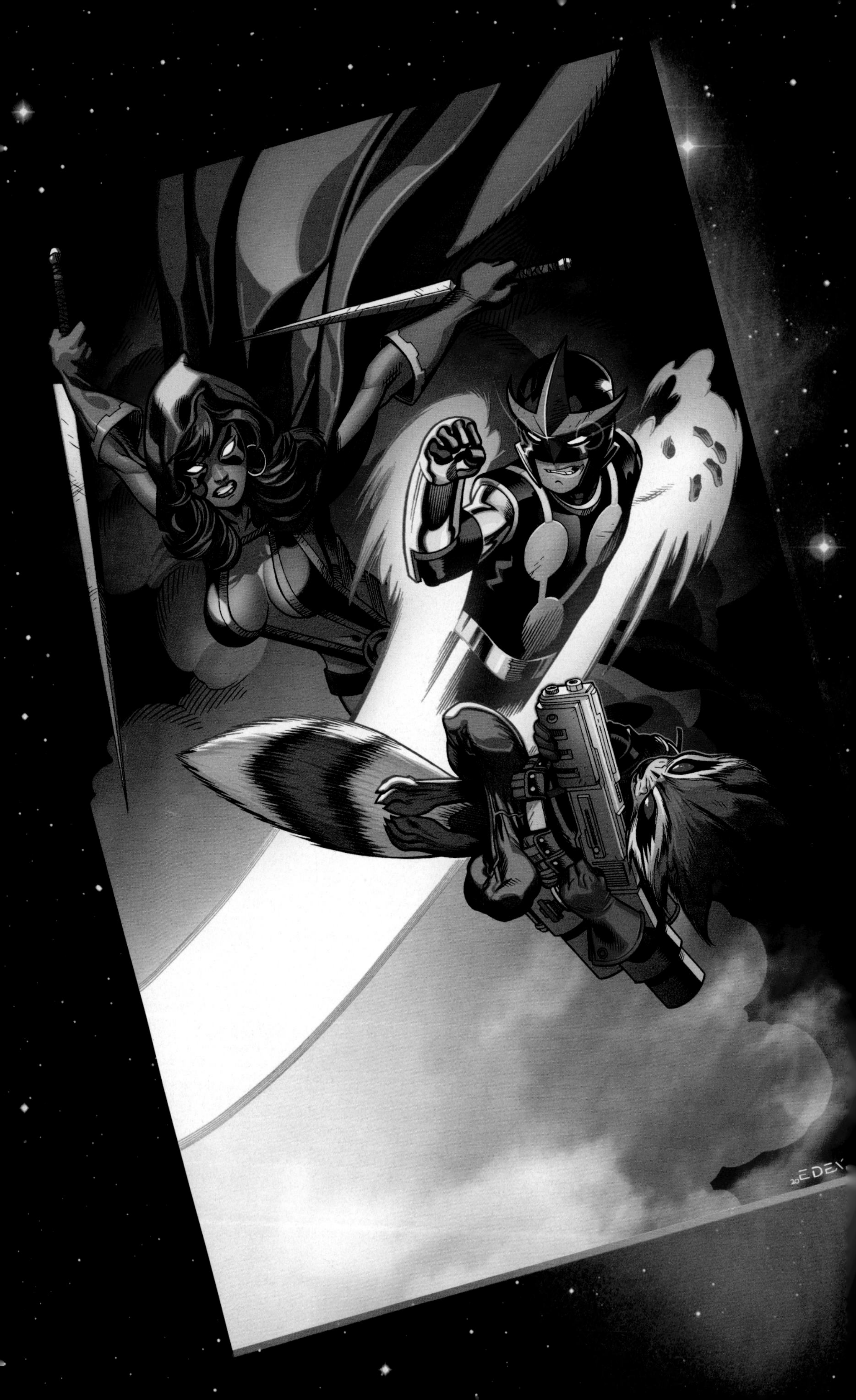

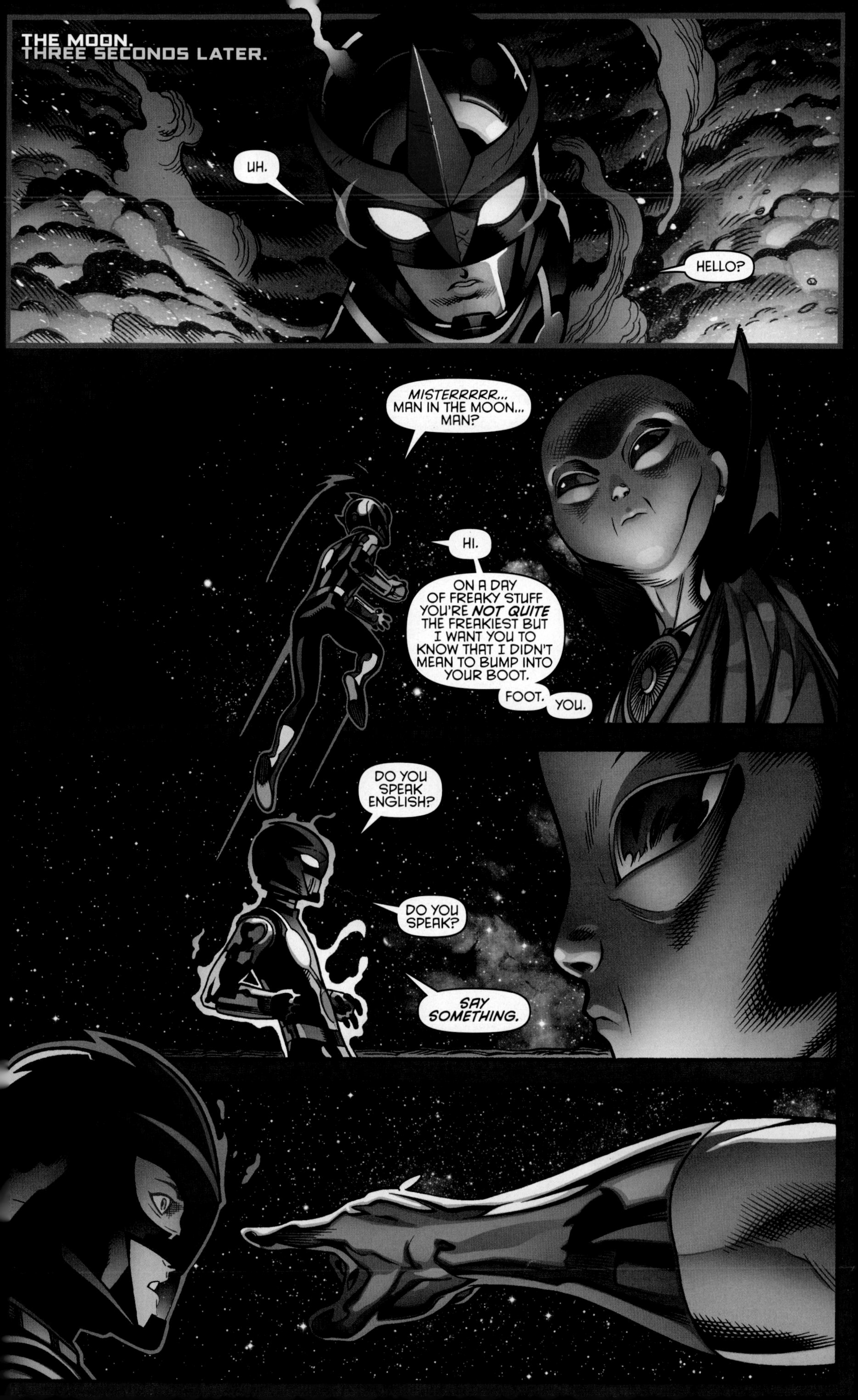

THE MOON.
THREE SECONDS LATER.
UH.
HELLO?
MISTERRRRR... MAN IN THE MOON... MAN?
HI.
ON A DAY OF FREAKY STUFF YOU'RE ***NOT QUITE*** THE FREAKIEST BUT I WANT YOU TO KNOW THAT I DIDN'T MEAN TO BUMP INTO YOUR BOOT.
FOOT.
YOU.
DO YOU SPEAK ENGLISH?
DO YOU SPEAK?
SAY SOMETHING.

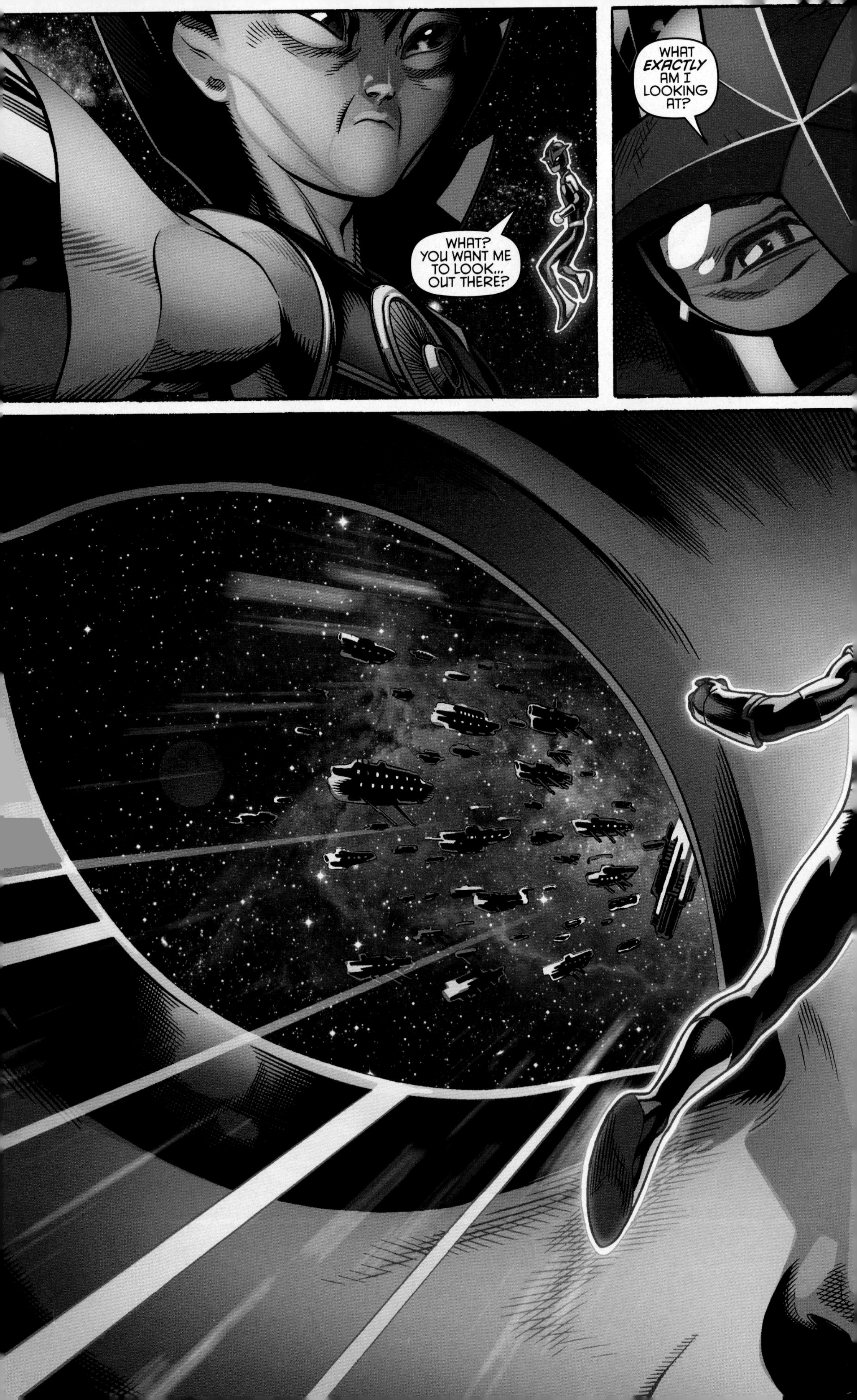
WHAT? YOU WANT ME TO LOOK... OUT THERE?
WHAT EXACTLY AM I LOOKING AT?

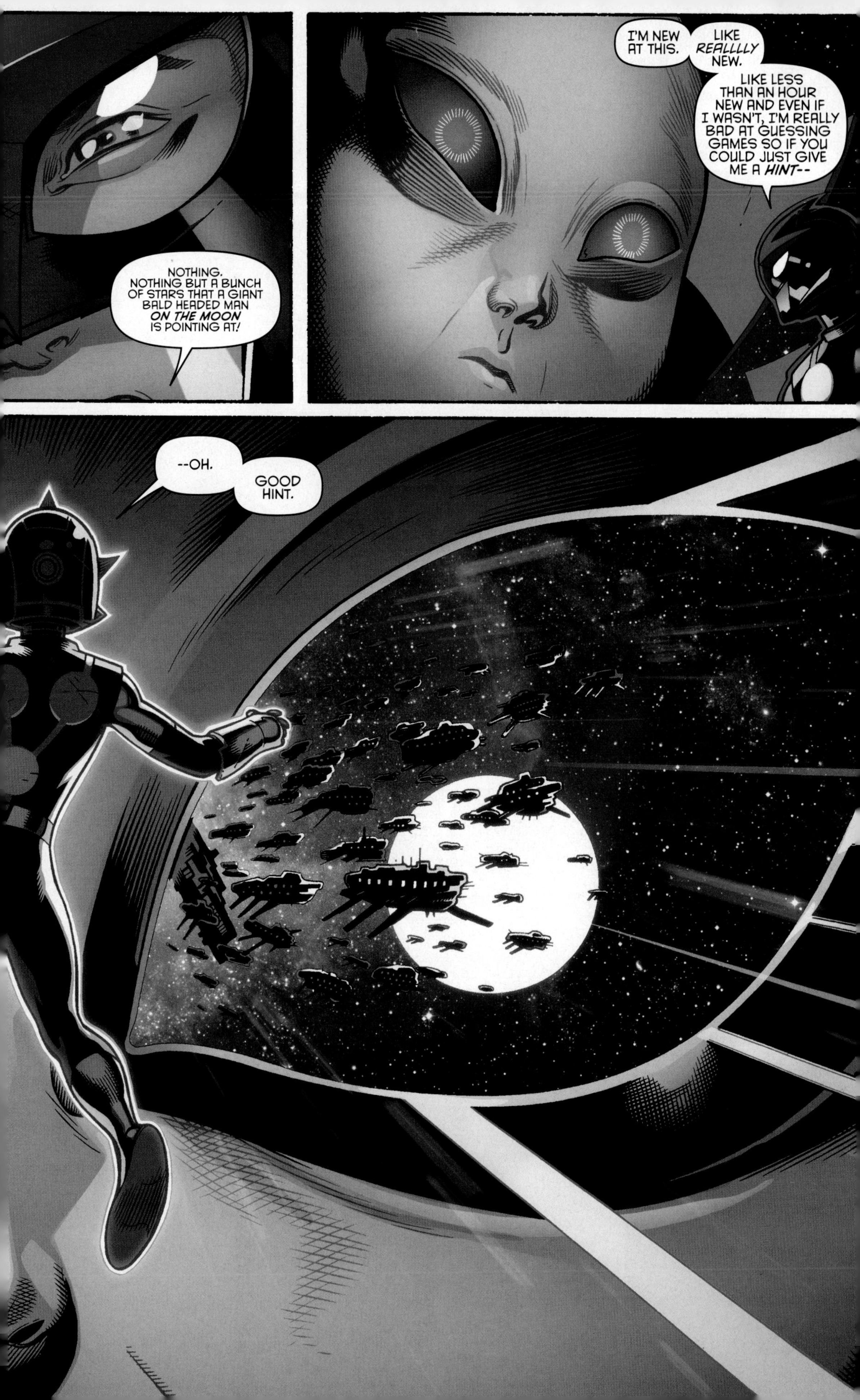
NOTHING. NOTHING BUT A BUNCH OF STARS THAT A GIANT BALD HEADED MAN *ON THE MOON* IS POINTING AT!
I'M NEW AT THIS.
LIKE *REALLLLY* NEW.
LIKE LESS THAN AN HOUR NEW AND EVEN IF I WASN'T, I'M REALLY BAD AT GUESSING GAMES SO IF YOU COULD JUST GIVE ME A *HINT*--
--OH.
GOOD HINT.

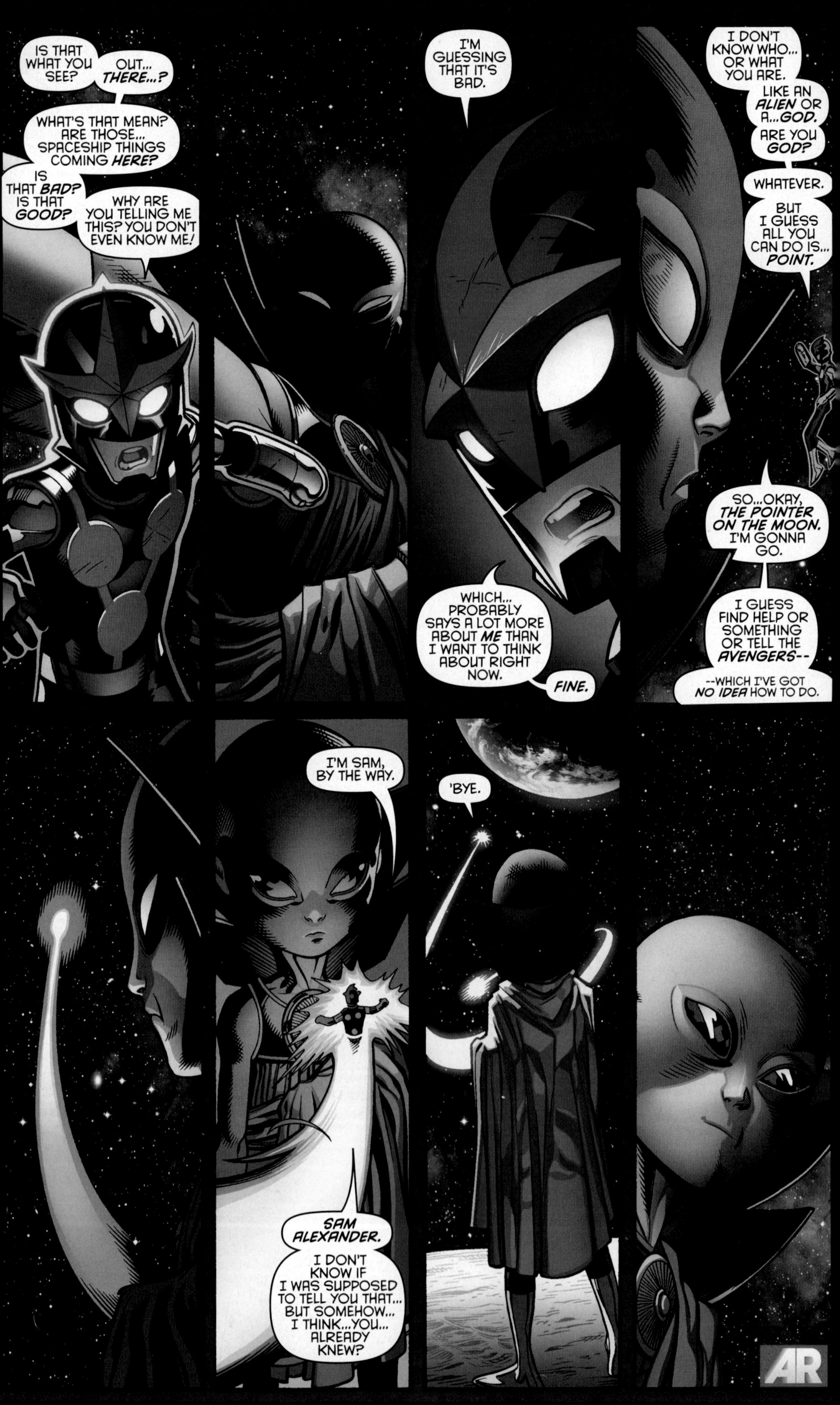

IS THAT WHAT YOU SEE?
OUT... THERE...?
WHAT'S THAT MEAN? ARE THOSE... SPACESHIP THINGS COMING HERE?
IS THAT BAD? IS THAT GOOD?
WHY ARE YOU TELLING ME THIS? YOU DON'T EVEN KNOW ME!
I'M GUESSING THAT IT'S BAD.
WHICH... PROBABLY SAYS A LOT MORE ABOUT ME THAN I WANT TO THINK ABOUT RIGHT NOW.
FINE.
I DON'T KNOW WHO... OR WHAT YOU ARE.
LIKE AN ALIEN OR A...GOD.
ARE YOU GOD?
WHATEVER.
BUT I GUESS ALL YOU CAN DO IS... POINT.
SO...OKAY, THE POINTER ON THE MOON. I'M GONNA GO.
I GUESS FIND HELP OR SOMETHING OR TELL THE AVENGERS--
--WHICH I'VE GOT NO IDEA HOW TO DO.
I'M SAM, BY THE WAY.
SAM ALEXANDER.
I DON'T KNOW IF I WAS SUPPOSED TO TELL YOU THAT... BUT SOMEHOW... I THINK...YOU... ALREADY KNEW?
'BYE.
AR

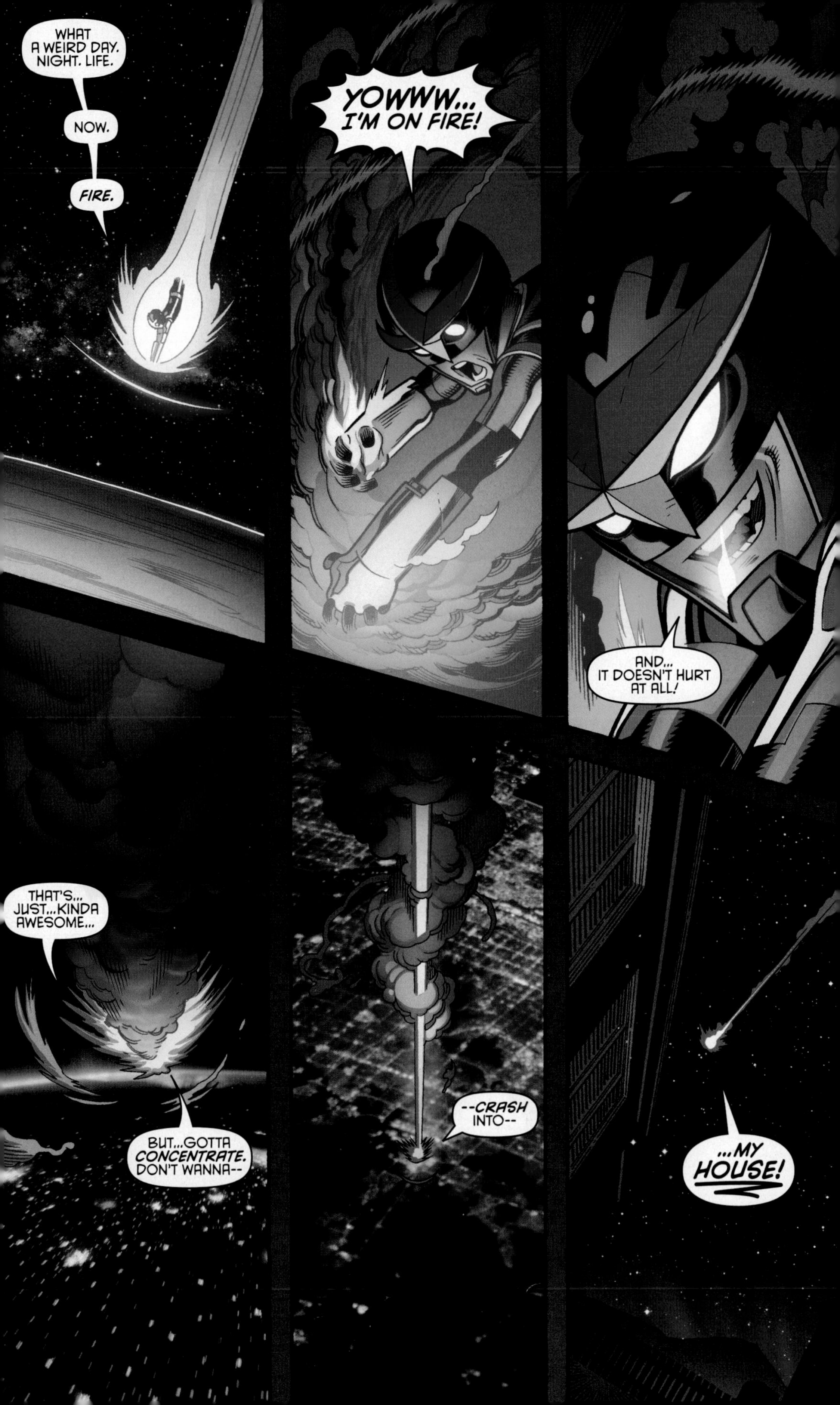
WHAT A WEIRD DAY. NIGHT. LIFE.
NOW.
FIRE.
YOWWW... I'M ON FIRE!
AND... IT DOESN'T HURT AT ALL!
THAT'S... JUST...KINDA AWESOME...
BUT...GOTTA CONCENTRATE. DON'T WANNA--
--CRASH INTO--
...MY HOUSE!

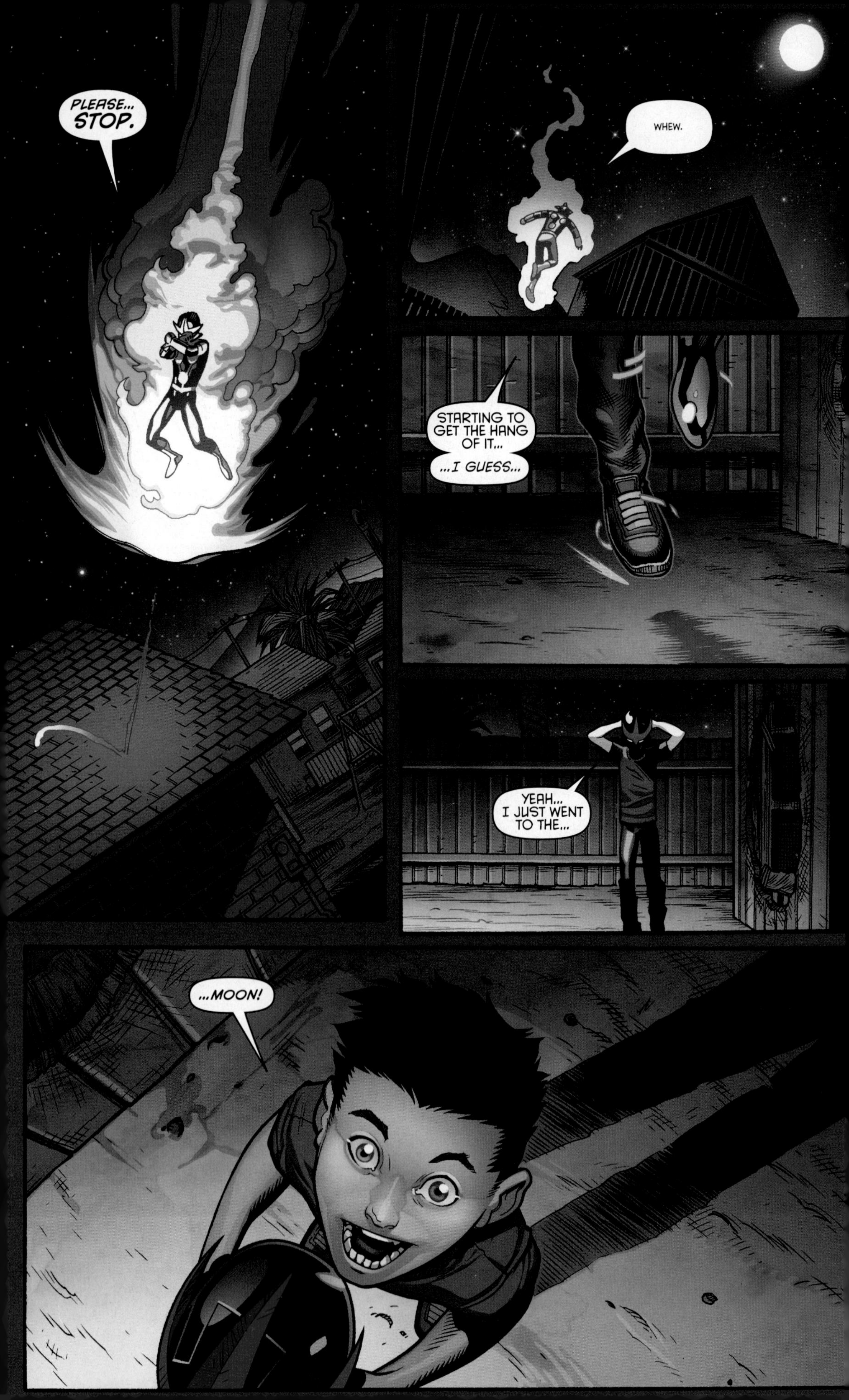
PLEASE... STOP.
WHEW.
STARTING TO GET THE HANG OF IT...
...I GUESS...
YEAH... I JUST WENT TO THE...
...MOON!

SAMUEL ALEJANDRO!

UH-OH.

¿DÓNDE TE HABÍAS METIDO? UM...

ACABAS DE SALIR DEL HOSPITAL.

MOM. *ENGLISH*. POR FAVOR.

¡TU HERMANA ESTABA DESEANDO PASAR UN RATO CONTIGO Y CUANDO VUELVO DE RECOGERLA RESULTA QUE HAS DESAPARECIDO!

I UNDERSTOOD *SOME* OR *NONE* OF THAT... BUT I GET IT.

YOU'RE MAD.

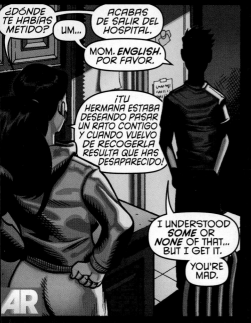

I WAS...OUT. IN THE GARAGE. LOOKING THROUGH DAD'S STUFF.

I THOUGHT. I THOUGHT I MIGHT FIND SOMETHING THAT WOULD HELP *US* FIND *HIM*. Y'KNOW LIKE WHERE HE WENT.

I MUST'VE FALLEN ASLEEP.

DO YOU WANT ME TO MAKE YOU SOMETHING TO EAT?

I'M OKAY.

TURN OUT THE LIGHTS WHEN YOU COME UP.

YOUR DAD. SOMETIMES HE'D GO... AWAY FOR A WHILE. LIKE THIS. MOSTLY BEFORE YOU WERE BORN.

NO MATTER WHAT ELSE YOU THINK OF HIM...

...AFTER *YOU* WERE BORN... HE TRIED SO HARD.

HE TRIED SO HARD TO BE A GOOD FATHER.

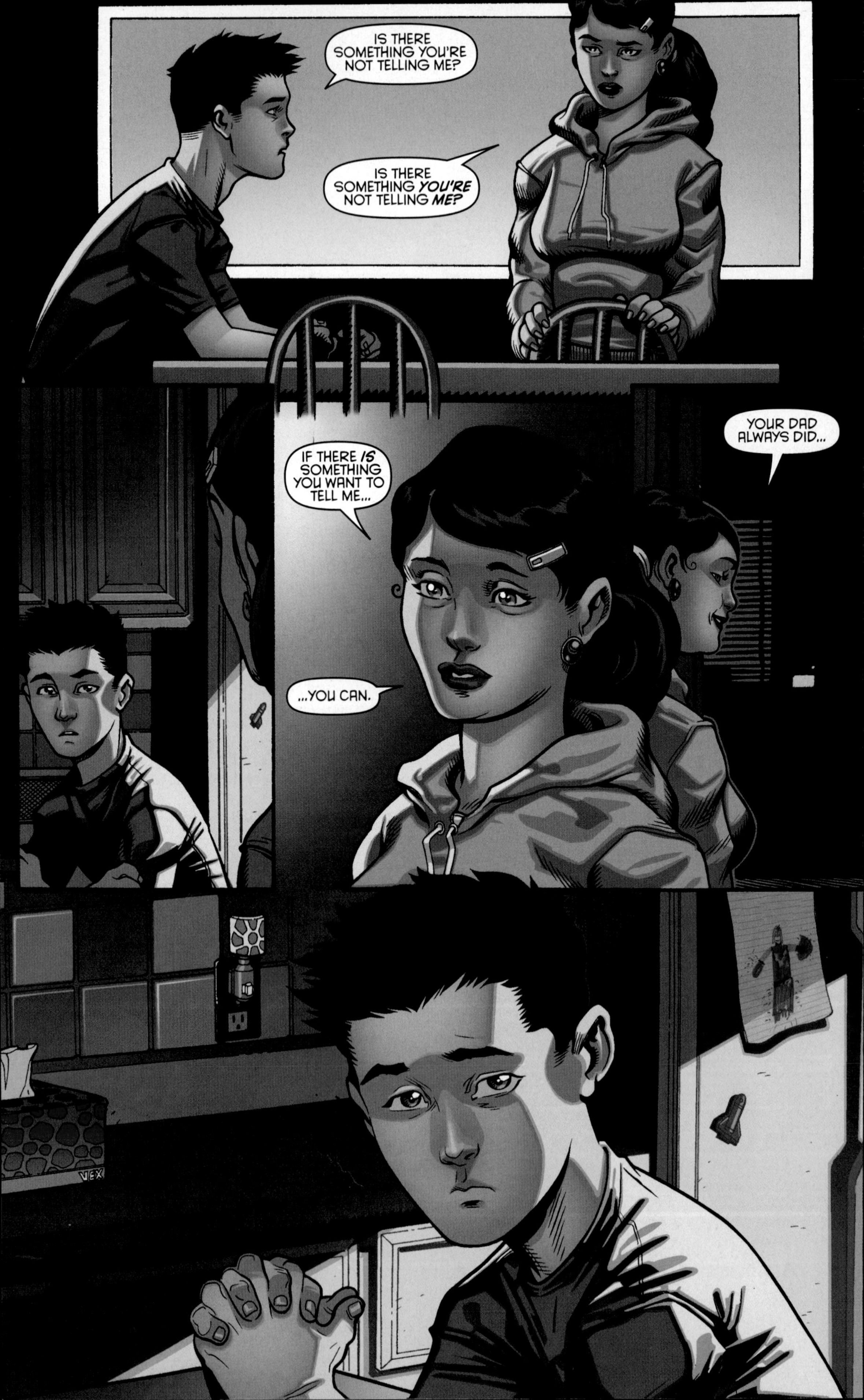
IS THERE SOMETHING YOU'RE NOT TELLING ME?
IS THERE SOMETHING *YOU'RE* NOT TELLING *ME?*
IF THERE *IS* SOMETHING YOU WANT TO TELL ME...
...YOU CAN.
YOUR DAD ALWAYS DID...
VEX

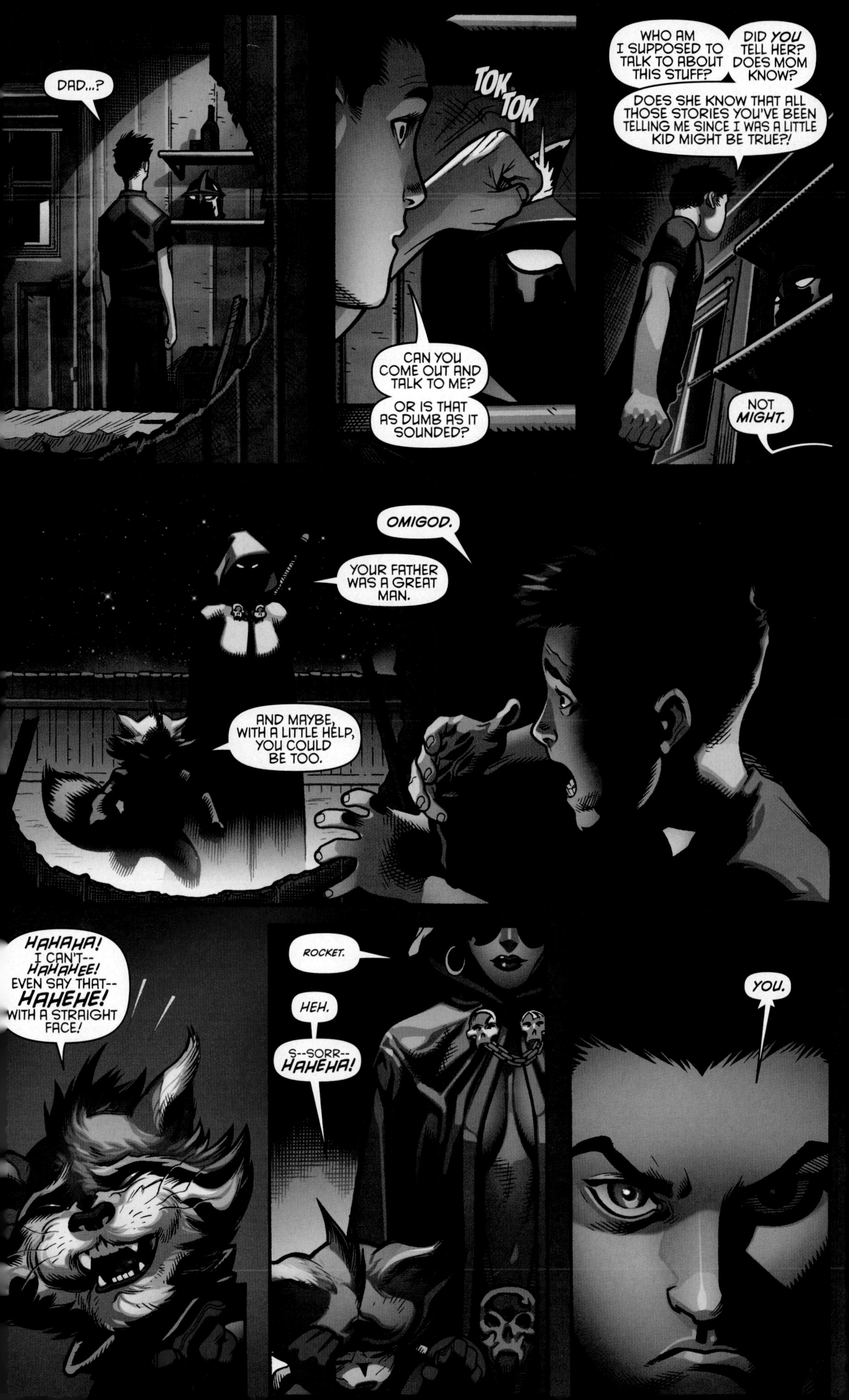
DAD...?
TOK TOK
CAN YOU COME OUT AND TALK TO ME?
OR IS THAT AS DUMB AS IT SOUNDED?
WHO AM I SUPPOSED TO TALK TO ABOUT THIS STUFF?
DID YOU TELL HER? DOES MOM KNOW?
DOES SHE KNOW THAT ALL THOSE STORIES YOU'VE BEEN TELLING ME SINCE I WAS A LITTLE KID MIGHT BE TRUE?!
NOT MIGHT.
OMIGOD.
YOUR FATHER WAS A GREAT MAN.
AND MAYBE, WITH A LITTLE HELP, YOU COULD BE TOO.
HAHAHA! I CAN'T-- HAHAHEE! EVEN SAY THAT-- HAHEHE! WITH A STRAIGHT FACE!
ROCKET.
HEH.
S--SORR-- HAHEHA!
YOU.

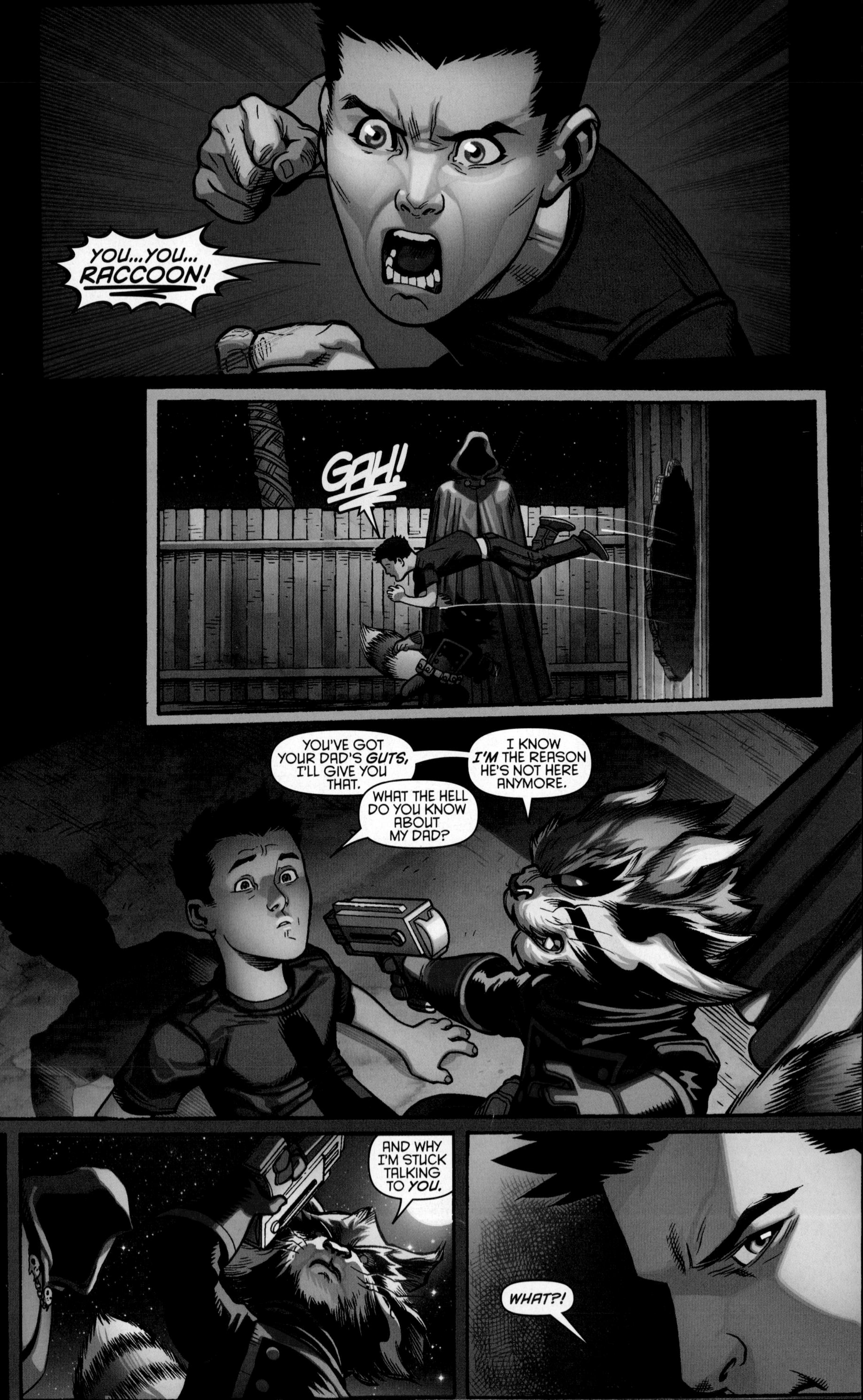
YOU...YOU...
RACCOON!
GAH!
YOU'VE GOT YOUR DAD'S GUTS, I'LL GIVE YOU THAT.
WHAT THE HELL DO YOU KNOW ABOUT MY DAD?
I KNOW I'M THE REASON HE'S NOT HERE ANYMORE.
AND WHY I'M STUCK TALKING TO YOU.
WHAT?!

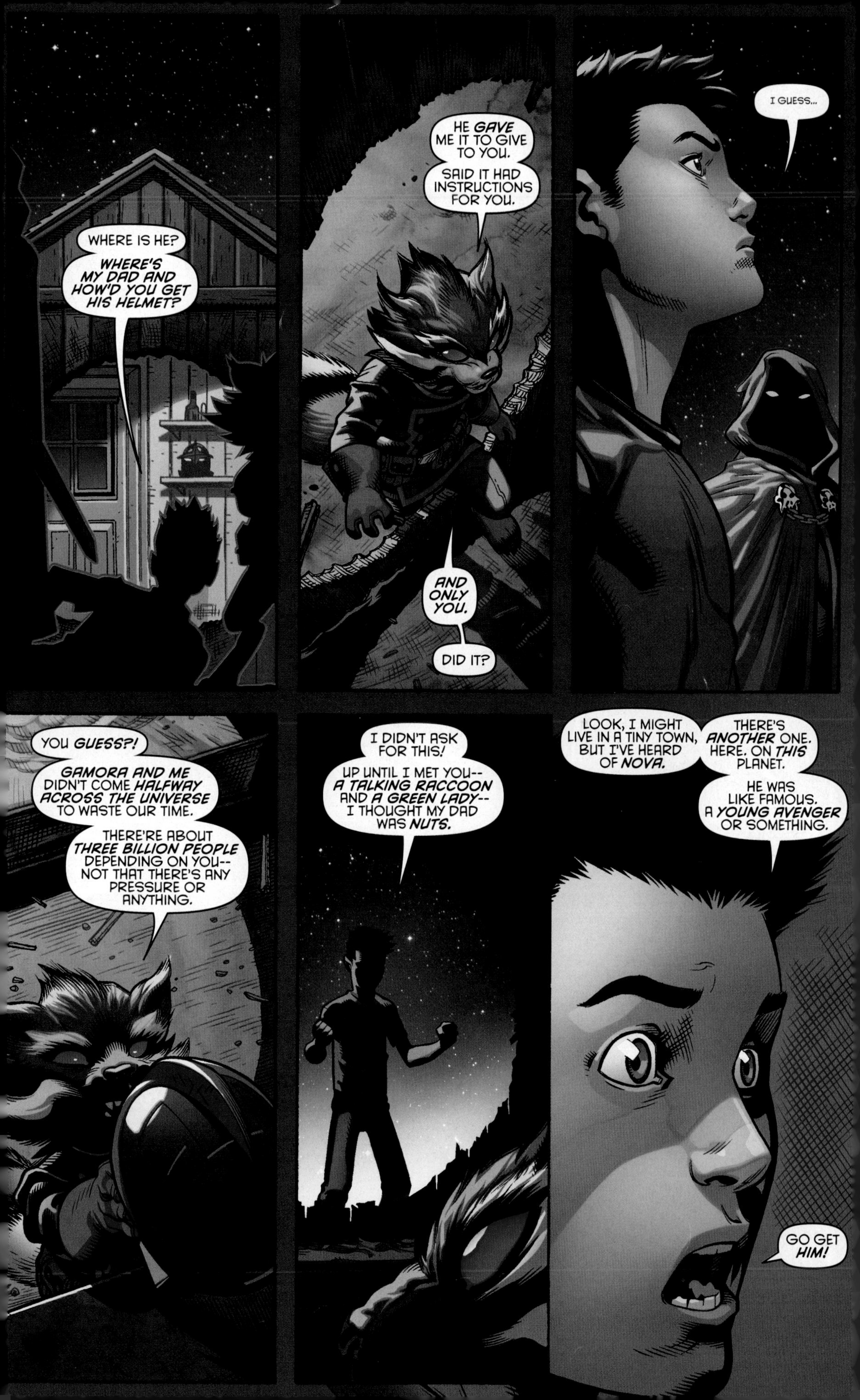

WHERE IS HE?
WHERE'S MY DAD AND HOW'D YOU GET HIS HELMET?
HE GAVE ME IT TO GIVE TO YOU.
SAID IT HAD INSTRUCTIONS FOR YOU.
AND ONLY YOU.
DID IT?
I GUESS...
YOU GUESS?!
GAMORA AND ME DIDN'T COME HALFWAY ACROSS THE UNIVERSE TO WASTE OUR TIME.
THERE'RE ABOUT THREE BILLION PEOPLE DEPENDING ON YOU-- NOT THAT THERE'S ANY PRESSURE OR ANYTHING.
I DIDN'T ASK FOR THIS!
UP UNTIL I MET YOU-- A TALKING RACCOON AND A GREEN LADY-- I THOUGHT MY DAD WAS NUTS.
LOOK, I MIGHT LIVE IN A TINY TOWN, BUT I'VE HEARD OF NOVA.
THERE'S ANOTHER ONE. HERE. ON THIS PLANET.
HE WAS LIKE FAMOUS. A YOUNG AVENGER OR SOMETHING.
GO GET HIM!

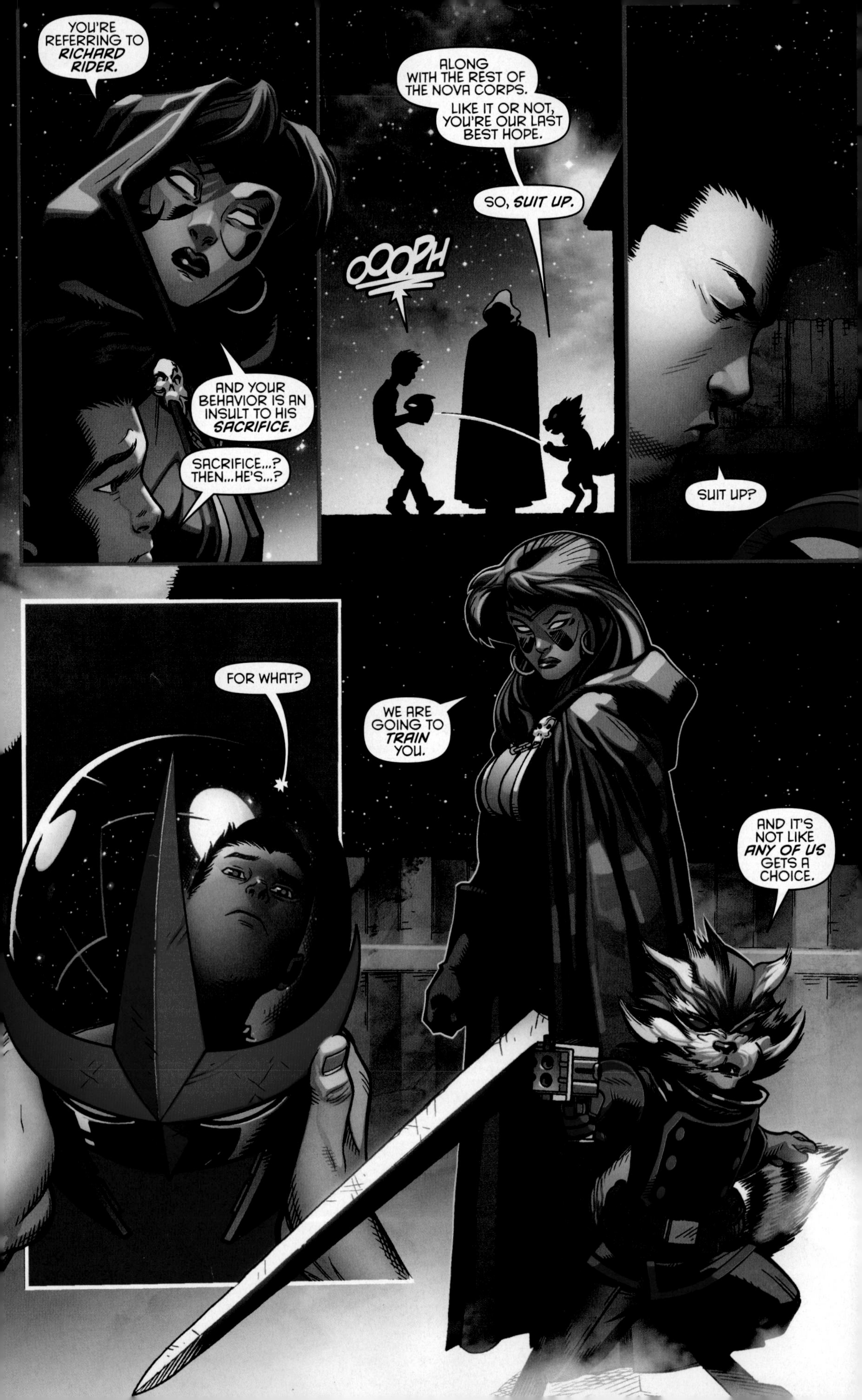
YOU'RE REFERRING TO *RICHARD RIDER.*
AND YOUR BEHAVIOR IS AN INSULT TO HIS *SACRIFICE.*
SACRIFICE...? THEN...HE'S...?
ALONG WITH THE REST OF THE NOVA CORPS.
LIKE IT OR NOT, YOU'RE OUR LAST BEST HOPE.
SO, *SUIT UP.*
OOOPH
SUIT UP?
FOR WHAT?
WE ARE GOING TO *TRAIN* YOU.
AND IT'S NOT LIKE *ANY OF US* GETS A CHOICE.

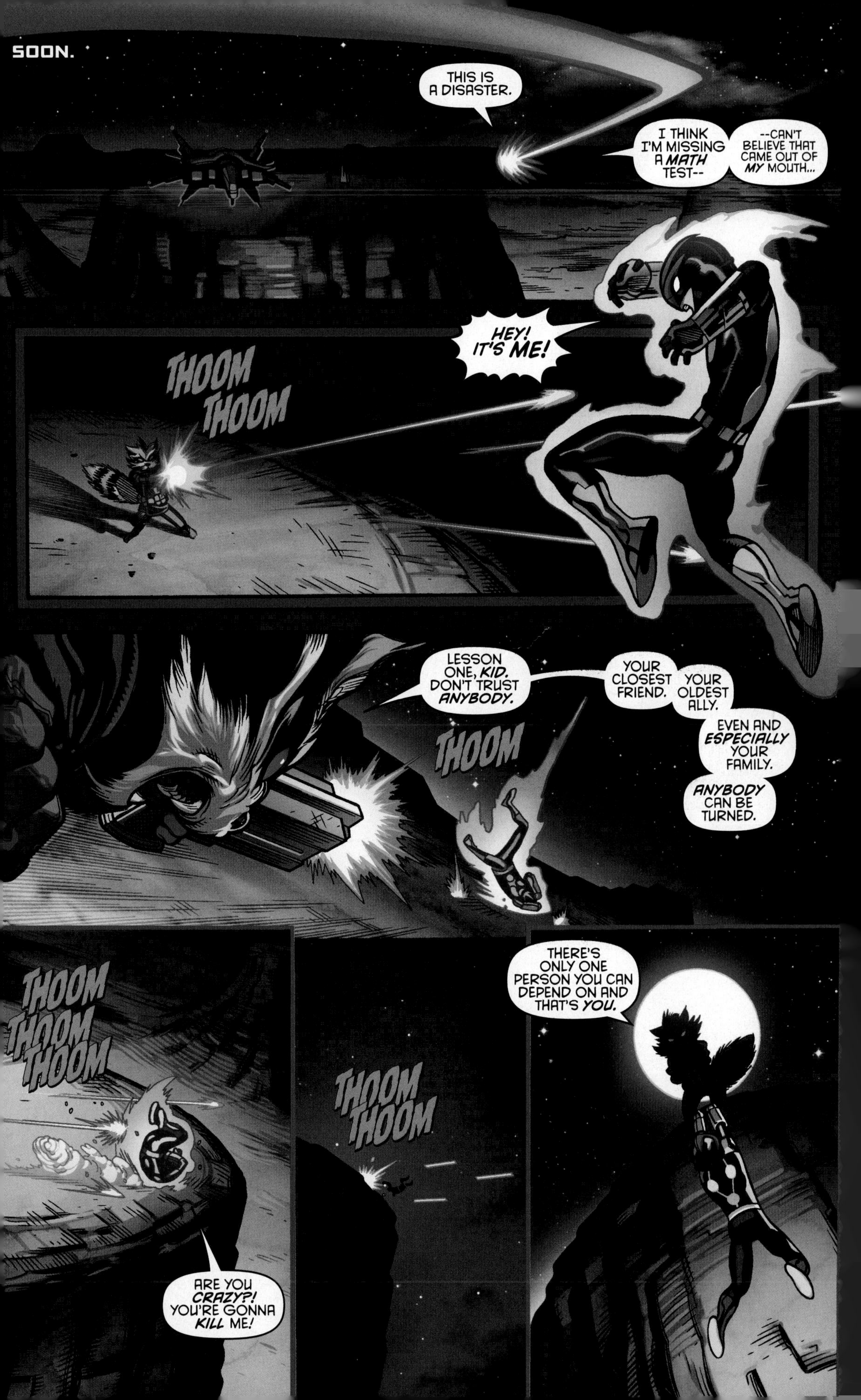
SOON.
THIS IS A DISASTER.
I THINK I'M MISSING A MATH TEST--
--CAN'T BELIEVE THAT CAME OUT OF MY MOUTH...
HEY! IT'S ME!
THOOM THOOM
LESSON ONE, KID. DON'T TRUST ANYBODY.
YOUR CLOSEST FRIEND.
YOUR OLDEST ALLY.
EVEN AND ESPECIALLY YOUR FAMILY.
ANYBODY CAN BE TURNED.
THOOM
THOOM THOOM THOOM
ARE YOU CRAZY?! YOU'RE GONNA KILL ME!
THOOM THOOM
THERE'S ONLY ONE PERSON YOU CAN DEPEND ON AND THAT'S YOU.

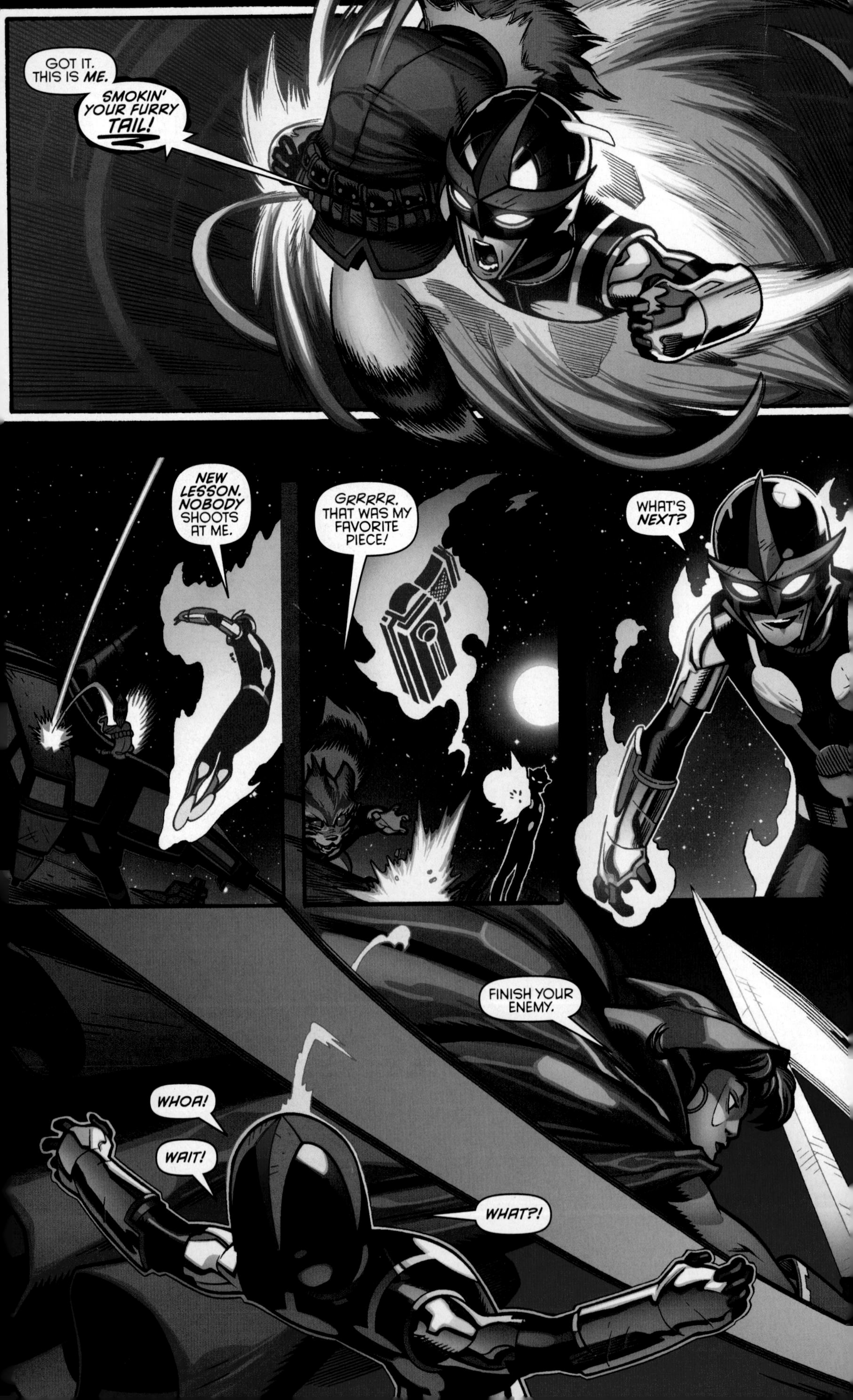
GOT IT. THIS IS *ME.*
SMOKIN' YOUR FURRY TAIL!
NEW LESSON. NOBODY SHOOTS AT ME.
GRRRRR. THAT WAS MY FAVORITE PIECE!
WHAT'S *NEXT?*
FINISH YOUR ENEMY.
WHOA!
WAIT!
WHAT?!

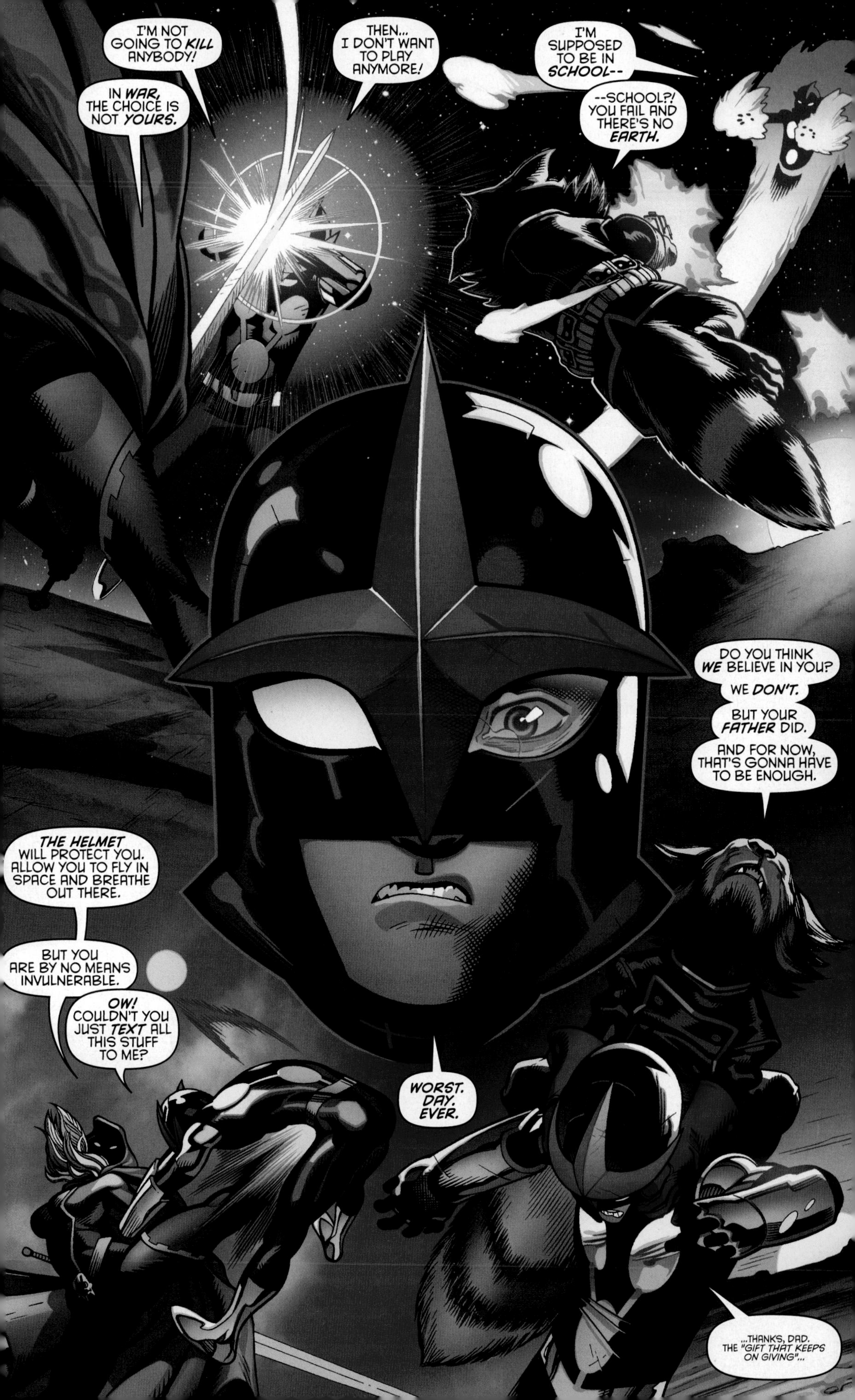
I'M NOT GOING TO KILL ANYBODY!
IN WAR, THE CHOICE IS NOT YOURS.
THEN... I DON'T WANT TO PLAY ANYMORE!
I'M SUPPOSED TO BE IN SCHOOL--
--SCHOOL?! YOU FAIL AND THERE'S NO EARTH.
DO YOU THINK WE BELIEVE IN YOU?
WE DON'T.
BUT YOUR FATHER DID.
AND FOR NOW, THAT'S GONNA HAVE TO BE ENOUGH.
THE HELMET WILL PROTECT YOU. ALLOW YOU TO FLY IN SPACE AND BREATHE OUT THERE.
BUT YOU ARE BY NO MEANS INVULNERABLE.
OW! COULDN'T YOU JUST TEXT ALL THIS STUFF TO ME?
WORST. DAY. EVER.
...THANKS, DAD. THE "GIFT THAT KEEPS ON GIVING"...

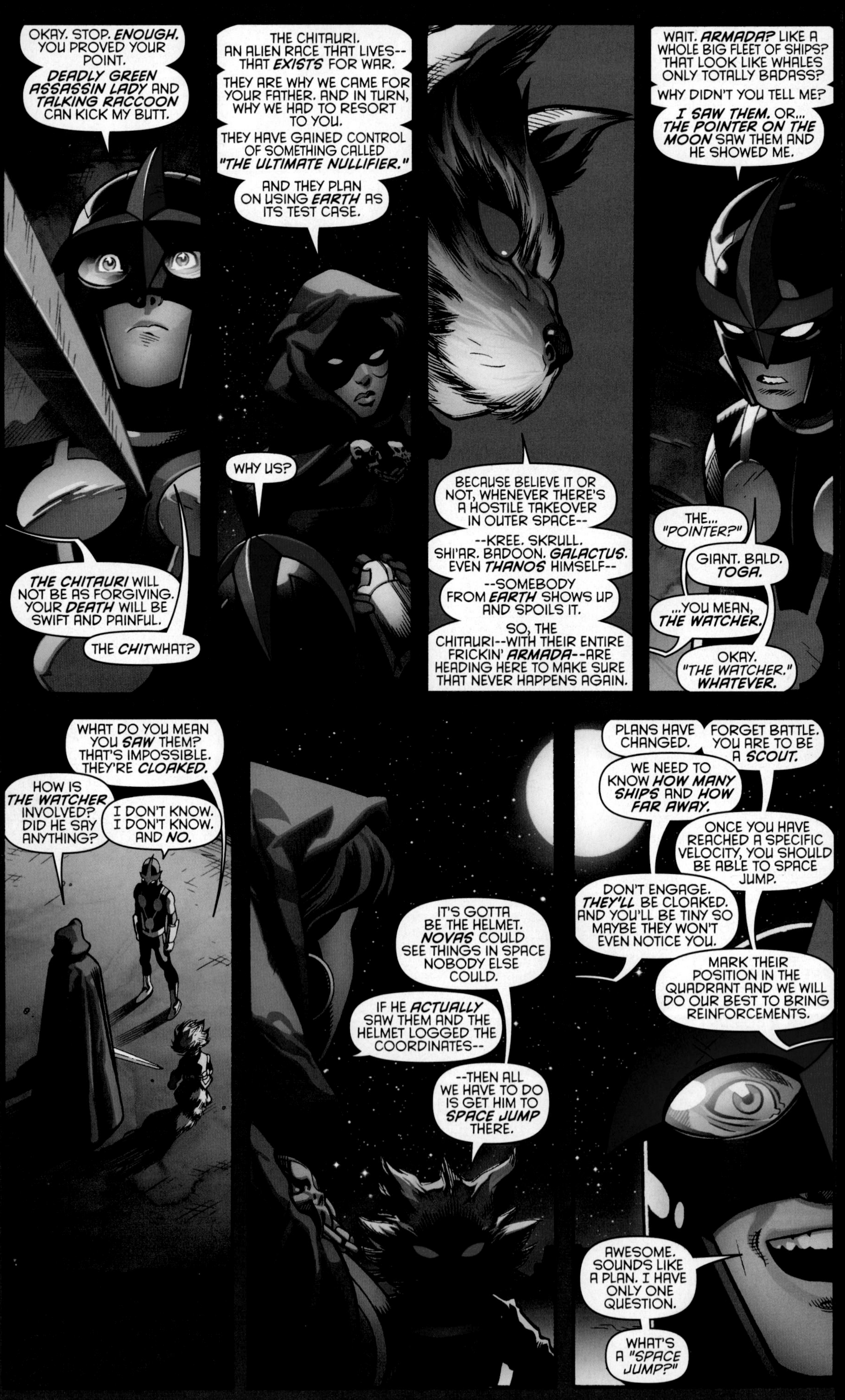
OKAY. STOP. ENOUGH. YOU PROVED YOUR POINT. DEADLY GREEN ASSASSIN LADY AND TALKING RACCOON CAN KICK MY BUTT.
THE CHITAURI WILL NOT BE AS FORGIVING. YOUR DEATH WILL BE SWIFT AND PAINFUL.
THE CHITWHAT?
THE CHITAURI. AN ALIEN RACE THAT LIVES-- THAT EXISTS FOR WAR.
THEY ARE WHY WE CAME FOR YOUR FATHER. AND IN TURN, WHY WE HAD TO RESORT TO YOU.
THEY HAVE GAINED CONTROL OF SOMETHING CALLED "THE ULTIMATE NULLIFIER."
AND THEY PLAN ON USING EARTH AS ITS TEST CASE.
WHY US?
BECAUSE BELIEVE IT OR NOT, WHENEVER THERE'S A HOSTILE TAKEOVER IN OUTER SPACE--
--KREE. SKRULL. SHI'AR. BADOON. GALACTUS. EVEN THANOS HIMSELF--
--SOMEBODY FROM EARTH SHOWS UP AND SPOILS IT.
SO, THE CHITAURI--WITH THEIR ENTIRE FRICKIN' ARMADA--ARE HEADING HERE TO MAKE SURE THAT NEVER HAPPENS AGAIN.
WAIT. ARMADA? LIKE A WHOLE BIG FLEET OF SHIPS? THAT LOOK LIKE WHALES ONLY TOTALLY BADASS?
WHY DIDN'T YOU TELL ME?
I SAW THEM. OR... THE POINTER ON THE MOON SAW THEM AND HE SHOWED ME.
THE... "POINTER?"
GIANT. BALD. TOGA.
...YOU MEAN, THE WATCHER.
OKAY. "THE WATCHER." WHATEVER.
WHAT DO YOU MEAN YOU SAW THEM? THAT'S IMPOSSIBLE. THEY'RE CLOAKED.
HOW IS THE WATCHER INVOLVED? DID HE SAY ANYTHING?
I DON'T KNOW. I DON'T KNOW. AND NO.
IT'S GOTTA BE THE HELMET. NOVAS COULD SEE THINGS IN SPACE NOBODY ELSE COULD.
IF HE ACTUALLY SAW THEM AND THE HELMET LOGGED THE COORDINATES--
--THEN ALL WE HAVE TO DO IS GET HIM TO SPACE JUMP THERE.
PLANS HAVE CHANGED.
FORGET BATTLE. YOU ARE TO BE A SCOUT.
WE NEED TO KNOW HOW MANY SHIPS AND HOW FAR AWAY.
ONCE YOU HAVE REACHED A SPECIFIC VELOCITY, YOU SHOULD BE ABLE TO SPACE JUMP.
DON'T ENGAGE. THEY'LL BE CLOAKED. AND YOU'LL BE TINY SO MAYBE THEY WON'T EVEN NOTICE YOU.
MARK THEIR POSITION IN THE QUADRANT AND WE WILL DO OUR BEST TO BRING REINFORCEMENTS.
AWESOME. SOUNDS LIKE A PLAN. I HAVE ONLY ONE QUESTION.
WHAT'S A "SPACE JUMP?"

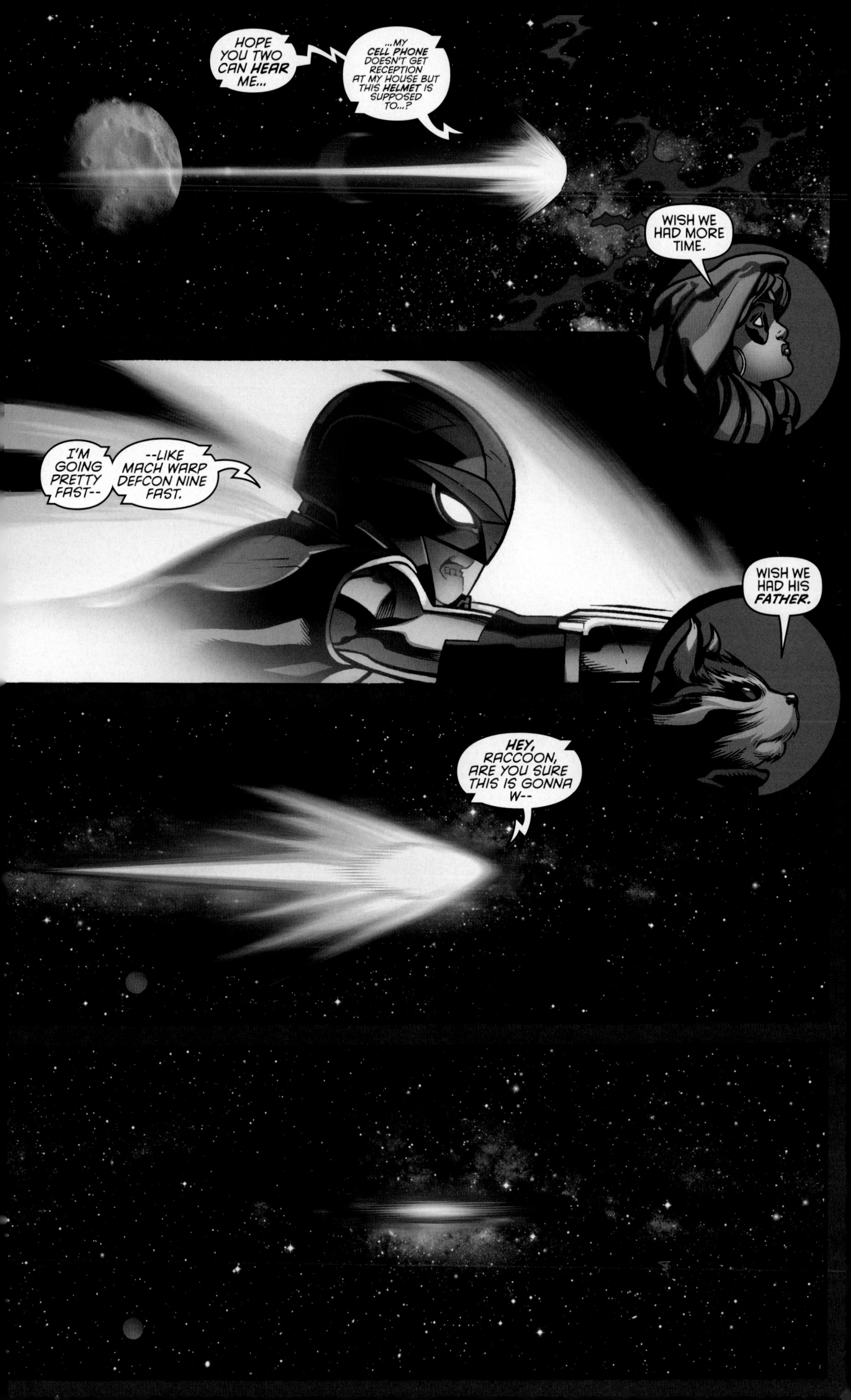
HOPE YOU TWO CAN HEAR ME...
...MY CELL PHONE DOESN'T GET RECEPTION AT MY HOUSE BUT THIS HELMET IS SUPPOSED TO...?
WISH WE HAD MORE TIME.
I'M GOING PRETTY FAST--
--LIKE MACH WARP DEFCON NINE FAST.
WISH WE HAD HIS FATHER.
HEY, RACCOON, ARE YOU SURE THIS IS GONNA W--

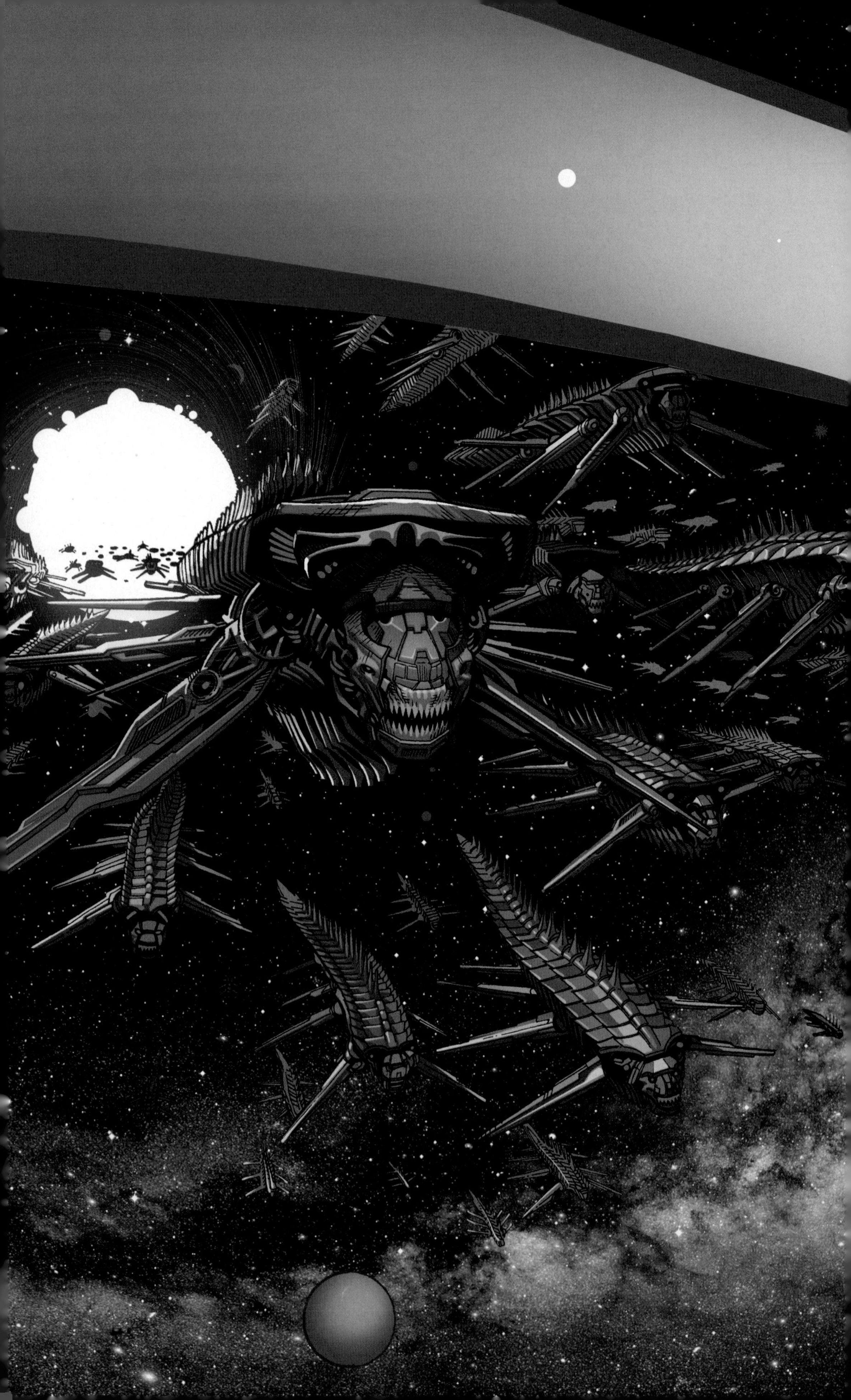

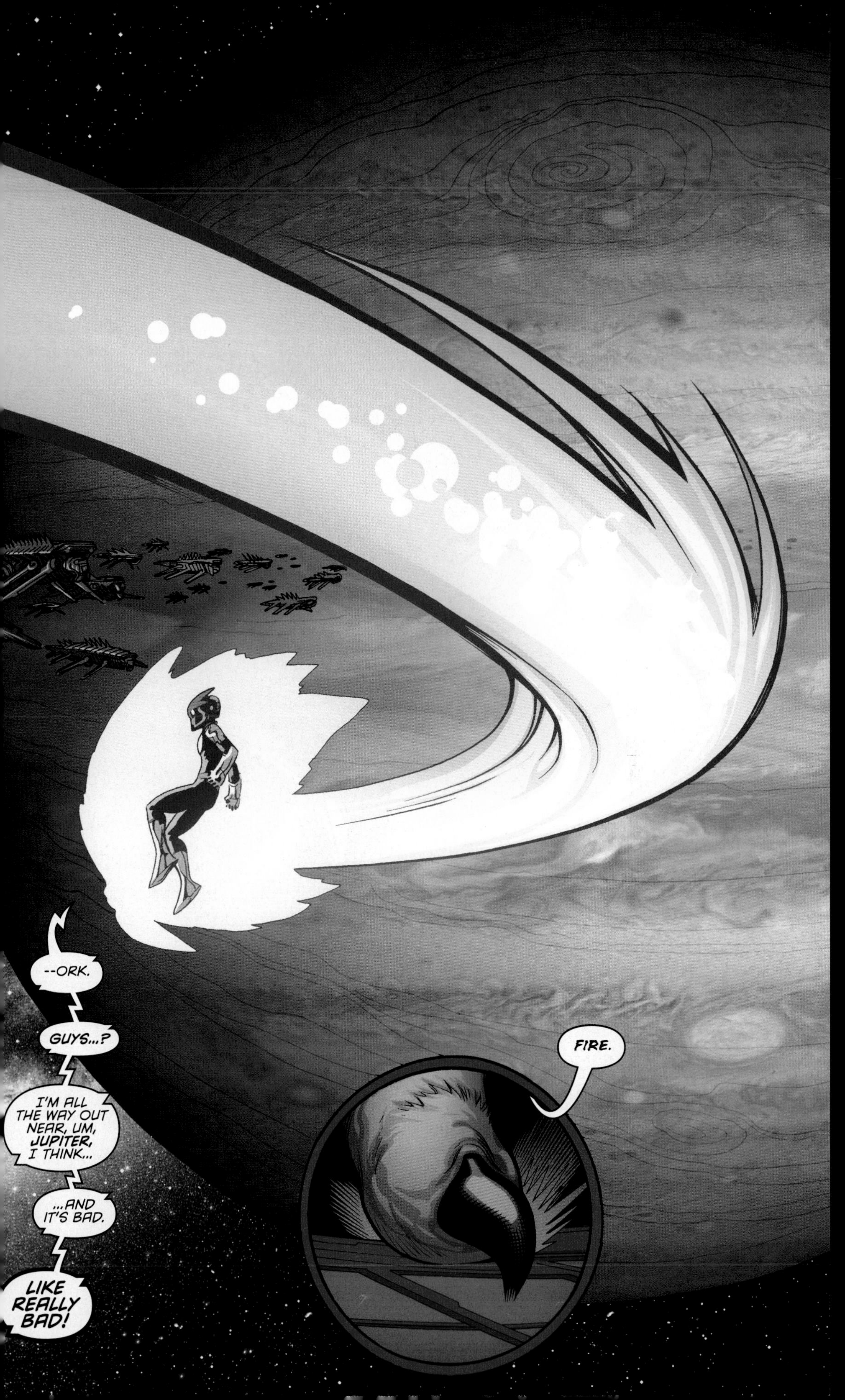
--ORK.
GUYS...?
I'M ALL THE WAY OUT NEAR, UM, JUPITER, I THINK...
...AND IT'S BAD.
LIKE REALLY BAD!
FIRE.

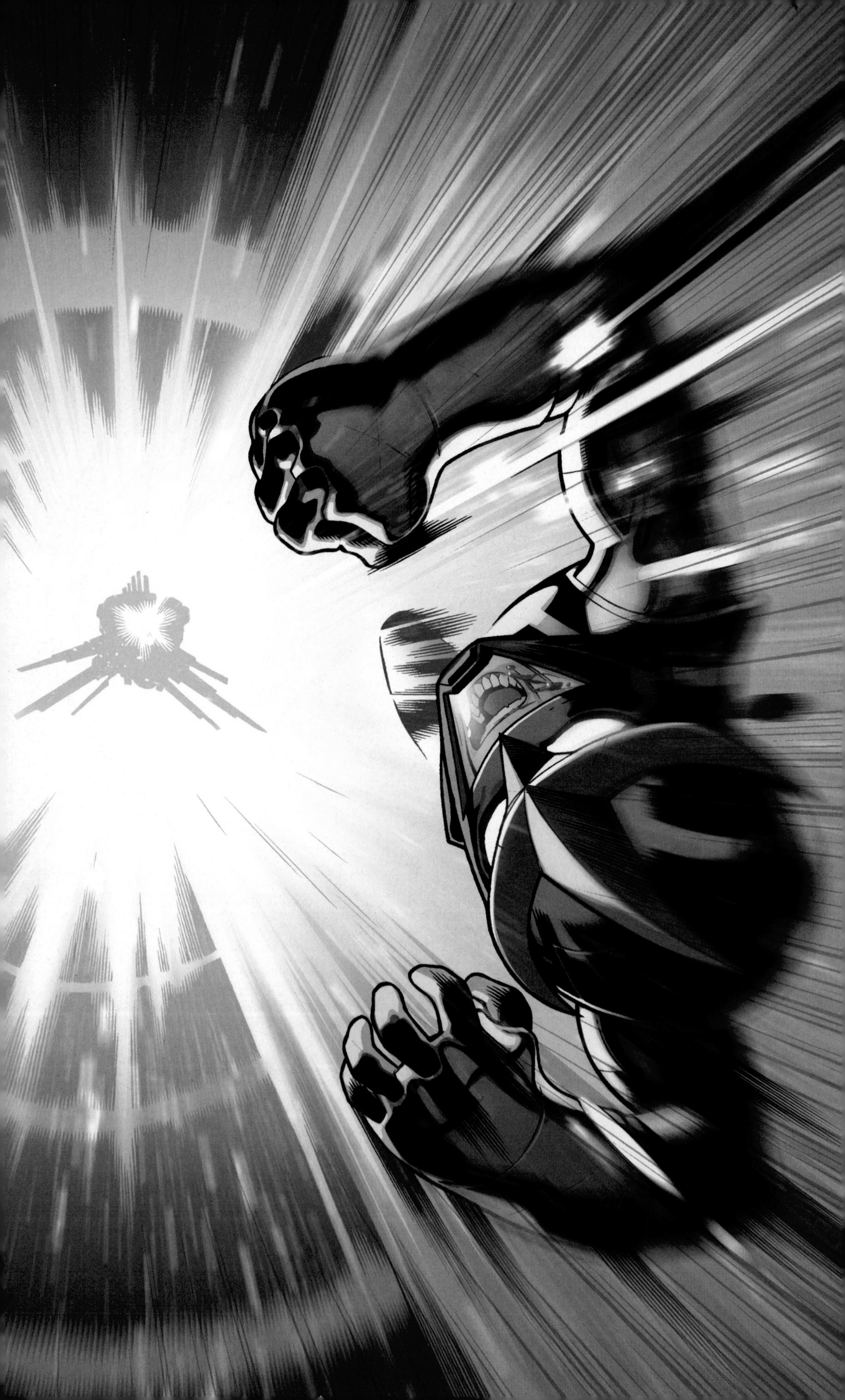

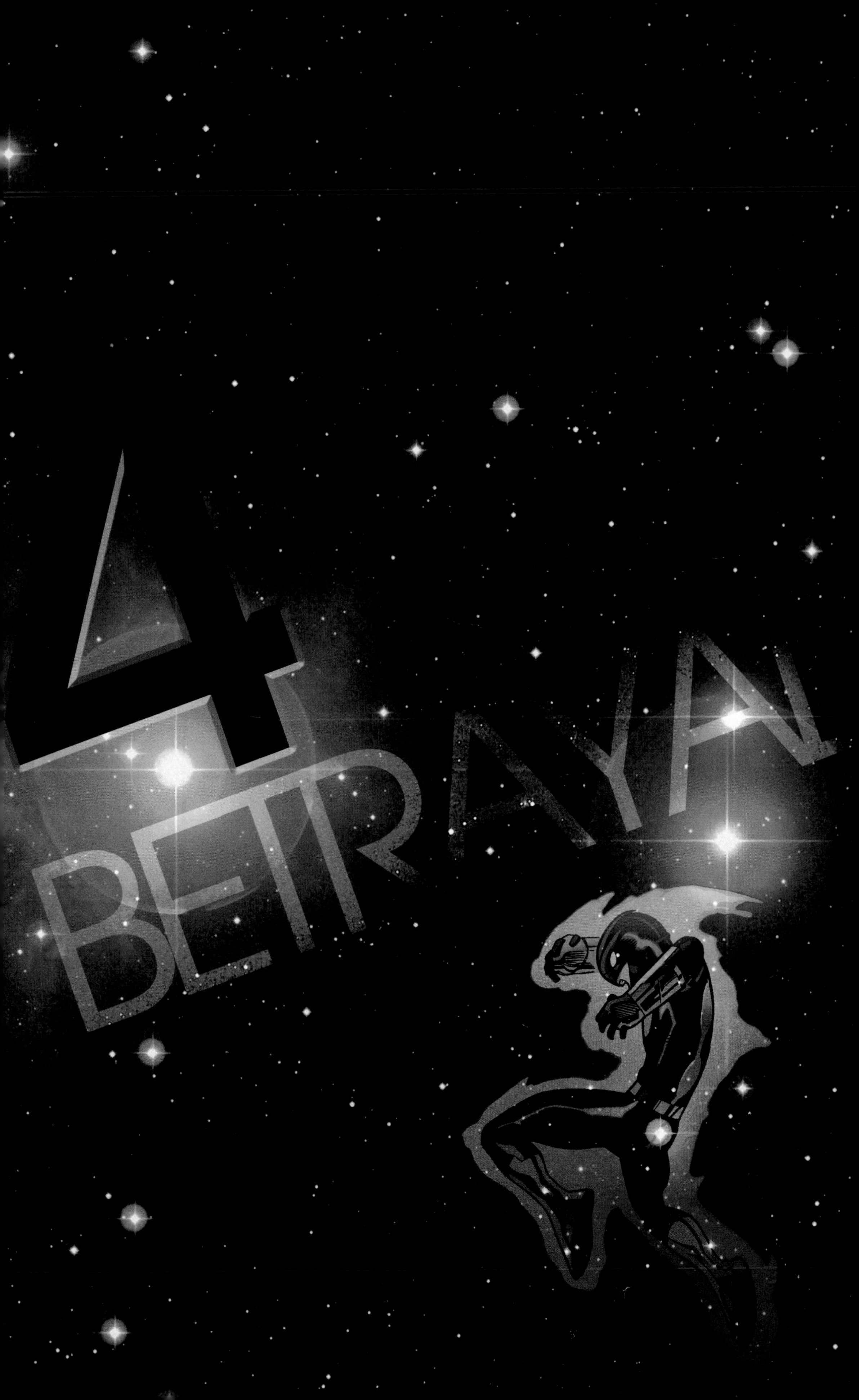
4
BETRAYAL

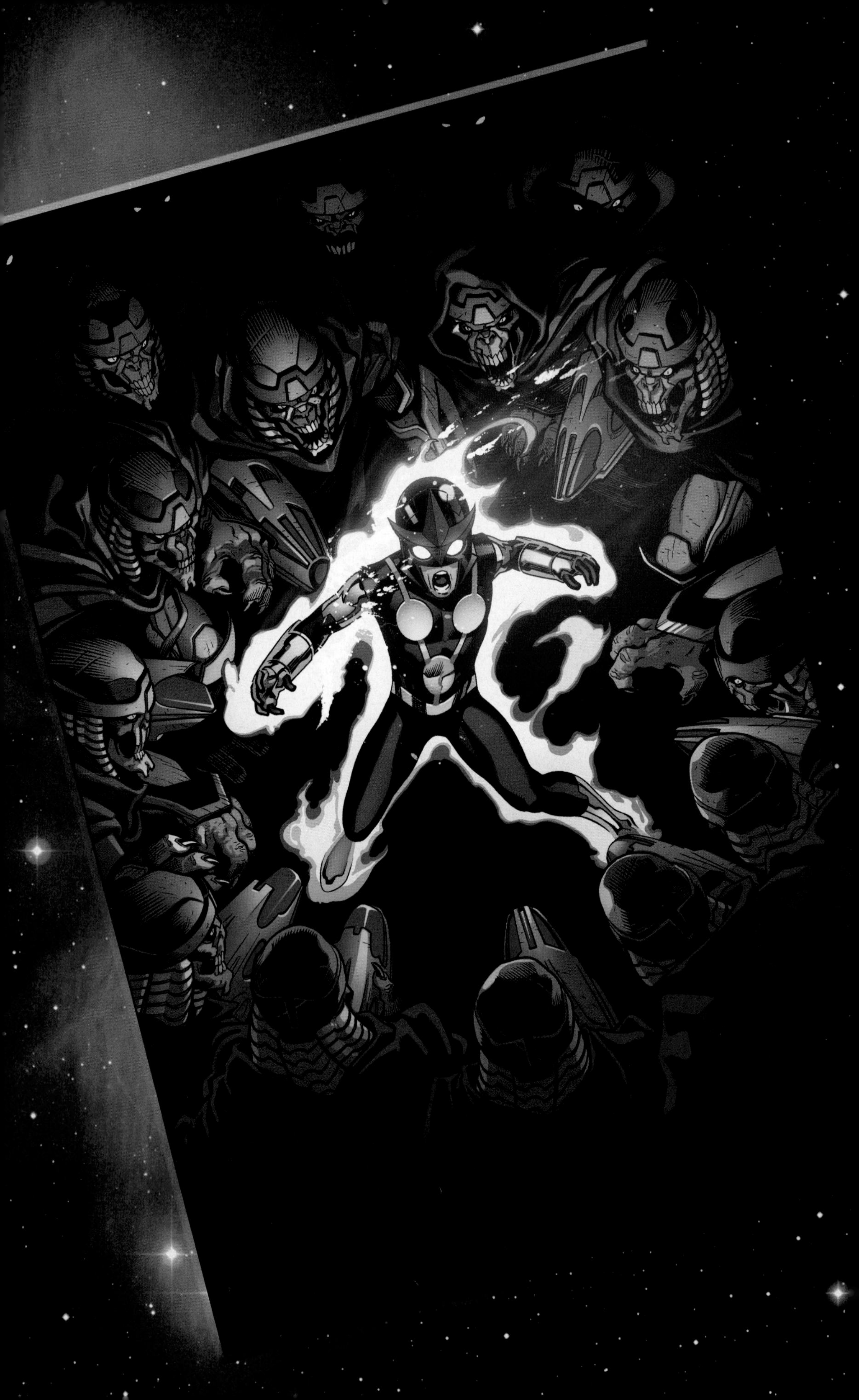

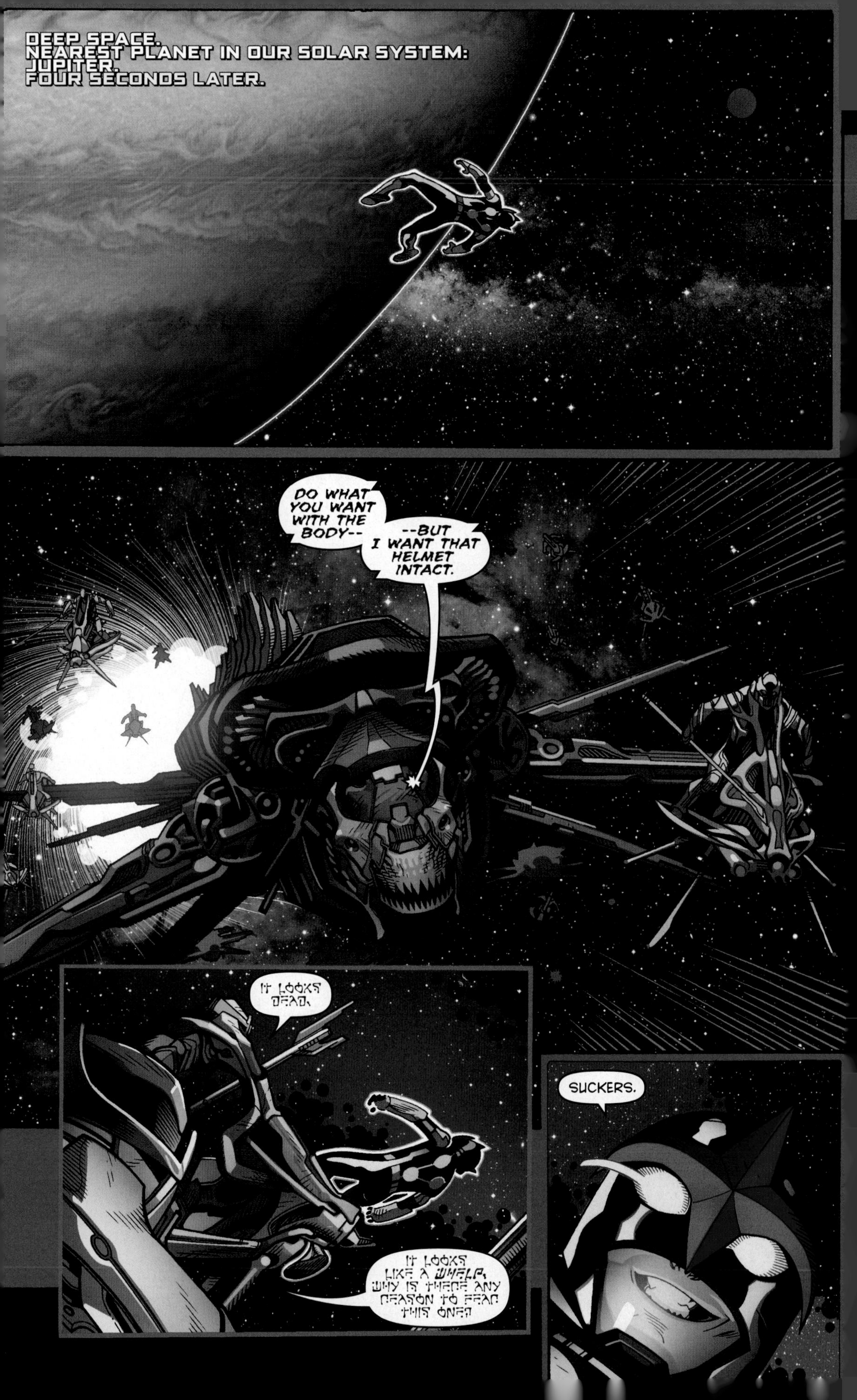
DEEP SPACE.
NEAREST PLANET IN OUR SOLAR SYSTEM: JUPITER.
FOUR SECONDS LATER.
DO WHAT YOU WANT WITH THE BODY--
--BUT I WANT THAT HELMET INTACT.
IT LOOKS DEAD.
IT LOOKS LIKE A WHELP. WHY IS THERE ANY REASON TO FEAR THIS ONE?
SUCKERS.

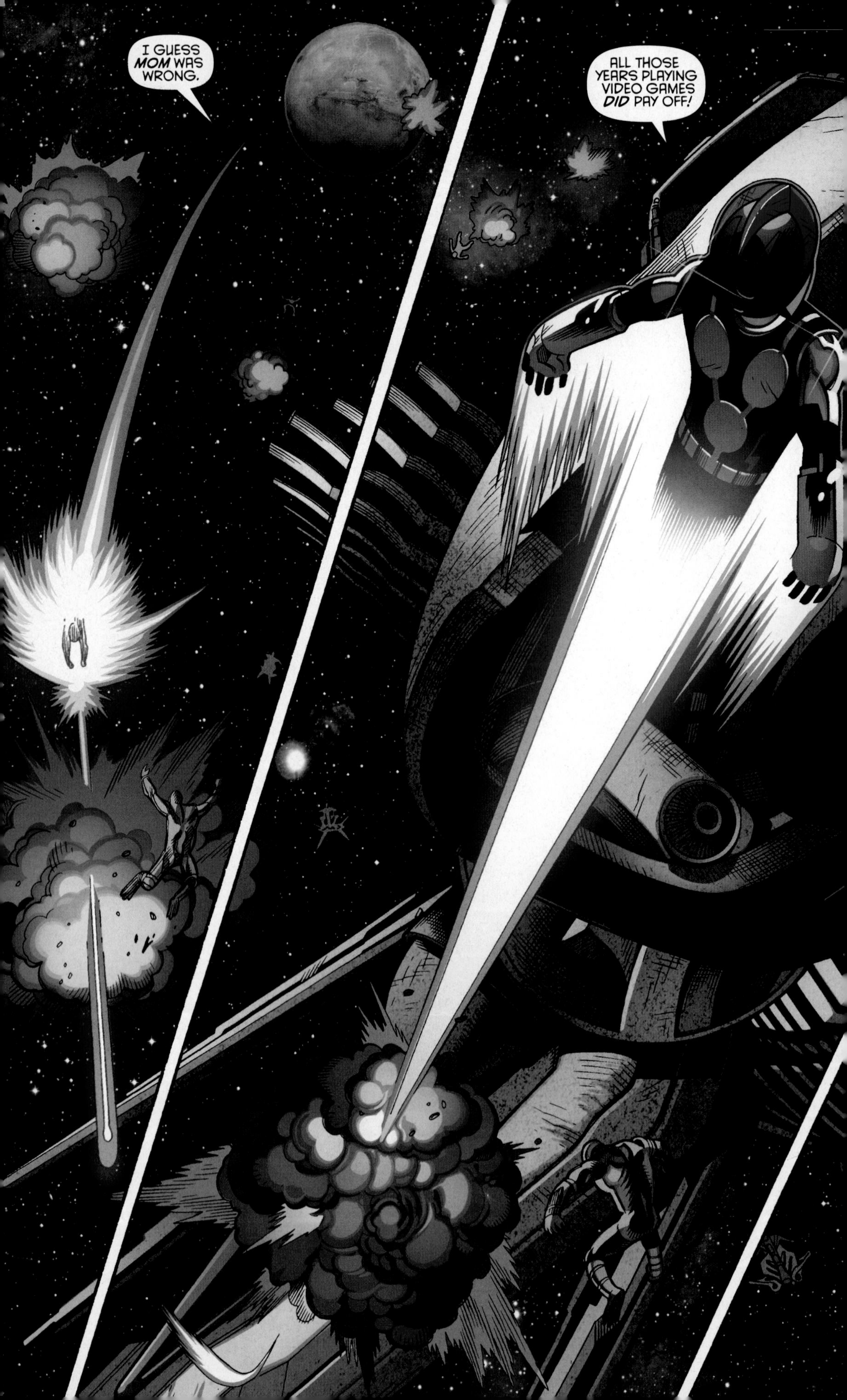
I GUESS MOM WAS WRONG.
ALL THOSE YEARS PLAYING VIDEO GAMES DID PAY OFF!

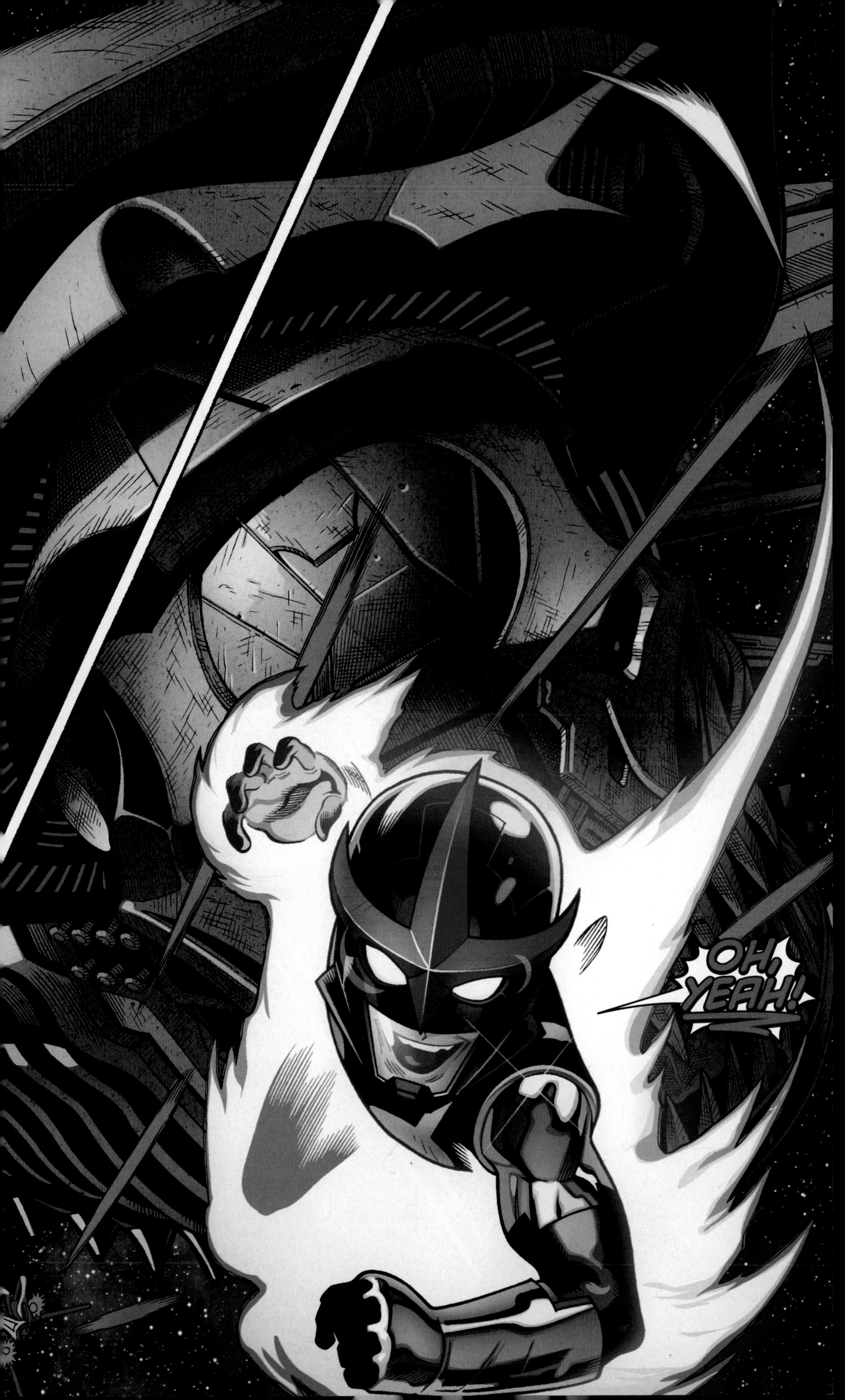
OH, YEAH!

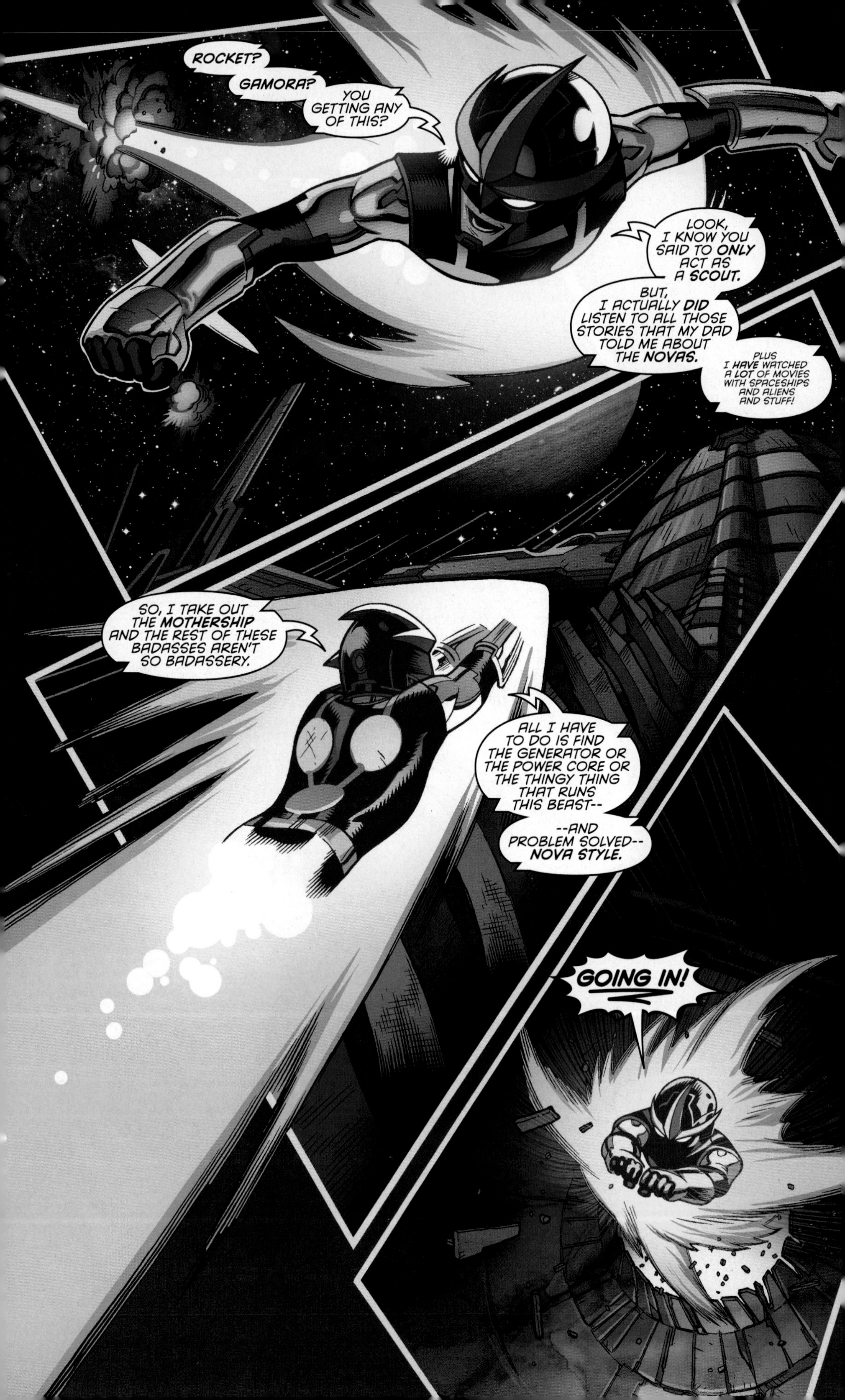
ROCKET?
GAMORA?
YOU GETTING ANY OF THIS?
LOOK, I KNOW YOU SAID TO ONLY ACT AS A SCOUT.
BUT, I ACTUALLY DID LISTEN TO ALL THOSE STORIES THAT MY DAD TOLD ME ABOUT THE NOVAS.
PLUS I HAVE WATCHED A LOT OF MOVIES WITH SPACESHIPS AND ALIENS AND STUFF!
SO, I TAKE OUT THE MOTHERSHIP AND THE REST OF THESE BADASSES AREN'T SO BADASSERY.
ALL I HAVE TO DO IS FIND THE GENERATOR OR THE POWER CORE OR THE THINGY THING THAT RUNS THIS BEAST--
--AND PROBLEM SOLVED-- NOVA STYLE.
GOING IN!

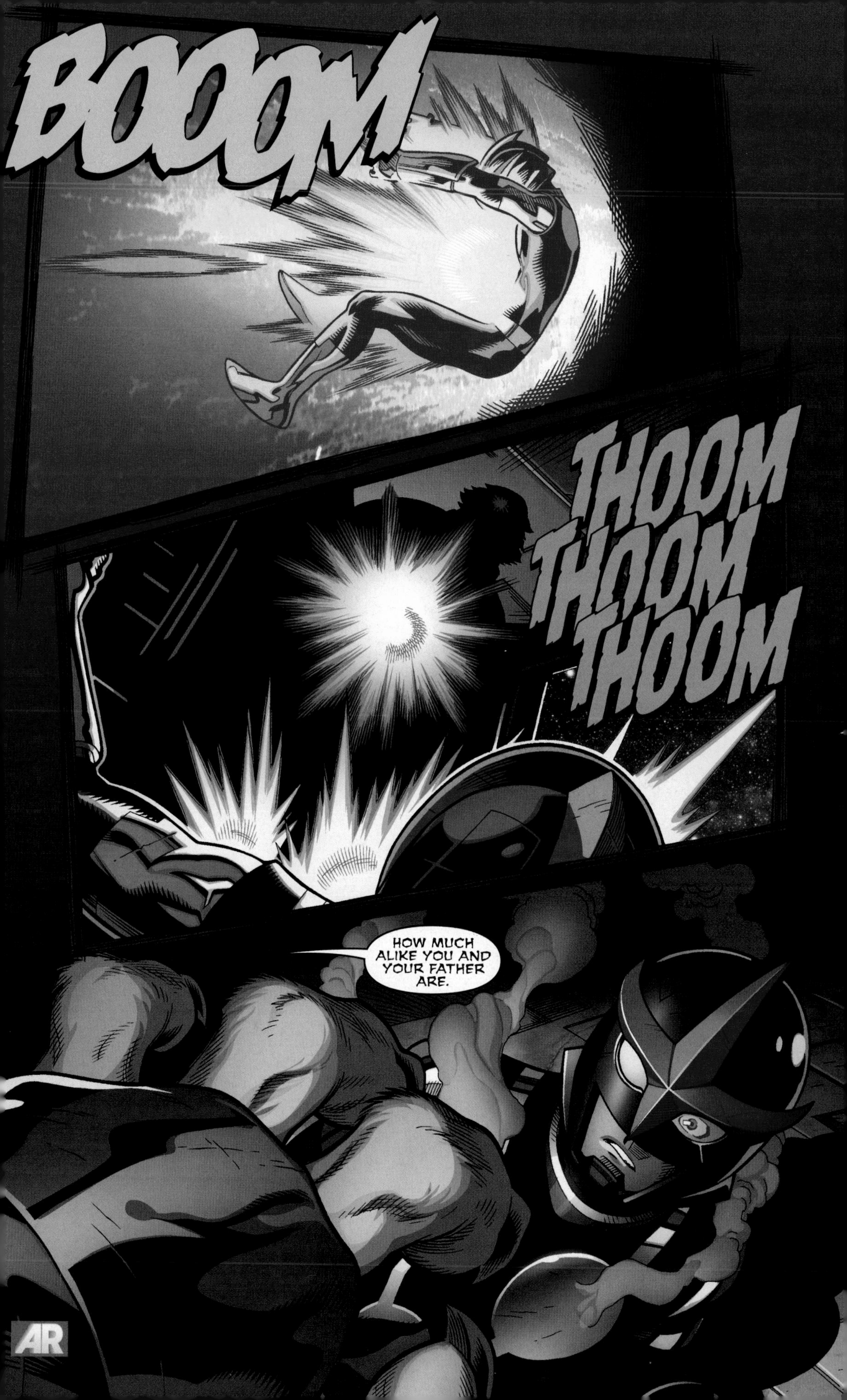
BOOOM
THOOM
THOOM
THOOM
HOW MUCH ALIKE YOU AND YOUR FATHER ARE.
AR

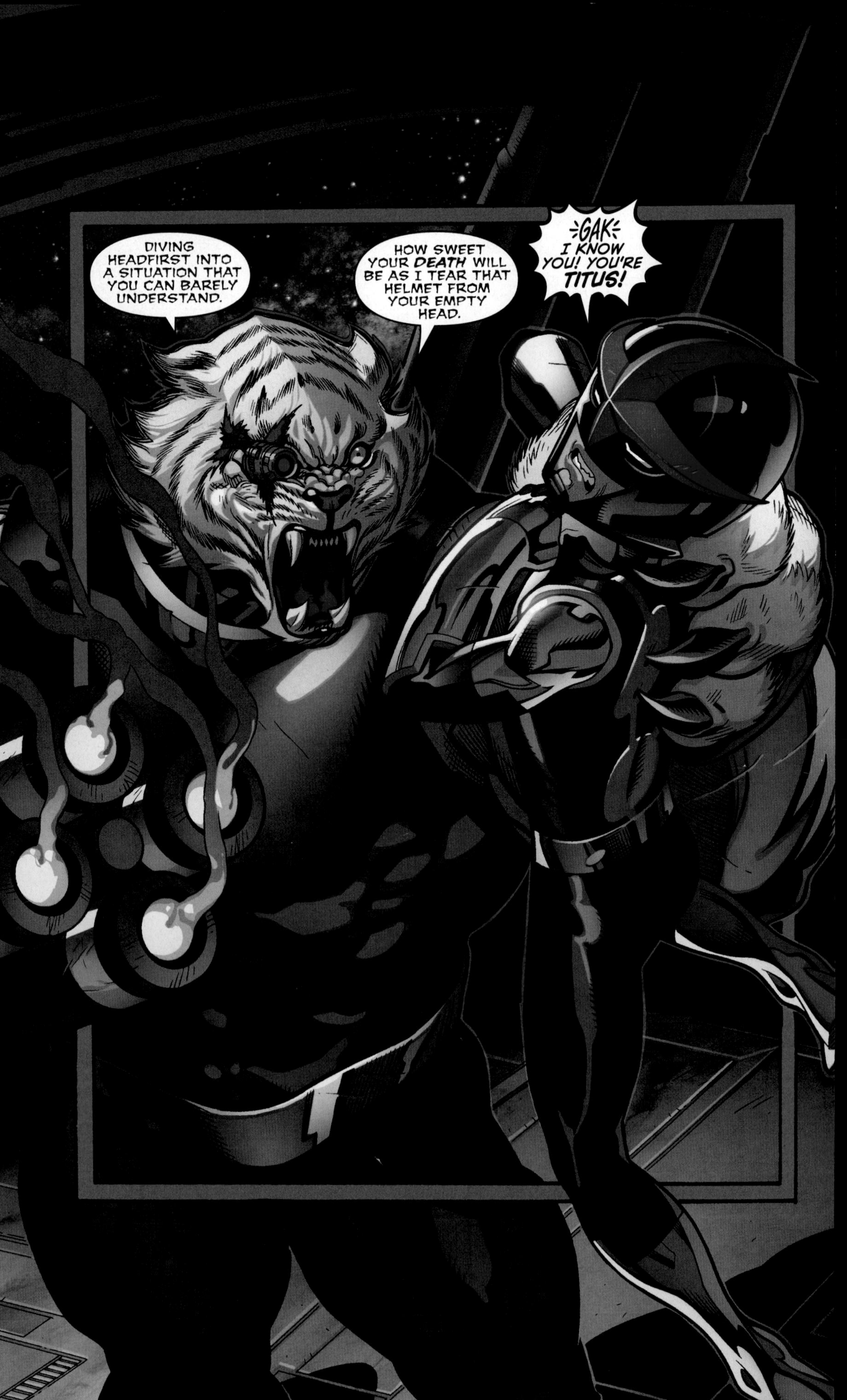
DIVING HEADFIRST INTO A SITUATION THAT YOU CAN BARELY UNDERSTAND.
HOW SWEET YOUR *DEATH* WILL BE AS I TEAR THAT HELMET FROM YOUR EMPTY HEAD.
GAK I KNOW YOU! YOU'RE ***TITUS!***

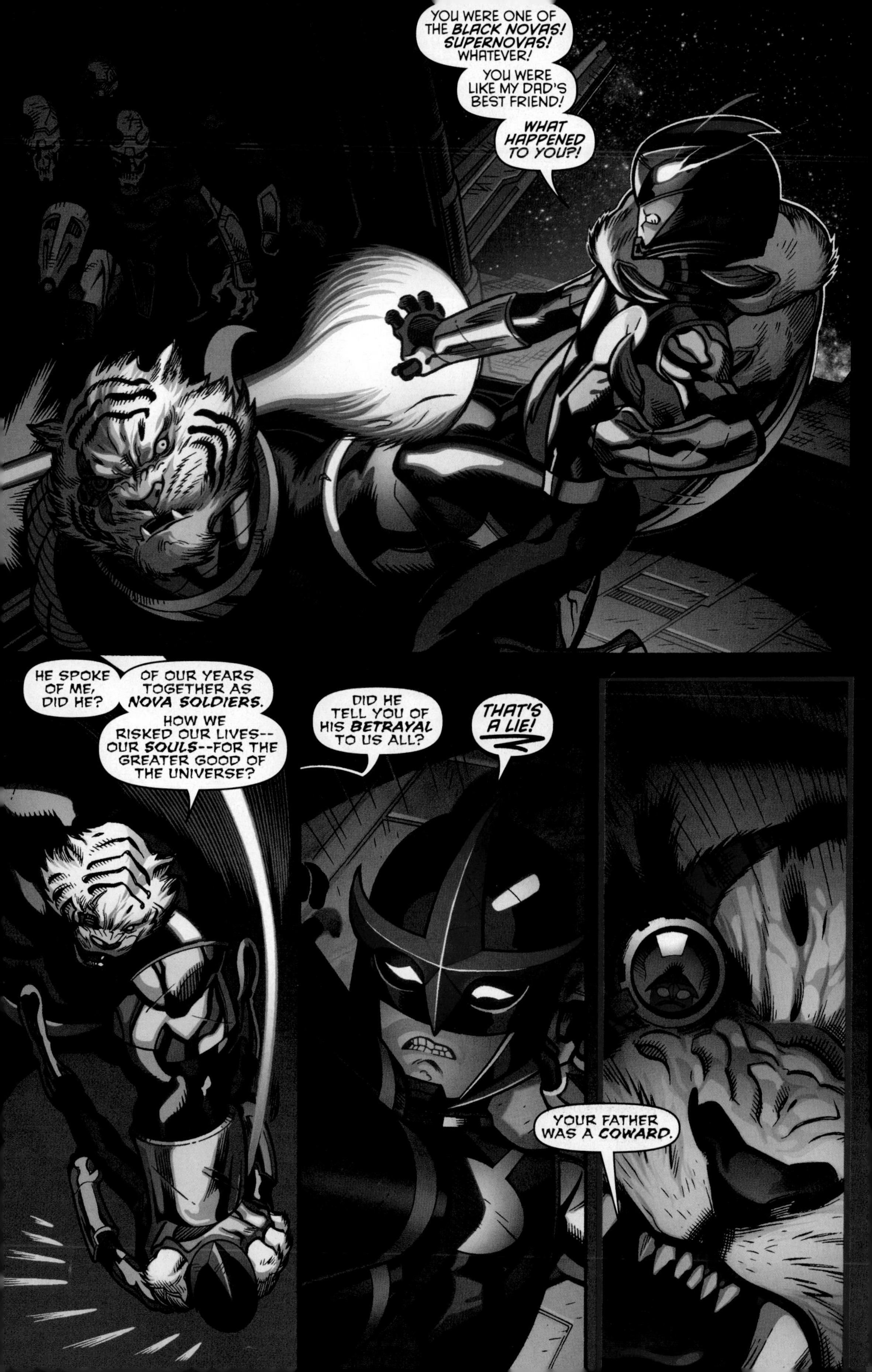
YOU WERE ONE OF THE BLACK NOVAS! SUPERNOVAS! WHATEVER!
YOU WERE LIKE MY DAD'S BEST FRIEND!
WHAT HAPPENED TO YOU?!
HE SPOKE OF ME, DID HE?
OF OUR YEARS TOGETHER AS NOVA SOLDIERS.
HOW WE RISKED OUR LIVES--OUR SOULS--FOR THE GREATER GOOD OF THE UNIVERSE?
DID HE TELL YOU OF HIS BETRAYAL TO US ALL?
THAT'S A LIE!
YOUR FATHER WAS A COWARD.

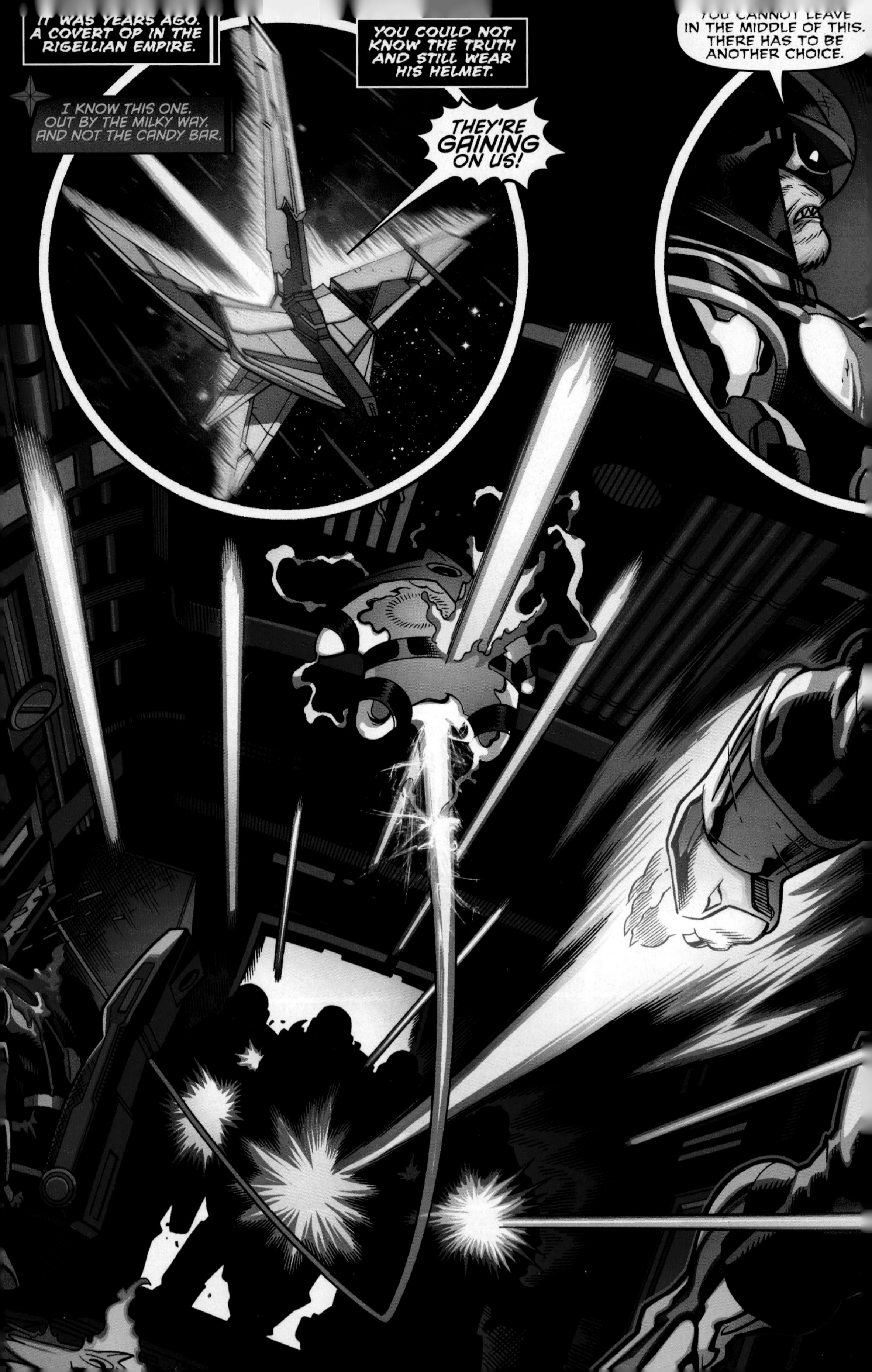
IT WAS YEARS AGO. A COVERT OP IN THE RIGELLIAN EMPIRE.
I KNOW THIS ONE. OUT BY THE MILKY WAY. AND NOT THE CANDY BAR.
YOU COULD NOT KNOW THE TRUTH AND STILL WEAR HIS HELMET.
THEY'RE GAINING ON US!
YOU CANNOT LEAVE IN THE MIDDLE OF THIS. THERE HAS TO BE ANOTHER CHOICE.

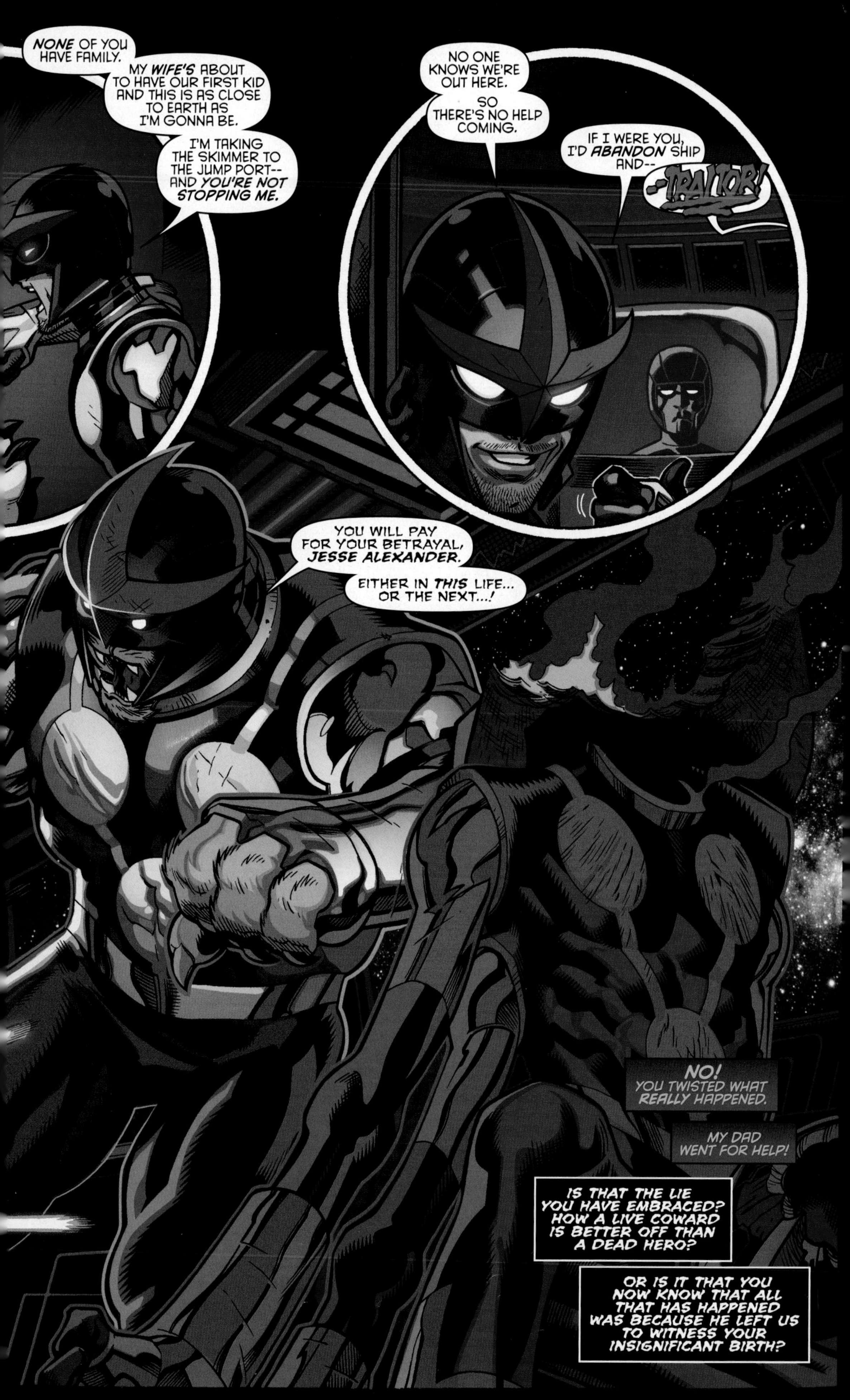
NONE OF YOU HAVE FAMILY.
MY WIFE'S ABOUT TO HAVE OUR FIRST KID AND THIS IS AS CLOSE TO EARTH AS I'M GONNA BE.
I'M TAKING THE SKIMMER TO THE JUMP PORT-- AND YOU'RE NOT STOPPING ME.
NO ONE KNOWS WE'RE OUT HERE.
SO THERE'S NO HELP COMING.
IF I WERE YOU, I'D ABANDON SHIP AND--
--TRAITOR!
YOU WILL PAY FOR YOUR BETRAYAL, JESSE ALEXANDER.
EITHER IN THIS LIFE... OR THE NEXT...!
NO! YOU TWISTED WHAT REALLY HAPPENED.
MY DAD WENT FOR HELP!
IS THAT THE LIE YOU HAVE EMBRACED? HOW A LIVE COWARD IS BETTER OFF THAN A DEAD HERO?
OR IS IT THAT YOU NOW KNOW THAT ALL THAT HAS HAPPENED WAS BECAUSE HE LEFT US TO WITNESS YOUR INSIGNIFICANT BIRTH?

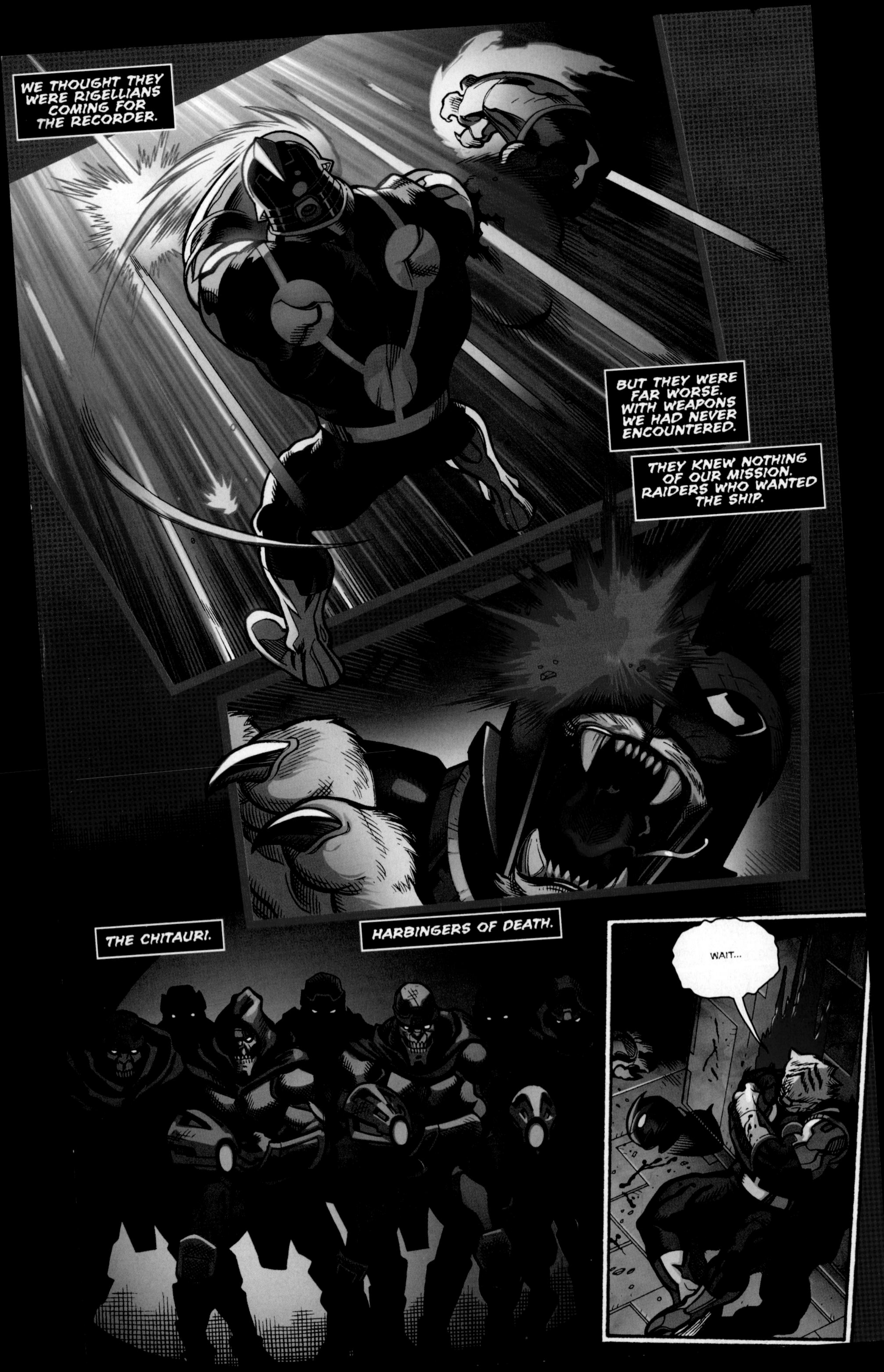
WE THOUGHT THEY WERE RIGELLIANS COMING FOR THE RECORDER.
BUT THEY WERE FAR WORSE. WITH WEAPONS WE HAD NEVER ENCOUNTERED.
THEY KNEW NOTHING OF OUR MISSION. RAIDERS WHO WANTED THE SHIP.
THE CHITAURI.
HARBINGERS OF DEATH.
WAIT...

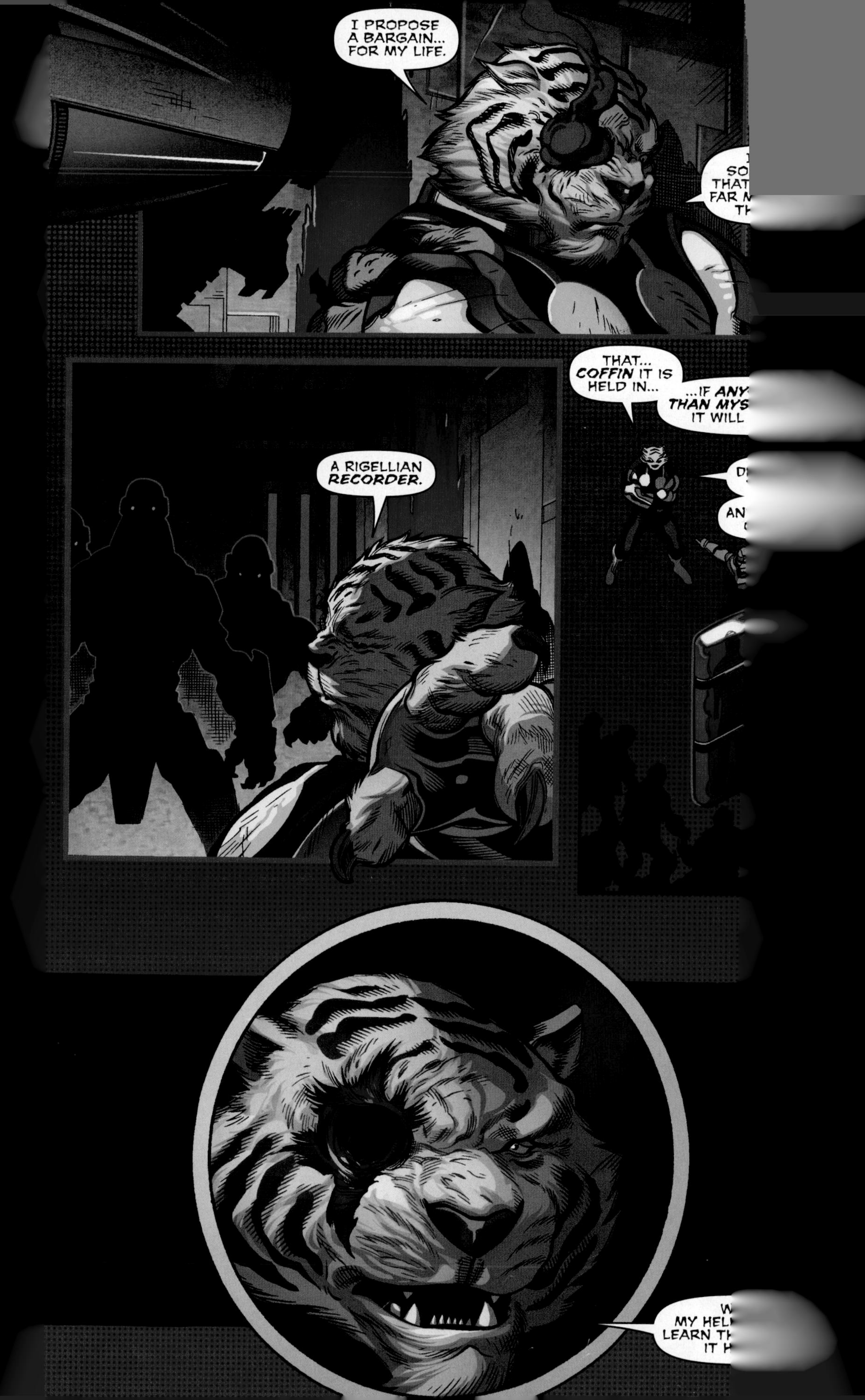
I PROPOSE A BARGAIN... FOR MY LIFE.
THAT... COFFIN IT IS HELD IN...
A RIGELLIAN RECORDER.

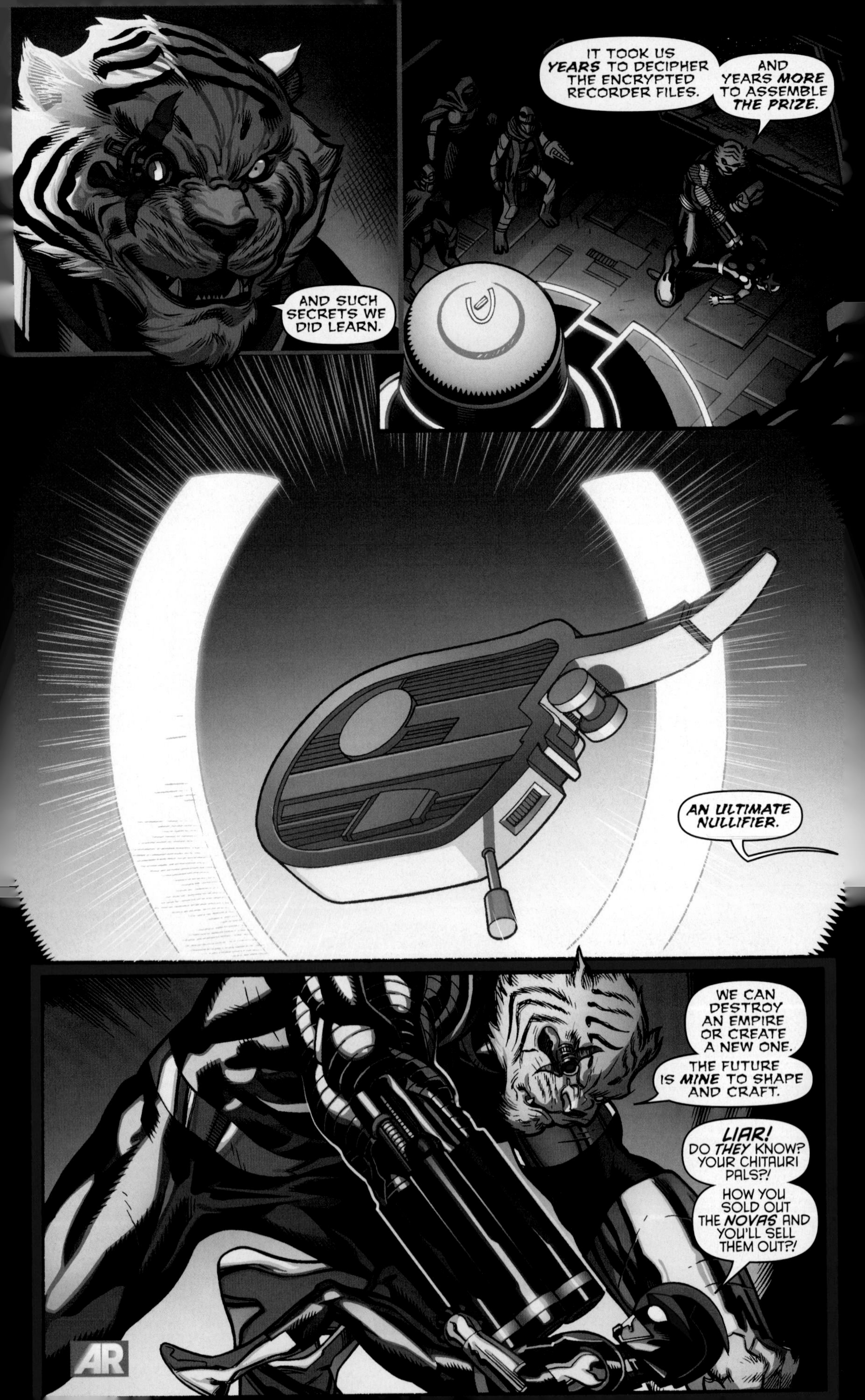
AND SUCH SECRETS WE DID LEARN.
IT TOOK US YEARS TO DECIPHER THE ENCRYPTED RECORDER FILES.
AND YEARS MORE TO ASSEMBLE THE PRIZE.
AN ULTIMATE NULLIFIER.
WE CAN DESTROY AN EMPIRE OR CREATE A NEW ONE.
THE FUTURE IS MINE TO SHAPE AND CRAFT.
LIAR! DO THEY KNOW? YOUR CHITAURI PALS?!
HOW YOU SOLD OUT THE NOVAS AND YOU'LL SELL THEM OUT?!
AR

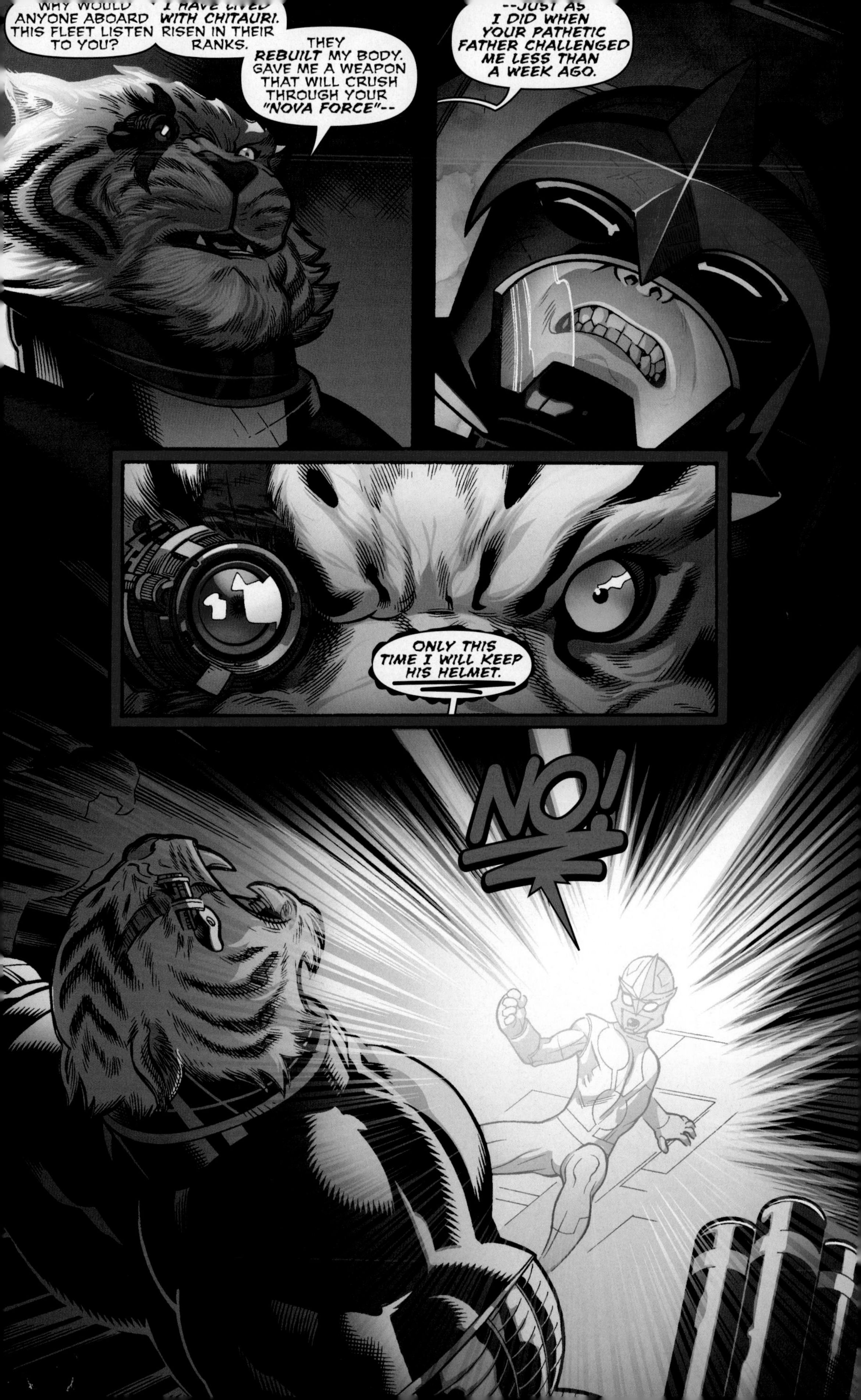
WHY WOULD ANYONE ABOARD THIS FLEET LISTEN TO YOU?
I HAVE LIVED WITH CHITAURI. RISEN IN THEIR RANKS.
THEY REBUILT MY BODY. GAVE ME A WEAPON THAT WILL CRUSH THROUGH YOUR "NOVA FORCE"--
--JUST AS I DID WHEN YOUR PATHETIC FATHER CHALLENGED ME LESS THAN A WEEK AGO.
ONLY THIS TIME I WILL KEEP HIS HELMET.
NO!

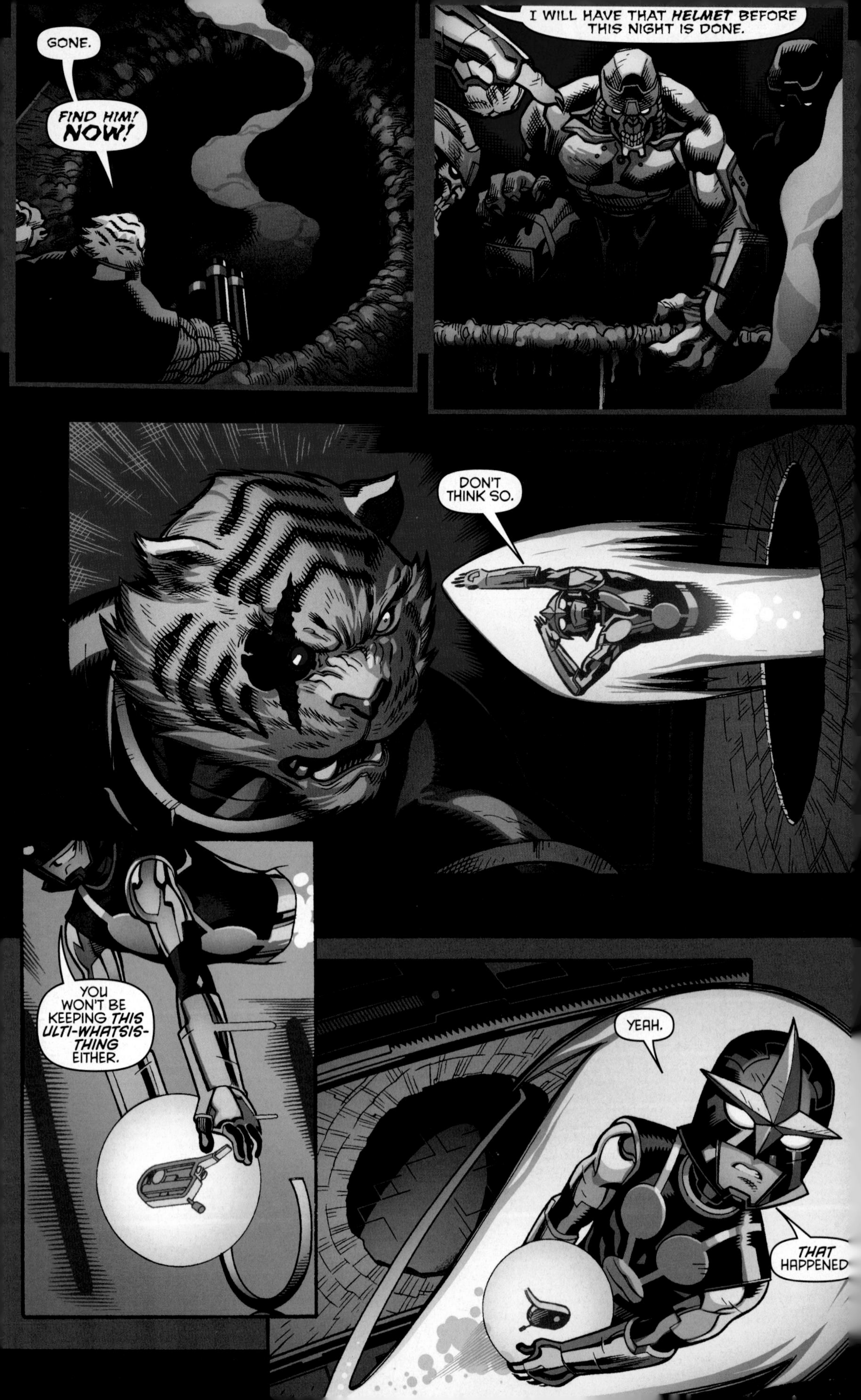
GONE.
FIND HIM! NOW!
I WILL HAVE THAT HELMET BEFORE THIS NIGHT IS DONE.
DON'T THINK SO.
YOU WON'T BE KEEPING THIS ULTI-WHATSIS-THING EITHER.
YEAH.
THAT HAPPENED

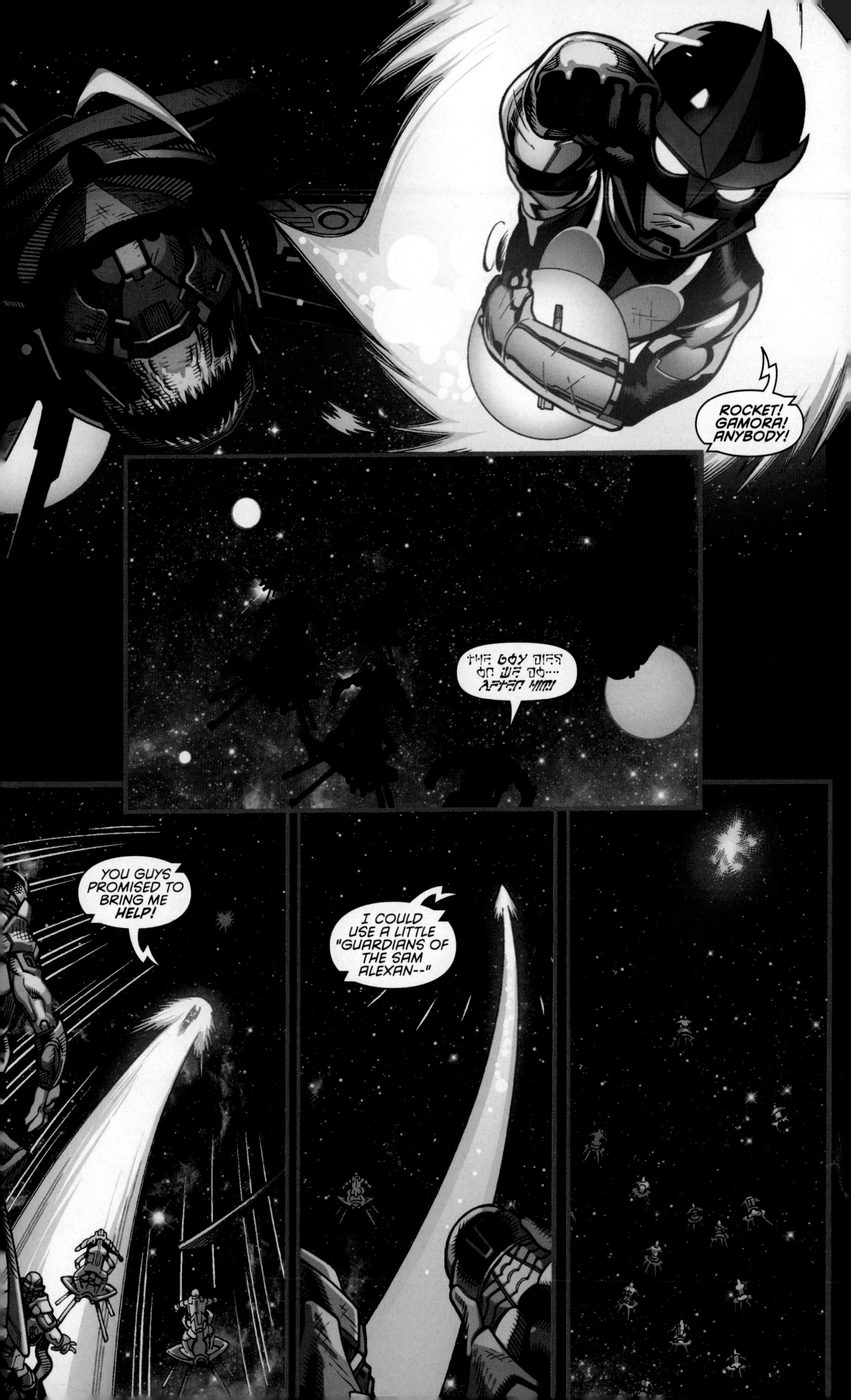
ROCKET! GAMORA! ANYBODY!
THE BOY DIES OR WE DO.... AFTER HIM!
YOU GUYS PROMISED TO BRING ME HELP!
I COULD USE A LITTLE "GUARDIANS OF THE SAM ALEXAN--"

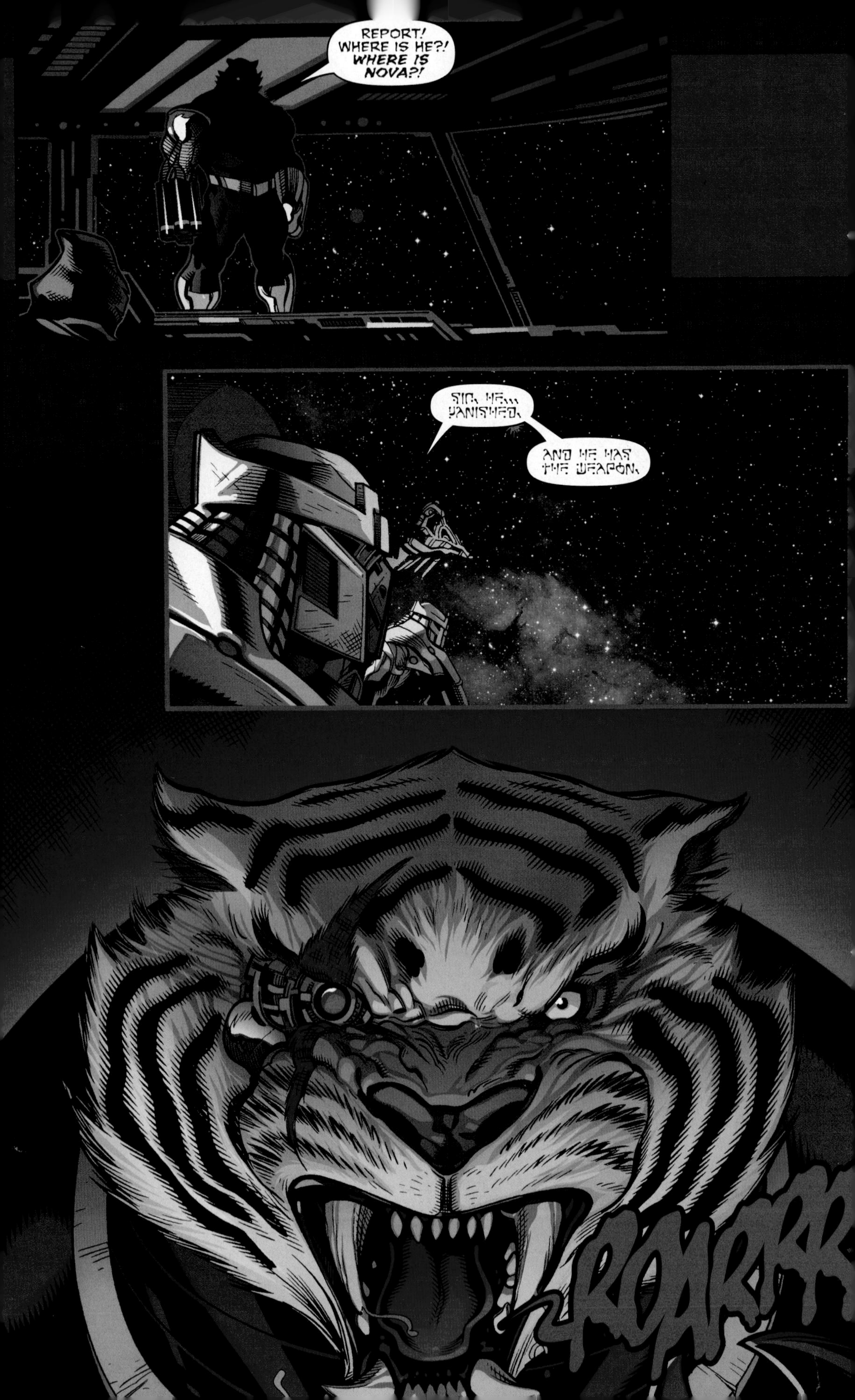
REPORT! WHERE IS HE?! WHERE IS NOVA?!
SIR, HE... VANISHED.
AND HE HAS THE WEAPON.
ROARRR

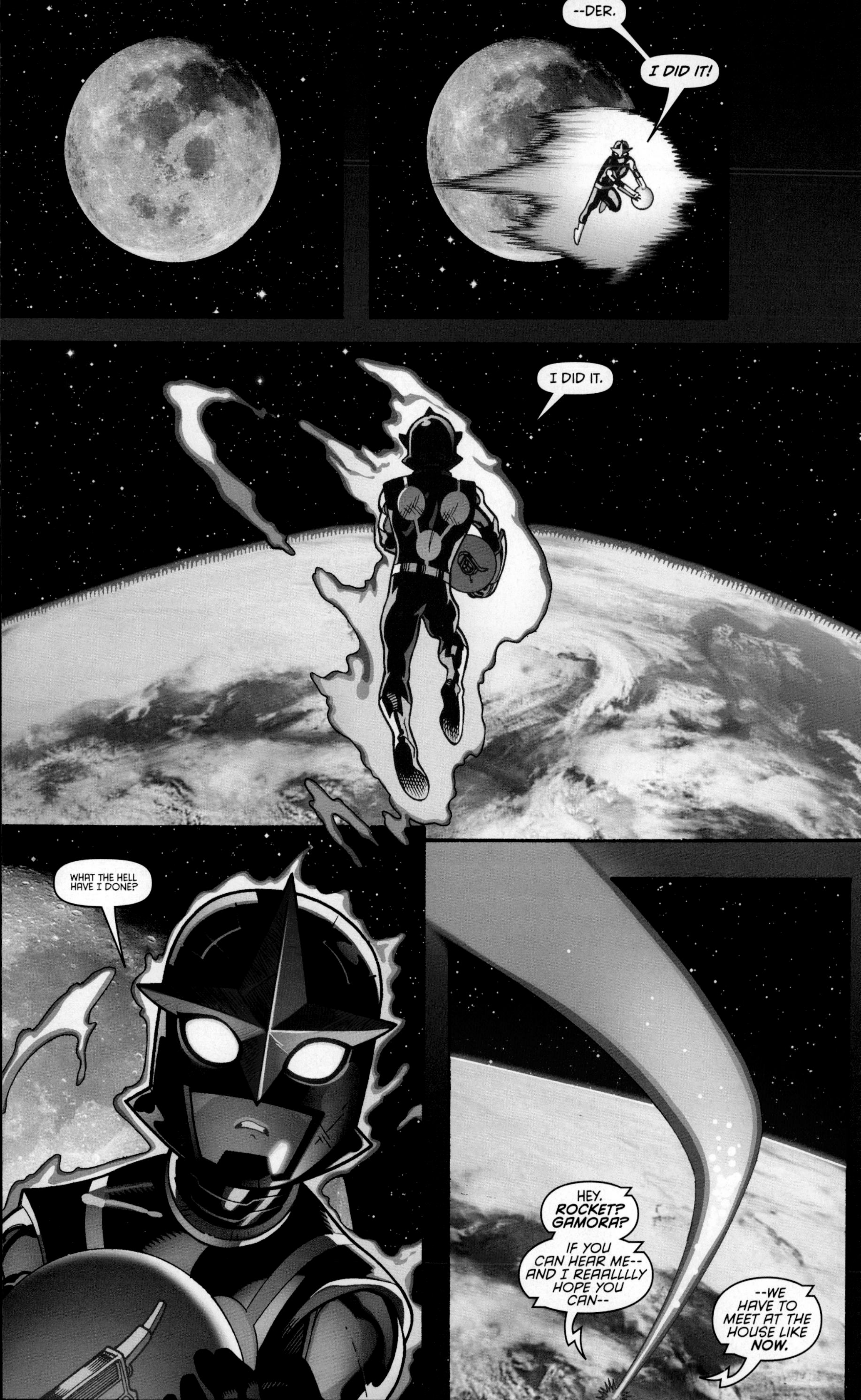
--DER.
I DID IT!
I DID IT.
WHAT THE HELL HAVE I DONE?
HEY. ROCKET? GAMORA?
IF YOU CAN HEAR ME-- AND I REAALLLLY HOPE YOU CAN--
--WE HAVE TO MEET AT THE HOUSE LIKE NOW.

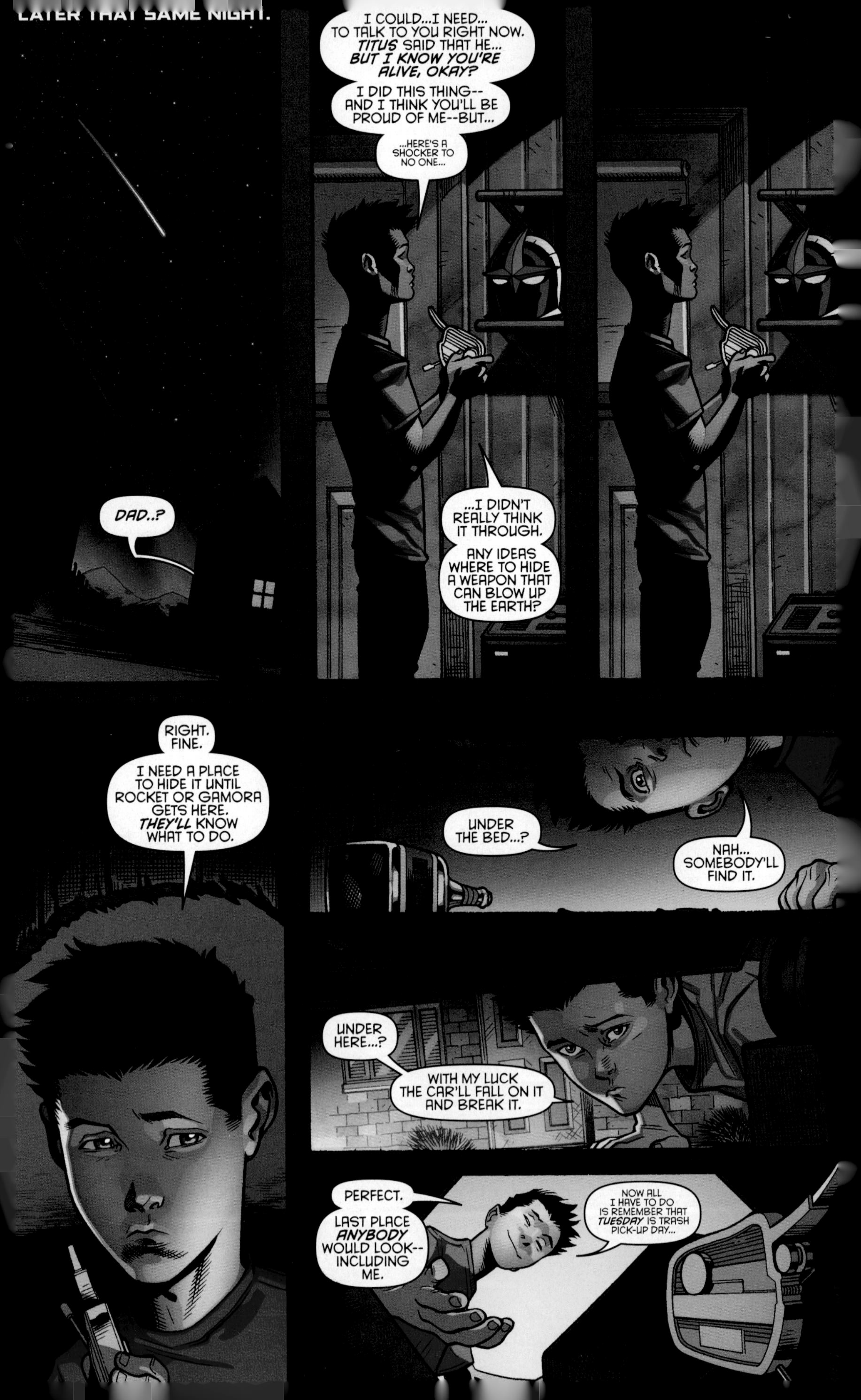
LATER THAT SAME NIGHT.
DAD..?
I COULD...I NEED... TO TALK TO YOU RIGHT NOW. TITUS SAID THAT HE... BUT I KNOW YOU'RE ALIVE, OKAY?
I DID THIS THING-- AND I THINK YOU'LL BE PROUD OF ME--BUT...
...HERE'S A SHOCKER TO NO ONE...
...I DIDN'T REALLY THINK IT THROUGH.
ANY IDEAS WHERE TO HIDE A WEAPON THAT CAN BLOW UP THE EARTH?
RIGHT. FINE.
I NEED A PLACE TO HIDE IT UNTIL ROCKET OR GAMORA GETS HERE. THEY'LL KNOW WHAT TO DO.
UNDER THE BED...?
NAH... SOMEBODY'LL FIND IT.
UNDER HERE...?
WITH MY LUCK THE CAR'LL FALL ON IT AND BREAK IT.
PERFECT.
LAST PLACE ANYBODY WOULD LOOK-- INCLUDING ME.
NOW ALL I HAVE TO DO IS REMEMBER THAT TUESDAY IS TRASH PICK-UP DAY...

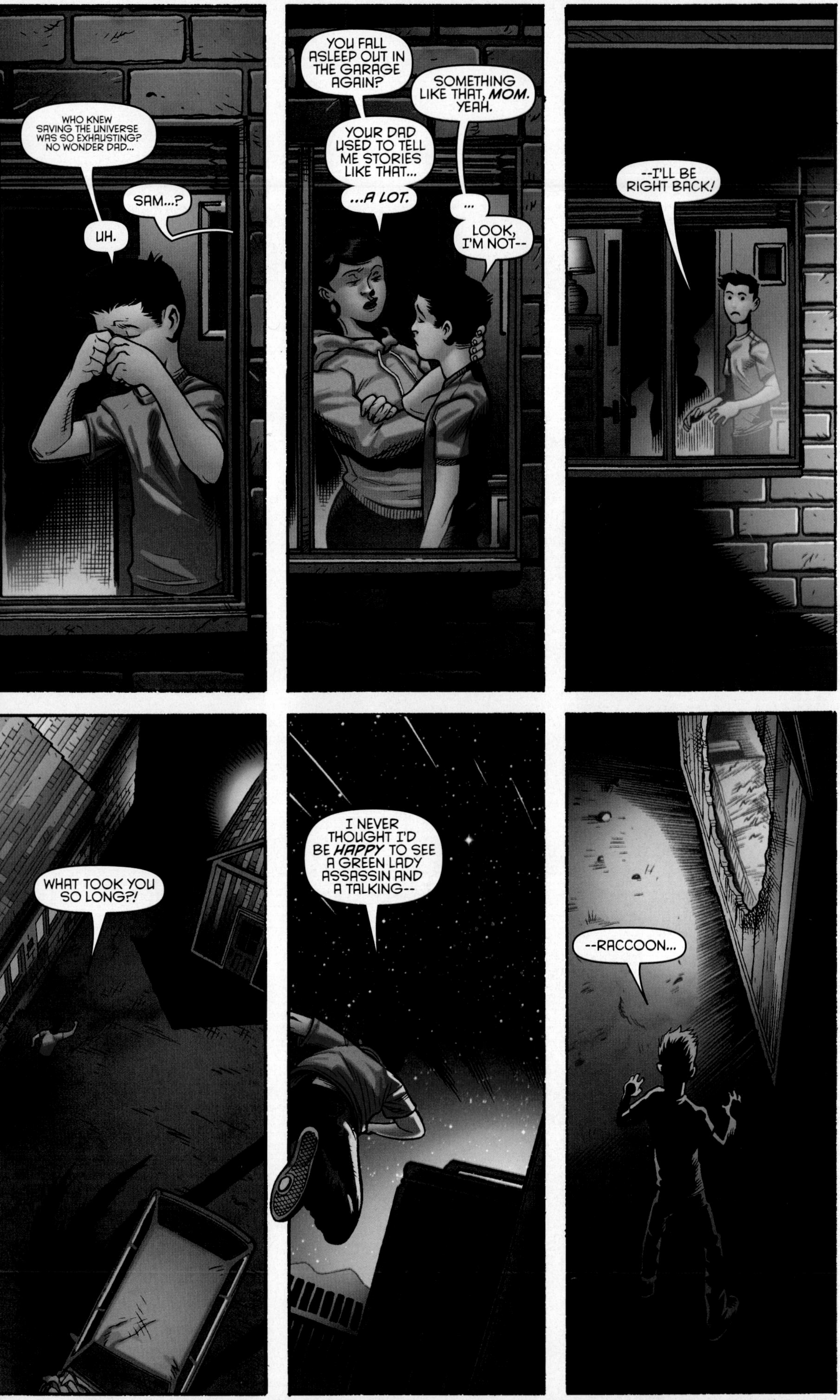
WHO KNEW SAVING THE UNIVERSE WAS SO EXHAUSTING? NO WONDER DAD...
SAM...?
UH.
YOU FALL ASLEEP OUT IN THE GARAGE AGAIN?
SOMETHING LIKE THAT, *MOM*. YEAH.
YOUR DAD USED TO TELL ME STORIES LIKE THAT...
...A LOT.
...
LOOK, I'M NOT--
--I'LL BE RIGHT BACK!
WHAT TOOK YOU SO LONG?!
I NEVER THOUGHT I'D BE *HAPPY* TO SEE A GREEN LADY ASSASSIN AND A TALKING--
--RACCOON...

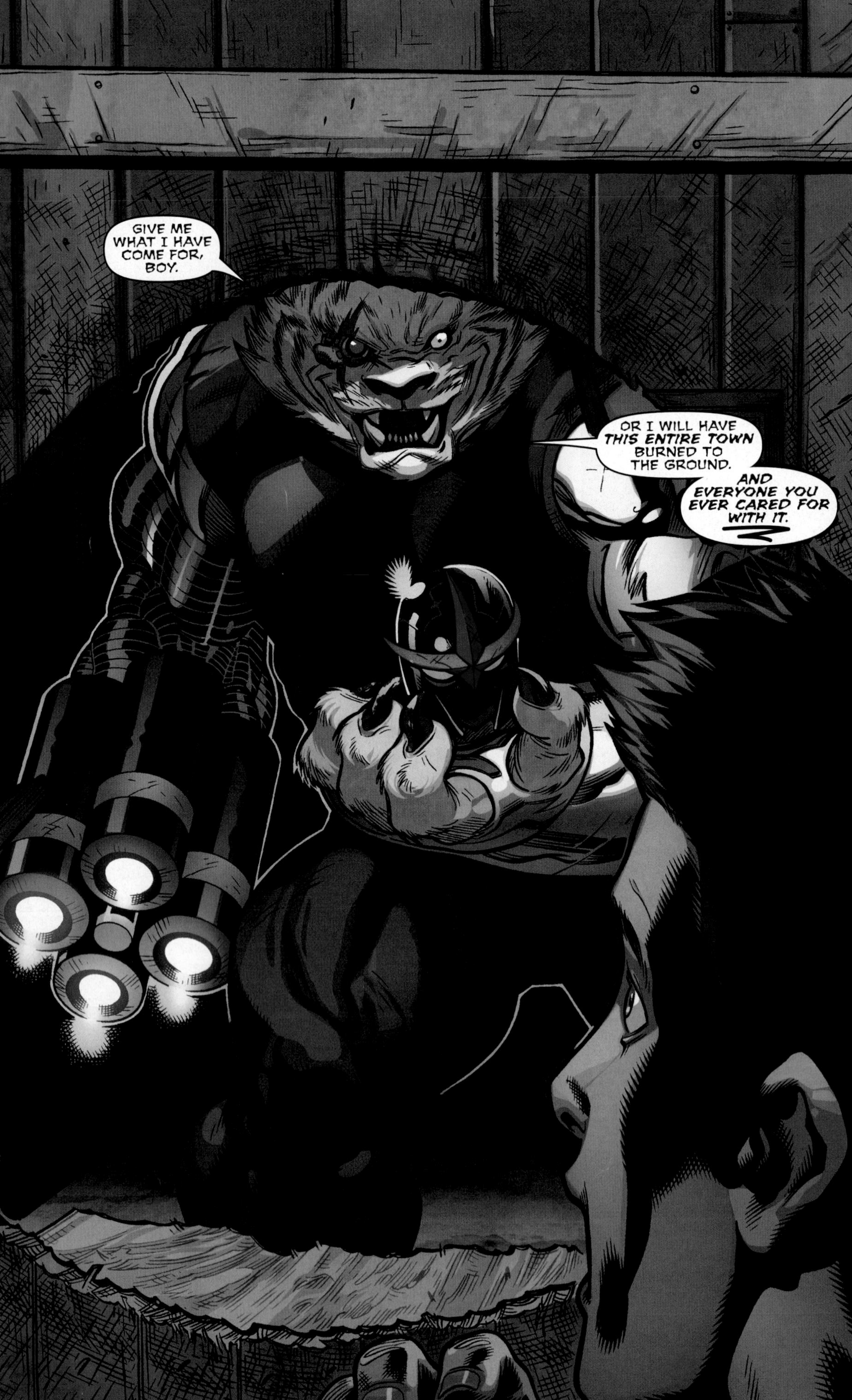
GIVE ME WHAT I HAVE COME FOR, BOY.
OR I WILL HAVE THIS ENTIRE TOWN BURNED TO THE GROUND.
AND EVERYONE YOU EVER CARED FOR WITH IT.

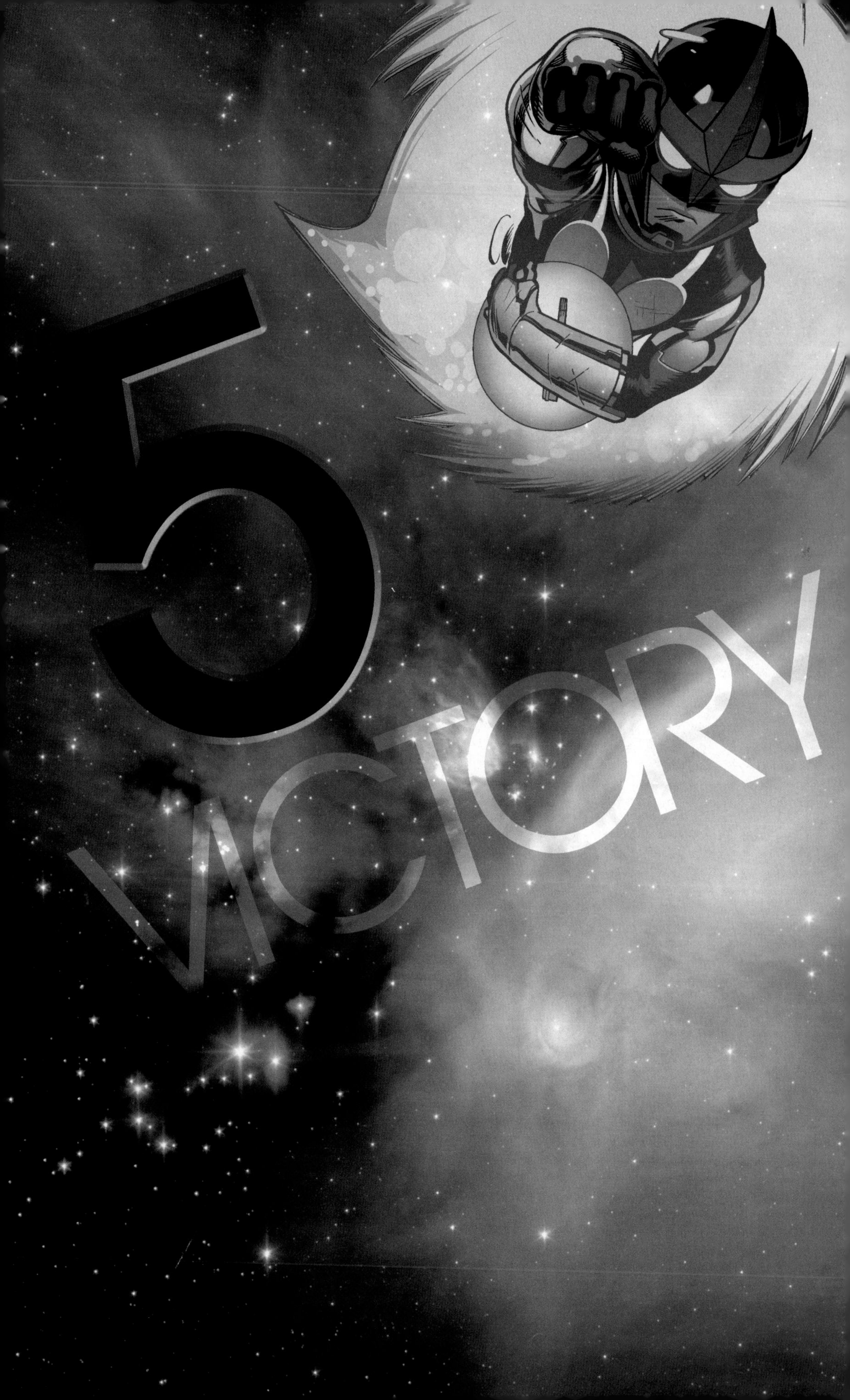
5
VICTORY

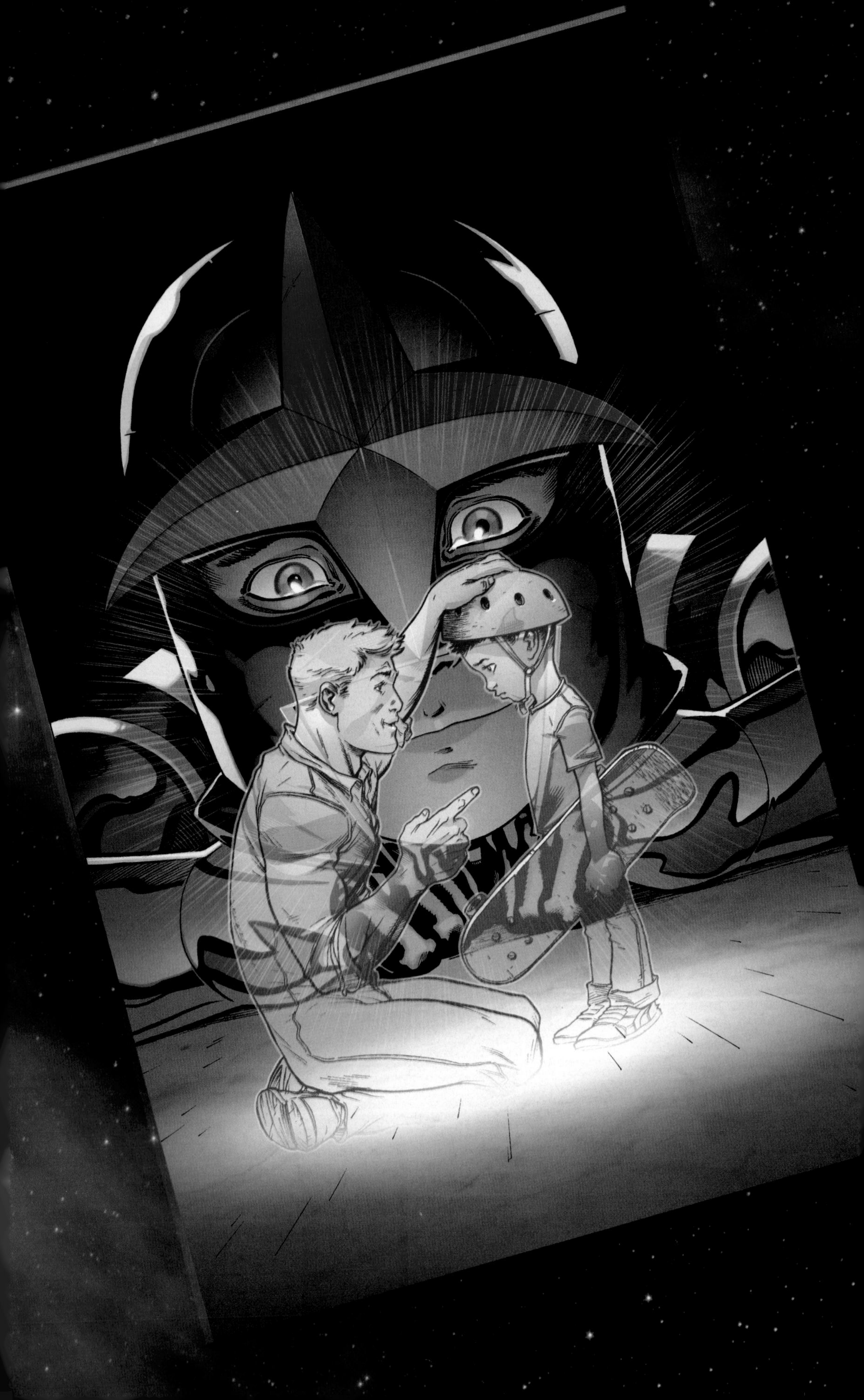

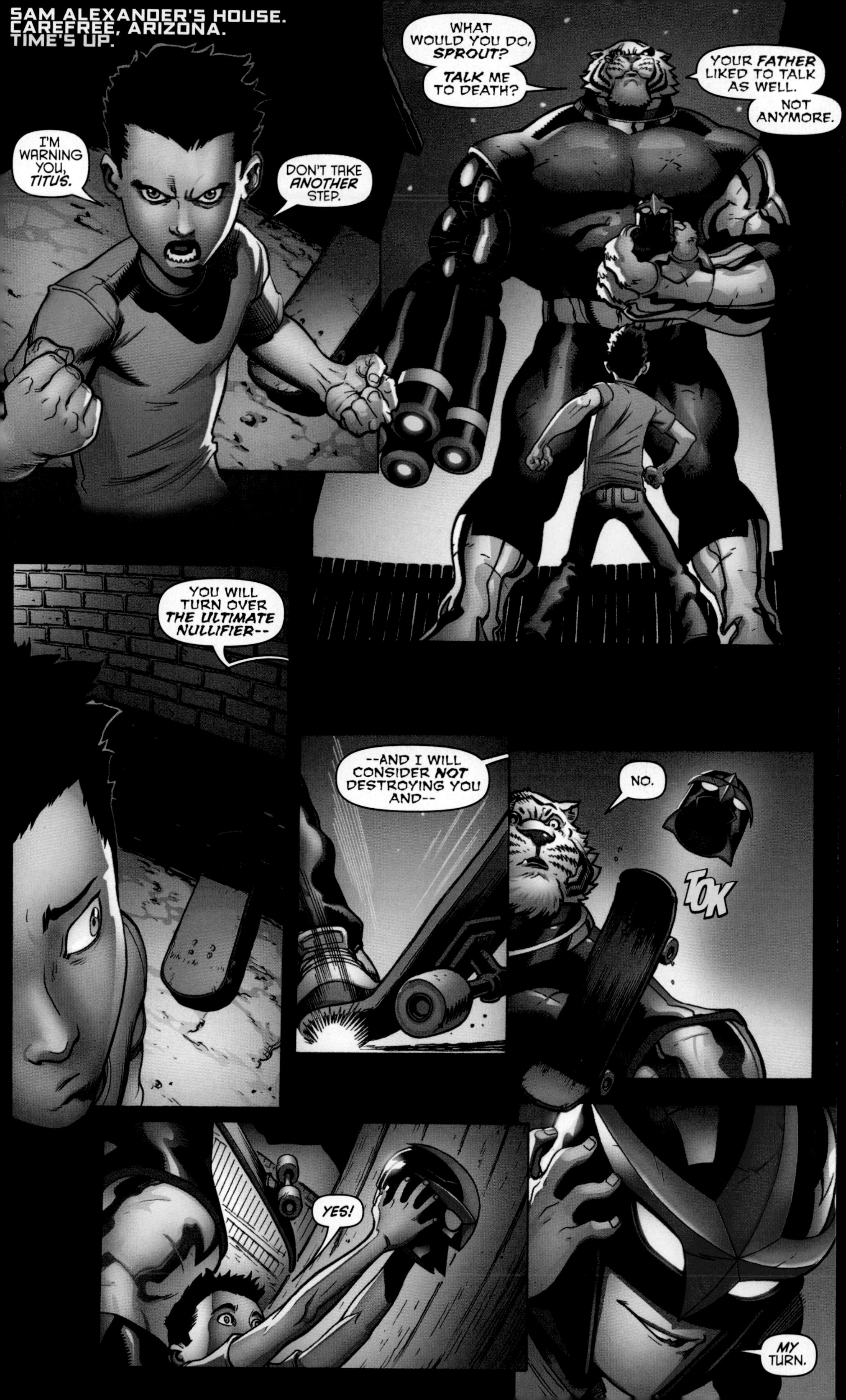
SAM ALEXANDER'S HOUSE.
CAREFREE, ARIZONA.
TIME'S UP.
I'M WARNING YOU, TITUS.
DON'T TAKE ANOTHER STEP.
WHAT WOULD YOU DO, SPROUT?
TALK ME TO DEATH?
YOUR FATHER LIKED TO TALK AS WELL.
NOT ANYMORE.
YOU WILL TURN OVER THE ULTIMATE NULLIFIER--
--AND I WILL CONSIDER NOT DESTROYING YOU AND--
NO.
TOK
YES!
MY TURN.

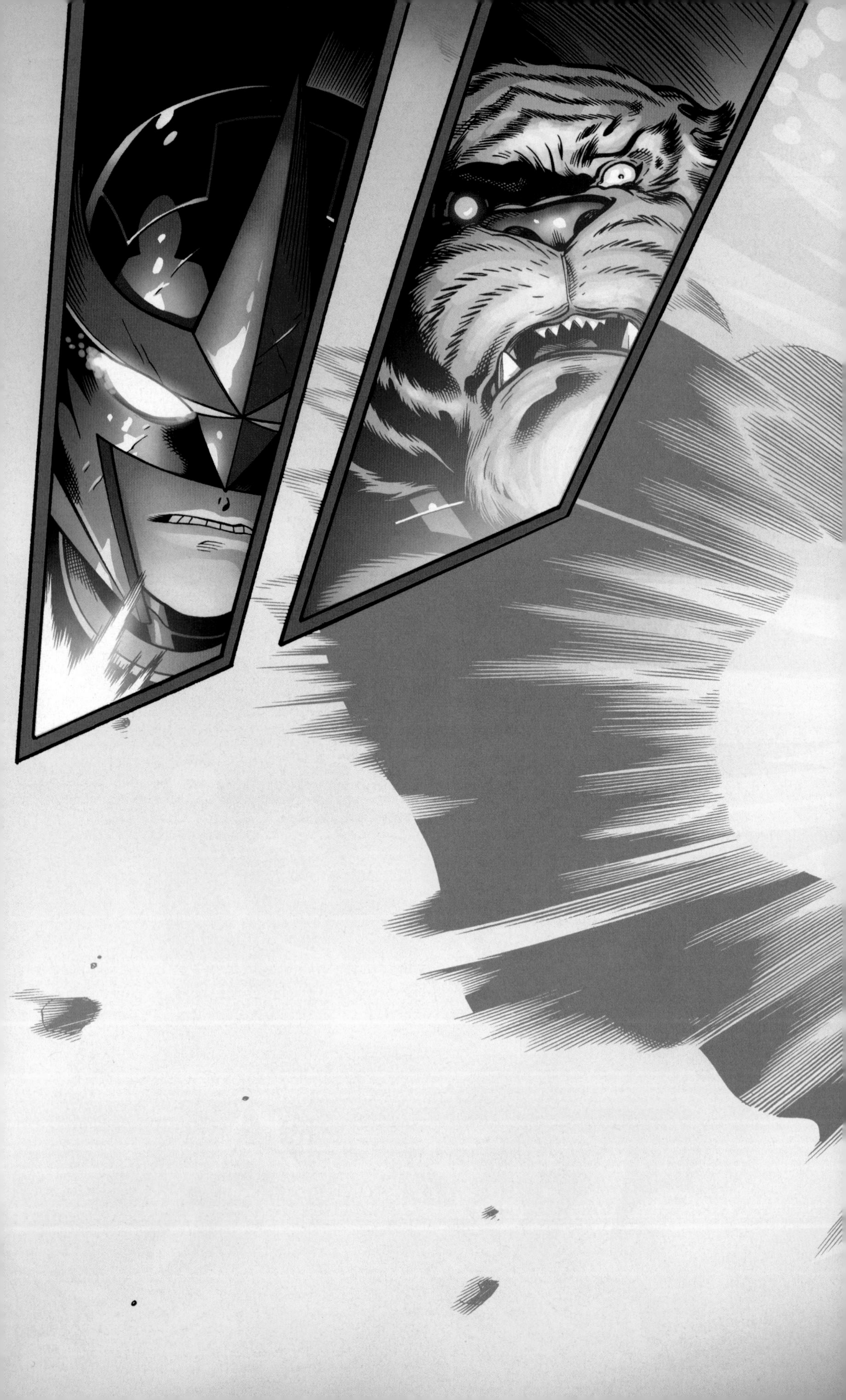

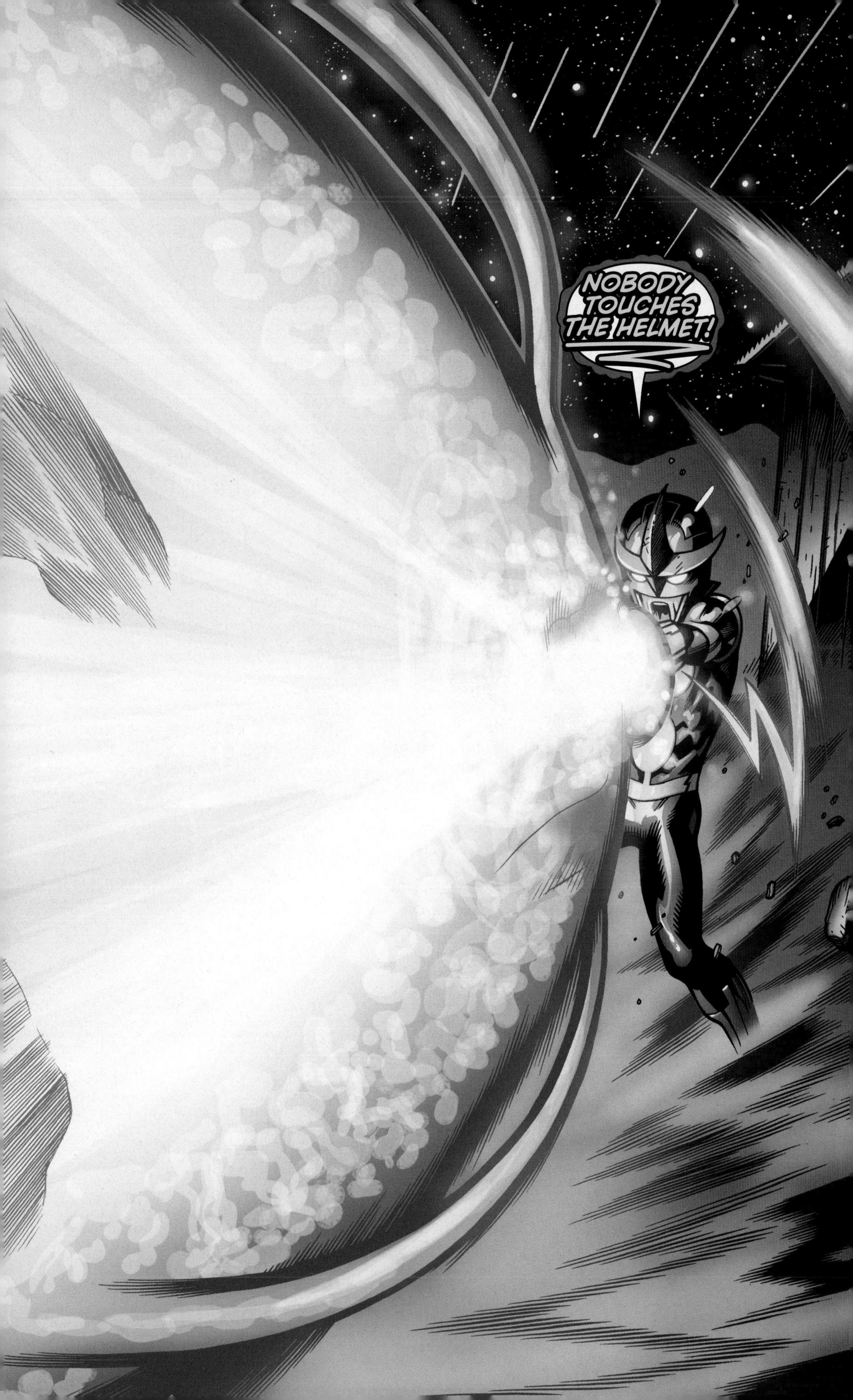
NOBODY TOUCHES THE HELMET!

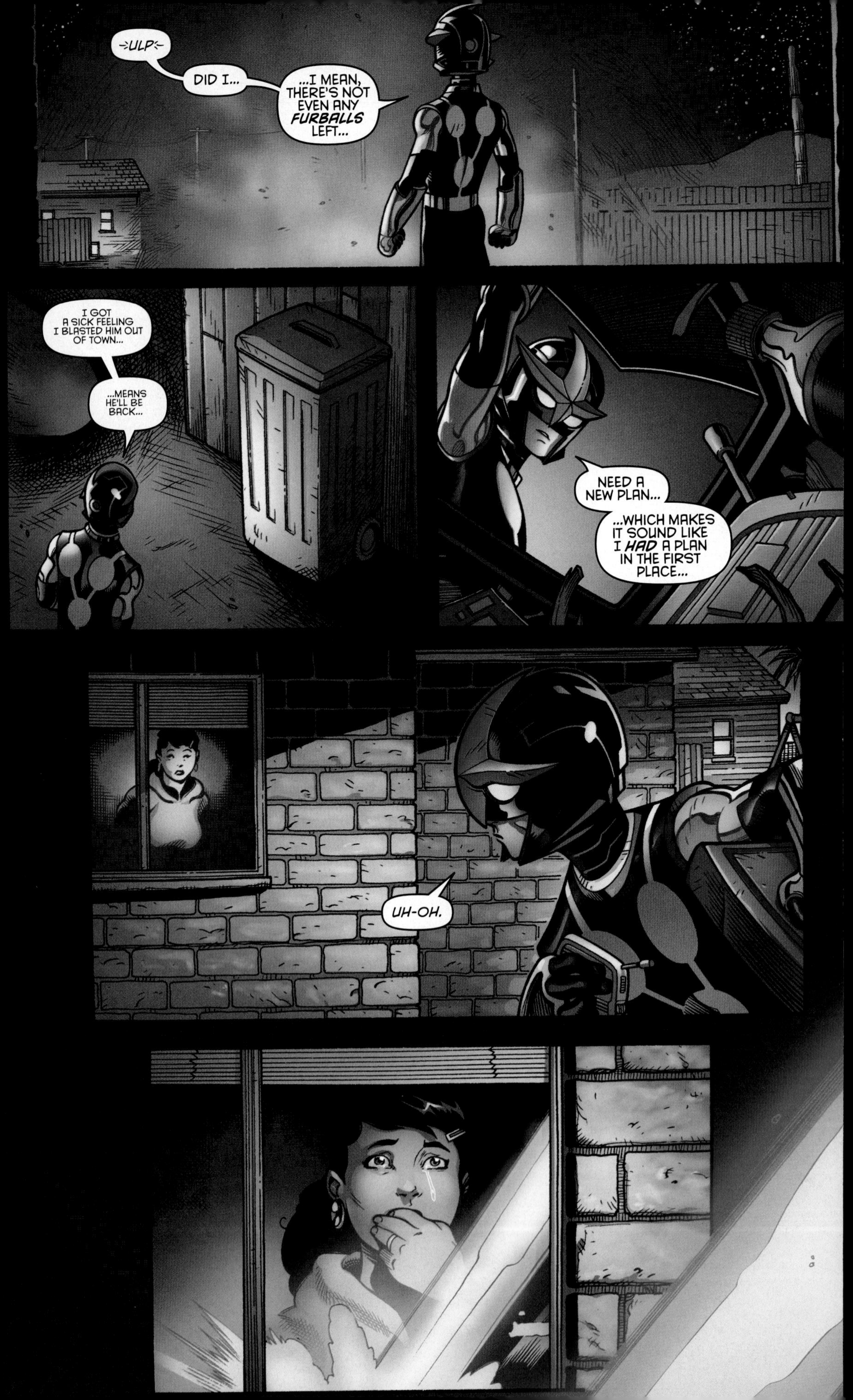
-ULP-
DID I...
...I MEAN, THERE'S NOT EVEN ANY FURBALLS LEFT...
I GOT A SICK FEELING I BLASTED HIM OUT OF TOWN...
...MEANS HE'LL BE BACK...
NEED A NEW PLAN...
...WHICH MAKES IT SOUND LIKE I HAD A PLAN IN THE FIRST PLACE...
UH-OH.

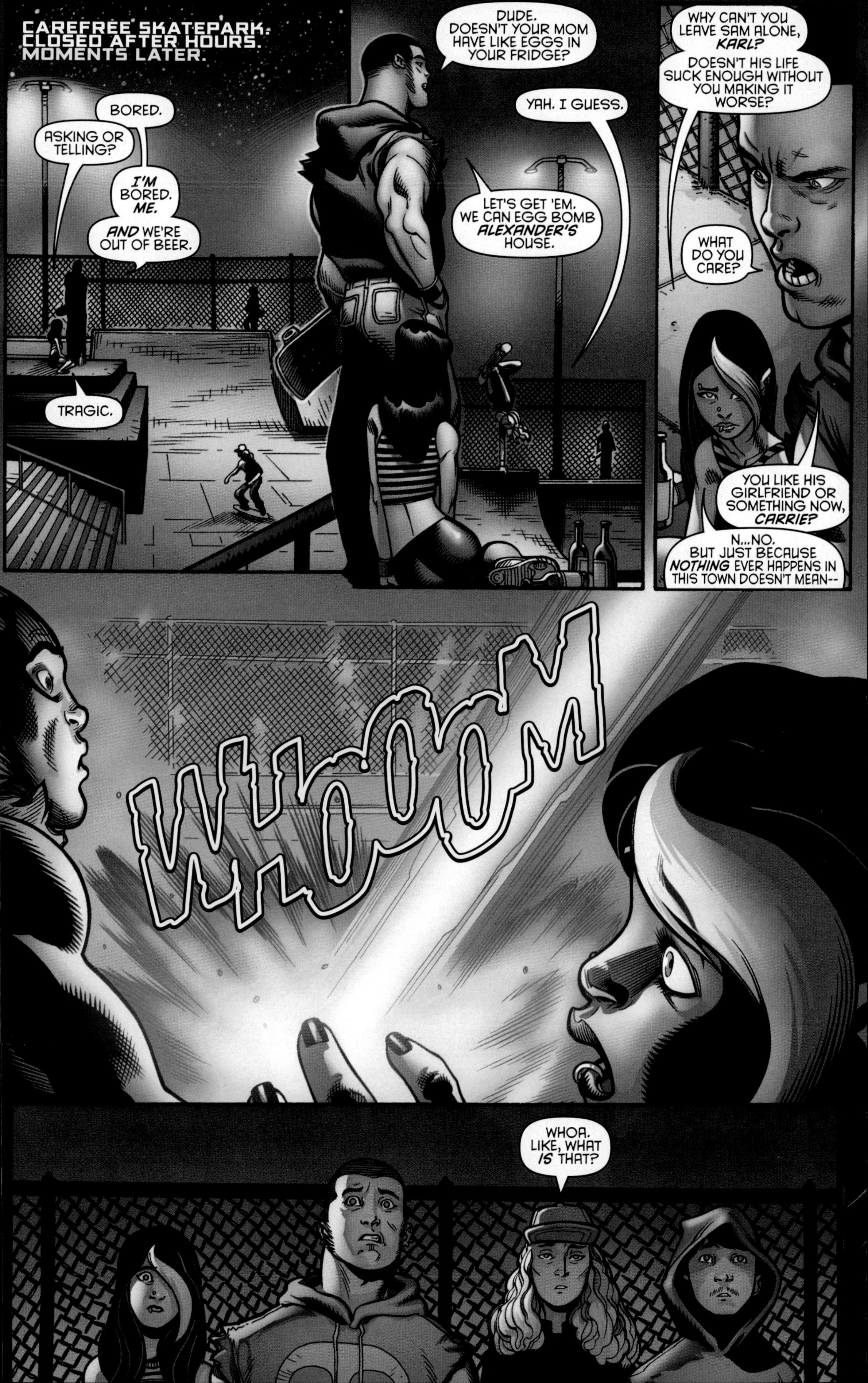
CAREFREE SKATEPARK. CLOSED AFTER HOURS. MOMENTS LATER.
BORED.
ASKING OR TELLING?
I'M BORED. ME.
AND WE'RE OUT OF BEER.
TRAGIC.
DUDE. DOESN'T YOUR MOM HAVE LIKE EGGS IN YOUR FRIDGE?
YAH. I GUESS.
LET'S GET 'EM. WE CAN EGG BOMB ALEXANDER'S HOUSE.
WHY CAN'T YOU LEAVE SAM ALONE, KARL?
DOESN'T HIS LIFE SUCK ENOUGH WITHOUT YOU MAKING IT WORSE?
WHAT DO YOU CARE?
YOU LIKE HIS GIRLFRIEND OR SOMETHING NOW, CARRIE?
N...NO. BUT JUST BECAUSE NOTHING EVER HAPPENS IN THIS TOWN DOESN'T MEAN--
WHOOOOM
WHOA. LIKE, WHAT IS THAT?

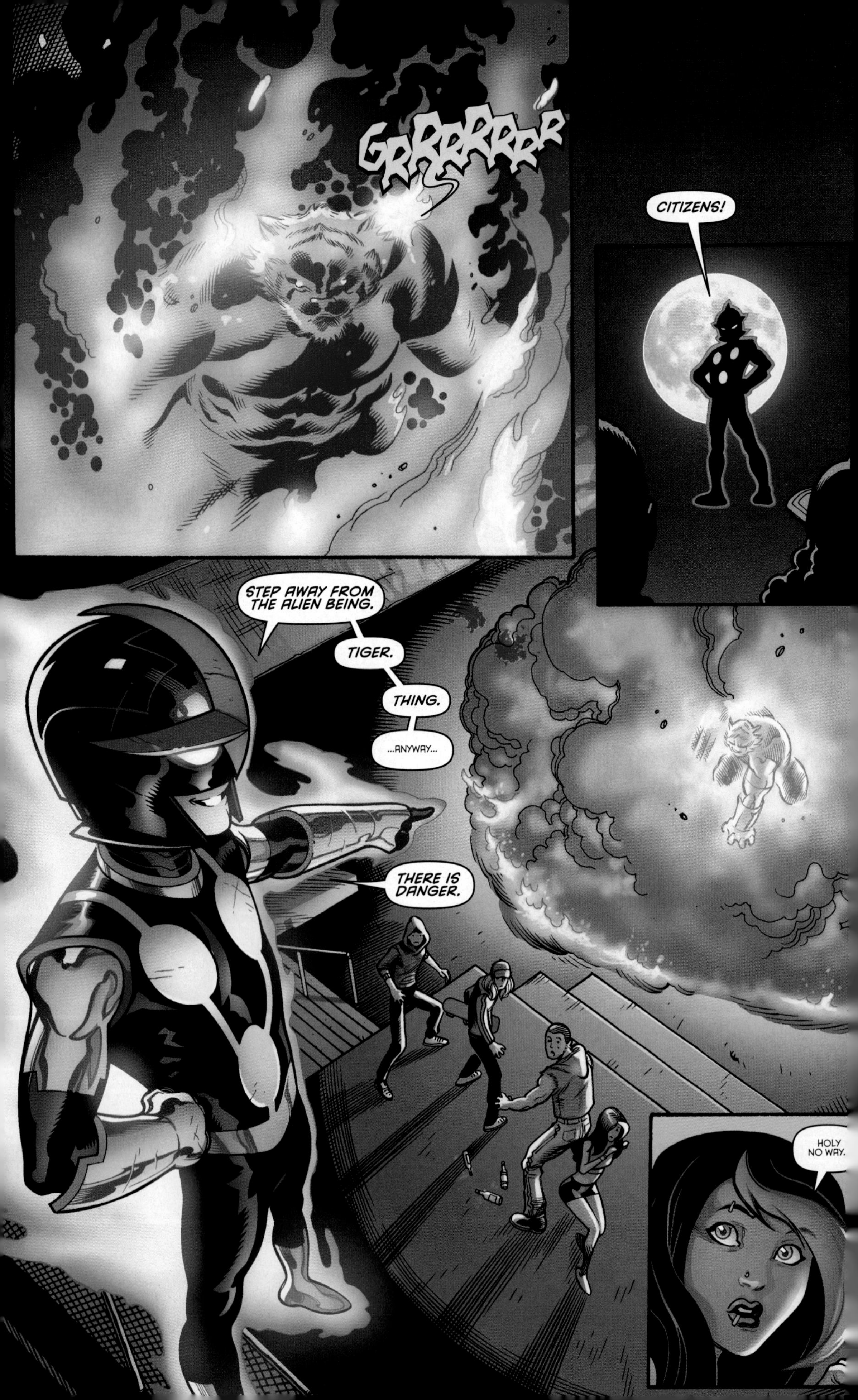
GRRRRRRR
CITIZENS!
STEP AWAY FROM THE ALIEN BEING.
TIGER.
THING.
...ANYWAY...
THERE IS DANGER.
HOLY NO WAY.

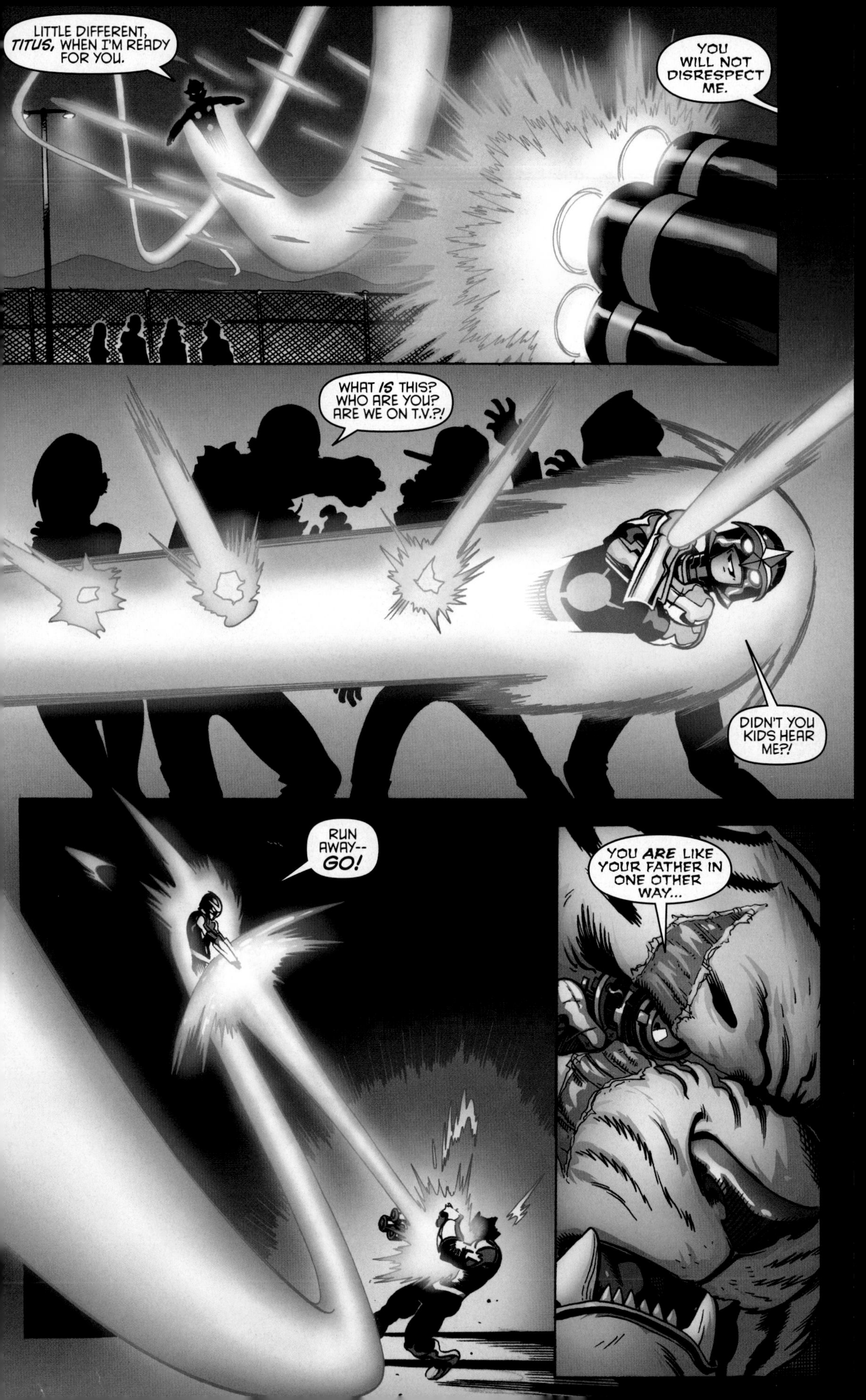
LITTLE DIFFERENT, *TITUS,* WHEN I'M READY FOR YOU.
YOU WILL NOT DISRESPECT ME.
WHAT *IS* THIS? WHO ARE YOU? ARE WE ON T.V.?!
DIDN'T YOU KIDS HEAR ME?!
RUN AWAY-- **GO!**
YOU **ARE** LIKE YOUR FATHER IN ONE OTHER WAY...

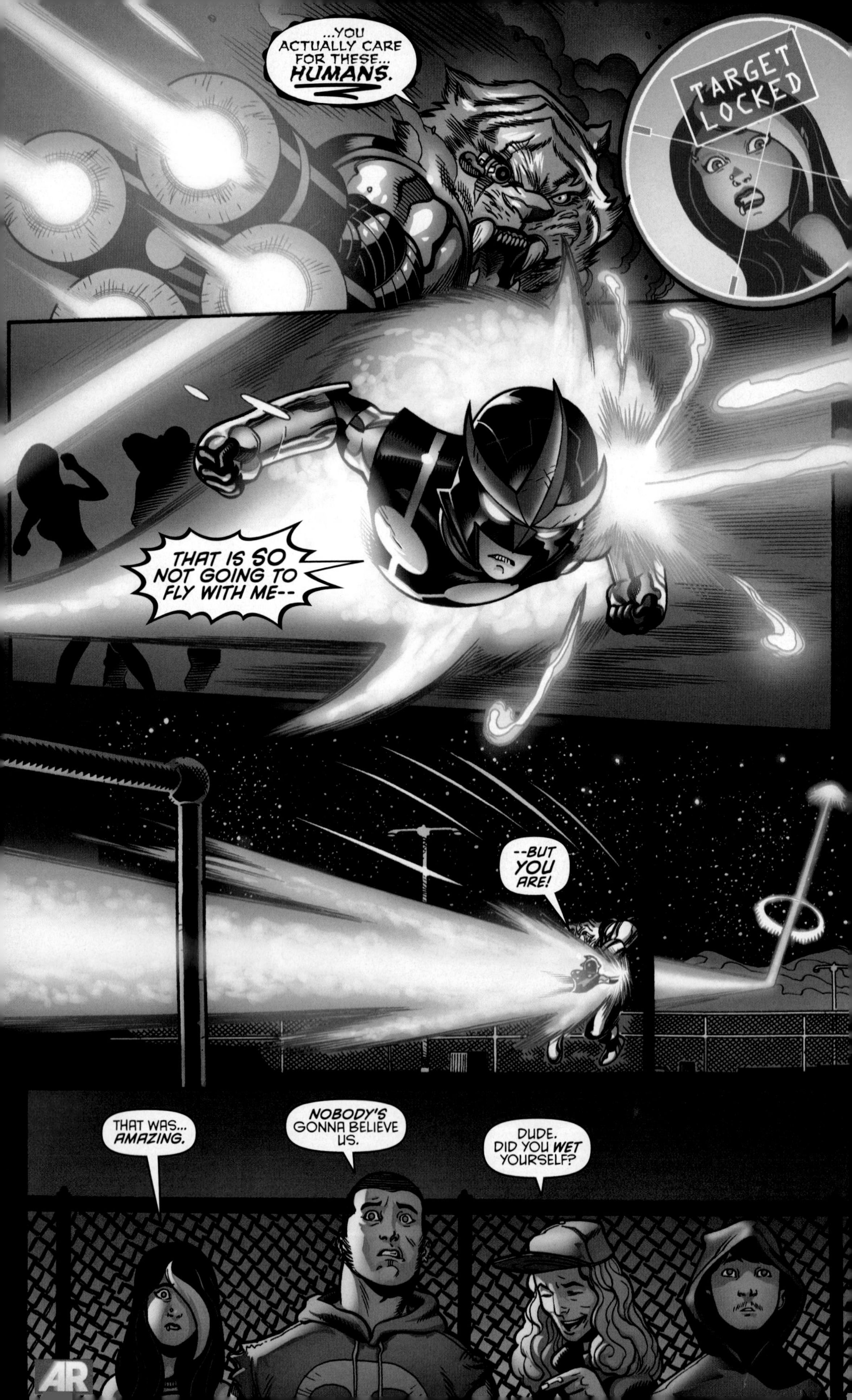
...YOU ACTUALLY CARE FOR THESE... HUMANS.
TARGET LOCKED
THAT IS SO NOT GOING TO FLY WITH ME--
--BUT YOU ARE!
THAT WAS... AMAZING.
NOBODY'S GONNA BELIEVE US.
DUDE. DID YOU WET YOURSELF?
AR

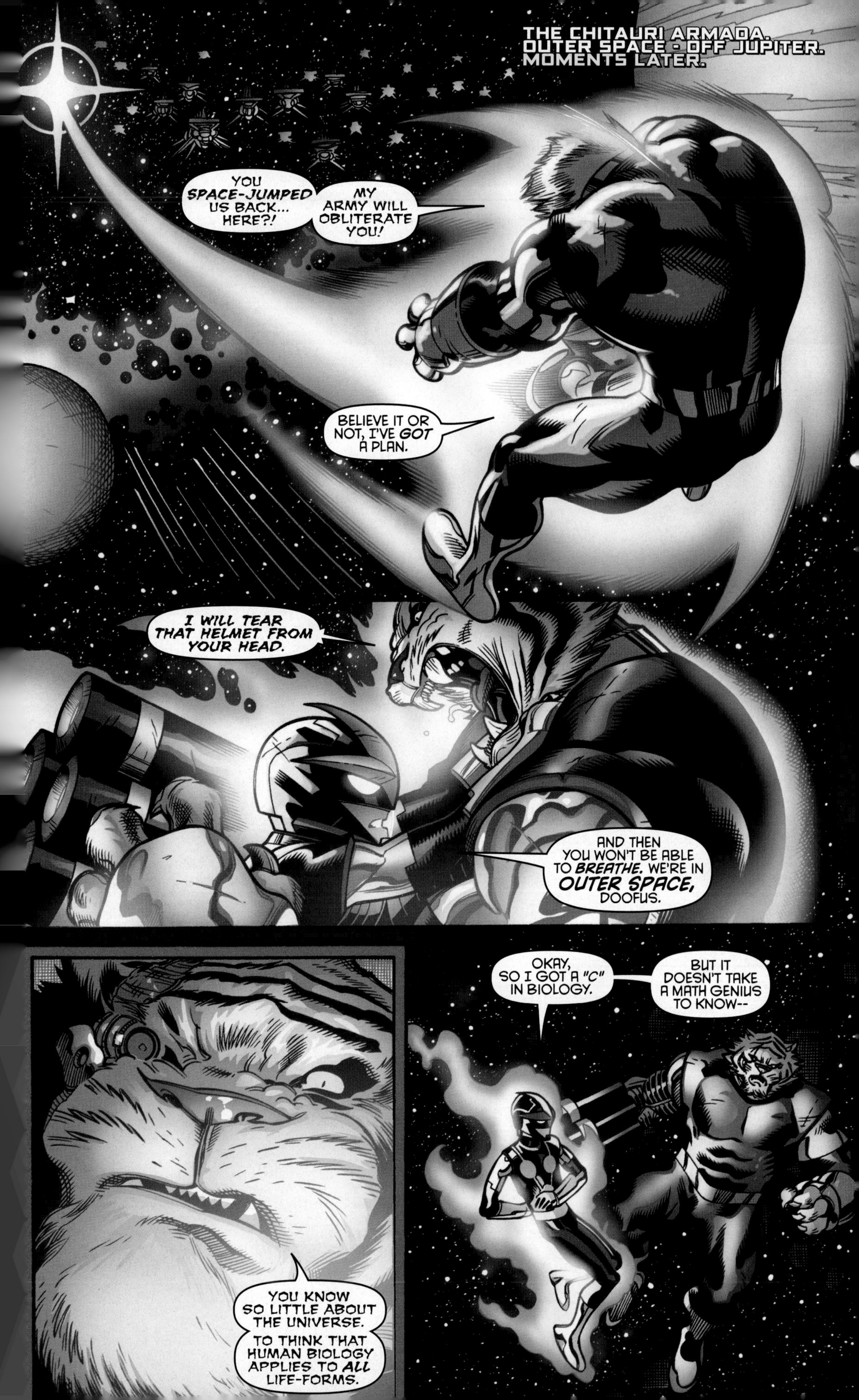
THE CHITAURI ARMADA. OUTER SPACE - OFF JUPITER. MOMENTS LATER.
YOU SPACE-JUMPED US BACK... HERE?!
MY ARMY WILL OBLITERATE YOU!
BELIEVE IT OR NOT, I'VE GOT A PLAN.
I WILL TEAR THAT HELMET FROM YOUR HEAD.
AND THEN YOU WON'T BE ABLE TO BREATHE. WE'RE IN OUTER SPACE, DOOFUS.
YOU KNOW SO LITTLE ABOUT THE UNIVERSE.
TO THINK THAT HUMAN BIOLOGY APPLIES TO ALL LIFE-FORMS.
OKAY, SO I GOT A "C" IN BIOLOGY.
BUT IT DOESN'T TAKE A MATH GENIUS TO KNOW--

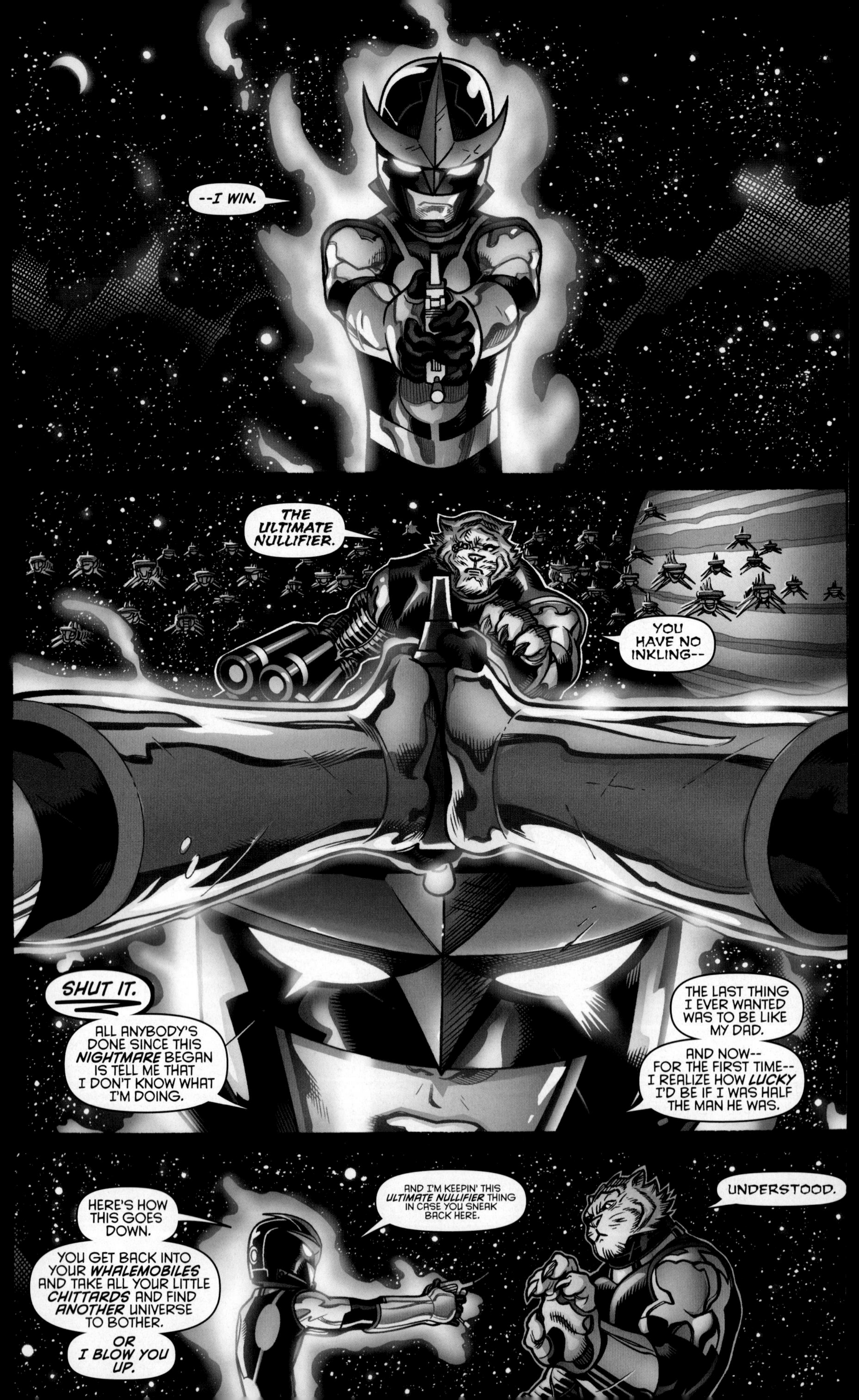
--I WIN.
THE ULTIMATE NULLIFIER.
YOU HAVE NO INKLING--
SHUT IT.
ALL ANYBODY'S DONE SINCE THIS NIGHTMARE BEGAN IS TELL ME THAT I DON'T KNOW WHAT I'M DOING.
THE LAST THING I EVER WANTED WAS TO BE LIKE MY DAD.
AND NOW-- FOR THE FIRST TIME-- I REALIZE HOW LUCKY I'D BE IF I WAS HALF THE MAN HE WAS.
HERE'S HOW THIS GOES DOWN.
YOU GET BACK INTO YOUR WHALEMOBILES AND TAKE ALL YOUR LITTLE CHITTARDS AND FIND ANOTHER UNIVERSE TO BOTHER.
OR I BLOW YOU UP.
AND I'M KEEPIN' THIS ULTIMATE NULLIFIER THING IN CASE YOU SNEAK BACK HERE.
UNDERSTOOD.

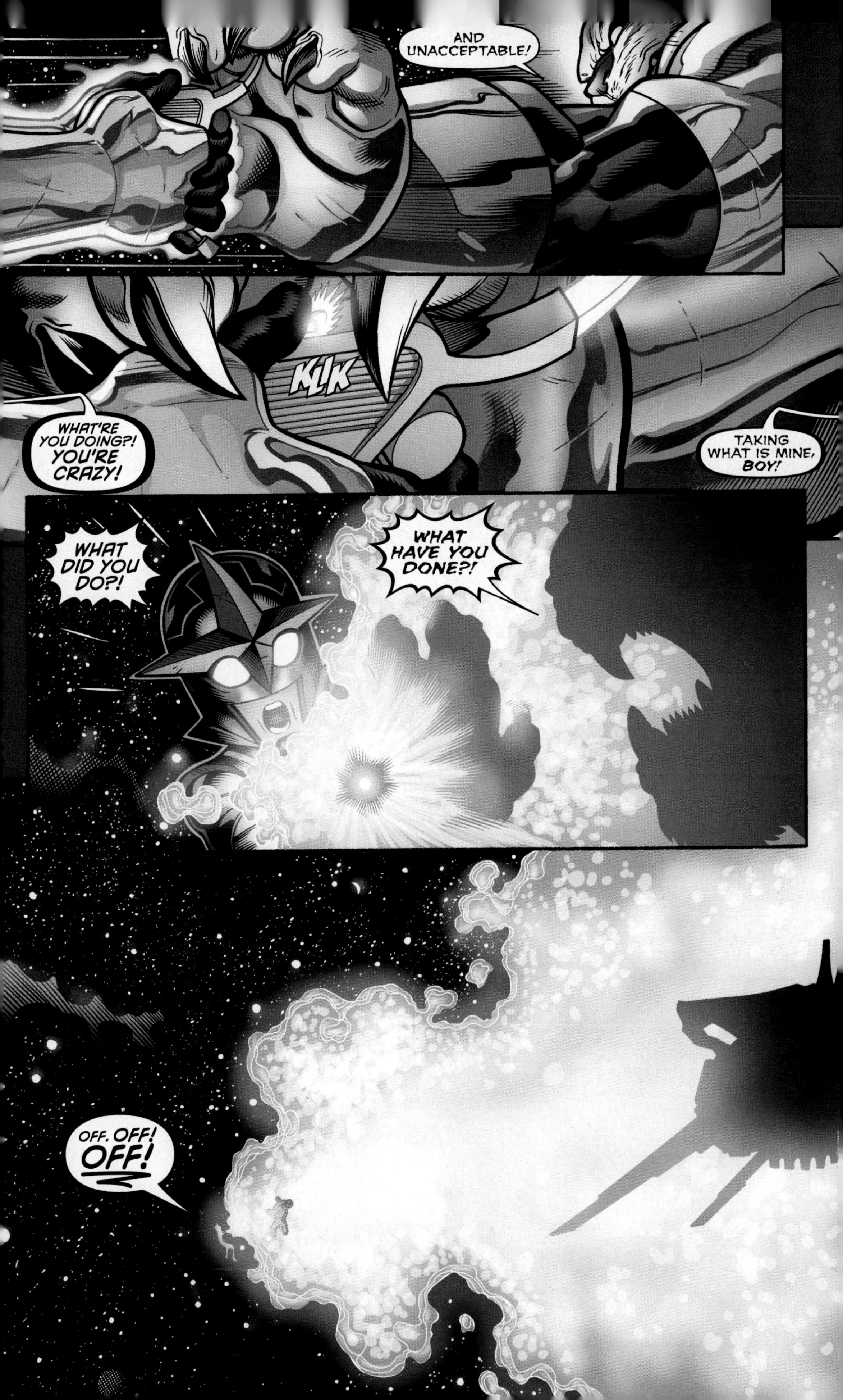
AND UNACCEPTABLE!
KLIK
WHAT'RE YOU DOING?! YOU'RE CRAZY!
TAKING WHAT IS MINE, BOY!
WHAT DID YOU DO?!
WHAT HAVE YOU DONE?!
OFF. OFF! OFF!

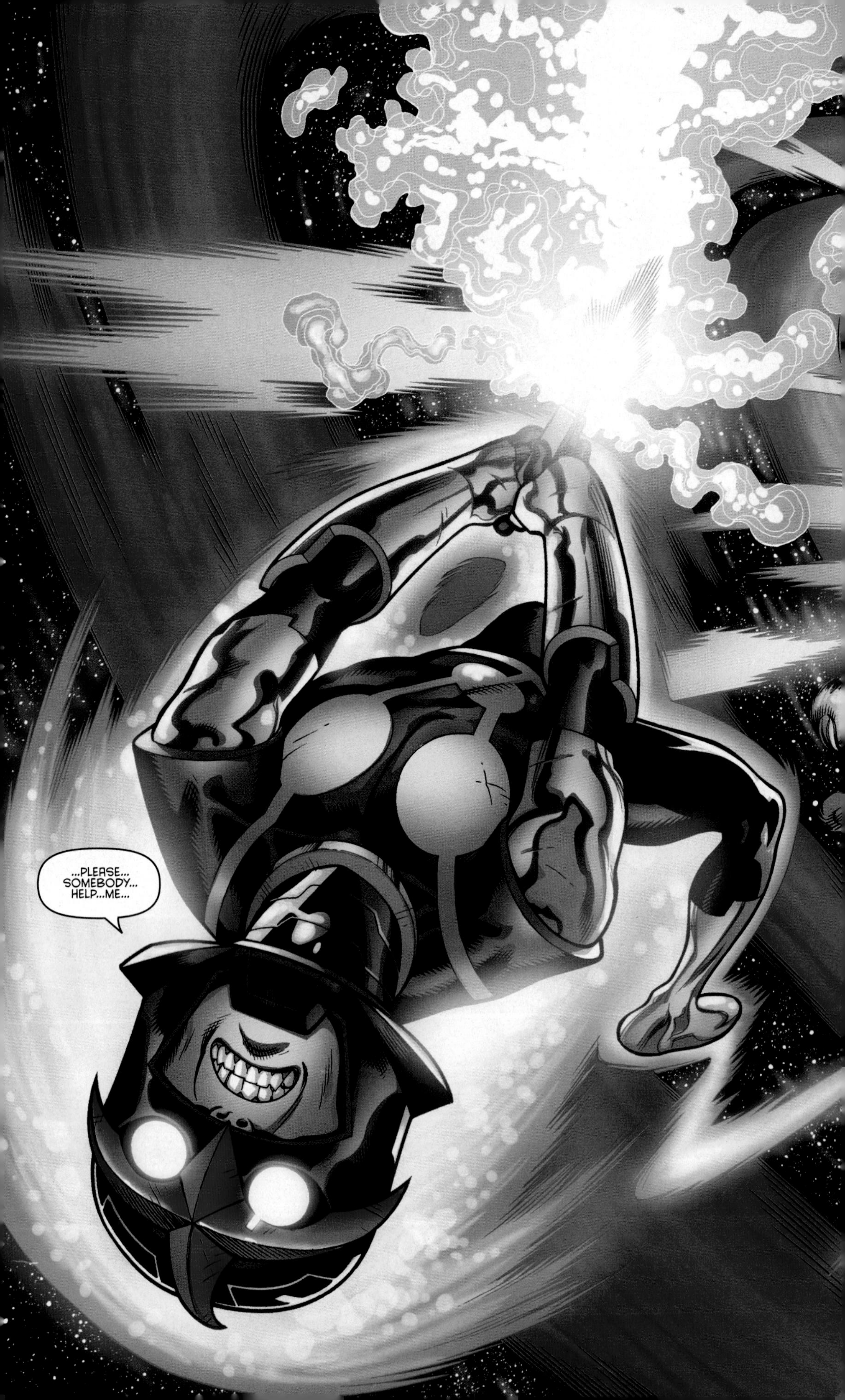
...PLEASE... SOMEBODY... HELP...ME...

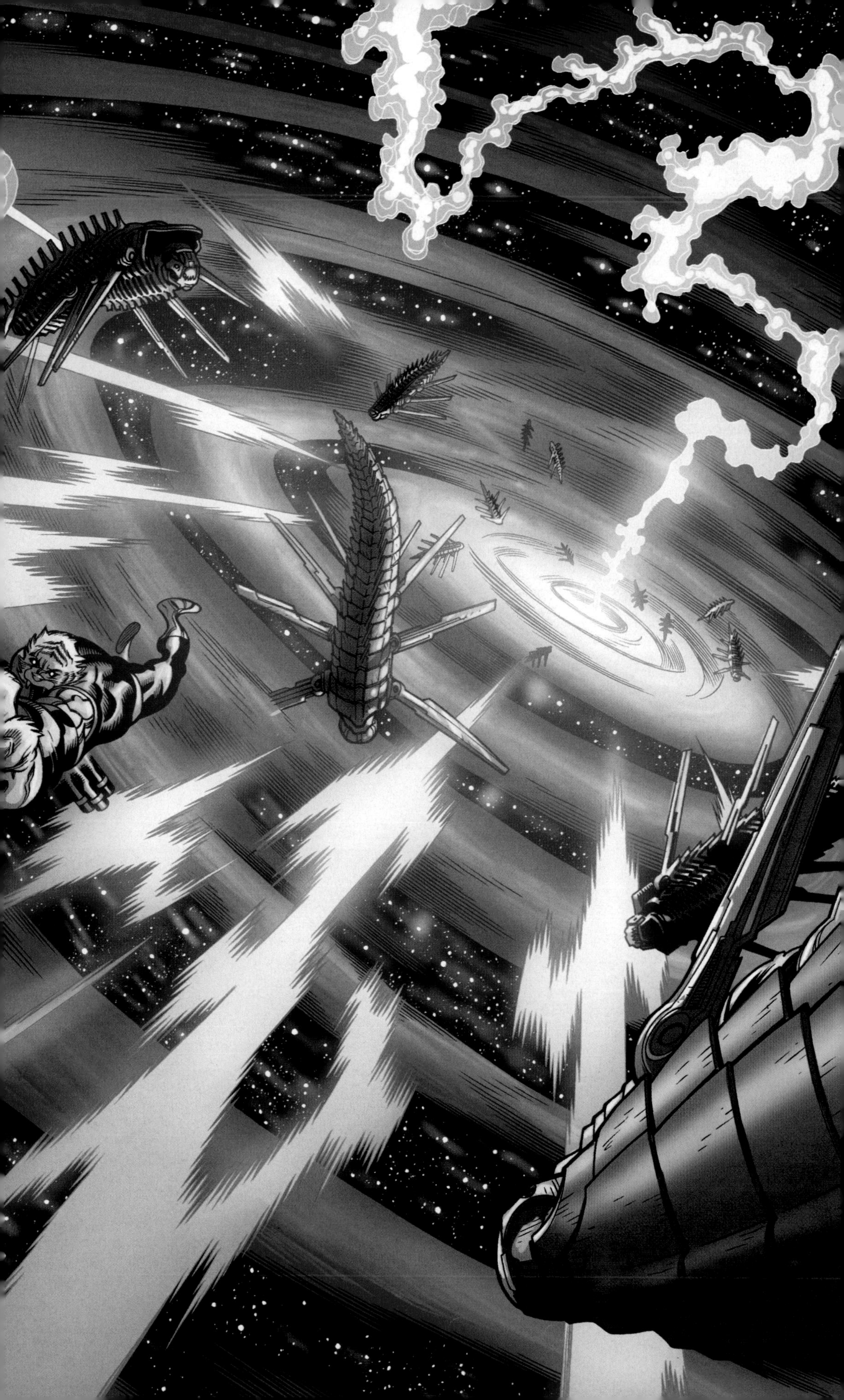

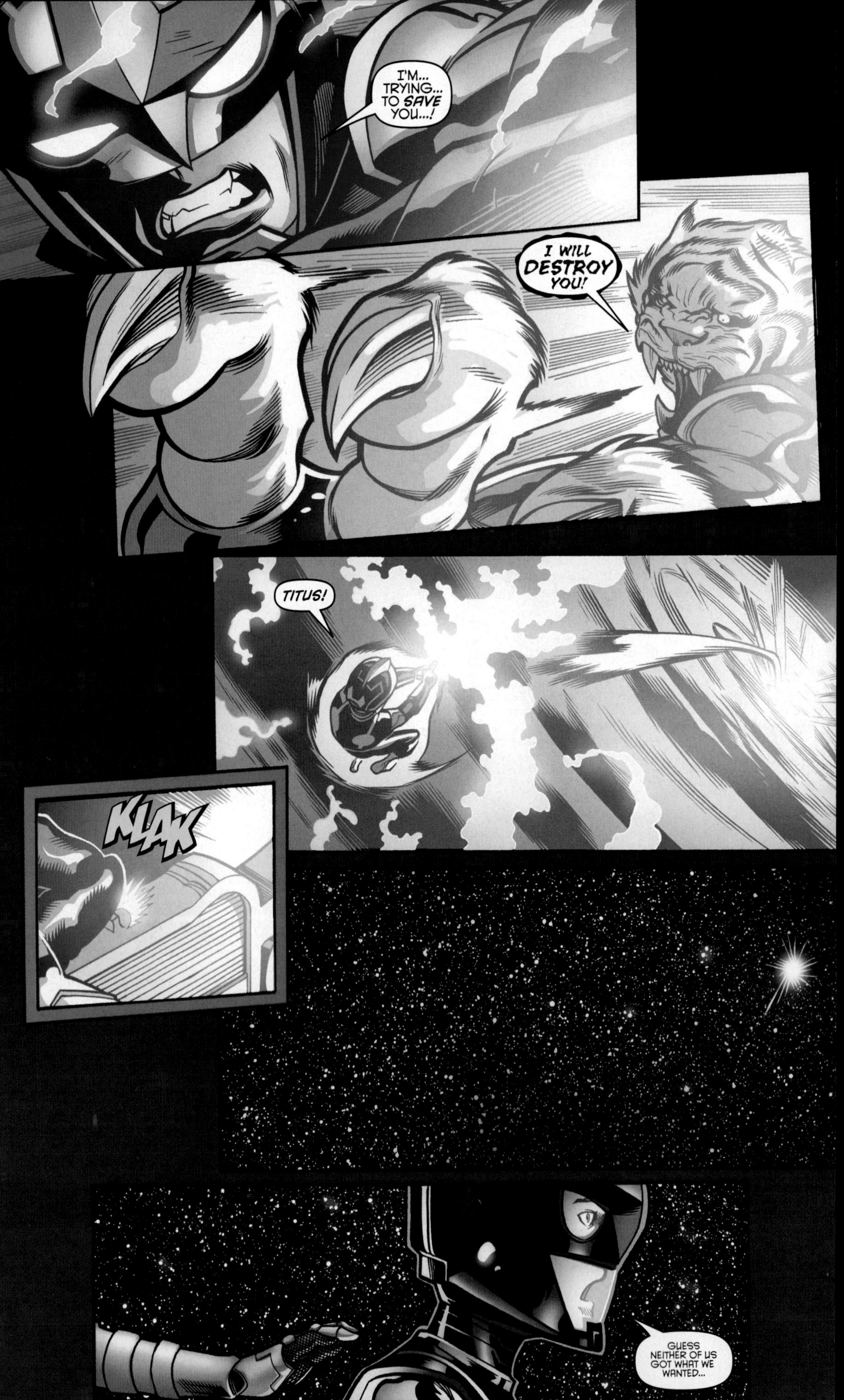
I'M... TRYING... TO SAVE YOU...!
I WILL DESTROY YOU!
TITUS!
KLAK
GUESS NEITHER OF US GOT WHAT WE WANTED...

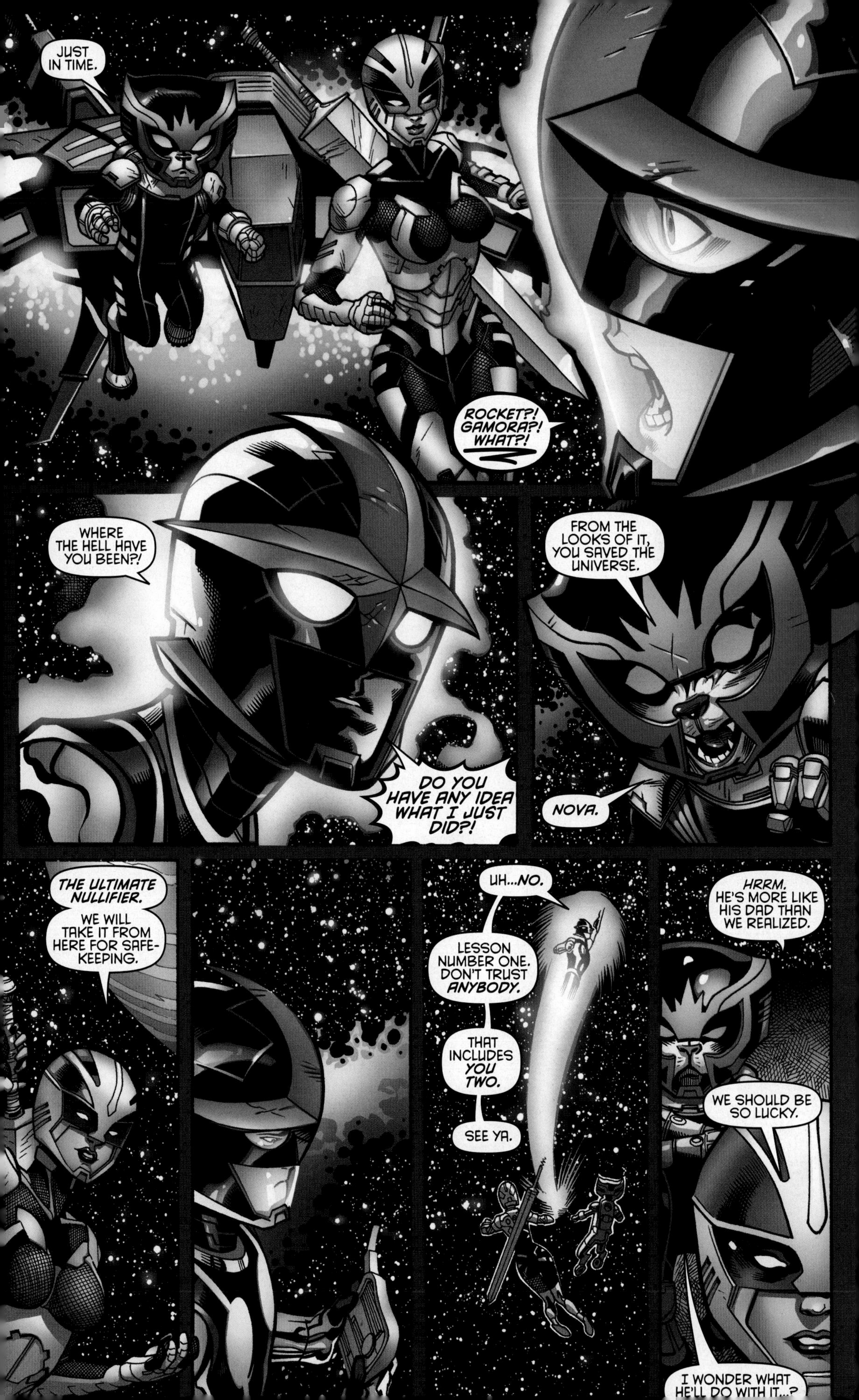
JUST IN TIME.
ROCKET?! GAMORA?! WHAT?!
WHERE THE HELL HAVE YOU BEEN?!
DO YOU HAVE ANY IDEA WHAT I JUST DID?!
FROM THE LOOKS OF IT, YOU SAVED THE UNIVERSE.
NOVA.
THE ULTIMATE NULLIFIER.
WE WILL TAKE IT FROM HERE FOR SAFE-KEEPING.
UH...NO.
LESSON NUMBER ONE. DON'T TRUST ANYBODY.
THAT INCLUDES YOU TWO.
SEE YA.
HRRM. HE'S MORE LIKE HIS DAD THAN WE REALIZED.
WE SHOULD BE SO LUCKY.
I WONDER WHAT HE'LL DO WITH IT...?

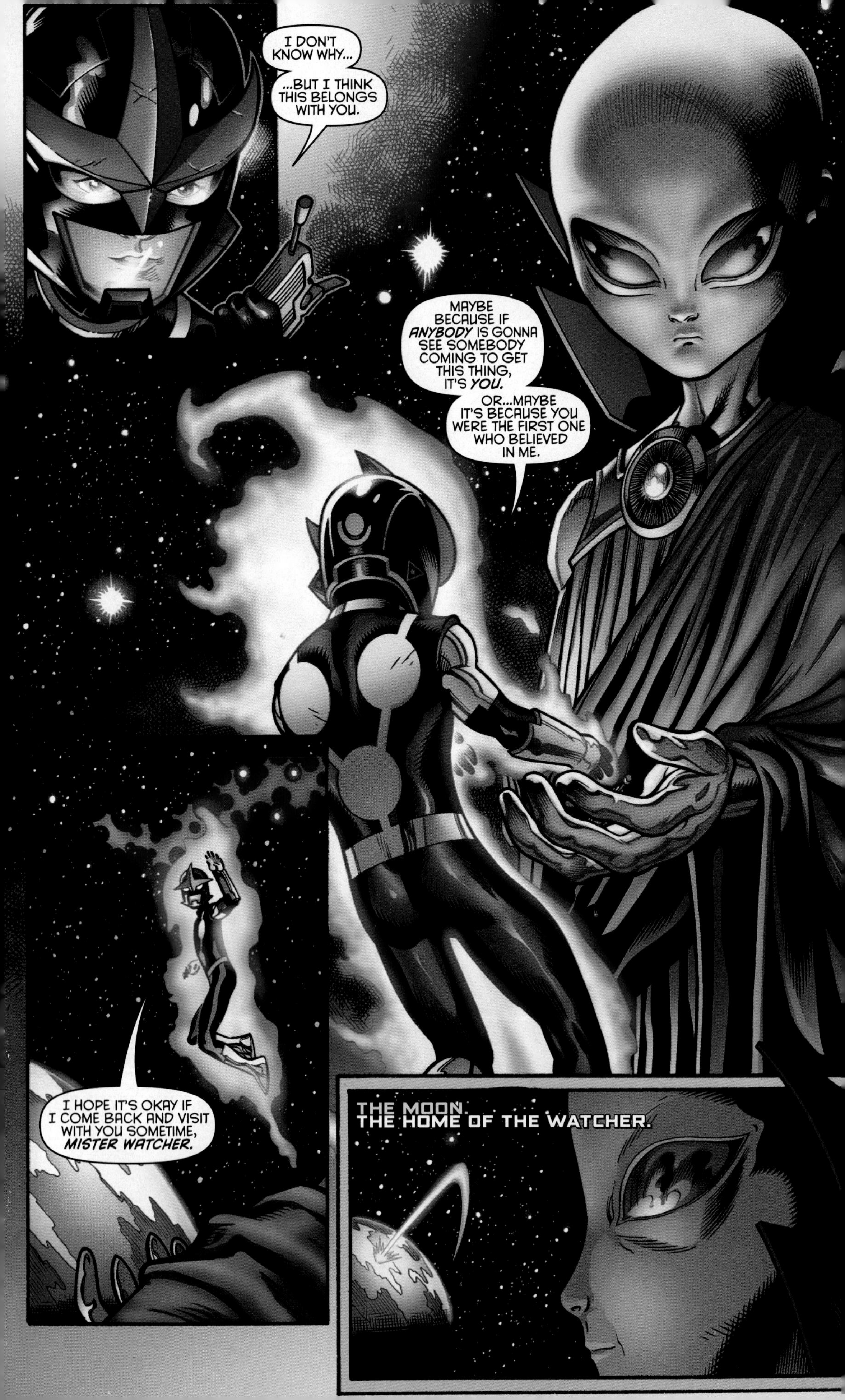
I DON'T KNOW WHY...
...BUT I THINK THIS BELONGS WITH YOU.
MAYBE BECAUSE IF *ANYBODY* IS GONNA SEE SOMEBODY COMING TO GET THIS THING, IT'S *YOU.*
OR...MAYBE IT'S BECAUSE YOU WERE THE FIRST ONE WHO BELIEVED IN ME.
I HOPE IT'S OKAY IF I COME BACK AND VISIT WITH YOU SOMETIME, *MISTER WATCHER.*
THE MOON.
THE HOME OF THE WATCHER.

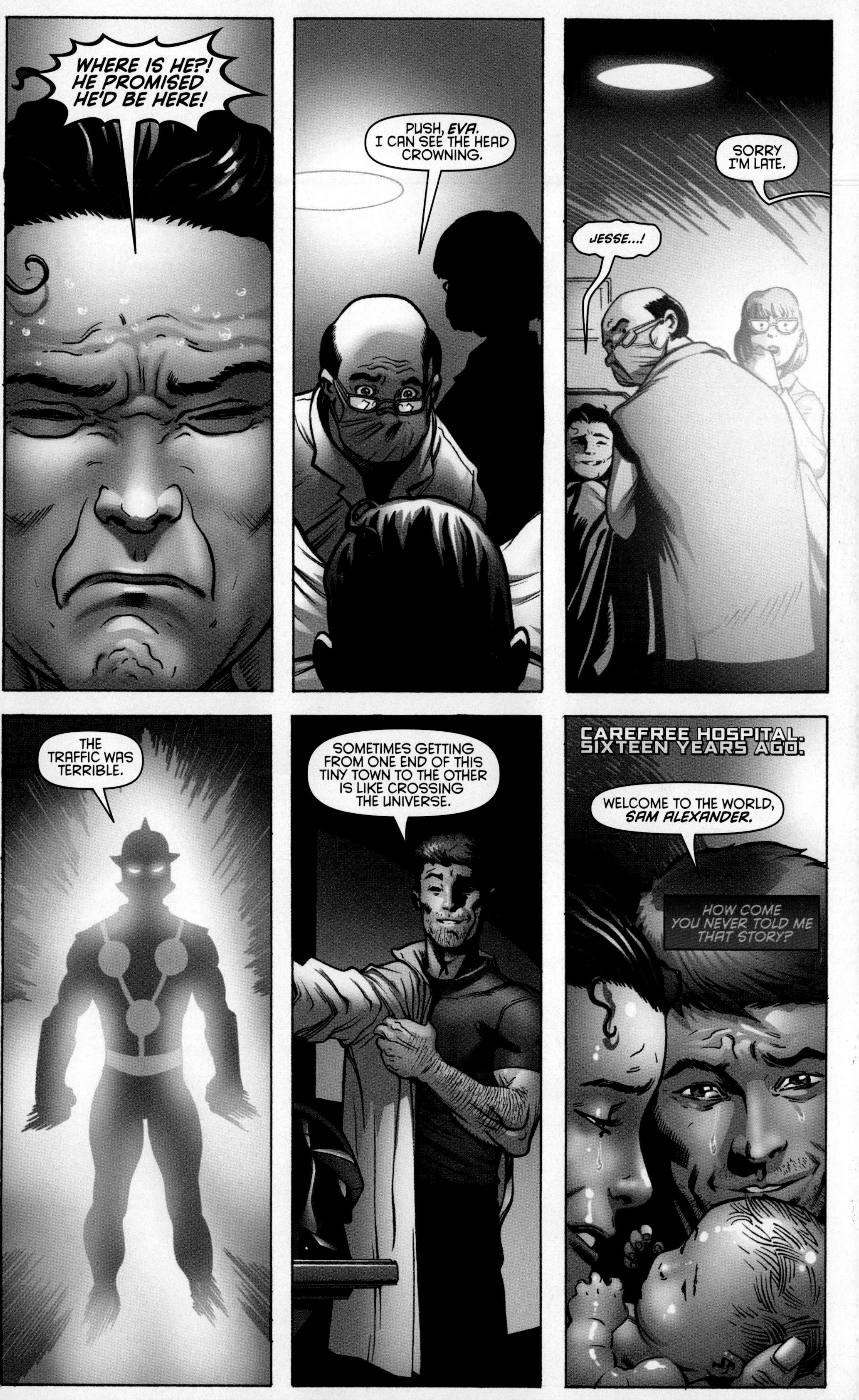
WHERE IS HE?! HE PROMISED HE'D BE HERE!
PUSH, EVA. I CAN SEE THE HEAD CROWNING.
SORRY I'M LATE.
JESSE...!
THE TRAFFIC WAS TERRIBLE.
SOMETIMES GETTING FROM ONE END OF THIS TINY TOWN TO THE OTHER IS LIKE CROSSING THE UNIVERSE.
CAREFREE HOSPITAL. SIXTEEN YEARS AGO.
WELCOME TO THE WORLD, SAM ALEXANDER.
HOW COME YOU NEVER TOLD ME THAT STORY?

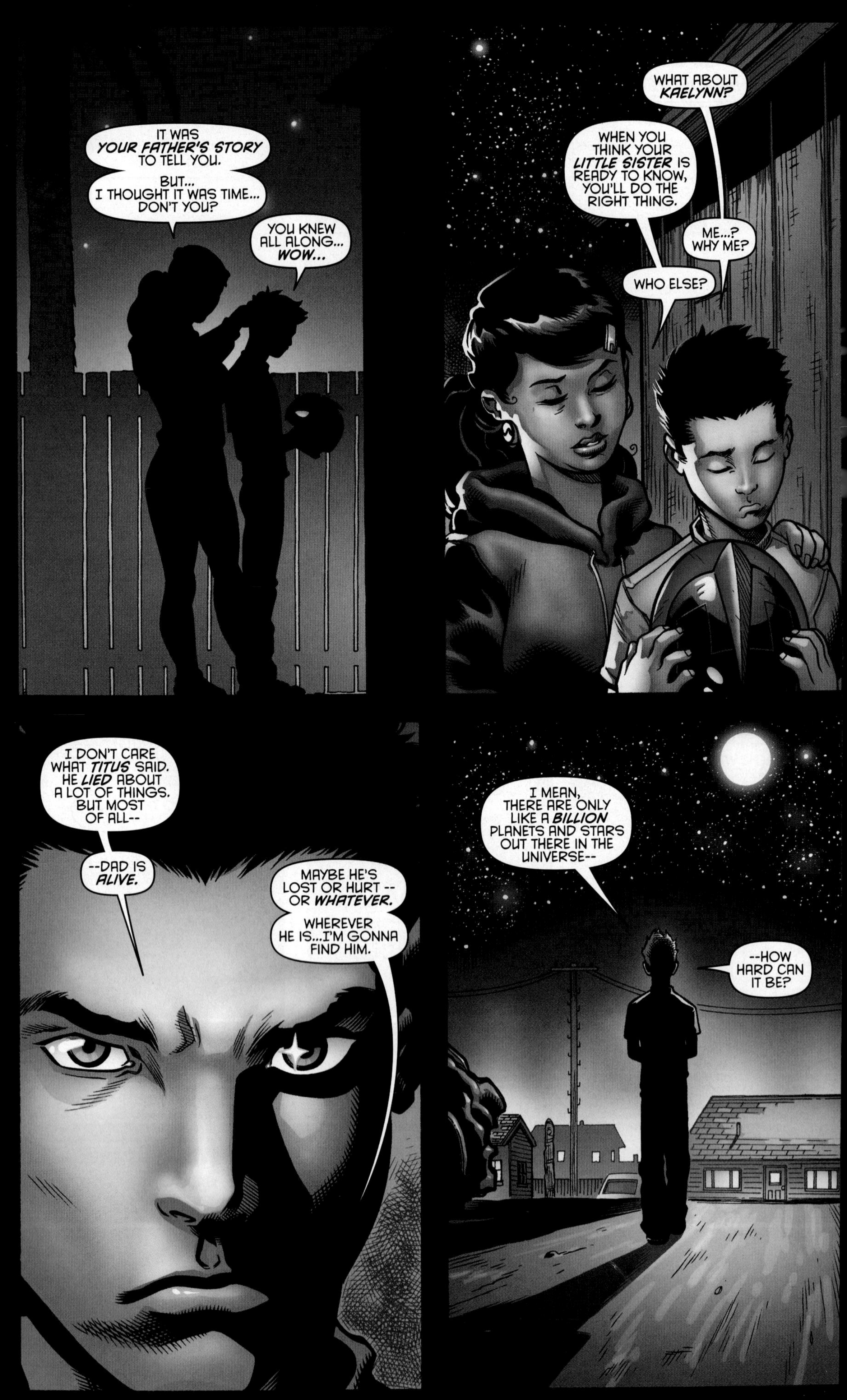
IT WAS YOUR FATHER'S STORY TO TELL YOU.
BUT... I THOUGHT IT WAS TIME... DON'T YOU?
YOU KNEW ALL ALONG... WOW...
WHAT ABOUT KAELYNN?
WHEN YOU THINK YOUR LITTLE SISTER IS READY TO KNOW, YOU'LL DO THE RIGHT THING.
ME...? WHY ME?
WHO ELSE?
I DON'T CARE WHAT TITUS SAID. HE LIED ABOUT A LOT OF THINGS. BUT MOST OF ALL--
--DAD IS ALIVE.
MAYBE HE'S LOST OR HURT -- OR WHATEVER.
WHEREVER HE IS...I'M GONNA FIND HIM.
I MEAN, THERE ARE ONLY LIKE A BILLION PLANETS AND STARS OUT THERE IN THE UNIVERSE--
--HOW HARD CAN IT BE?

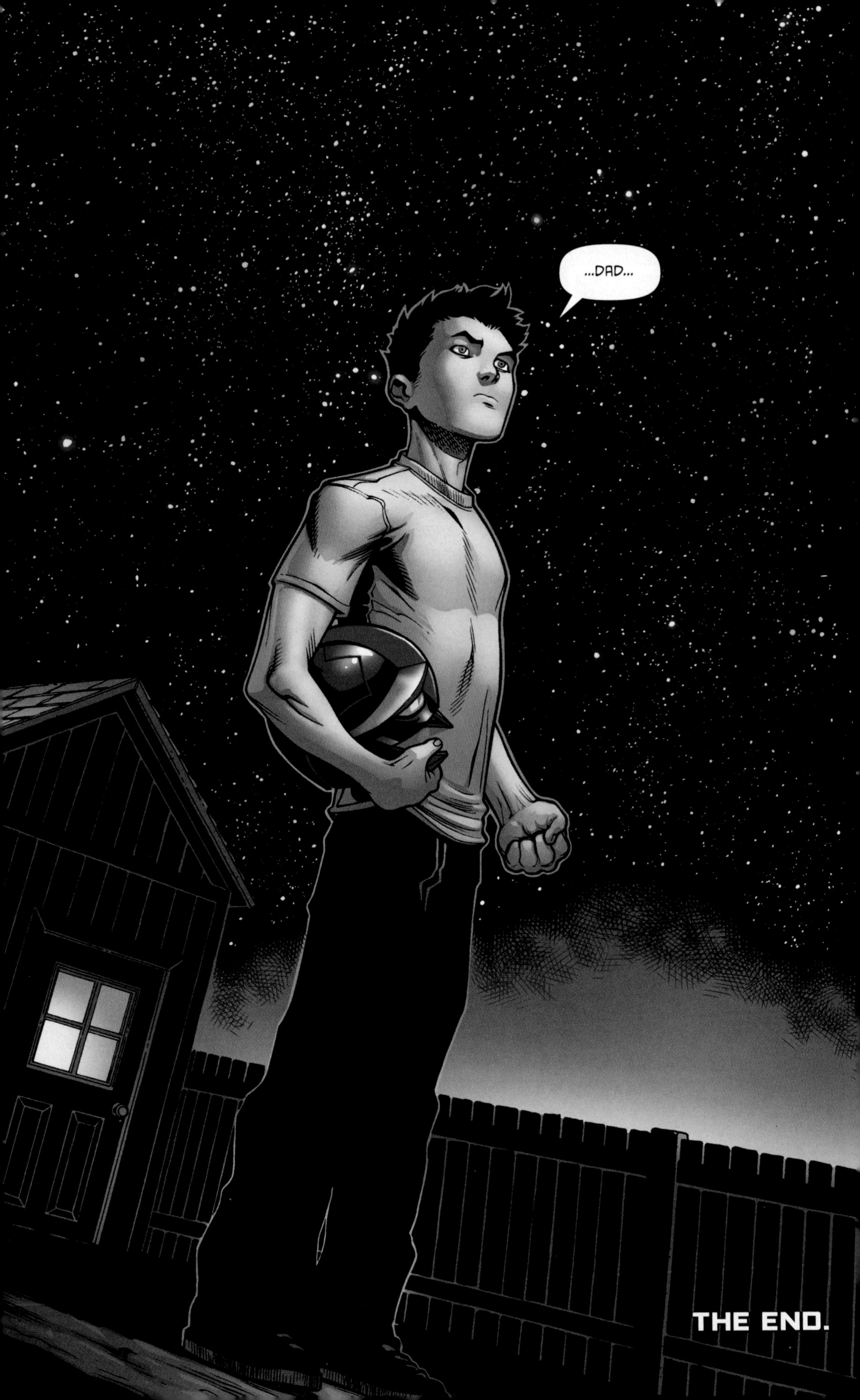
...DAD...
THE END.

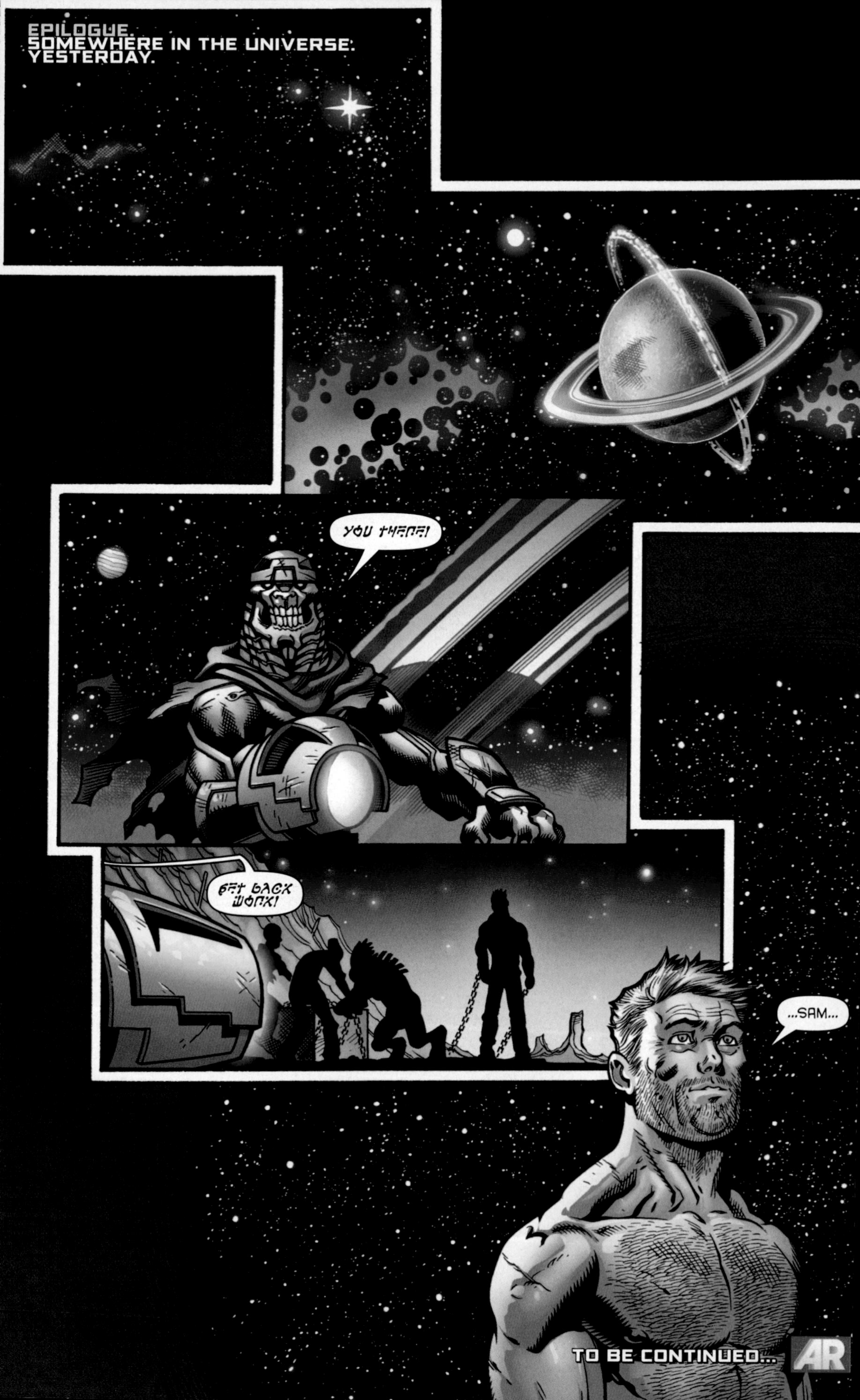
EPILOGUE.
SOMEWHERE IN THE UNIVERSE:
YESTERDAY.
YOU THERE!
GET BACK WORK!
...SAM...
TO BE CONTINUED...

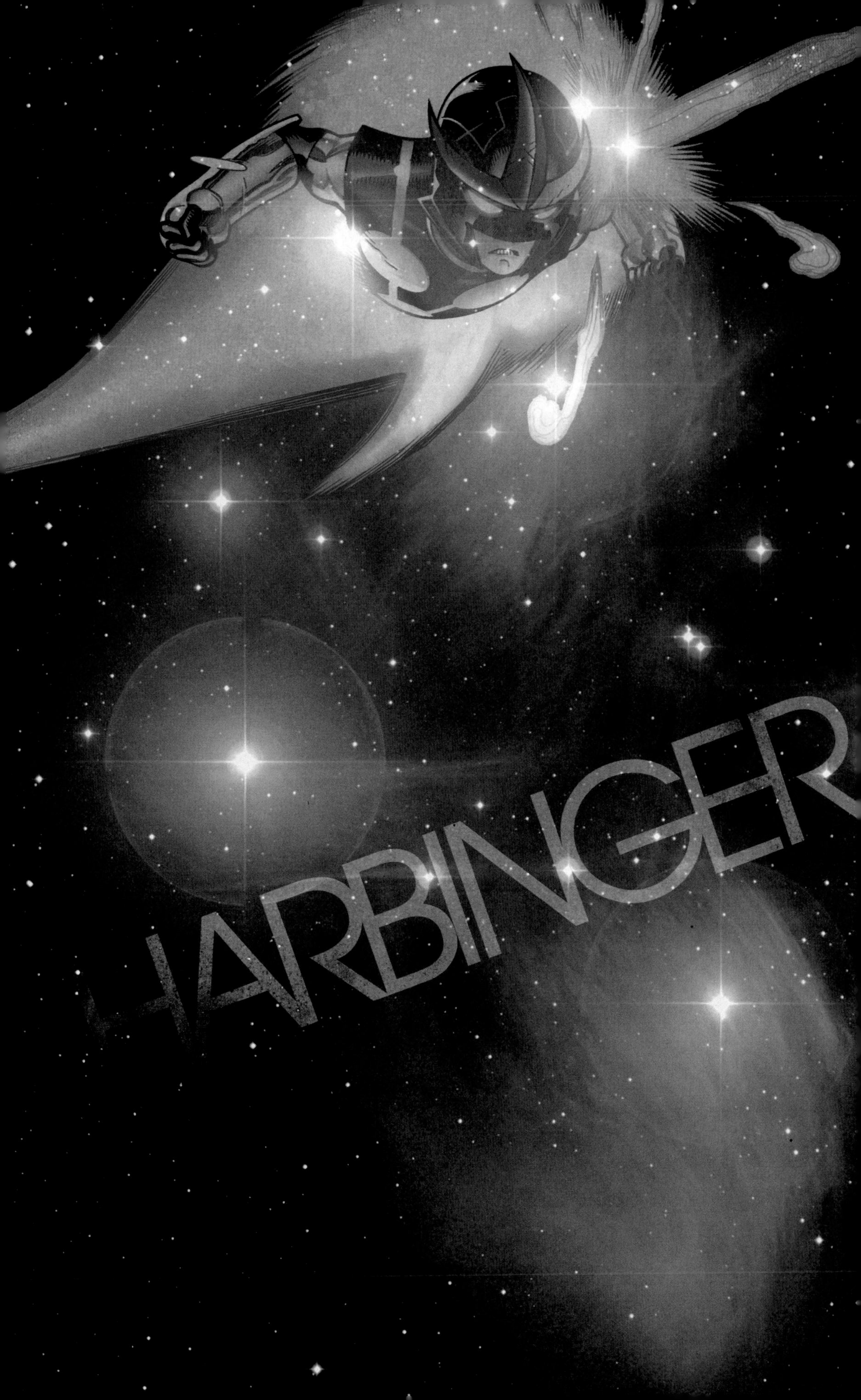
HARBINGER

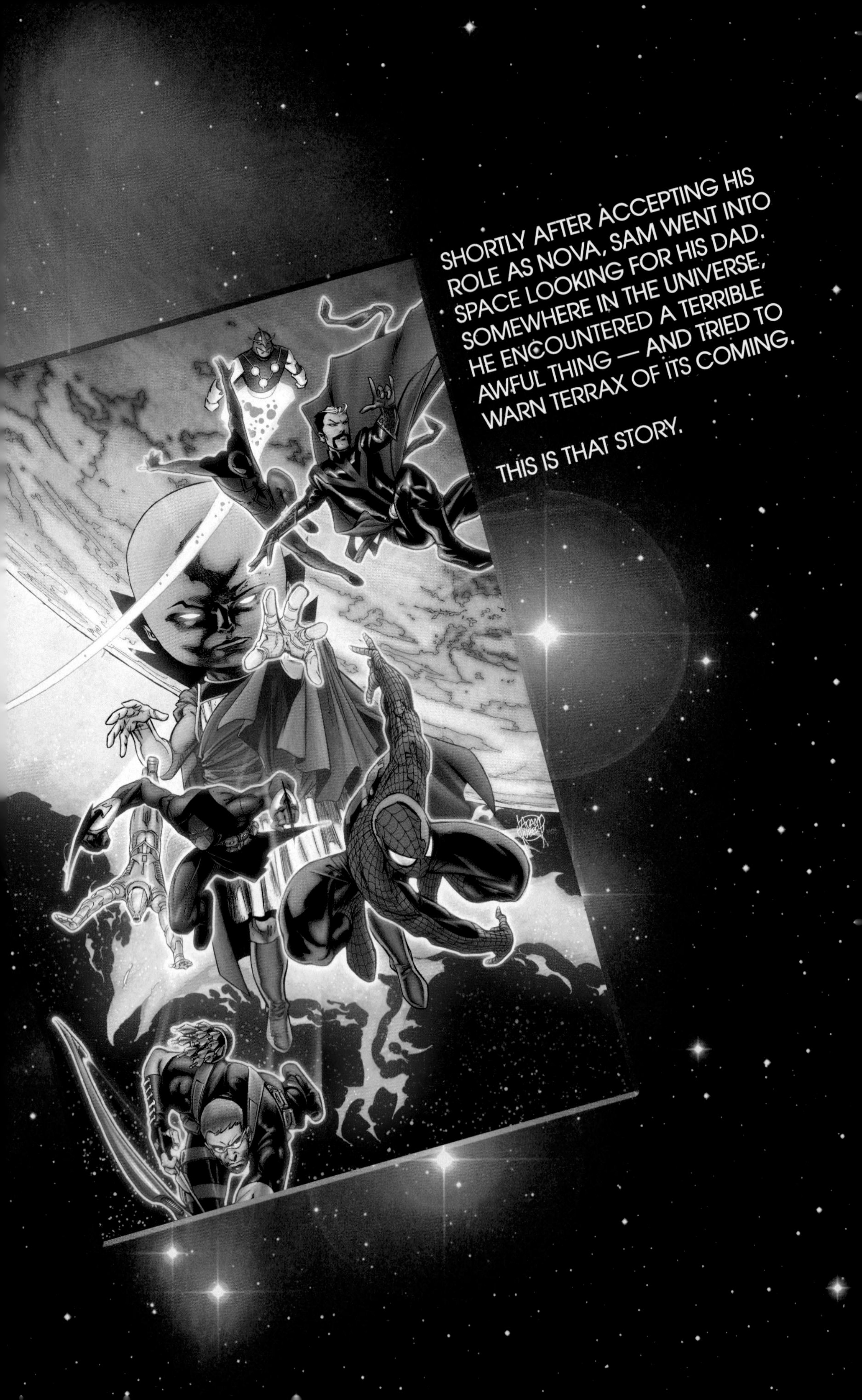

SHORTLY AFTER ACCEPTING HIS ROLE AS NOVA, SAM WENT INTO SPACE LOOKING FOR HIS DAD. SOMEWHERE IN THE UNIVERSE, HE ENCOUNTERED A TERRIBLE AWFUL THING — AND TRIED TO WARN TERRAX OF ITS COMING.

THIS IS THAT STORY.

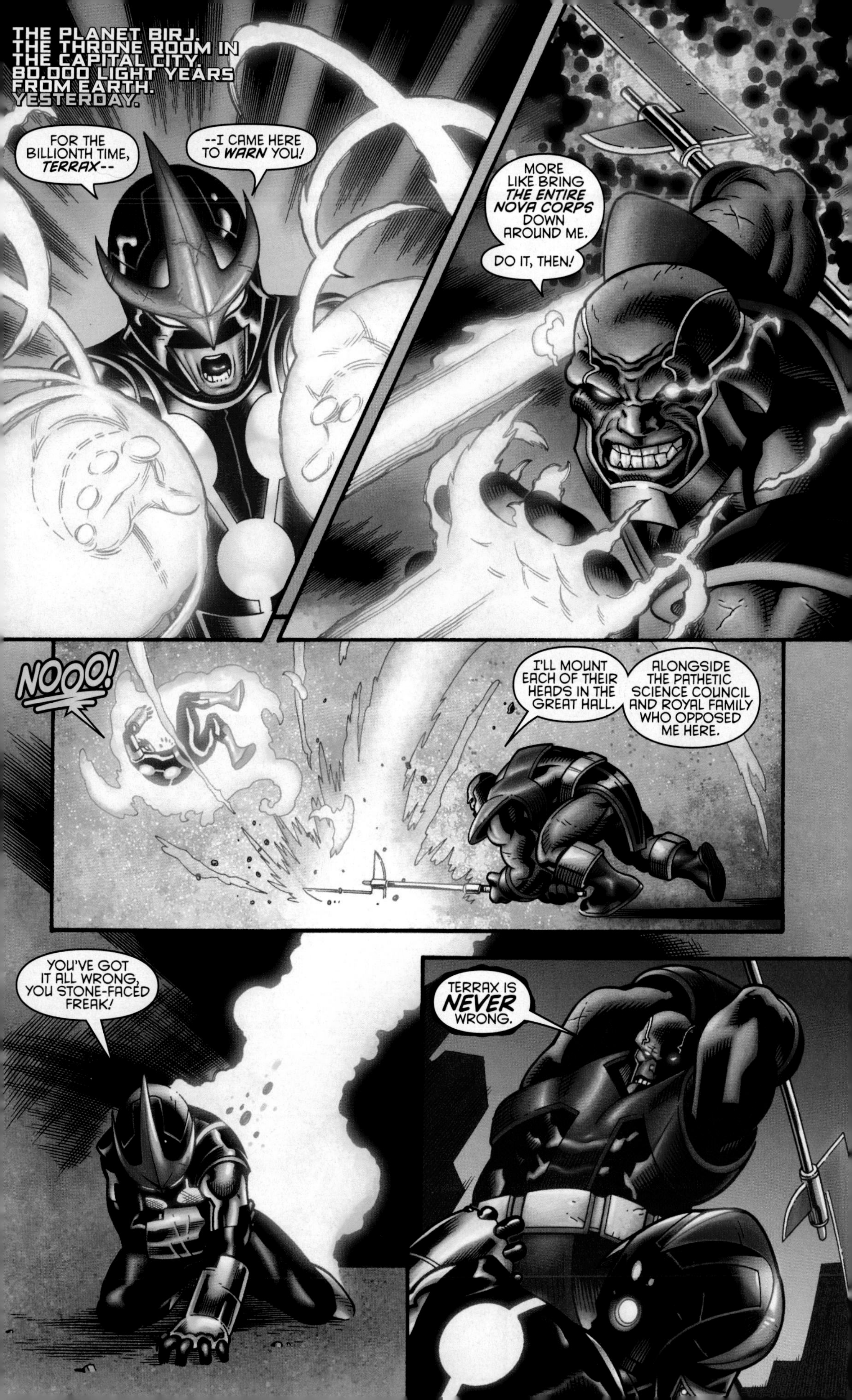
THE PLANET BIRJ. THE THRONE ROOM IN THE CAPITAL CITY. 80,000 LIGHT YEARS FROM EARTH. YESTERDAY.
FOR THE BILLIONTH TIME, TERRAX--
--I CAME HERE TO WARN YOU!
MORE LIKE BRING THE ENTIRE NOVA CORPS DOWN AROUND ME.
DO IT, THEN!
NOOO!
I'LL MOUNT EACH OF THEIR HEADS IN THE GREAT HALL.
ALONGSIDE THE PATHETIC SCIENCE COUNCIL AND ROYAL FAMILY WHO OPPOSED ME HERE.
YOU'VE GOT IT ALL WRONG, YOU STONE-FACED FREAK!
TERRAX IS NEVER WRONG.

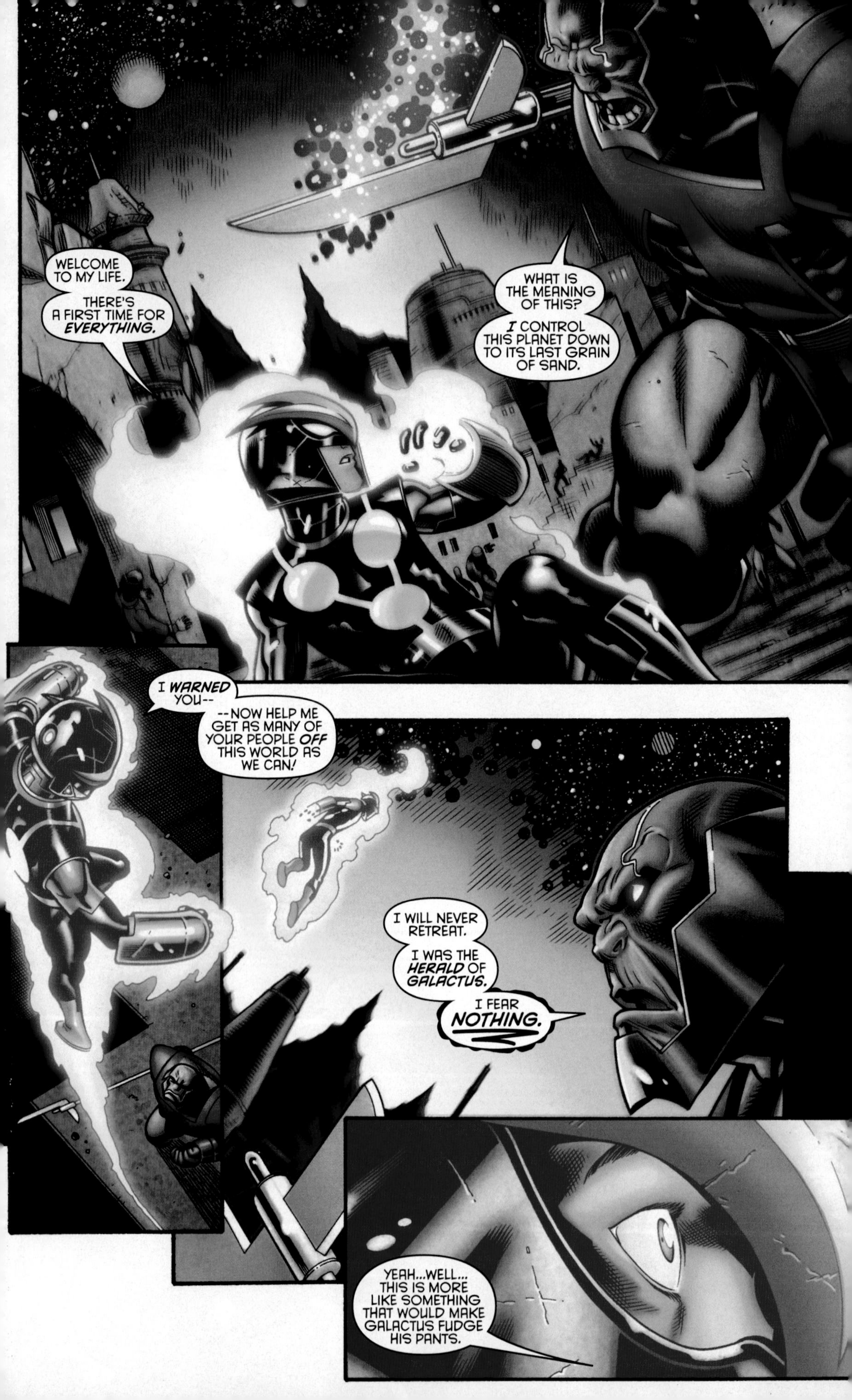
WELCOME TO MY LIFE.
THERE'S A FIRST TIME FOR EVERYTHING.
WHAT IS THE MEANING OF THIS?
I CONTROL THIS PLANET DOWN TO ITS LAST GRAIN OF SAND.
I WARNED YOU--
--NOW HELP ME GET AS MANY OF YOUR PEOPLE OFF THIS WORLD AS WE CAN!
I WILL NEVER RETREAT.
I WAS THE HERALD OF GALACTUS.
I FEAR NOTHING.
YEAH...WELL... THIS IS MORE LIKE SOMETHING THAT WOULD MAKE GALACTUS FUDGE HIS PANTS.

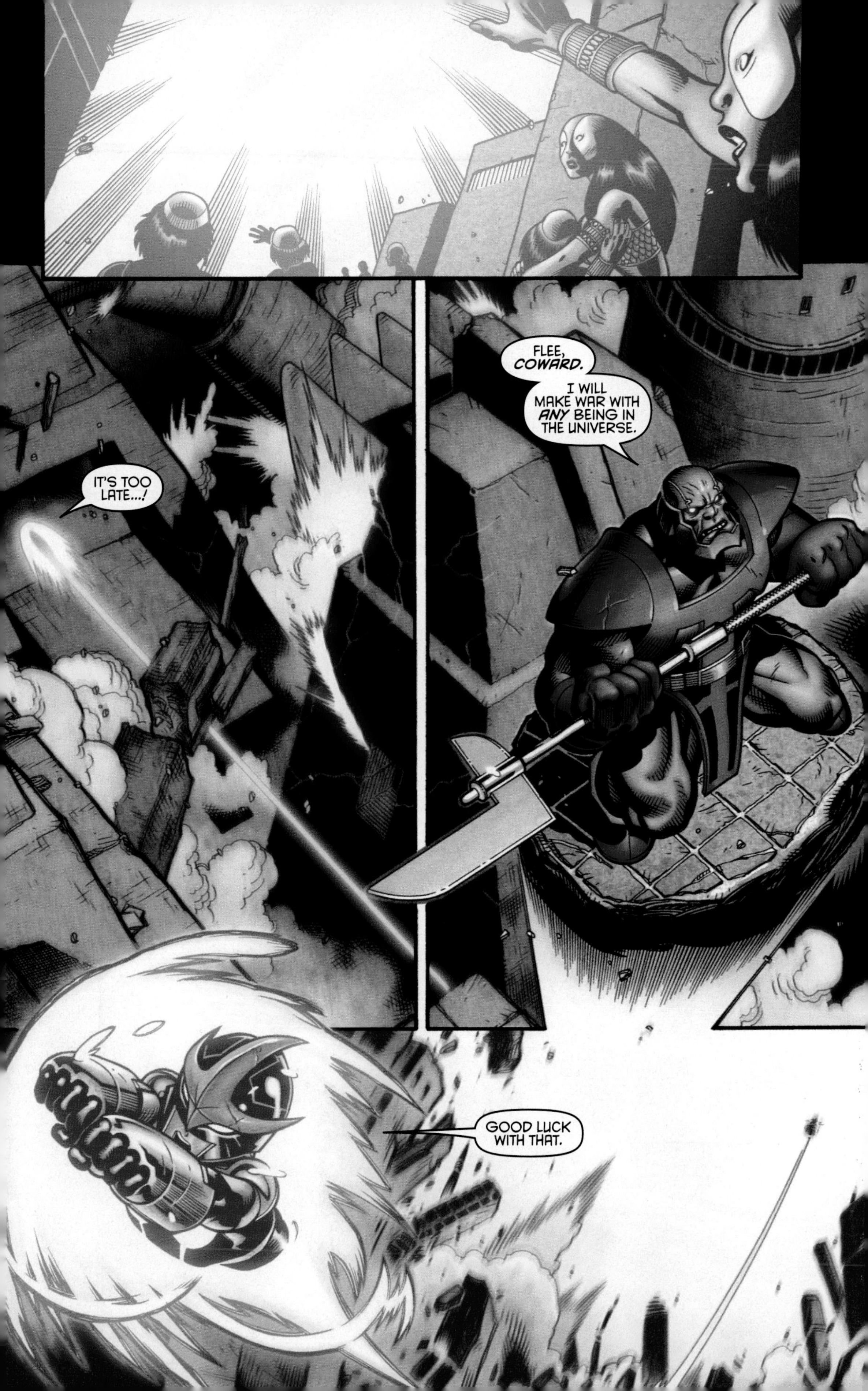
IT'S TOO LATE...!
FLEE, COWARD.
I WILL MAKE WAR WITH ANY BEING IN THE UNIVERSE.
GOOD LUCK WITH THAT.

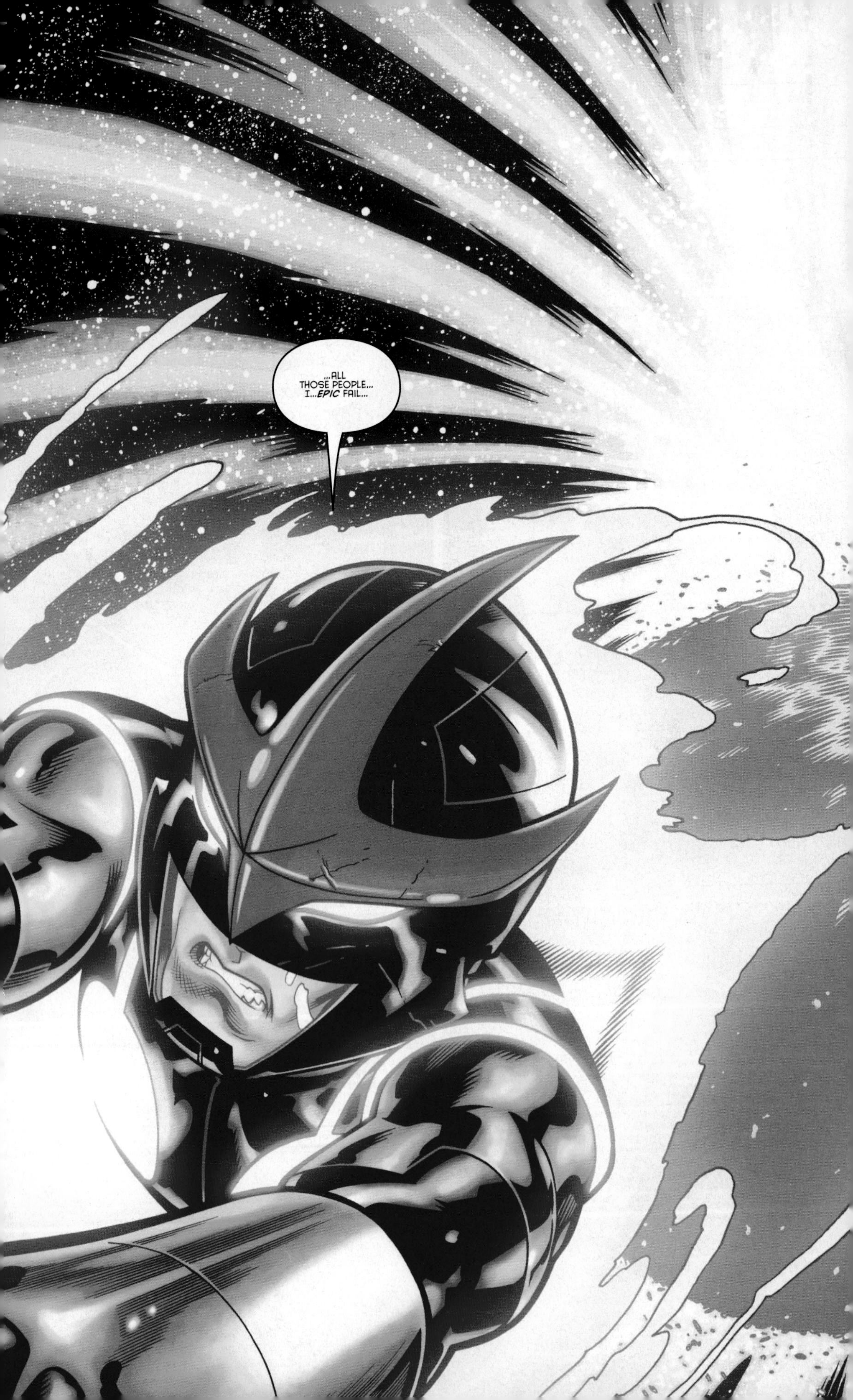
...ALL THOSE PEOPLE... I...*EPIC* FAIL...

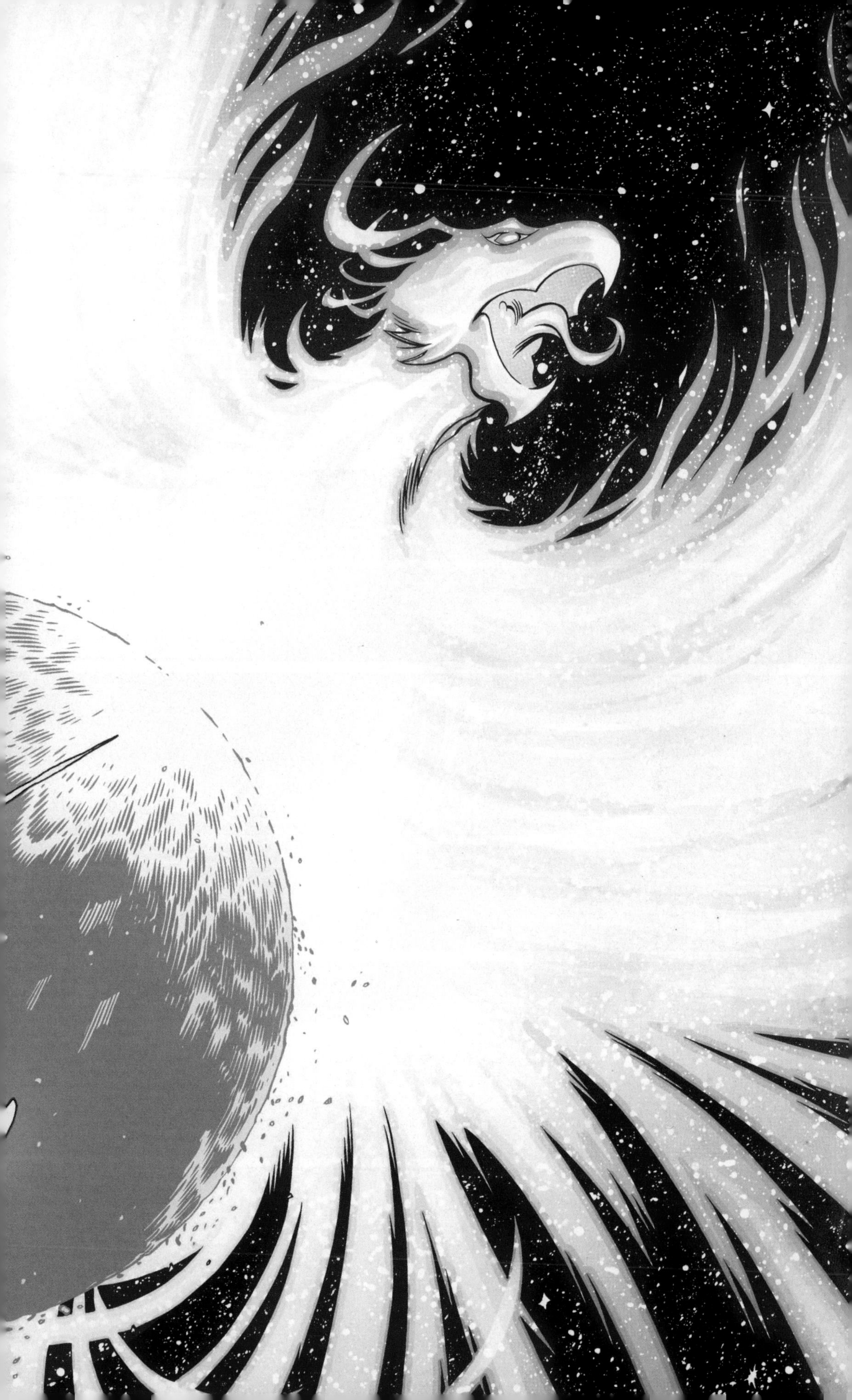

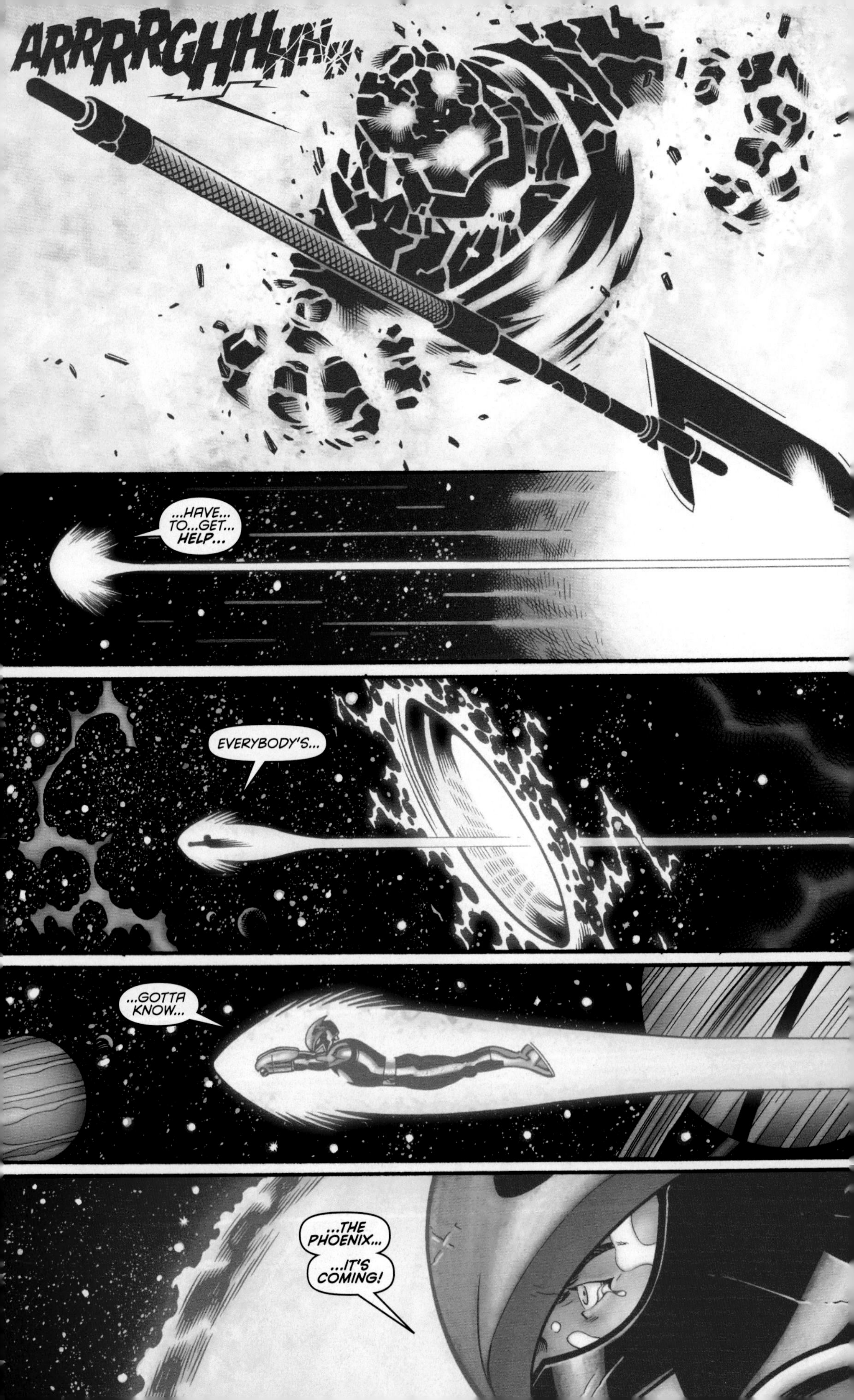
ARRRRGHHHHH
...HAVE... TO...GET... HELP...
EVERYBODY'S...
...GOTTA KNOW...
...THE PHOENIX...
...IT'S COMING!

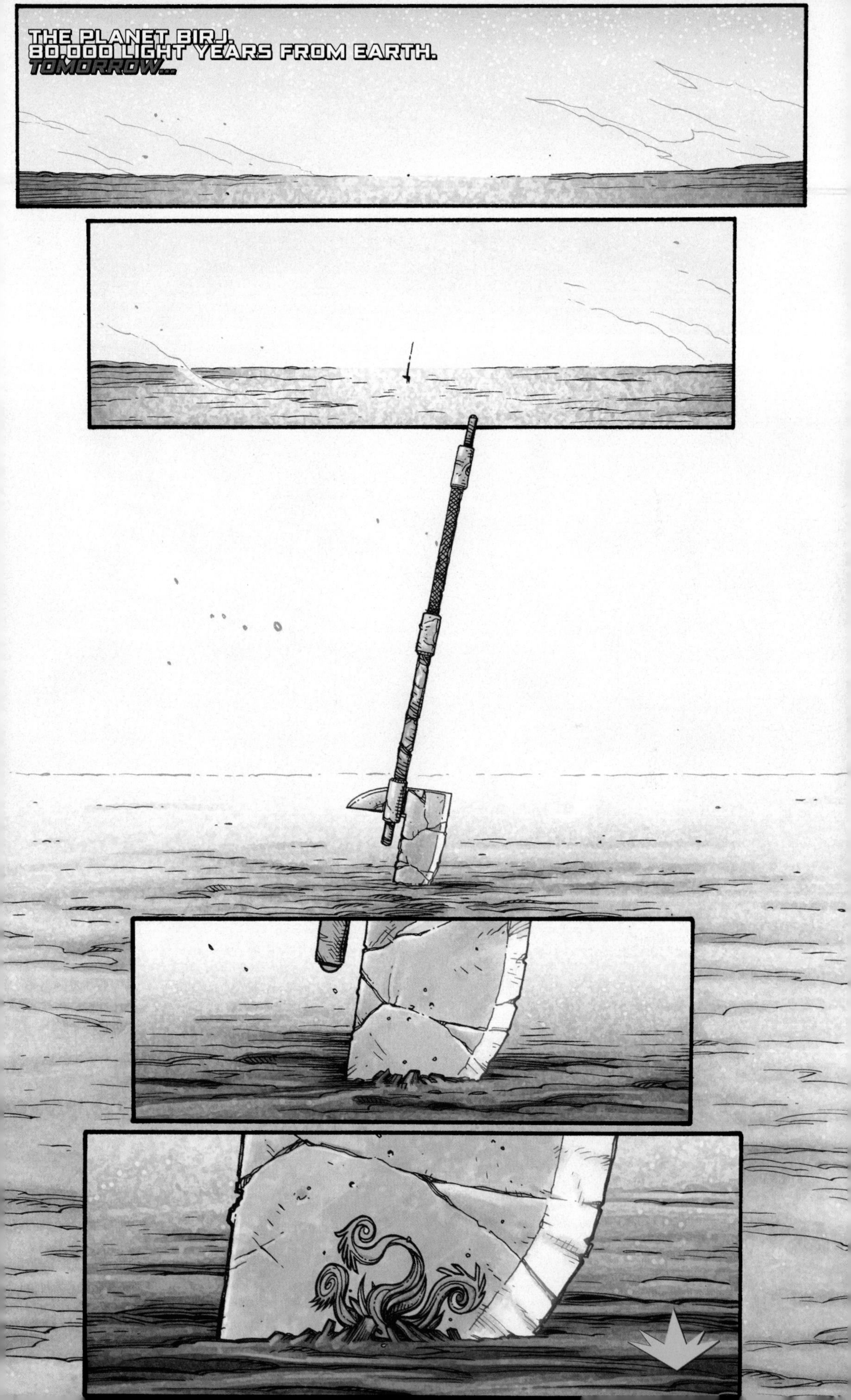
THE PLANET BIRJ.
80,000 LIGHT YEARS FROM EARTH.
TOMORROW...

DIAMONDHEAL

NOVA SAVED THE WORLD AGAIN — TWICE! ALONGSIDE THE AVENGERS, HE WAS CRUCIAL IN DEFEATING THE PHOENIX FROM CONSUMING EARTH. HIS ACTIONS WERE SO AMAZING THAT THOR, THE GOD OF THUNDER, ASKED HIM TO JOIN THE AVENGERS.

THIS IS WHAT HAPPENED NEXT...

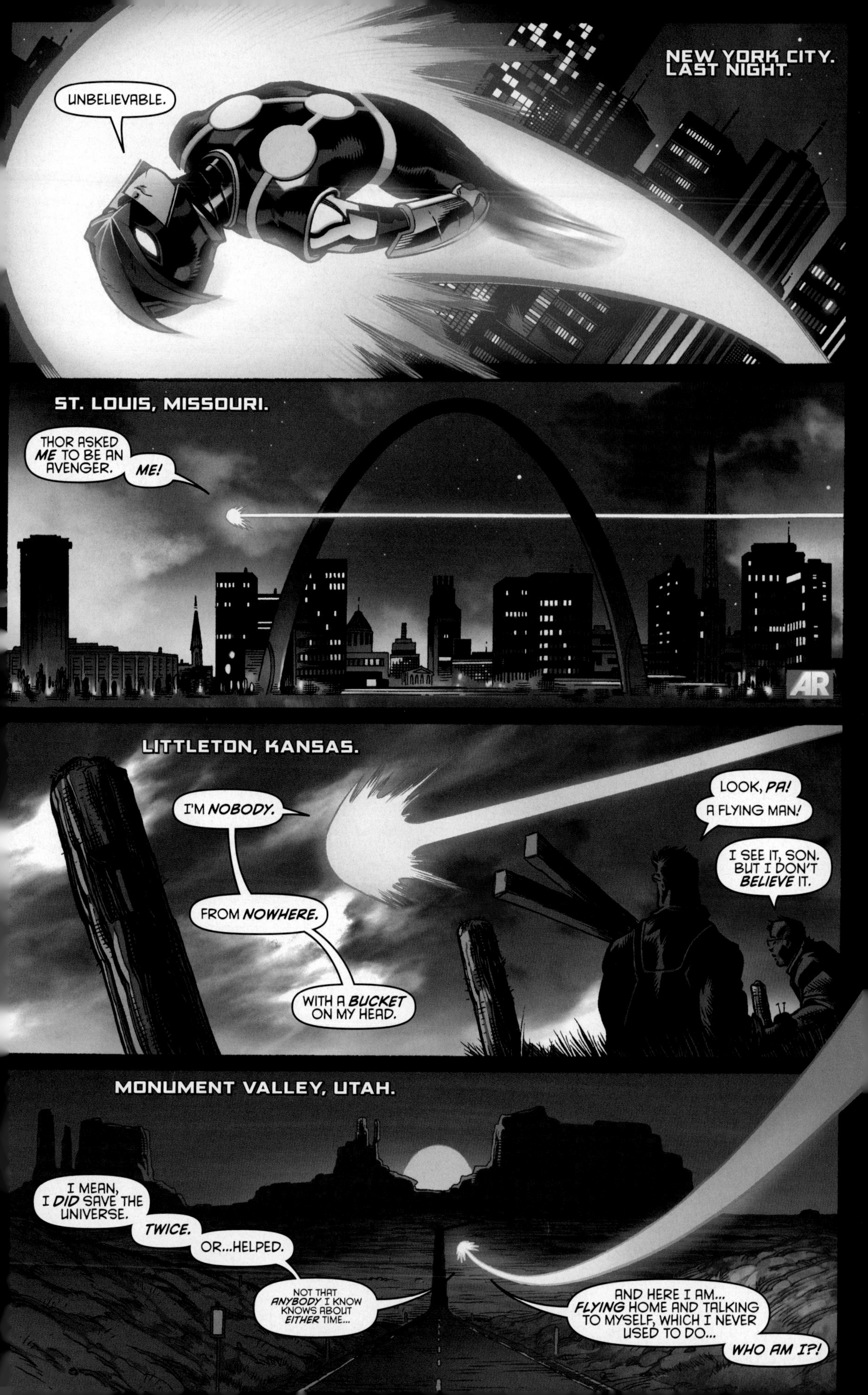
NEW YORK CITY. LAST NIGHT.
UNBELIEVABLE.
ST. LOUIS, MISSOURI.
THOR ASKED *ME* TO BE AN AVENGER.
ME!
AR
LITTLETON, KANSAS.
I'M *NOBODY.*
FROM *NOWHERE.*
WITH A *BUCKET* ON MY HEAD.
LOOK, *PA!*
A FLYING MAN!
I SEE IT, SON. BUT I DON'T *BELIEVE* IT.
MONUMENT VALLEY, UTAH.
I MEAN, I *DID* SAVE THE UNIVERSE.
TWICE.
OR...HELPED.
NOT THAT *ANYBODY* I KNOW KNOWS ABOUT *EITHER* TIME...
AND HERE I AM... *FLYING* HOME AND TALKING TO MYSELF, WHICH I NEVER USED TO DO...
WHO AM I?!

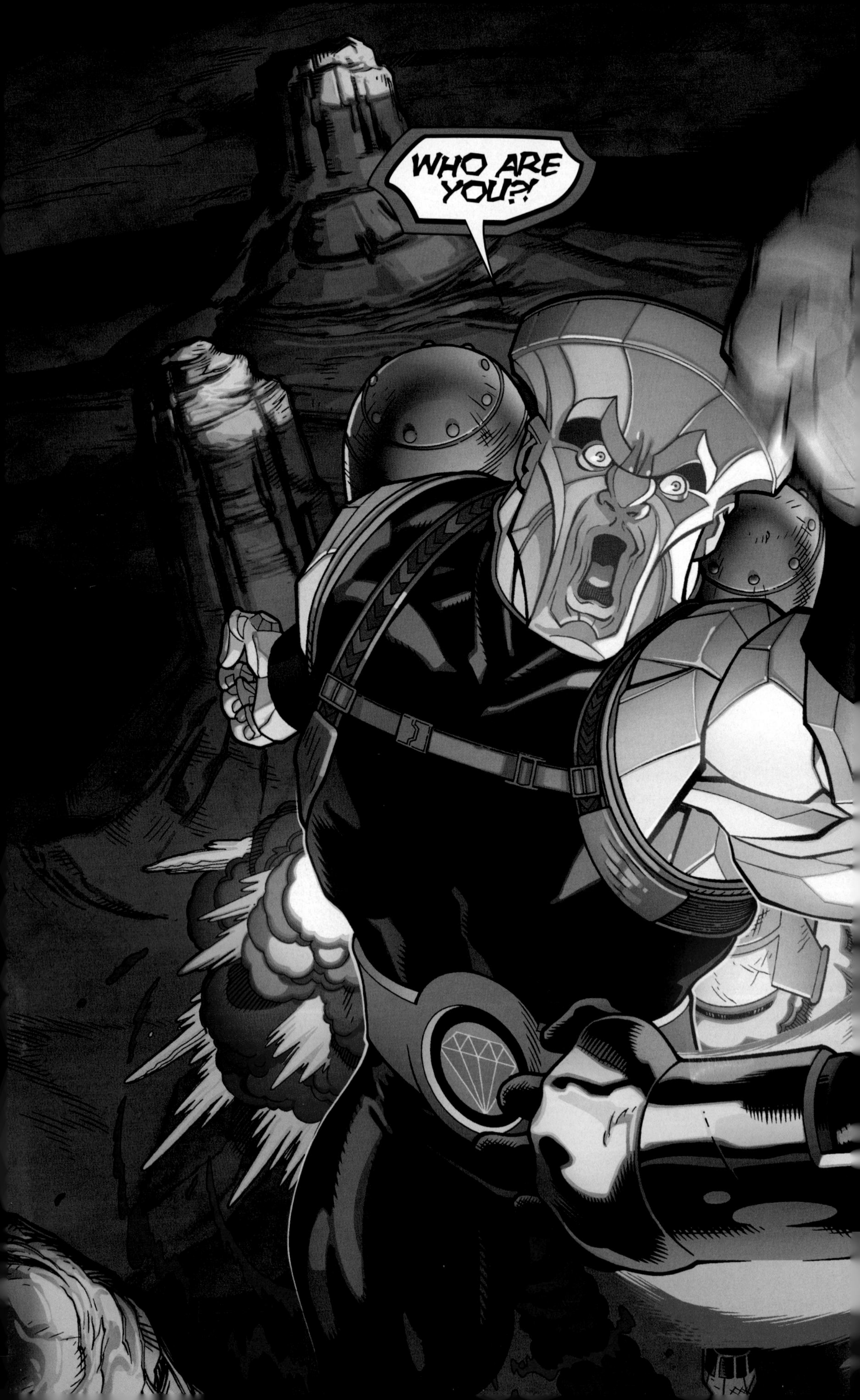
WHO ARE YOU?!

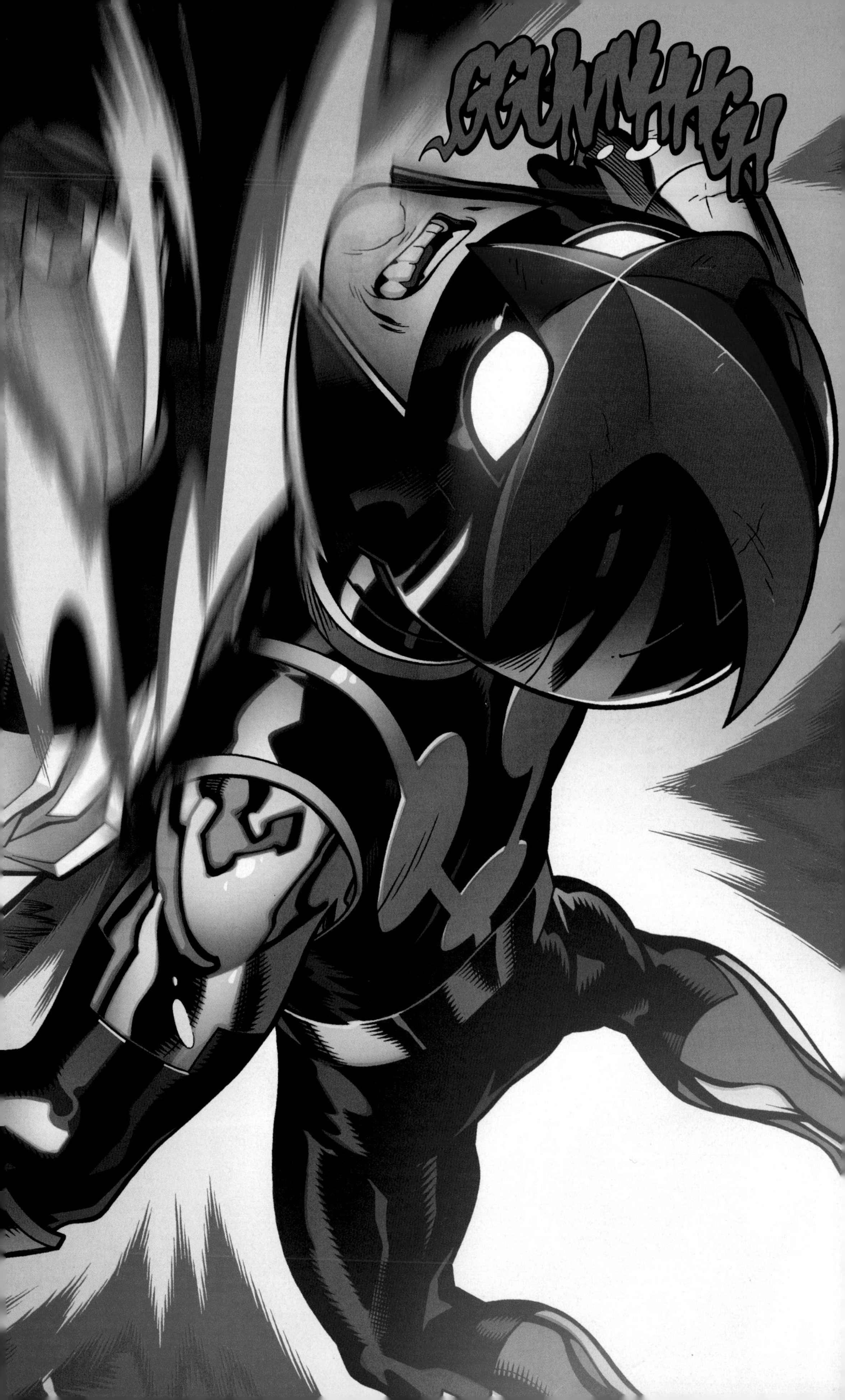
GGUNNHGH

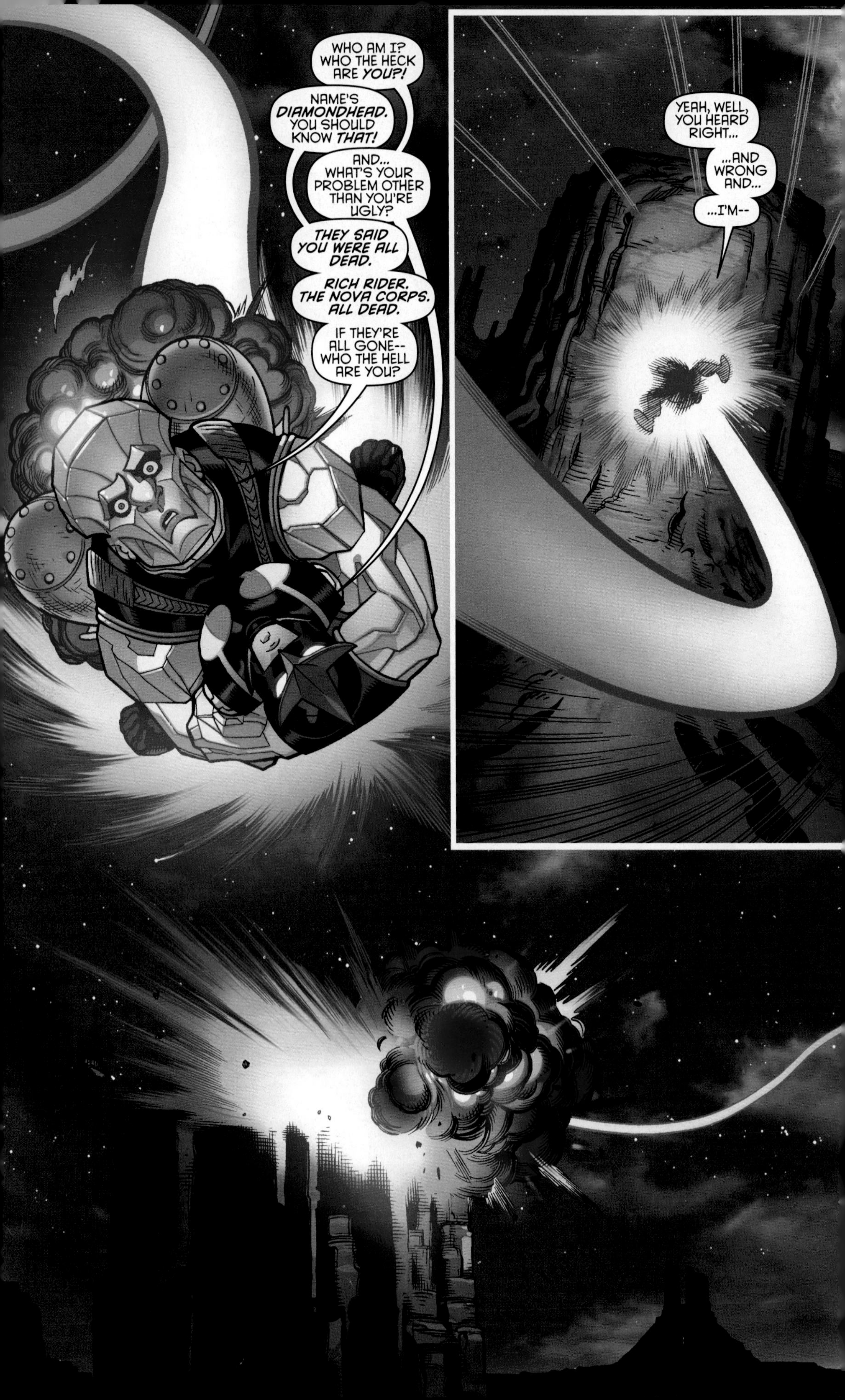
WHO AM I? WHO THE HECK ARE YOU?!
NAME'S DIAMONDHEAD. YOU SHOULD KNOW THAT!
AND... WHAT'S YOUR PROBLEM OTHER THAN YOU'RE UGLY?
THEY SAID YOU WERE ALL DEAD.
RICH RIDER. THE NOVA CORPS. ALL DEAD.
IF THEY'RE ALL GONE-- WHO THE HELL ARE YOU?
YEAH, WELL, YOU HEARD RIGHT...
...AND WRONG AND...
...I'M--

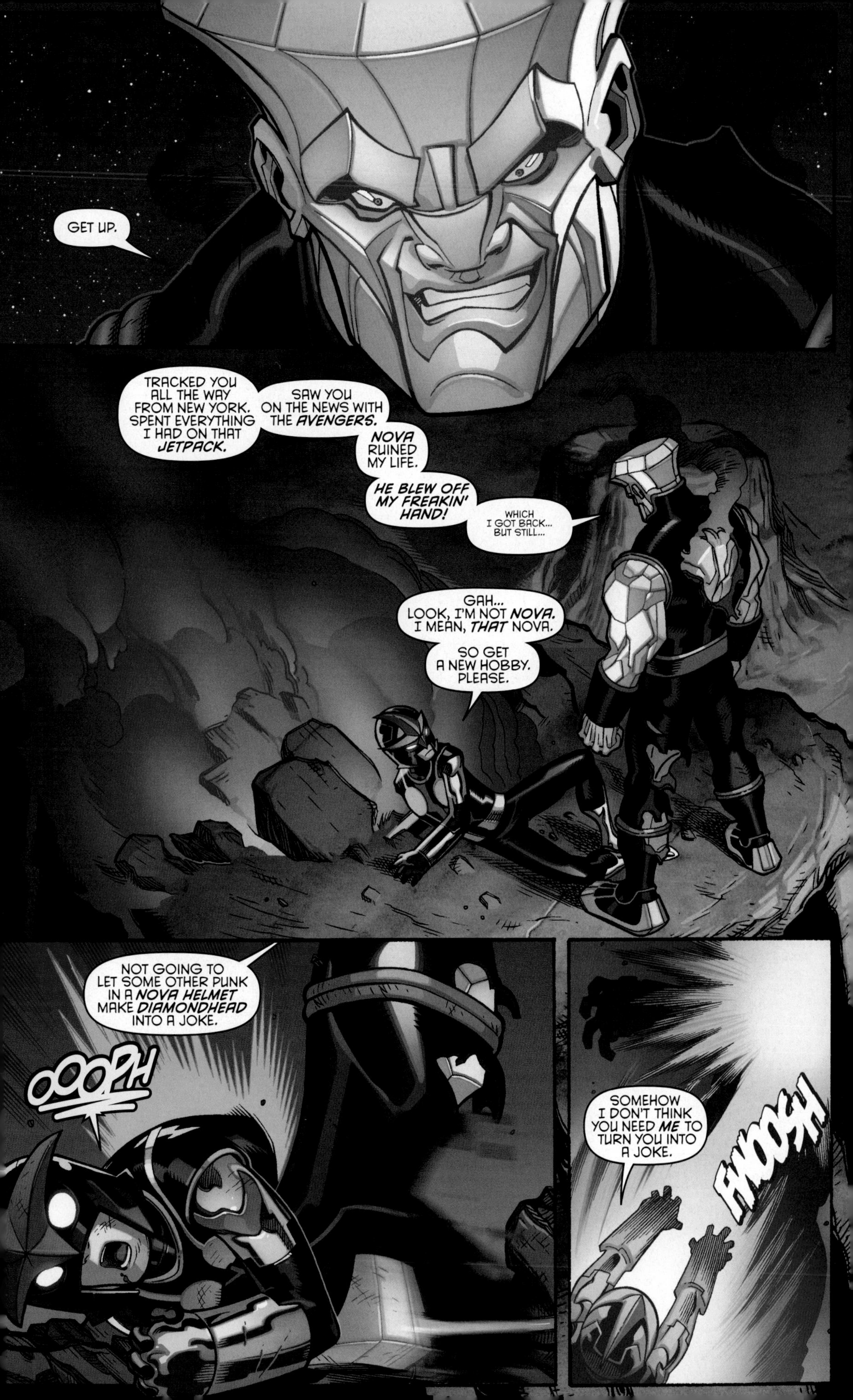
GET UP.
TRACKED YOU ALL THE WAY FROM NEW YORK. SPENT EVERYTHING I HAD ON THAT JETPACK.
SAW YOU ON THE NEWS WITH THE AVENGERS.
NOVA RUINED MY LIFE.
HE BLEW OFF MY FREAKIN' HAND!
WHICH I GOT BACK... BUT STILL...
GAH... LOOK, I'M NOT NOVA. I MEAN, THAT NOVA.
SO GET A NEW HOBBY. PLEASE.
NOT GOING TO LET SOME OTHER PUNK IN A NOVA HELMET MAKE DIAMONDHEAD INTO A JOKE.
OOOPH
SOMEHOW I DON'T THINK YOU NEED ME TO TURN YOU INTO A JOKE.
FWOOSH

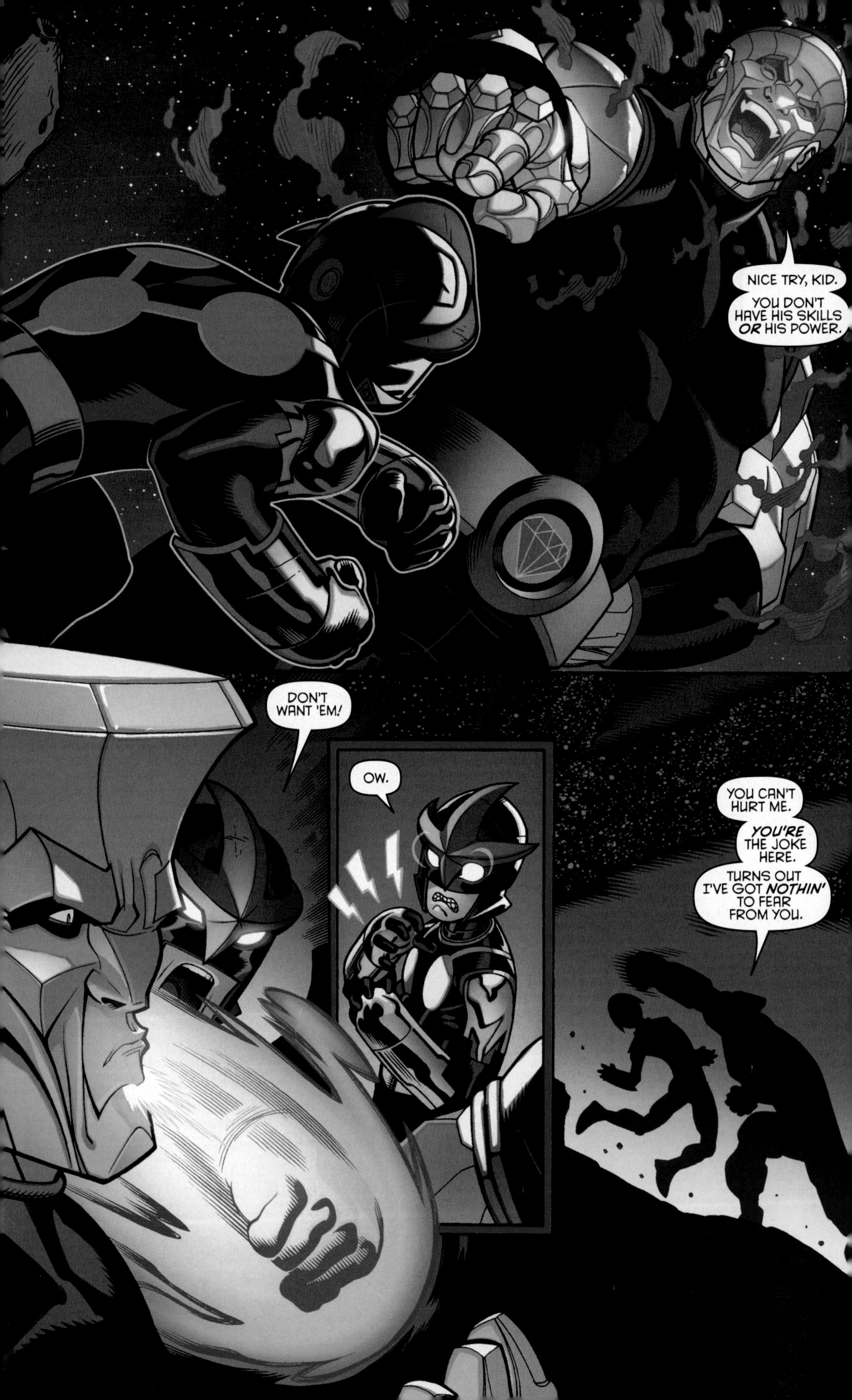
NICE TRY, KID.
YOU DON'T HAVE HIS SKILLS *OR* HIS POWER.
DON'T WANT 'EM!
OW.
YOU CAN'T HURT ME.
YOU'RE THE JOKE HERE.
TURNS OUT I'VE GOT *NOTHIN'* TO FEAR FROM YOU.

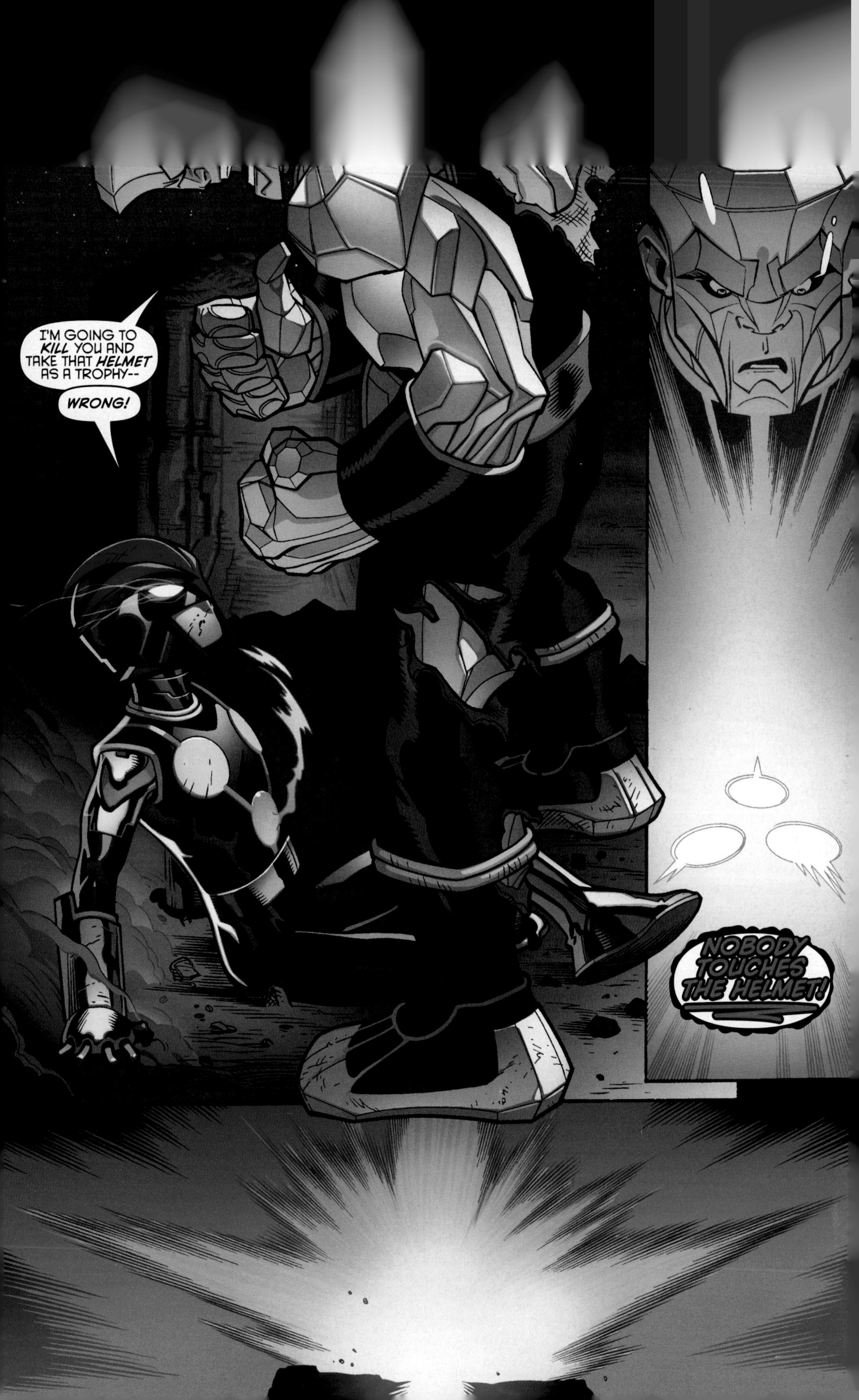
I'M GOING TO KILL YOU AND TAKE THAT HELMET AS A TROPHY--
WRONG!
NOBODY TOUCHES THE HELMET!

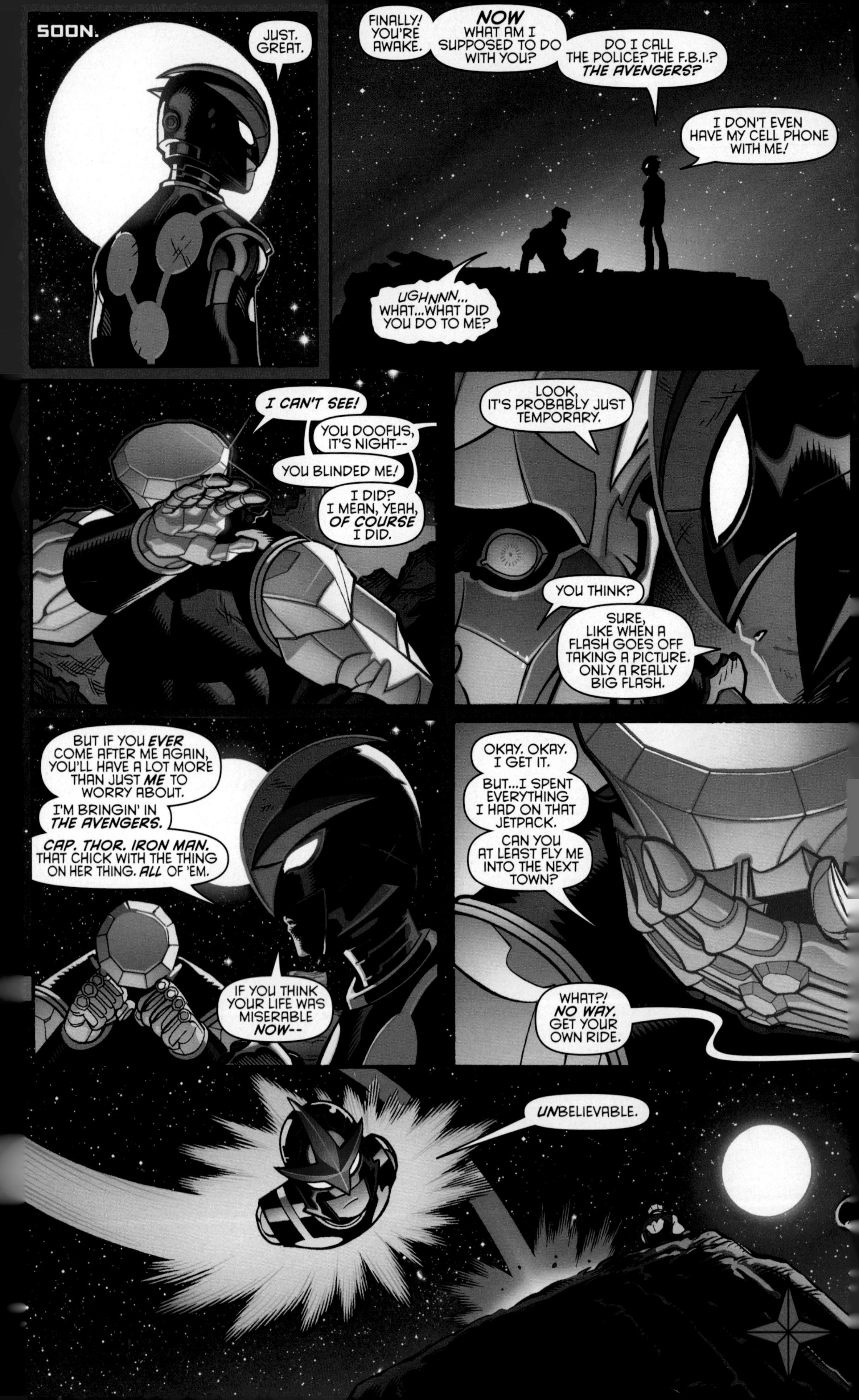
SOON.
JUST. GREAT.
FINALLY! YOU'RE AWAKE.
NOW WHAT AM I SUPPOSED TO DO WITH YOU?
DO I CALL THE POLICE? THE F.B.I.? THE AVENGERS?
I DON'T EVEN HAVE MY CELL PHONE WITH ME!
UGHNNN... WHAT...WHAT DID YOU DO TO ME?
I CAN'T SEE!
YOU DOOFUS, IT'S NIGHT--
YOU BLINDED ME!
I DID? I MEAN, YEAH, OF COURSE I DID.
LOOK, IT'S PROBABLY JUST TEMPORARY.
YOU THINK?
SURE, LIKE WHEN A FLASH GOES OFF TAKING A PICTURE. ONLY A REALLY BIG FLASH.
BUT IF YOU EVER COME AFTER ME AGAIN, YOU'LL HAVE A LOT MORE THAN JUST ME TO WORRY ABOUT.
I'M BRINGIN' IN THE AVENGERS.
CAP. THOR. IRON MAN. THAT CHICK WITH THE THING ON HER THING. ALL OF 'EM.
IF YOU THINK YOUR LIFE WAS MISERABLE NOW--
OKAY. OKAY. I GET IT.
BUT...I SPENT EVERYTHING I HAD ON THAT JETPACK.
CAN YOU AT LEAST FLY ME INTO THE NEXT TOWN?
WHAT?! NO WAY. GET YOUR OWN RIDE.
UNBELIEVABLE.

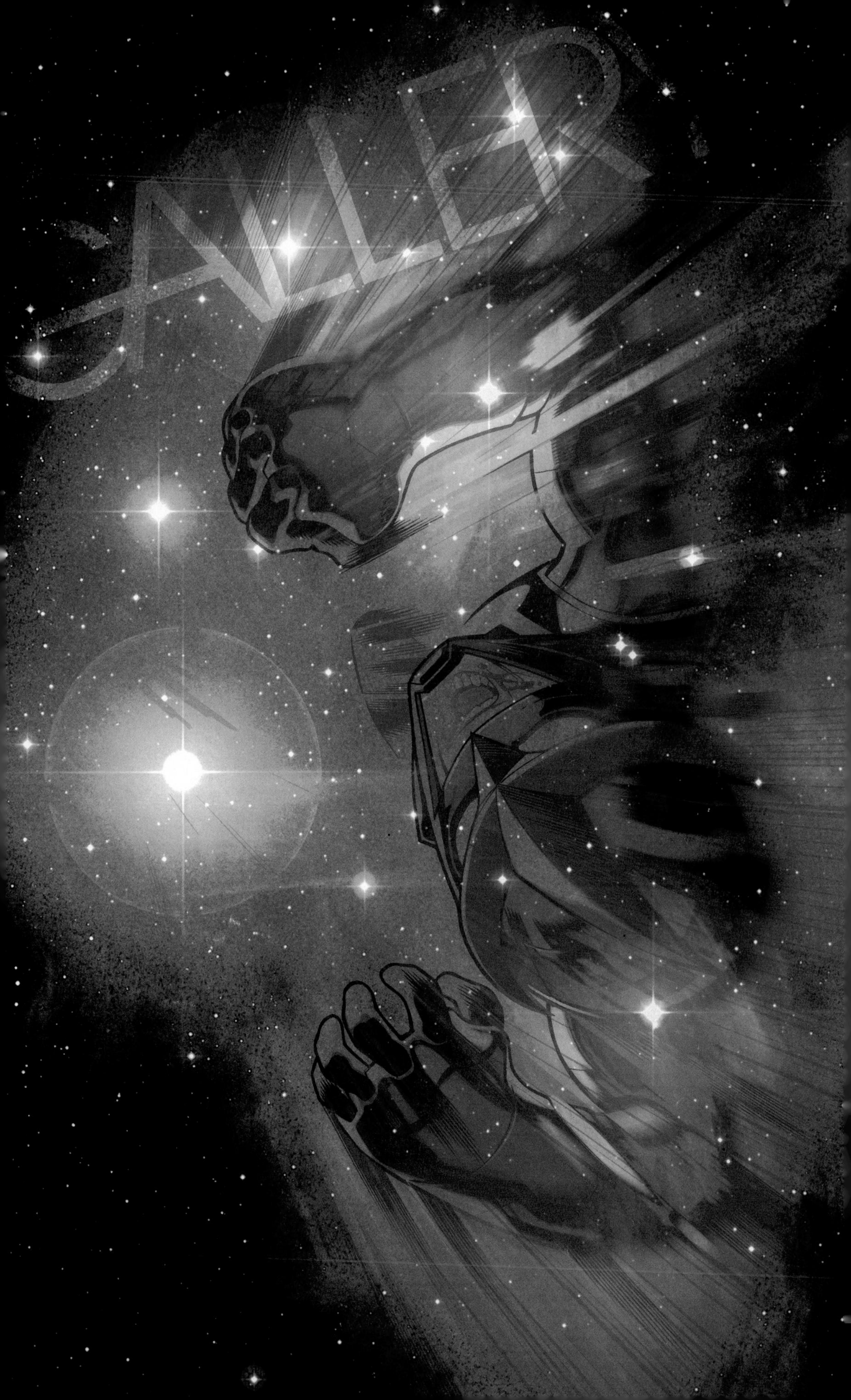

ISSUE #1 VARIANT COVER SKOTTIE YOUNG

ISSUE #1 VARIANT COVER
JOE QUESADA, DANNY MIKI & RICHARD ISANOVE

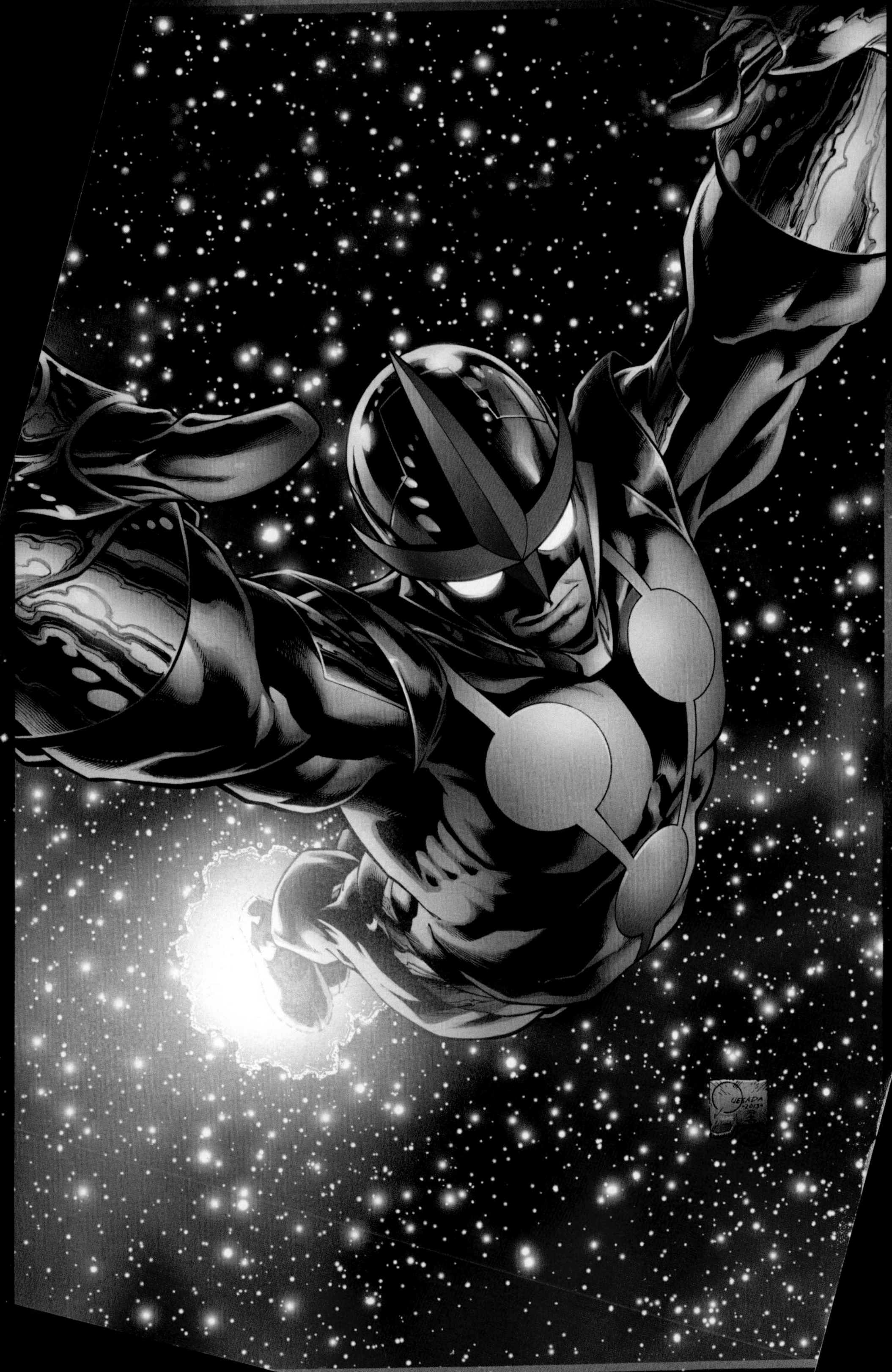

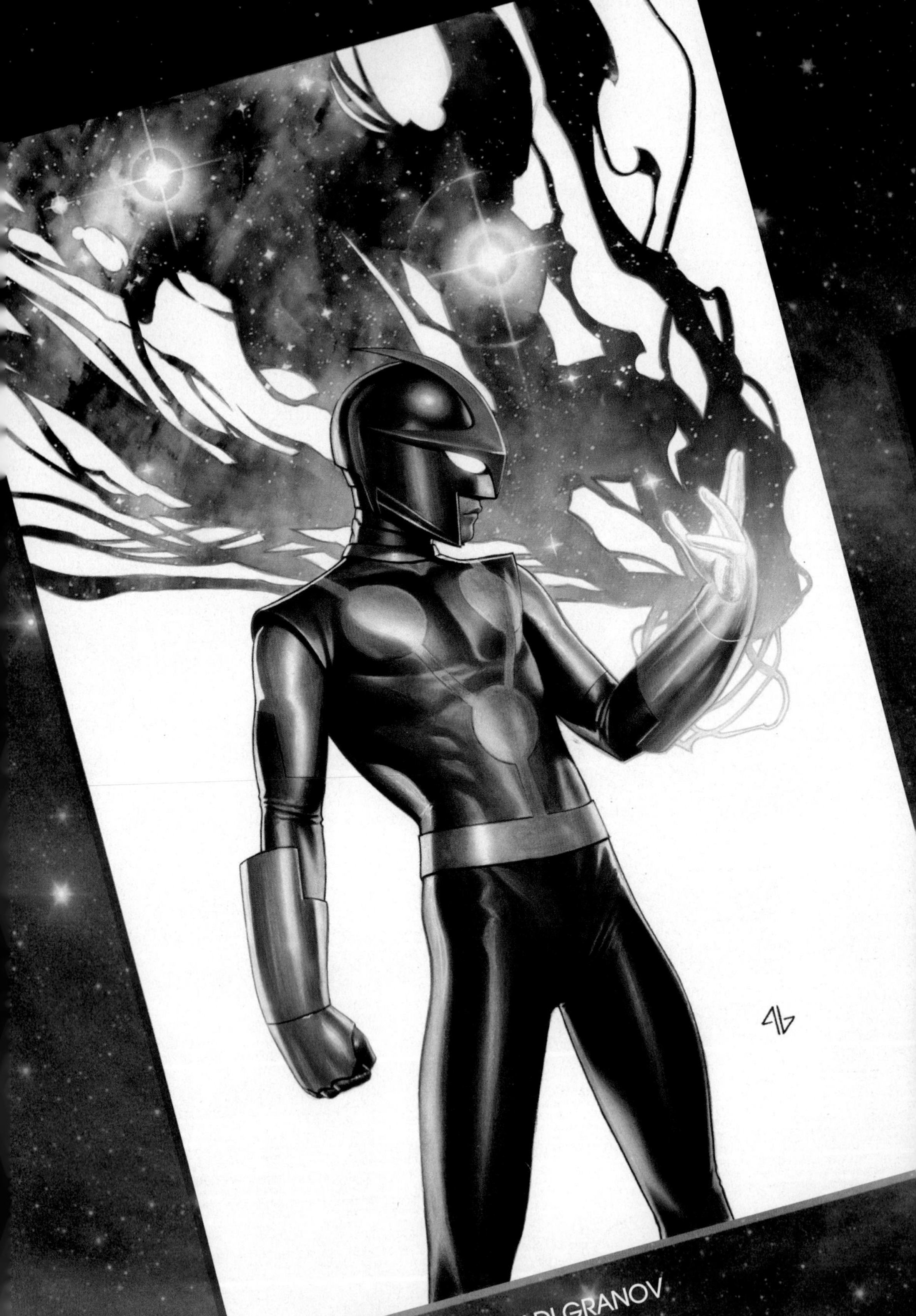

ISSUE #1 VARIANT COVER ADI GRANOV

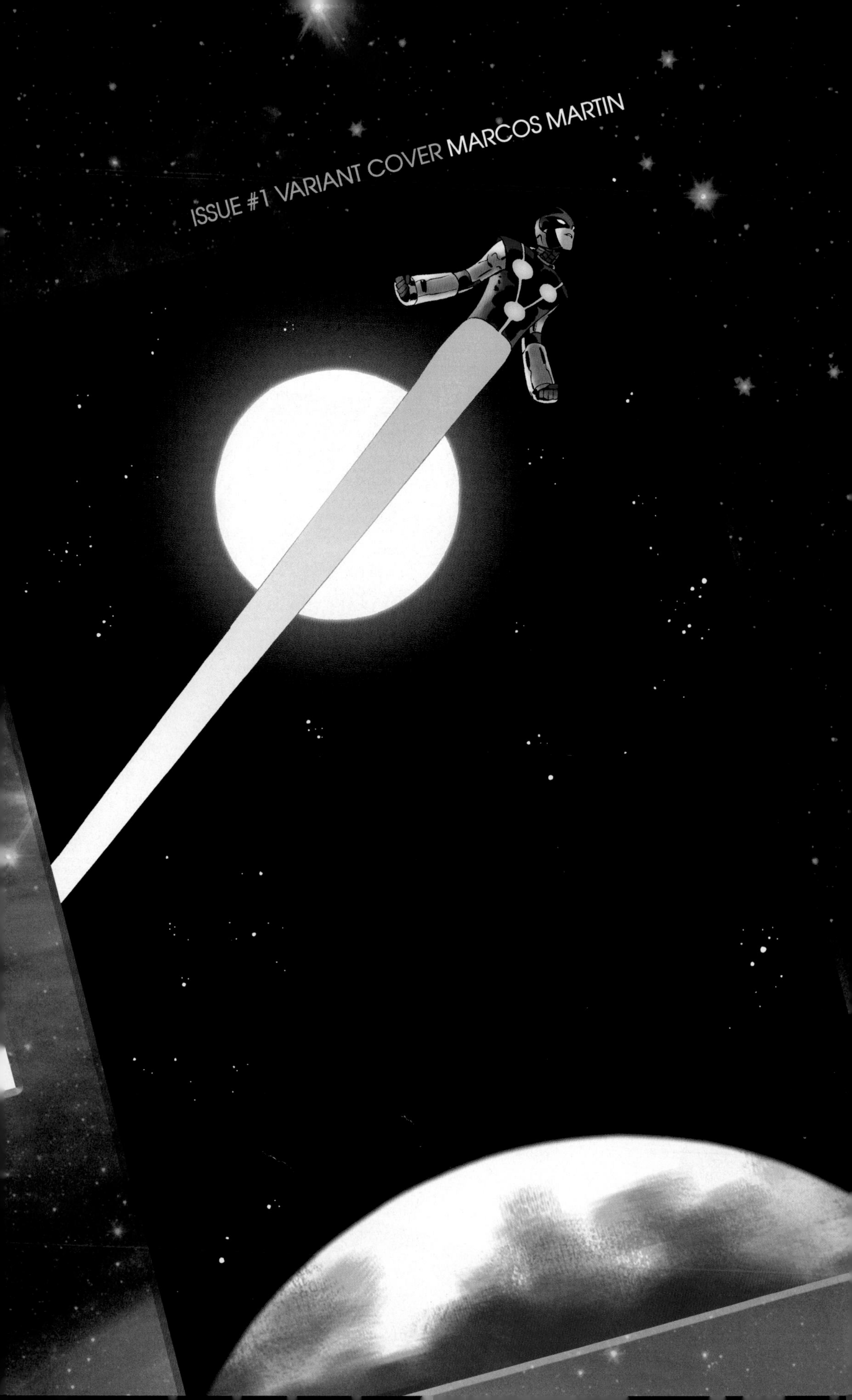
ISSUE #1 VARIANT COVER MARCOS MARTIN

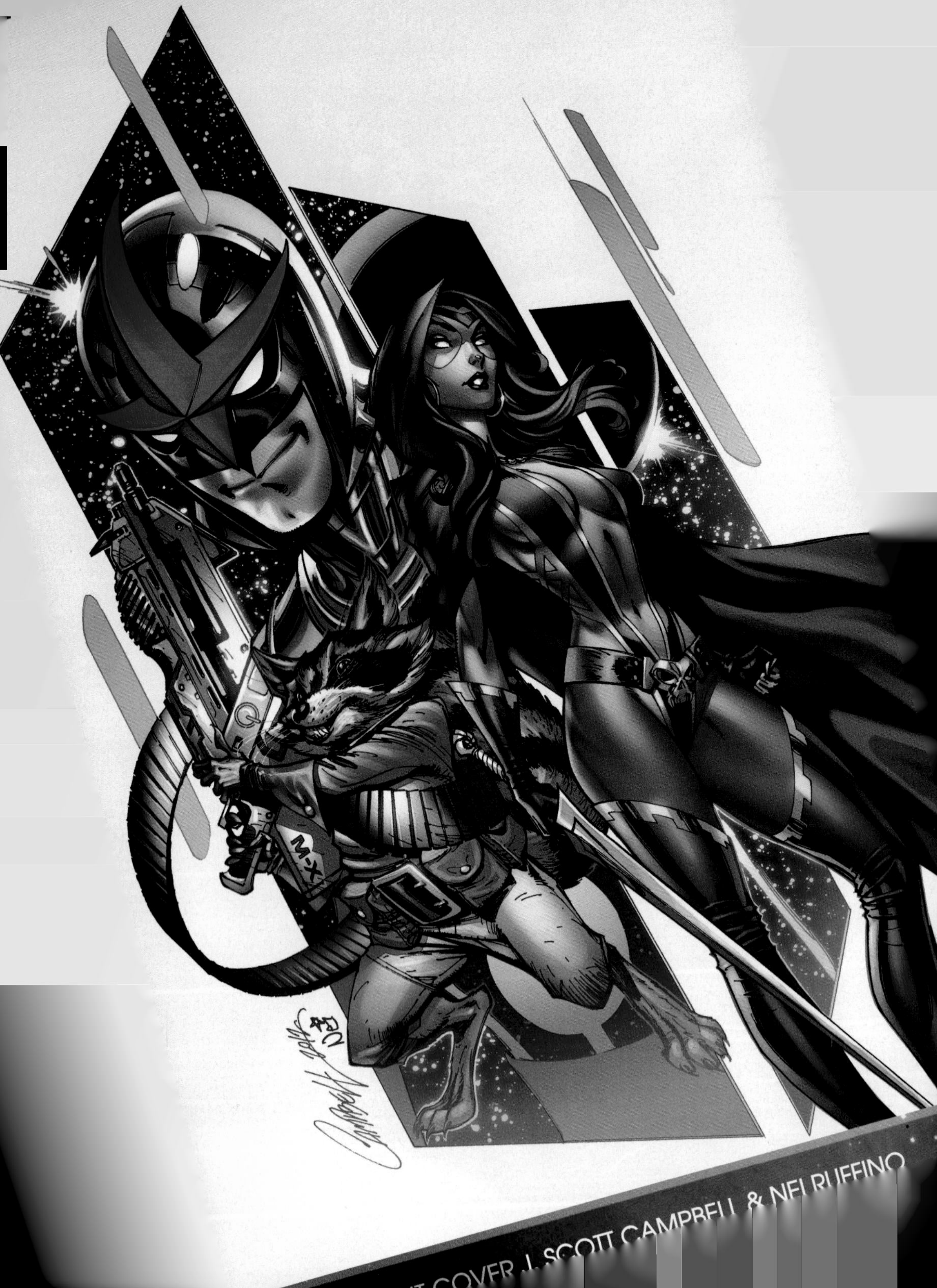
M-X

ISSUE #2 VARIANT COVER J. SCOTT CAMPBELL & NEI RUFFINO

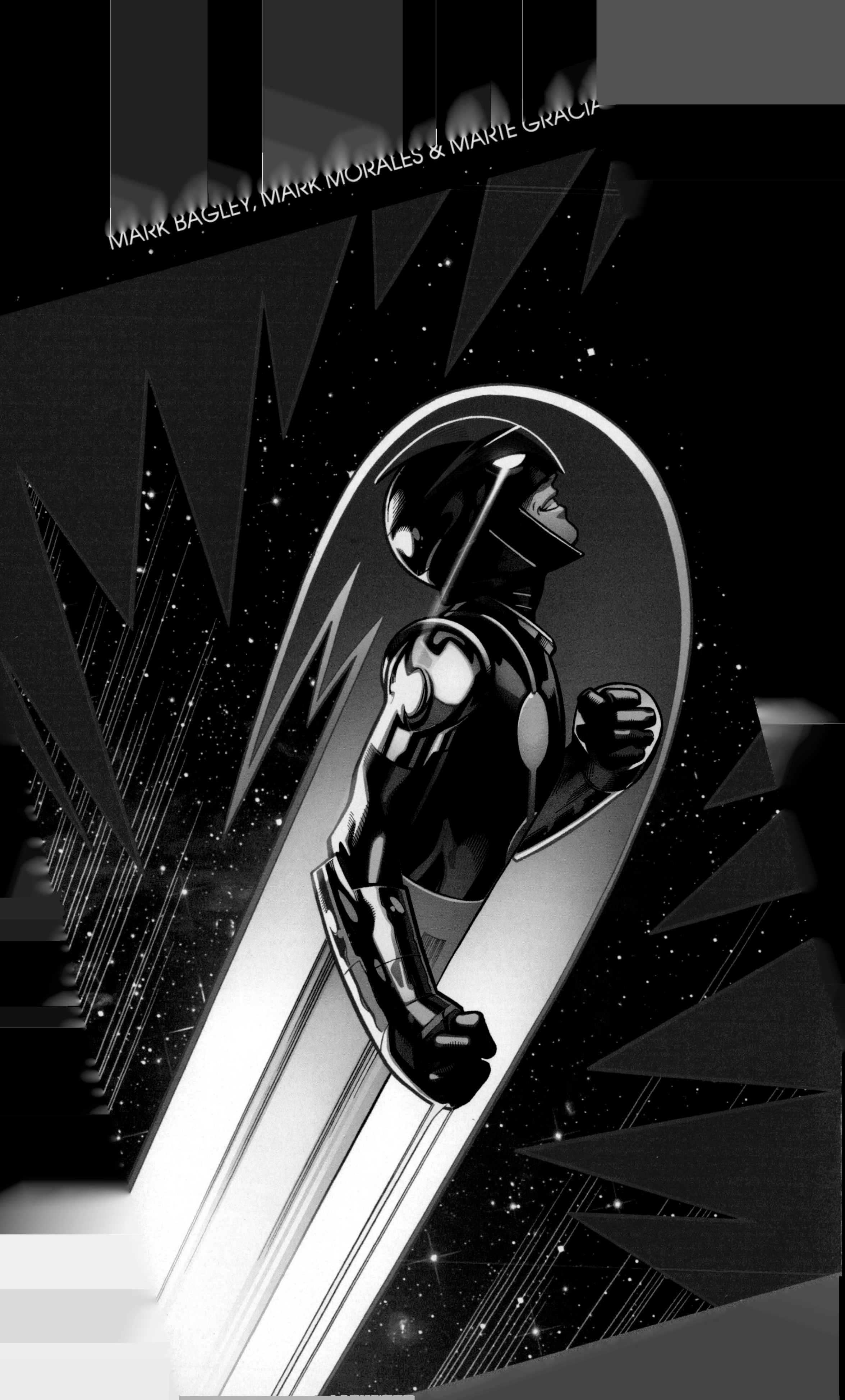
MARK BAGLEY, MARK MORALES & MARTE GRACIA

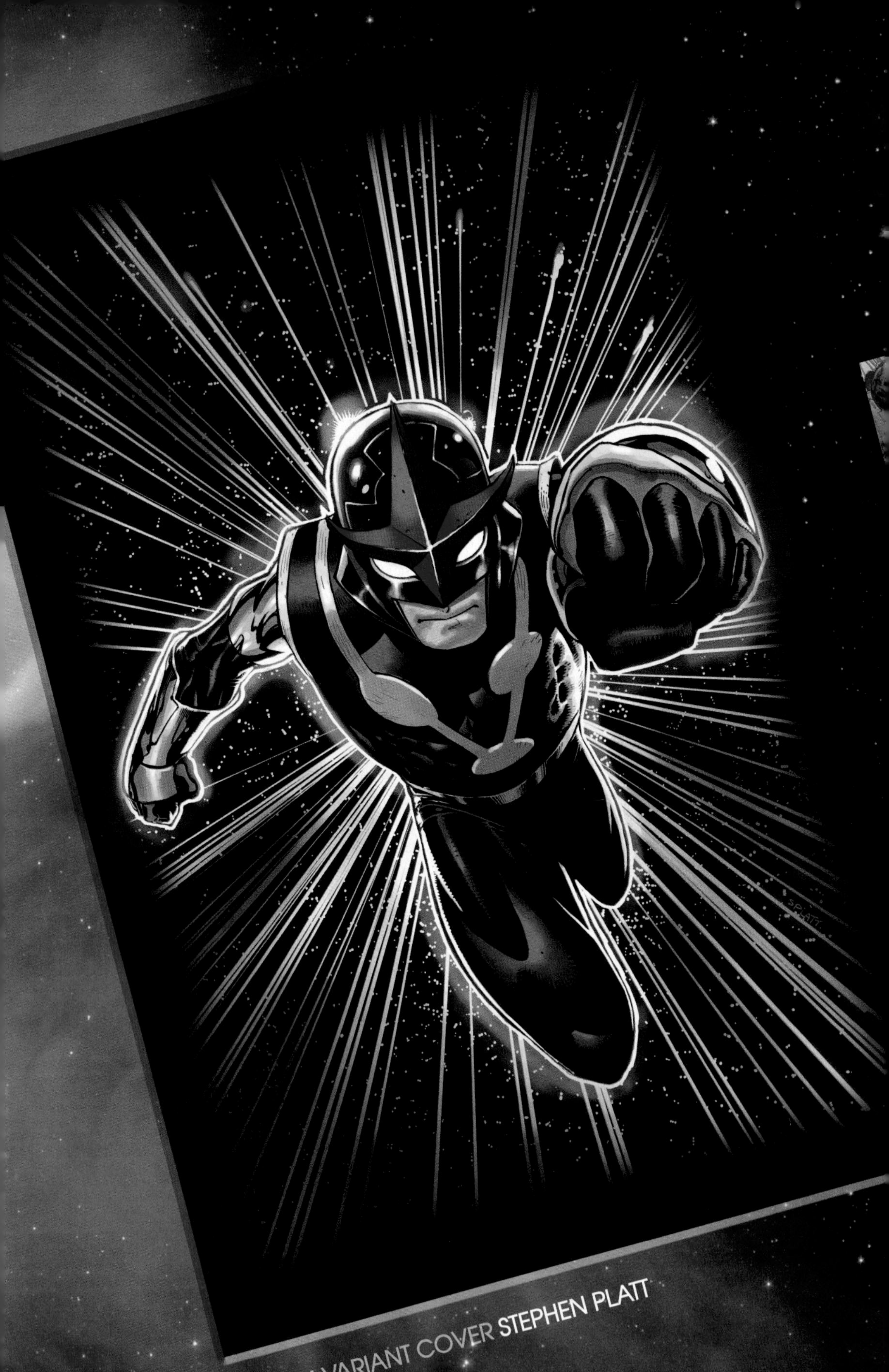

ISSUE #4 VARIANT COVER STEPHEN PLATT

ISSUE #5 VARIANT COVER MR GARCIN

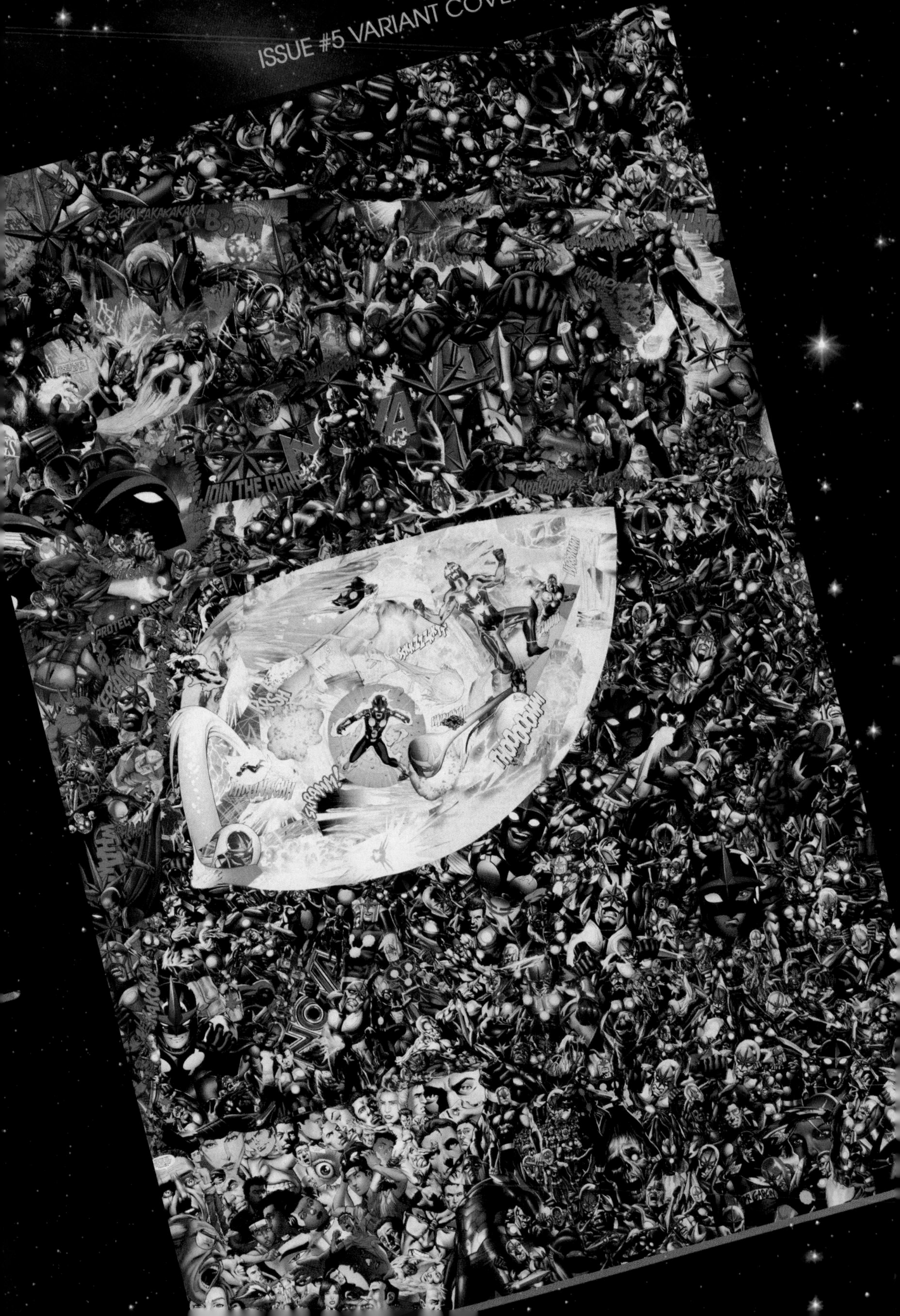

ED McGUINNESS' SKETCH

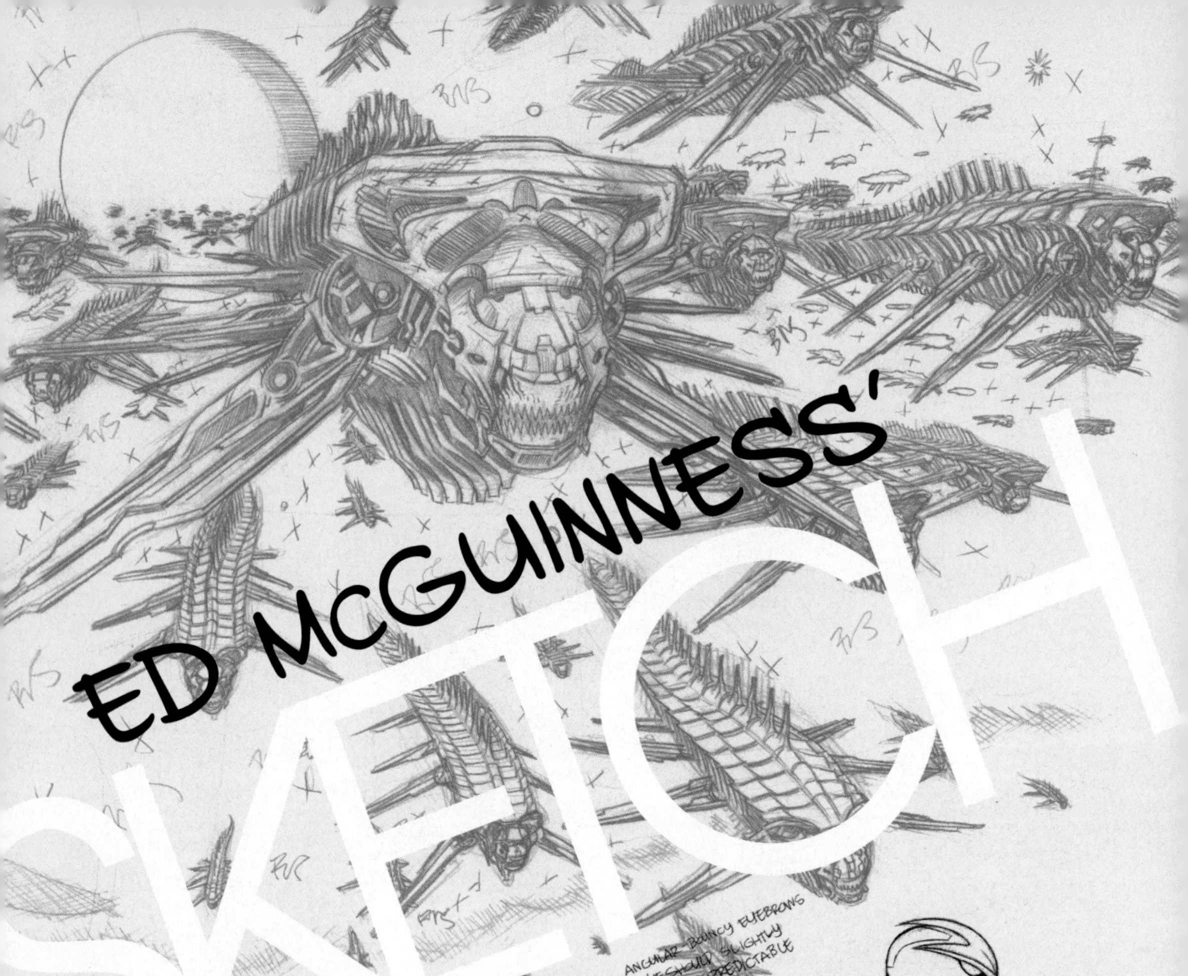

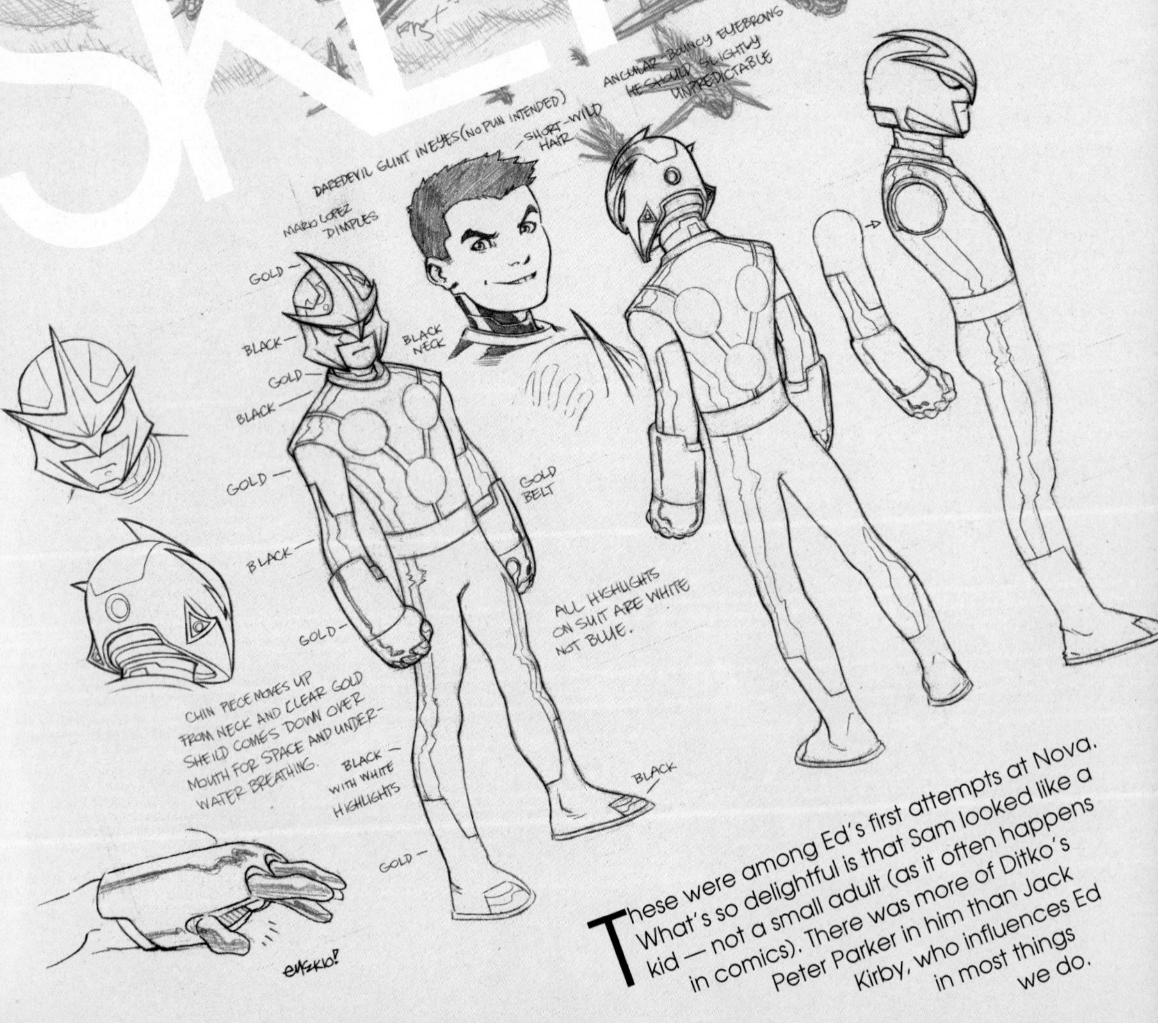

ANGULAR BOUNCY EYEBROWS
SLIGHTY UNPREDICTABLE
DAREDEVIL GLINT IN EYES (NO PUN INTENDED)
SHORT-WILD HAIR
MARIO LOPEZ DIMPLES
GOLD
BLACK
BLACK NECK
GOLD
BLACK
GOLD
GOLD BELT
BLACK
ALL HIGHLIGHTS ON SUIT ARE WHITE NOT BLUE.
GOLD
CHIN PIECE MOVES UP FROM NECK AND CLEAR GOLD SHEILD COMES DOWN OVER MOUTH FOR SPACE AND UNDER-WATER BREATHING.
BLACK WITH WHITE HIGHLIGHTS
BLACK
GOLD

These were among Ed's first attempts at Nova. What's so delightful is that Sam looked like a kid — not a small adult (as it often happens in comics). There was more of Ditko's Peter Parker in him than Jack Kirby, who influences Ed in most things we do.

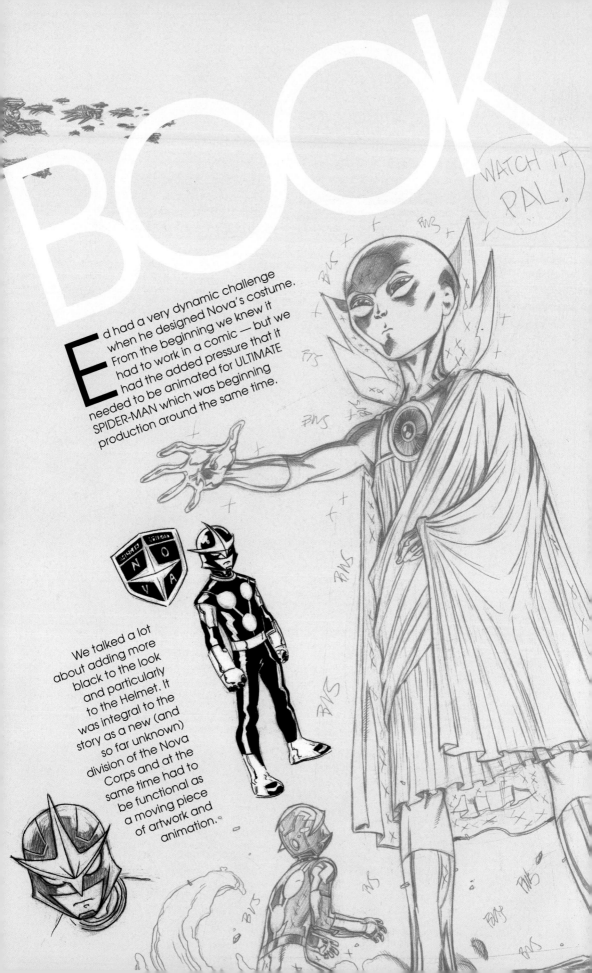

BOOK

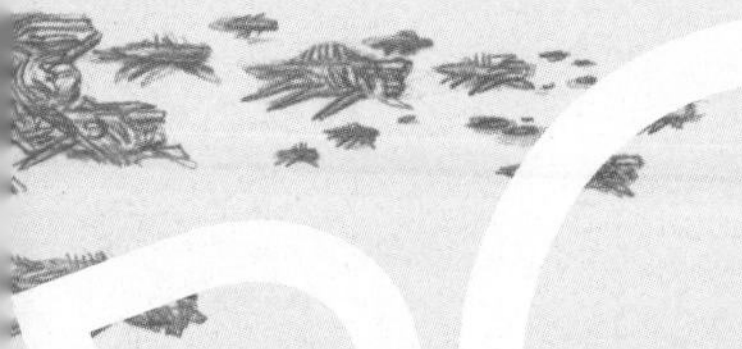

Ed had a very dynamic challenge when he designed Nova's costume. From the beginning we knew it had to work in a comic — but we had the added pressure that it needed to be animated for ULTIMATE SPIDER-MAN which was beginning production around the same time.

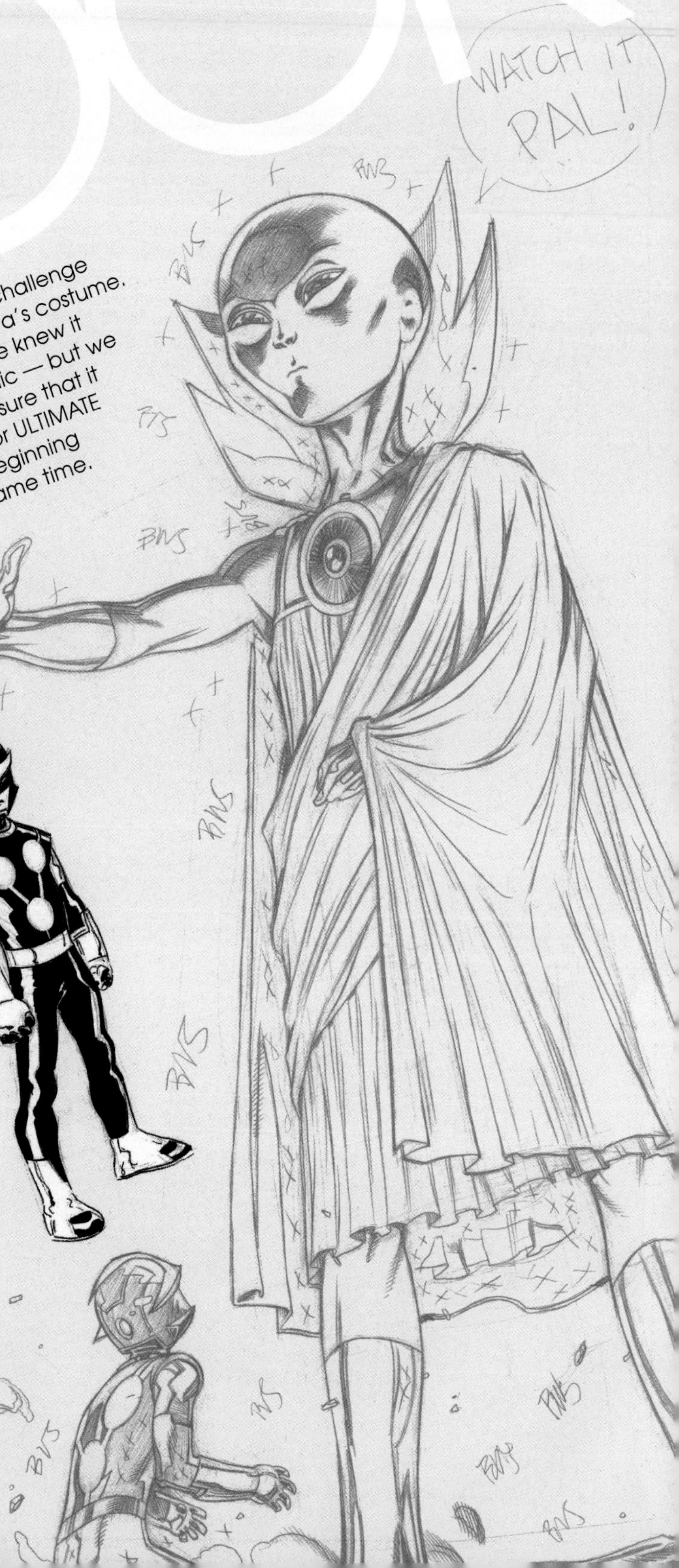
WATCH IT PAL!

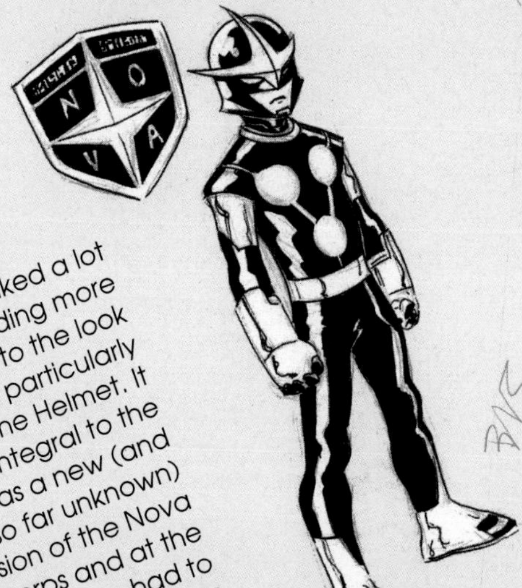
N O V A

We talked a lot about adding more black to the look and particularly to the Helmet. It was integral to the story as a new (and so far unknown) division of the Nova Corps and at the same time had to be functional as a moving piece of artwork and animation.

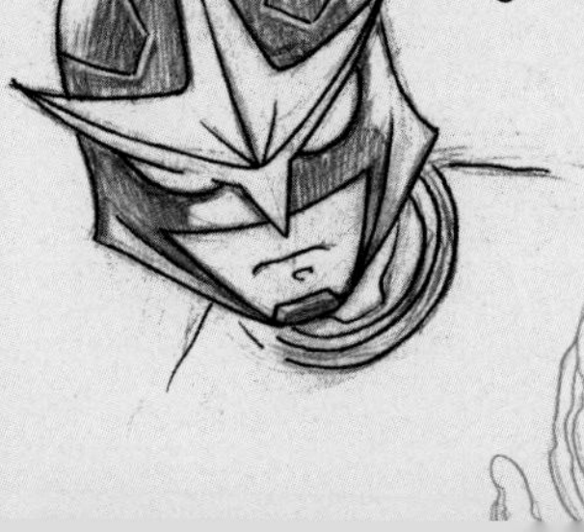

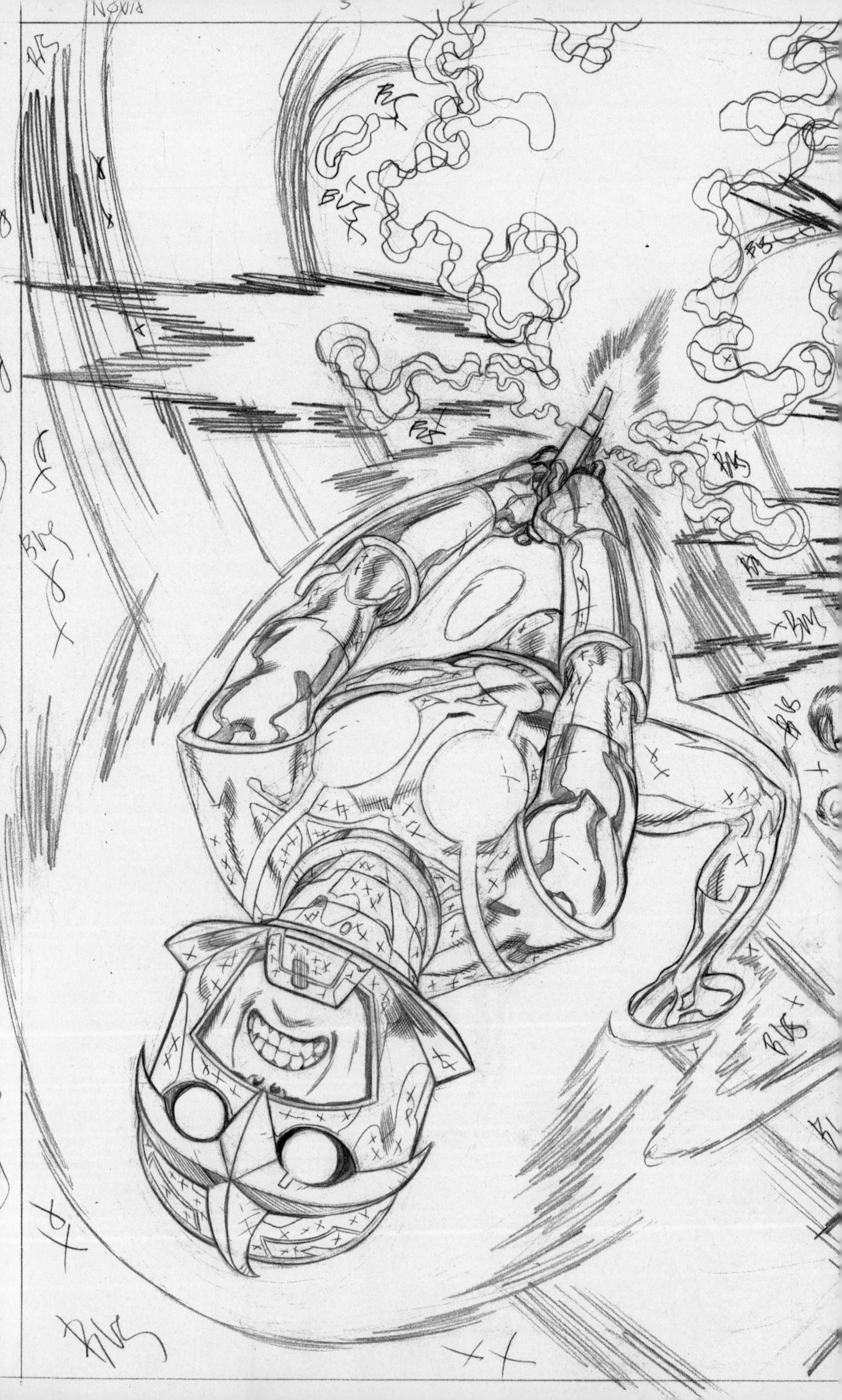

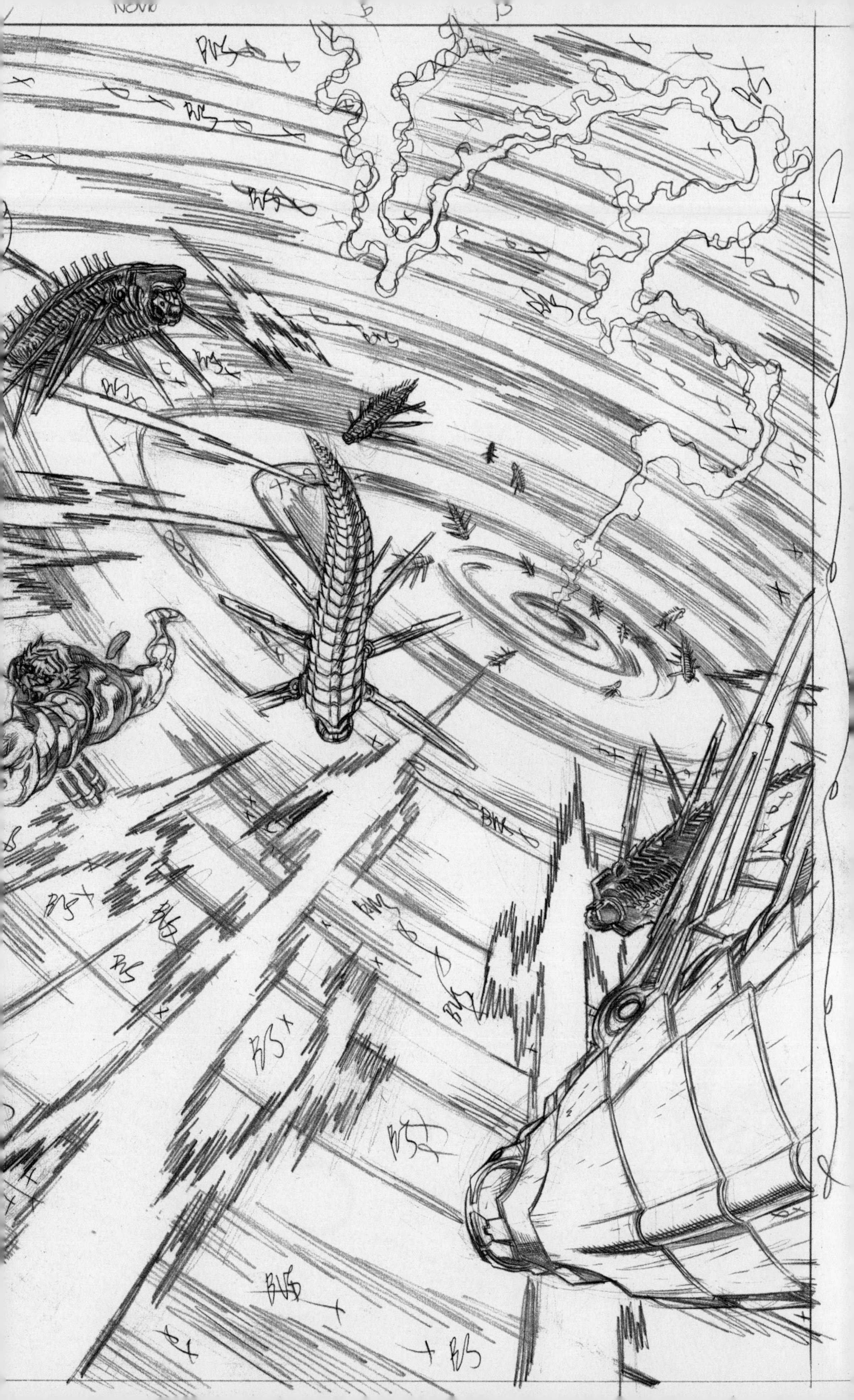

COVER DESIGN

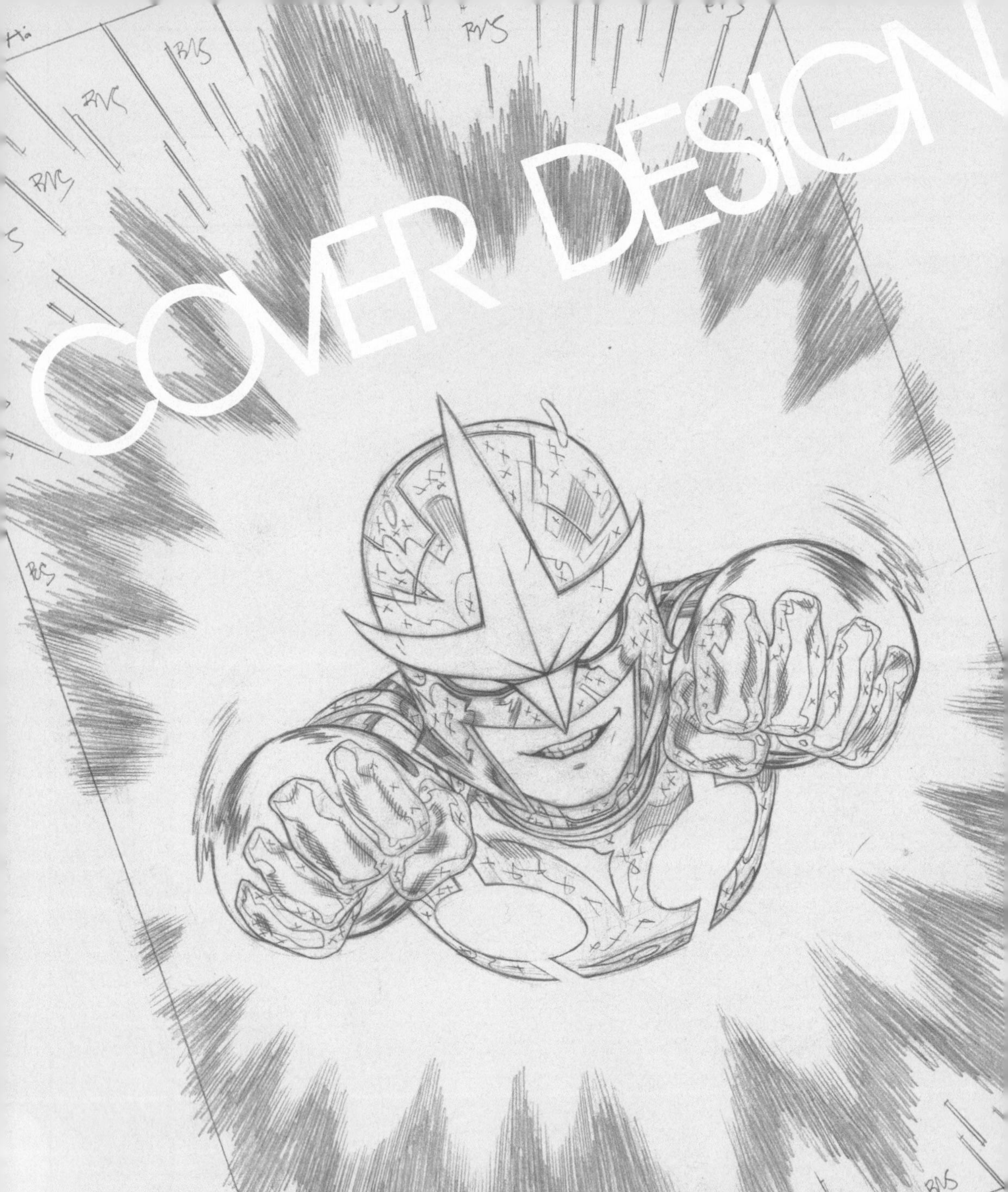

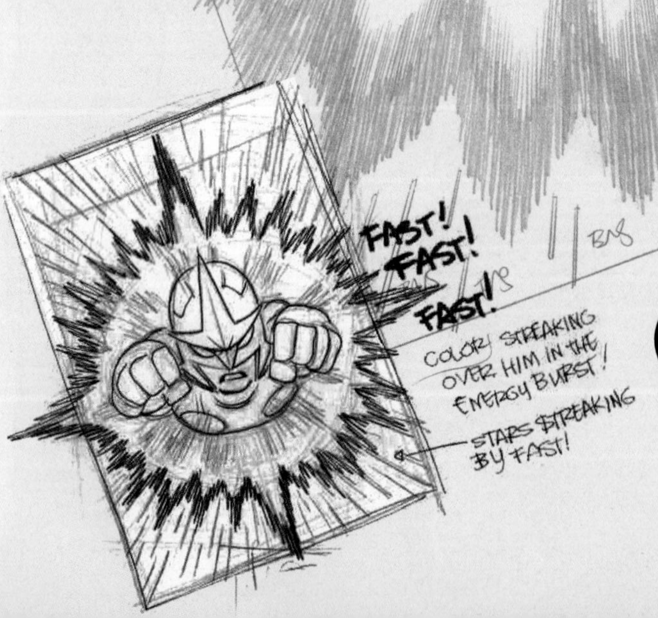
FAST!
FAST!
FAST!
COLOR STREAKING OVER HIM IN THE ENERGY BURST!
STARS STREAKING BY FAST!

Covers are one of Ed's many strengths: bold, clean images. When talking about the first issue, we wanted Nova to be coming right at you and Ed nailed it. But what makes the cover so much fun (as editor Steve Wacker loves to point out) is the sly grin on Sam's face. It's a small, pure character thing that really gives you a sense that he's not like any Nova we've seen before.

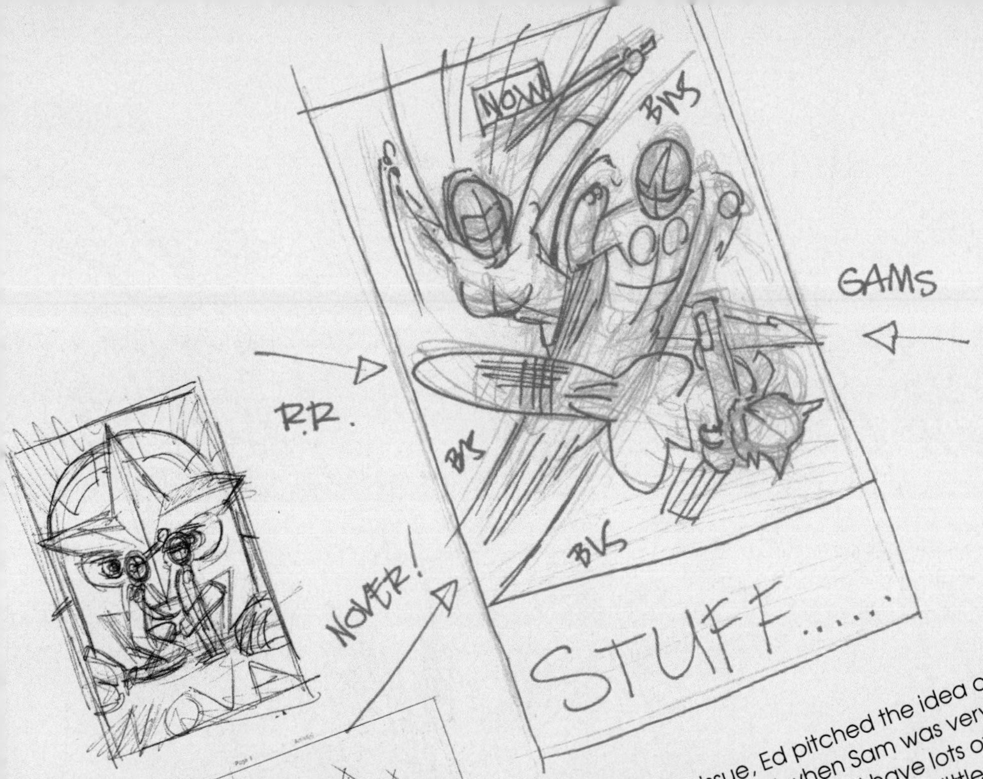
NOW
BVS
GAMS
R.R.
NOVER!
STUFF.....

For our last issue, Ed pitched the idea of seeing Sam and his Dad when Sam was very little. As fathers, both Ed and I have lots of photos of us with our kids when they were little and this was an attempt to capture some of that. Because the ending was hopefully going to be very emotional, Ed wanted a cover that would depict one of those quiet, sweet moments between a father and a son.

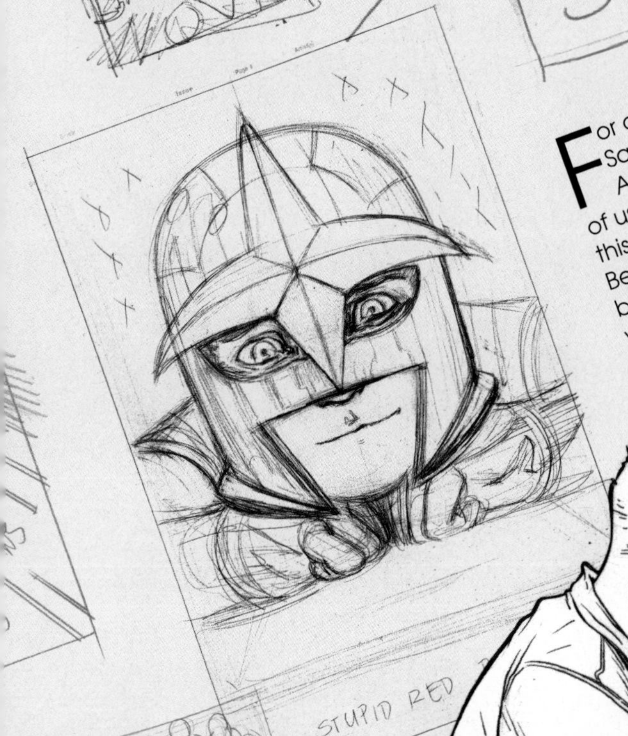
STUPID RED

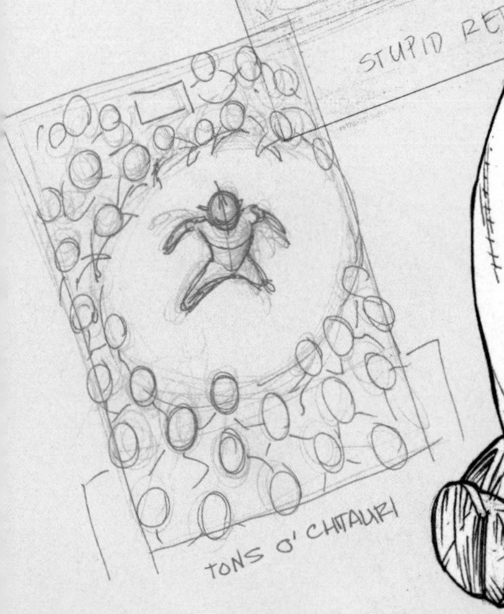
TONS O' CHITAURI

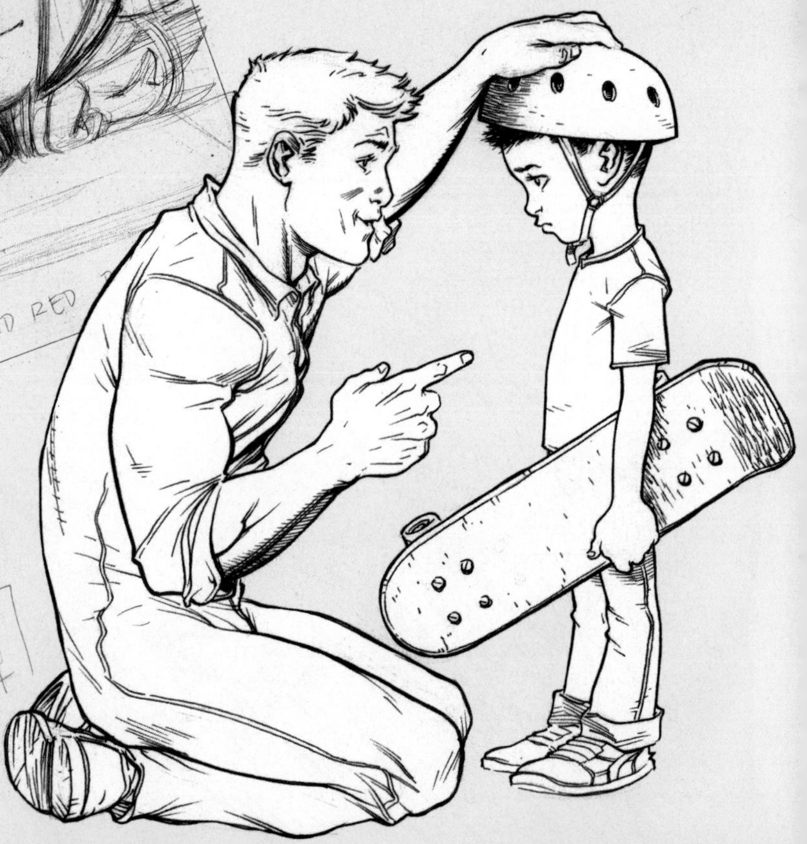

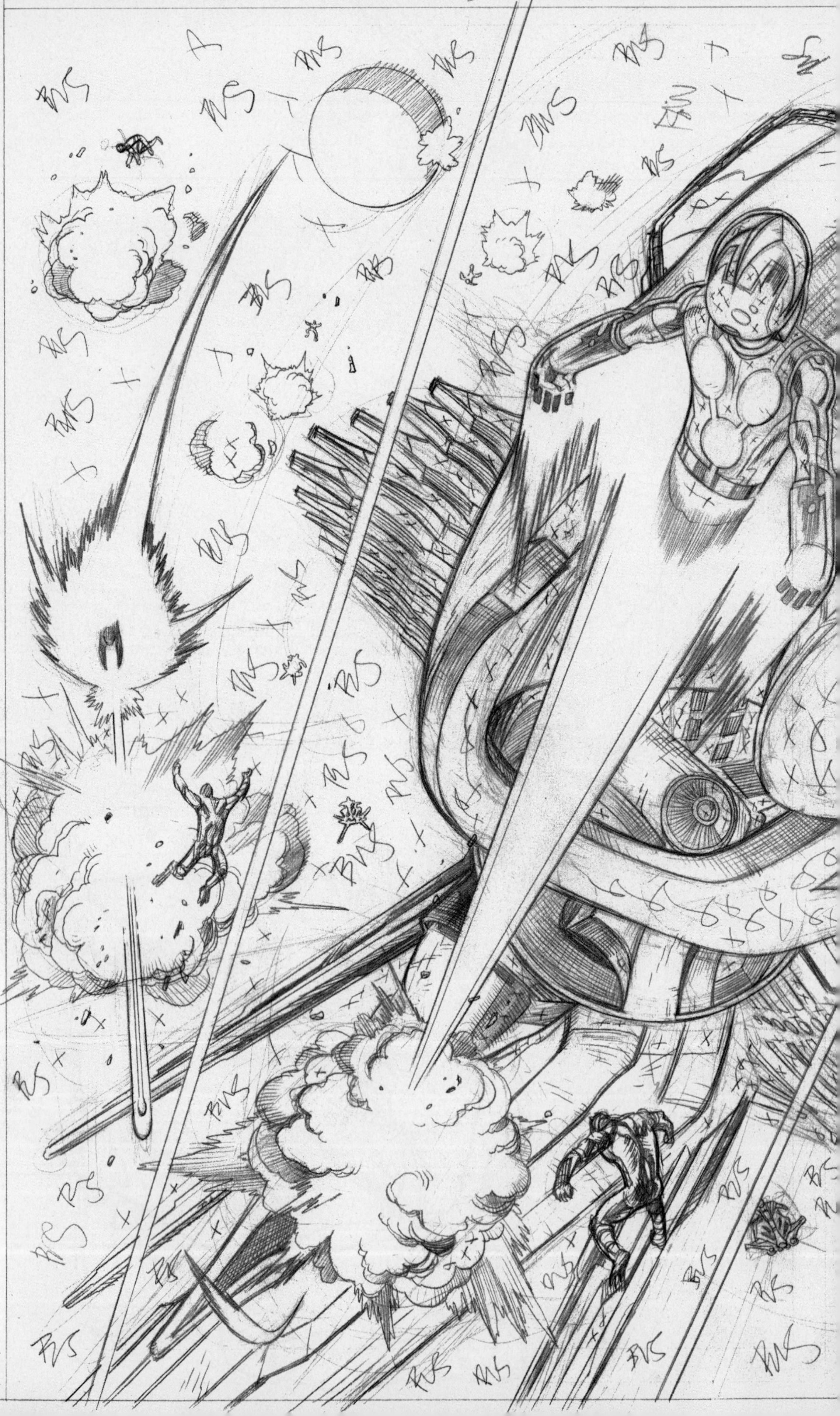

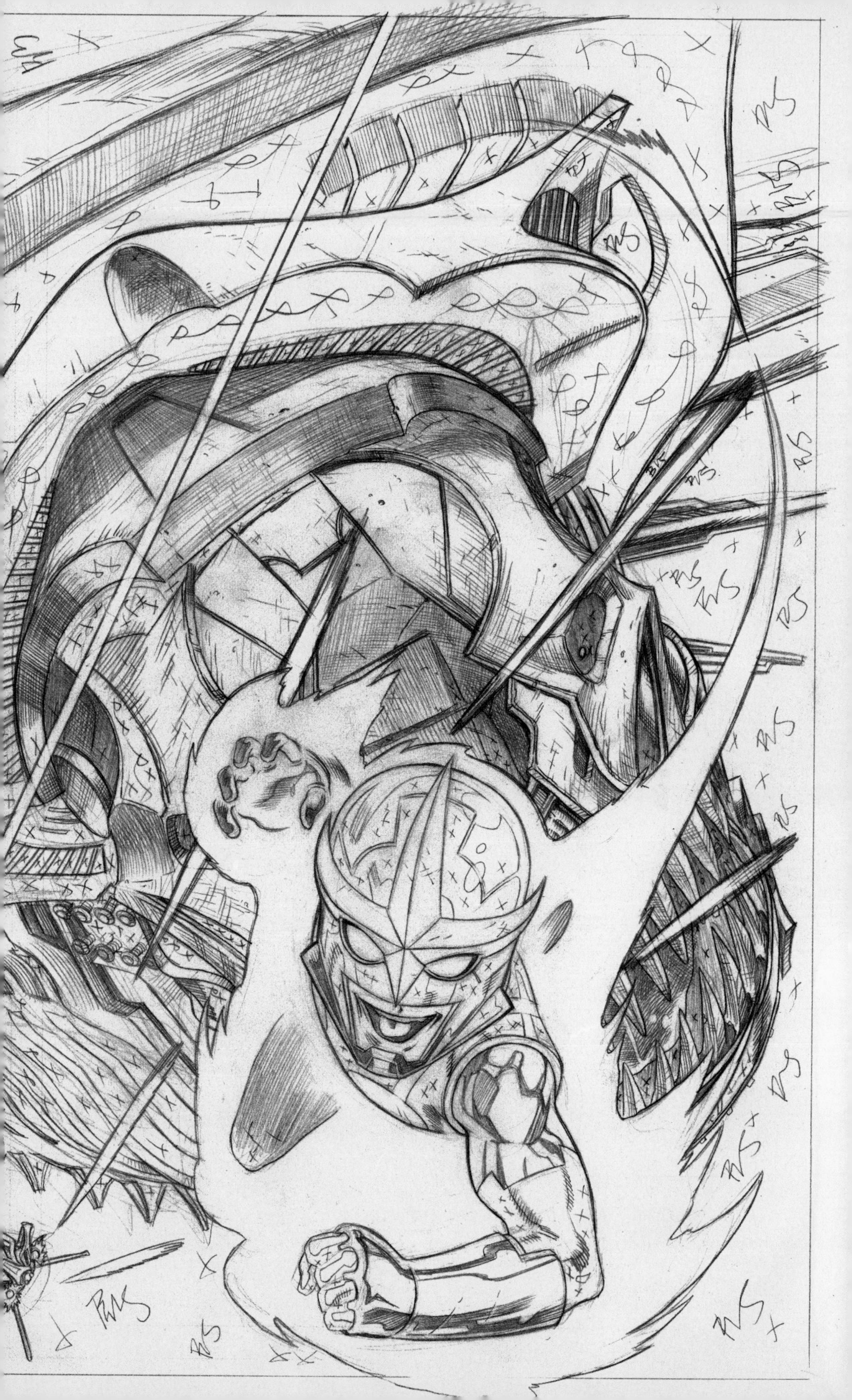

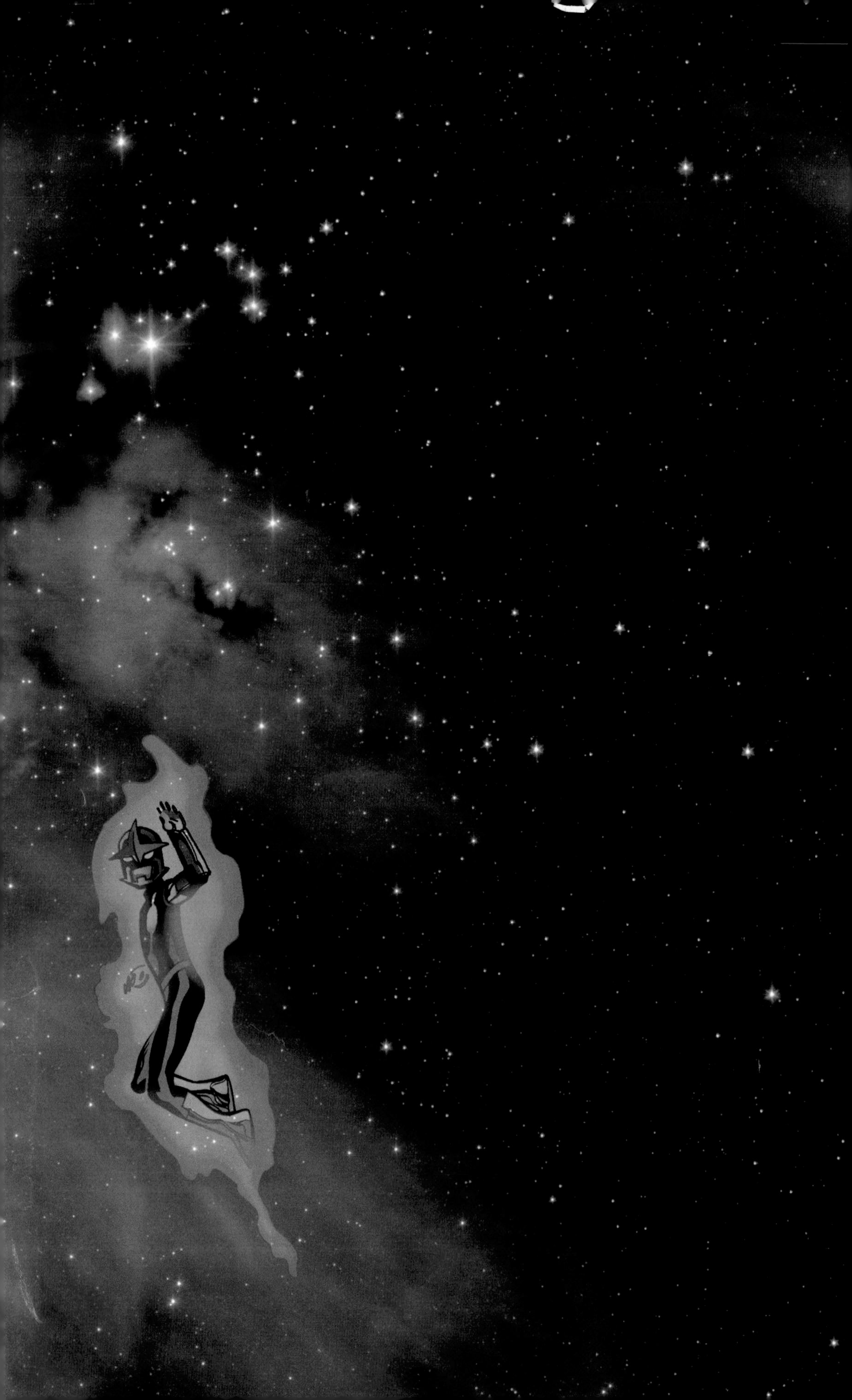

TO ACCESS THE FREE *MARVEL AUGMENTED REALITY APP* THAT ENHANCES AND CHANGES THE WAY YOU EXPERIENCE COMICS:

1. Download the app for free via marvel.com/ARapp
2. Launch the app on your camera-enabled Apple iOS® or Android™ device*
3. Hold your mobile device's camera over any cover or panel with the AR graphi
4. Sit back and see the future of comics in action!

*Available on most camera-enabled Apple iOS® and Android™ devices. Content subject to change and availability.

NOVA AR INDEX

TMAHTJG9NQFK

TO REDEEM YOUR CODE FOR A FREE DIGITAL COPY:

1. GO TO MARVEL.COM/REDEEM. OFFER EXPIRES ON 7/3/15.
2. FOLLOW THE ON-SCREEN INSTRUCTIONS TO REDEEM YOUR DIGITAL COPY.
3. LAUNCH THE MARVEL COMICS APP TO READ YOUR COMIC NOW!
4. YOUR DIGITAL COPY WILL BE FOUND UNDER THE *MY COMICS* TAB.
5. READ & ENJOY!

YOUR FREE DIGITAL COPY WILL BE AVAILABLE ON

MARVEL COMICS APP FOR APPLE® iOS DEVICES

MARVEL COMICS APP FOR ANDROID™ DEVICES

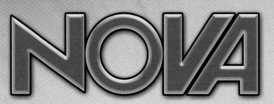

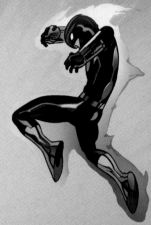